ALL THE CHILDREN OF THE BIBLE

The "All" Series by Dr. Lockyer . . .

All the Apostles of the Bible

All the Books and Chapters of the Bible

All the Children of the Bible

All the Divine Names and Titles in the Bible

All the Doctrines of the Bible

All the Holy Days and Holidays

All the Kings and Queens of the Bible

All the Men of the Bible

All the Messianic Prophecies of the Bible

All the Miracles of the Bible

All the Parables of the Bible

All the Prayers of the Bible

All the Promises of the Bible

All the Trades and Occupations of the Bible

All the Women of the Bible

All About Bible Study

More than 500,000 copies of the "All" series are now in print.

ALL THE CHILDREN OF THE BIBLE

by

HERBERT LOCKYER, D.D.

All the Children of the Bible

Grand Rapids, Michigan

Twelfth printing October 1981
ISBN 0-310-28030-3

Library of Congress Catalog Card Number: 70-120052

Appreciation is expressed to The Macmillan Company for permission to quote from *The New Testament in Modern English.*

Printed in the United States of America

Dedicated
to all those who,
by life, lip, and literature,
bring children to Jesus, and
present Jesus to children

CONTENTS

INTRODUCTION

It may come as a great surprise to many lovers of the Bible to learn that it is, primarily, a Book about children. From beginning to end, the holy Child Jesus, dominates its sacred pages; and the terms, "child" and "children," occur almost 2,000 times in the sixty-six books forming the Holy Bible. Thus, for anyone to attempt a reference book on *all* the children of the Bible would indeed be a prodigious task. The purpose of our study is simply to classify what the Bible says concerning divine and human estimates of children; to examine the relationship between parents and children; and to consider some of the Bible characters whose childhood is especially mentioned. Attention will also be given to the symbolic use of some of the terms used.

The countless thousands of named and unnamed persons crowding the Bible were all children once — boys and girls, desired and undesired — with the exception of the first two parents of the human race. Adam and Eve had no childhood. Adam was never a boy, and Eve was never a girl. Adam appeared as a perfect man, fresh from the Creator's hand. Out of Adam, Eve came forth a perfect woman, fashioned by the Lord God Almighty, the Source of Life. Thereafter, Adam and Eve became the world's first parents; and together, the fountainhead of humanity. Boys and girls came fast, and all Bible children were real boys and girls like those romping around us today.

What does it matter that they are separated from us by thousands of years! We can embrace them in heart, and love them as if we had actually known them. Their stories make us alive with interest, and we find ourselves grieved at their wrongs and grateful for their deliverances. It doesn't take us long to find out that many of these Bible children are much like those in our own homes; that in their history, as in a mirror, we have the reflection of our children. It is thus that the dry bones in the Bible become clothed with flesh, and live before us, although the customs of their day differ from ours.

Several years ago a company of workmen preparing the foundations for a house in Rome, laid bare a child's sepulcher, at least 2,000 years old. The diggers were touched with kindly feeling as they unearthed a large number of objects belonging to dolls' housekeeping. Such treasure would have given as much joy to their own little girls as it gave to its first possessor. More than one visitor has been moved to tears visiting the great museum at Naples by finding, among the curiosities dug out of Pompeii, a long row of childrens' savings banks with a slit in the top to let in the money, just like your child's "piggy bank." More than a hundred years ago antiquarians found in an old British tower built by the Picts, a boy's toy boat in the deep earth outside — just like a boat a boy today would scoop out of a piece of wood.

What do these facts, and similar ones, prove? Is it not the actuality that children are just children in every age and nation? Dress, language, and color of skin may differ, but all have the same beating heart, whose heart-blood is red; the same dreams and fancies; the same little heartaches and tears; the same craving for parental love. The boys and girls of the Bible are not foreigners, but simply those of bygone years who were part of the same great family of each succeeding generation who come to make a *home* – one of the sweetest words in any language. Do you remember the lines of Longfellow on *Children?*

> Ye are better than all the ballads
> That ever were sung or said;
> For ye are living poems,
> And all the rest are dead.

Our purpose in this volume is to classify all that the Bible has to say on the care and conduct, traits and training of children; and to interpret for the children of today some of the outstanding pictures of child life in the Bible. A study, such as we have undertaken, proves how up-to-date the Bible is and how its writings anticipated a good deal that is taught today in child psychology, and whose command, "Feed My Lambs" has never been withdrawn. This present study is to lead us to obey one of His chief commands to parents and teachers, and to all who have the spiritual welfare of children at heart! How solemn was the warning of Reuben, "Do not sin against the child" (Gen. 42:22). For all who have close contact with children, John Keble has the exhortation –

> O ye who wait with hearts too light
> By Font or Cradle, – fear in time!
> Oh let not all your dreams be bright
> Here in Earth's wayward clime!
>
> From the foul dew, the blighting air,
> Watch well your treasure newly won;
> Heaven's Child and yours, uncharm'd by Prayer,
> May prove Perdition's Son!

EVALUATION

The Planets of Space

The Prominence of Earth

The Purpose of Creation

The Perversion of Satan

The Provision of Restoration

The Primacy of Children

1
EVALUATION

In our appraisal of the importance of the child we seldom pause to consider the vital connection between the creation and children. Paul could write about God's "own purpose and grace, which was given us in Christ Jesus *before the world began*" (II Tim. 1:9) and of the "hope of eternal life . . . promised *before the world began*" (Tit. 1:2). When it came to the beginning of the world, "Through faith we understand that the worlds were framed by the word of God" (Heb. 11:3) – the Word being God's eternal Son (Heb. 1:2; John 1:1-3). These august truths imply that in the dateless past eternity the mind of God conceived the plan of a universe and the part earth should have in that plan.

The opening chapters of Genesis make it clear that when God made the heavens and the earth the earth was to be His masterpiece and that the heavens with all their hosts were to function for the benefit of earth. No information is given as to the manner of the creation of the other planets more immense than the earth, but we are given a detailed account of the creation of the earth with all its necessary light, vapor and water, land and sea, plants and trees, animals, birds and fish, all for the well-being of man, the climax of God's creature ability and for all the children to spring from man.

The Planets of Space

How overwhelming is the fact that all the marvelous galaxies of the universe are only incidental to earth, and that the bulk of the Bible is taken up with earth, and with God's purpose in creating it. The colossal heavenly bodies are seldom mentioned in Scripture. Job refers to Orion, Pleiades, Mazzaroth and Arcturus (9:9; 38:31-33). The moon and the stars are referred to as "the ordinances of heaven" (Job 38:33; Jer. 31:35-37). The sun, most glorious of all the planets, is in the majority of references dealt with as a symbol. For instance, "The Lord God is a sun." In order to emphasize the importance of earth as the only planet assigned by God as the only birthplace of children, let us refresh our minds by briefly viewing the enormous galaxies in space, designed for the welfare of earth.

A multimillion starred galaxy dwarfs the globe on which we live and makes man seem very small. The universe about us is vast beyond our comprehension. It is infinite and inconceivably immense, with new universes of stars out in space being discovered constantly. When we read the majestic sentence opening in the Bible, "In the beginning God created the heaven and the earth" (Gen. 1:1), we know that the Hebrew word for heaven is in the plural, and implies the entire solar system, or all the planets in space to the remotest extent. Moses wrote, "Thus the heavens and the earth were finished, and all the host of them" (Gen. 2:1). The spheres in space form a host, and host is the symbol of the vast, of the magnificent, of the mighty. The heavenly bodies form a host (II Chron. 33:3). The angels are a host (Gen. 32:2). The occupants of the deep are also a host (Gen. 1:21).

Such language indicates that there is nothing in the activities of God that suggests that He is scanty in His provision. The marvels of the universe cannot be measured. They defy all human reckoning. No matter where we turn we are confronted with the generosity and the infinite resourcefulness of God. Further, the word used for host is in the singular number, and therefore implies the oneness of creation. All in the great expanse of the universe is the provision of one mind. While each planet was created for a purpose, "the host of them" taken collectively reveals unity of divine purpose, and the product of a supreme intelligence. Professor Beattie, an eminent philosopher who lived in Aberdeen a decade ago, sought to give his small son a simple lesson in first principles, and this is how he did it:

One spring day Dr. Beattie traced with his finger in the soil of his garden the name, *John Beattie,* and then sowed in the lines some seed of mustard and cress. About two weeks later his little son ran into the study exclaiming –

"Father! my name is coming up in the garden!"

"Nonsense!" said his father, "don't talk like that!"

"Come and see!" urged the boy.

The father went out with him, and there beheld "John Beattie" outlined in living green.

"Well! how strange that such a thing should have come by chance!"

"Oh, Father," replied the boy, "it could never have come by chance; someone must have done it."

Then the wise father replied: "You are quite right, my boy; it could not have come by chance; I sowed the seed."

It was then easy for Dr. Beattie to speak to his little son about the divine designer whose existence is revealed by the wealth and variety of His works in the wide realm of the heavens and the earth. Does not the discovery in the heart of that child represent the ultimate feeling in the soul of universal mankind?

Identifying some of the galaxies in the host of heaven we have –

1. The Sun

This brilliant star keeps all the other planets under control and dominates and dwarfs the solar family of nine major planets, namely, Pluto, Neptune, Uranus, Saturn, Jupiter, Mars, Earth, Venus and Mercury. After millenniums of shining, it still rules the days and imparts all necessary light and heat for the benefit of earth. The planets nearest the sun are Mercury, Venus, Earth and Mars. The Sun is about ninety-three million miles from the earth, with a diameter over a hundred times that of the earth. Although it is so distant from the earth, the light of the sun takes only eight minutes to reach the earth.

Because of the energy generated by nuclear fusion and its incandescent gases, temperatures on the sun are so terrific that they are difficult to imagine. The surface is about 6,000° centigrade, while the temperature at the center may be anything from fifteen to twenty million degrees Centigrade. One Centigrade is a hundred degrees. Why did God create this tremendous ball of fire and light? Was it not for the good of man, beast, grass and trees of earth? (Gen. 1:11, 12, 16, 17). Without all that accrues from the sun, this earth of ours would pass into oblivion. God knew that the millions upon millions of children who would be born on the earth He had created would be dependent upon the light, heat and power of a sun, and so He flung one into space. He then reminded the inhabitants of the earth that as they cannot live physically and materially without the provisions of the sun, so they cannot exist aright without dependence upon Him who is our "sun" and "shield" (Ps. 84:11). Tennyson wrote of –

> The shining table-lands
> To which our God Him-
> self is Moon and Sun.

Oliver Wendell Holmes, in his poem, *Lord of All Being,* has the verse –

> Sun of our life, Thy quickening ray
> Sheds on our path the glow of day;
> Star of our hope, Thy softened light
> Cheers the long watches of the night.

2. The Moon

Because of the recent, remarkable achievements of brave astronauts, universal attention has focused upon –

> The moon, the governess
> of floods,
> Pale in her anger, washes
> all the air –

as Shakespeare described the only satellite in the solar system of a size comparable to the earth. In the spaceship *Apollo 8,* its three intrepid American crew were the first in the history of the world to conquer space and journey over 230,000 miles to circle around the moon at about fifty miles from its surface. Frank Borman, chief of the three moon travelers spoke of it as "a vast, forbidding expanse of nothing."

More than a quarter of a million miles from the earth, the moon is in diameter about one quarter of the earth's, and has a surface area less than half of that of the Atlantic Ocean. It is without atmosphere and has great degrees of temperature making the existence of human life impossible. While man is now able to land on the moon, he would not be able to live on it because the daytime temperature at its surface rises to 100° centigrade, as high as that of boiling water, and at night the temperature sinks to -180° centigrade, as low as that of liquid air.

As with the sun, this further lamp of heaven was hung out at God's command for the express purpose of guiding the seasons and illuminating the earth like living things who are conscious of the glorious function they have to perform (Ps. 104:19). To the Jews and to the ancients, the moon was "the arbiter of festivals" (Ps. 81:3). This is why the psalmist wrote of it "as a faithful witness in heaven" (Ps. 89:37). The festivals observed by Israel were signs of the Covenant, consequently the moon is likened to a witness in heaven. When God fashioned the moon He declared that its function would be to give light upon the earth, and as the lesser light to rule the night (Gen. 1:15, 16). This luminary has no light of its own. What it receives from the sun it reflects to earth. Is there not a spiritual lesson here for the Church which is symbolized as being as "fair as the moon"? (S. of S. 6:10).

Fascinating though it would be, to enumerate and examine all the other planets in the immense solar system, we have confined ourselves to a consideration of the sun and moon only, seeing these two galaxies are specifically mentioned as being related to the earth. Whatever the place in space which the larger satellites, along with the thousands upon thousands of smaller planets called "asteroids" may have, we are not told. They must have their function otherwise God would not have created them. Emphasis is upon the "two great lights" which He especially fashioned for the profit of human, animal and vegetable life on earth (Gen. 1:14-31).

Lord of all being, throned afar,
Thy glory flames from sun and star,
Center and soul of every sphere
Yet to each loving heart how dear.

The Prominence of Earth

Attention has already been drawn to the fact that "the host of heaven" is a phrase implying all large planets and multitudinous stars in space, and that the earth is given separate notice – "the heavens *and the earth*." After the record of the creation of the galaxies, the emphasis is on the earth, and on the process of its transformation as an abode suitable to all who are to be born in it. The supreme purpose of creation was for procreation, or the birth and well-being of children on the earth. Thus, after the initial and summary statement at the opening of the Bible, the process of the creative work of six days was necessary to bring the earth into a condition of habitation for its first occupants and for all the children to come from them. God made the earth, and the earth only, for man, then created man for the earth.

"Purpose," it has been said, "is the autograph of mind," and such an autograph is seen in all the works of God, particularly in this material universe of ours. After "The generations of the heavens and the earth" (Gen. 2:4-7) are traced up to the great fountainhead of the creation – God – then comes His final work of the creation of man for the place he was to occupy in the economy of the world. Man, therefore, was a necessary complement of the divine plan in creation. There was not a man to till the good earth God had made, and in Adam's task as a gardener we have the first reference in Scripture to the use of human instrumentality in the divine economy. God could have made the fields fruitful without human instrumentality, but this was not His plan. The work of man was to co-operate with God, and work was introduced before the curse.

Further, earth – hung and held in space by the omnipotent Creator of the rolling spheres – is the only one containing personal beings who can think, love, hate, hope, fear, choose and determine. All other planets are ruled out as the habitations of humans. They are either too far away – hence too cold – or too close to the sun – hence too hot. Alas! they are either too small or too large, and have either too little or no atmosphere, or have a poisonous atmosphere of the heavier gases, making life impossible. The earth, then, is the only member of the sun's family known to have living creatures upon it, and the human family forms a most vital part of the universe in which it exists.

Jupiter, for instance, the largest of the planets, measuring some 89,000 miles across, 484 million miles from the sun, and roughly about 1,300 times the size of the earth, is believed to have an atmosphere made up mainly of hydrogen, methane and clouds of ammonia. It is also terribly cold, about -130°C., a temperature in which life could never exist.

Uranus, Neptune and Pluto are all likewise too cold and their atmosphere too deadly poisonous for any life to be found on them.

Mercury, the planet nearest to the sun, is consequently too hot for either man or beast to live there. On its sunlit side it is believed to reach 500° centigrade. Nothing could live in such fierce heat.

Mars, "the red planet" between earth and Jupiter, which is almost half the size of the earth, about 4,200 miles in diameter, is often thought of as the planet most likely to support life. But because of the thin, icy air of Mars – the atmosphere containing only a very small amount of oxygen – man could not survive there. It is only on our tiny planet that life has been created and developed, and the Bible identifies man only with earth. Had there been life on any of the other galaxies in the universe, God would have said so. Herein, then, is earth privileged.

Earth. When the astronauts looked back at earth from the moon on that Christmas, 1968, they saw a beautiful paradise, "a shimmering disc set against a black velvet backdrop." Frank Borman cried as he saw the earth at a distance of some 230,000 miles – "the *good* earth!" To those men in space the boundaries between nations, the political struggles, the wars, the sins and sufferings were invisible. They saw "a planet cocooned against the fierce heat and deadly radiation of the sun by the atmosphere, a natural haven in which humans can live, work, rest, play, laugh and be happy, love and create." Away from earth they recognized what riches such a marvelous world contains.

Facts concerning the dimensions of the earth are known to every schoolboy. It has a total surface area of almost 200,000,000 square miles – a land area of some 58,500,000 square miles – a sea area of something like 139,-440,000 square miles. Its total mass weight is reckoned to be 6,600 million million million tons. Some weight to hang on nothing! The earth travels at a speed of 18.5 miles per second, or roughly 66,600 miles per hour, and takes approximately 365 days to complete its orbit. In comparison with the other planets our world is really a promised land with resources that man has barely tapped as yet. Only about three percent of this world of ours has so far been occupied or brought under control. Experts tell us that twice as much could be cultivated with very little effort and thereby eliminate starvation. Untapped riches beneath deserts, icecaps, sea-beds and mountains await man's discovery. For instance, it is estimated that Brazil has iron ore reserves of 35,000,000,000 tons – enough to make 140,000,000,000 family cars.

Further, "the cocktail of gases wrapped around the earth" are most vital to us. The atmosphere protects the earth from the fierce heat of the sun and the freezing cold of space. Water covers 70.6 percent of the world, and of this only about 2 percent is being exploited. It is said that a fortune of diamonds – 75,000 carats of them – is being brought up each month from the sea-bed off southwest Africa; and that other treasure troves are hidden under the oceans. When God made the earth He made it capable of producing all that would be necessary for the good of the countless children born on it.

The presence of humans, then, on our planet takes us back to the place God assigned to it among the galaxies, and to His purpose in its creation. For centuries man believed the earth to be the center of creation, but the fact is that it is only a small galaxy among millions in a universe as boundless as it is awe-inspiring. The latest scientific observation has so far probed only a fraction of it. As man probes deeper into the universe, the number of planets seem to grow as immense as the space through which they hurtle. Yet the fact remains that it is earth that is central in the eternal counsels of God, for before the worlds began He determined that earth should be the one world He would love and give His Son to die for the sins of its inhabitants (John 3:16).

The Purpose of Creation

In a past eternity, before time began, God conceived the master plan of a universe, with an earth planet as the only sphere on which to exhibit His transcendant attributes of grace, love, righteousness and mercy. To such a world He would send His only begotten Son as the culmination of the revelation of all His virtues and purposes. Thus, when Jesus came from heaven to earth, He could say, "He that hath seen me hath seen the Father" (John 14:9). Before God laid the foundation of the earth, or fashioned the heavens by His hands, (Heb. 1:10) He designed the plan of having a family of humans He could endow with eternal life, and have with Himself forever (Tit. 1:2). So, when it came to creation, He prepared the earth as the place for man's habitation and instituted the means by which it was to be populated.

The grand object in the creation of the universe, particularly the earth, and then the creation of man was to show forth and make visible to the entire cosmos God's own unseen glory and perfection. It was His will that man on earth was to have points of resemblance to his Creator, and to prove in all his character and conduct that he was indeed created in God's image. In the domination he was to have over the earth, man was to exhibit the sovereignty and power of God as the King and Ruler of the universe. Often under the midnight sky of Palestine, brilliant with stars, David, a great lover of nature, often mused upon things deep and high, on the marvels and mysteries of the immense solar system on the one hand, and on the rest of creation on the other.

Is this not the feature expressed in the perfect yet simple poem of the eighth psalm, which is a lyric echo of the creation record in Genesis? Overwhelmed by the glorious host of galaxies above him, David came to see the insignificance and weakness of man when compared with the majestic march of the colossal worlds in space and exclaimed, "What is man?" How infinitesimal he seemed alongside the grandeur of the heavens! As Thomas Carlyle expressed it – "When I gazed into these stars, have they not looked down upon me as if with pity from their serene faces, like eyes glistening with heavenly tears over the little lot of man?"

Yet the rolling spheres were created by God for the well-being of man although He made him a little lower than the angels. An interesting feature of this great psalm is the way David brought "creation" and "children" together. He speaks of the way the lisping tongues of infants, in simple and innocent wonder, worship and offer praise to God as the Creator (Ps. 8:2; Matt. 21:16). God accomplishes the greatest things and reveals His glory by means of the weakest instruments.

The psalmist then goes on to declare the intention of the Creator to give the creature dominion over all His works (8:6) – a distinction man still retains in a remarkable degree – but alas he is often less subservient to this purpose of his being than the brutes that he controls (Isa. 1:3). His power to dominate nature would have been greater but for the weakness sin has produced. Jesus, because He was perfect Man, could completely control nature (I Cor. 15:24; Heb. 2:8). During the millennium, full dignity and power will be restored to man as foreshadowed by the psalmist, "The upright shall have dominion . . . in the morning" (Ps. 49:14). David thus touches the two poles in the eighth psalm – human frailty on the one hand, and the glory of human destiny on the other. As Pascal exclaimed, "O the grandeur and the littleness, the excellence and the corruption, the majesty and the meanness, of man."

What must not be forgotten is the fact that the essential greatness of man and his superiority in creation was to be his by reason of his moral sense and his spiritual likeness to God. Further, in his moral powers he was meant to reveal God's righteousness and holiness, and reflect His light, inaccessible and full of glory. Then in the remarkable mental powers with which man was endowed, God fitted him for his responsibilities as an earth dweller. There was to be seen the image of God as the all-wise.

In the creation of home life on earth, with its love of husband and wife, parent and child, God designed to represent the love and blessedness of His home in heaven. At the heart of creation was His purpose to people earth with human beings through whom the fullness of His love might flow out.

> "As the Loving one He is
> the Fountain of Life;
> As the Living One He is
> the Fountain of Love."

Male and female were thus made in the divine image, that their whole life might be a life of love, and that in the children they bore, God's love might flow through the parents to their children. In the constitution of the human family God meant the mystery and blessedness of a life of love and fellowship to be understood. The parental relationship and human fatherhood were designed to reflect the fatherhood of God. "The Father . . . of whom the whole family in heaven and earth is named" (Eph. 3:14, 15). As Dr. Andrew Murray puts it in his appealing volume, *The Children for Christ* –

> Of this Fatherhood the father of the family on earth is to be the image and the likeness. In the life he imparts to his child, in the image he sees reflected, in the unity of which he is conscious, in the loving care he exercises, in the obedience and trust he sees rendered to himself, in the love in which family life finds its happiness, the home and the fatherhood of earth are the image of the heavenly. What a solemn and what a blessed view this gives us of the parental relationship!

The whole of the universe was a perfect creation and requires no further attention on the part of its Creator, but with the earth it is different, for being the sphere most precious to His heart, it has His constant care and thought, for the man He planted on it was made in His own image and likeness. Charles Wesley has taught us to sing of the –

> "Love Divine, all loves excelling
> Joy of heaven, to earth come down,"

for the express purpose of fixing in us His humble dwelling. Although God is able to tell the number of the myriads of stars and can call them all by their names yet it is upon the circle of our earth that He sits, indicating that it is circular in shape and that He is intimately associated with all its affairs (Ps. 147:3, 4; Isa. 40:22, 26). Not only is He the God of the starry heavens but also the God of sorrowing hearts. Creator of the universe, He yet condescends to give power to the faint (Isa. 40:28; 42:5).

The Perversion of Satan

To God, earth is most precious. It is His pearl of great price. An integral part of His marvelous universe, earth was a specific creation to fulfill a specific concept. Prepared atmospherically, geologically and biologically for the propagation of a human race, earth is the only planet peopled with those able to receive the revelation of God as the Creator and Father. Ours alone is the world among the worlds in space into which the Creator's beloved Son came as a child; the only world to be given the Holy Oracles of God and the privilege of converse with Him. How great is the sum of benefits He has loaded upon the earth which He ever loves! Its original condition in the primary creation was one of unequalled freshness and beauty, with no groans of suffering as the result of sin to mar the harmony of the song of "the morning stars" as they sang together (Job 38: 7). There was no slimy trail of the serpent to mar the perfections of the Creator's handiwork. Then tragedy overtook an unstained earth on which our first parents walked in cloudless fellowship with their Creator.

An iniquitous rebel appeared in Paradise to challenge the plan and supremacy of God and sin raised its horrid head against God, and with sin there came death. If Satan had not intruded to mar the bliss of man there would have been no sin, no death, no graves. As it was God's purpose in the creation of Adam and Eve to multiply and thereby fill the earth with children, one wonders what would have become of an enormous sinless race having no death to limit population? As death came by sin, then had there been no sin there would have been no death. If children, then, born into the world, were born sinless and remained so, would they have continued living on in undisturbed bliss or would they have been translated to heaven at God's bidding as Enoch was who walked with God?

The sorrow is that man did not remain innocent. Expelled from heaven because of his pride, Lucifer, an archangel of the highest order, became Satan, the adversary of God and man. Entering the Garden as the god of this world, and likewise its prince, as well as the prince of the power of the air, he concentrated all his efforts upon the destruction of God's desires for the perfect humanity. Satan has no relation with other planets seeing they are destitute of angelic or human beings to tempt and seduce. It was God's intention that the love and blessing of the home He had created should be as a ladder up which our first parents would climb nearer the great Father-heart in heaven. The heavens and the earth He had created were to be in correspondence with each other – the home in heaven, with the Father there, the original of the home on earth, with its loved ones living in complete harmony with each other, and with their Father above. But Satan came and thwarted the divine ideal, and, as Andrew Murray writes –

> How terrible the curse and the power of sin! Fatherhood in the likeness of God, the communication to any being of a life that was to be immortal and ever blessed, and the establishment of a home of love like that in heaven, was to have been the high privilege of man, as God created him. Alas! sin came in, and wrought a fearful ruin. The father makes the child the partaker of a sinful nature; the father feels himself too sinful to be a blessing to his child; and the home, alas! is too often the path not to heaven, but to hell.

As the result of the transgression of Adam and Eve there came about the hereditary corruption that Scripture constantly affirms, but which modern man, especially the humanist, denies. When David said, "Behold, I was shapen in iniquity, and in sin did my mother conceive me" (Ps. 51:5), he did not imply that he was conceived in a moment of passionate lust out of wedlock, but that he was the inheritor of the innate proneness to sin in every child of man from Adam down. (See Ps. 58:3). This is what is known as "original sin," or inbred sin. Every child is born with a bias toward evil, and as the child is a sinner by birth, he becomes a sinner by practice when, reaching the years of discernment between good and evil, he follows and obeys the pull of inherited sin. Within every child, then, from the first child, Cain, down, every child born into the world, with the exception of Jesus, was by nature a child of wrath (Eph. 2:3. See Job 14:4; Rom. 5:12).

When God fashioned the earth, and then created man to live upon it, it was with the design of having an unending race of holy beings to inhabit it. Satan, however, through his deception, succeeded in enticing Adam and Eve to eat of the forbidden tree, and with the birth of their first child he has had a foothold in every child born into the world since then. But what must be made clear is the fact that God does not hold a child responsible for inherited sin, only for practiced sins. As original sin is covered by the blood, a child, dying before reaching the years of moral choice and the power to discern between right and wrong, passes right into the presence of Jesus in virtue of His atoning work upon the cross. The incurable mentally deficient child enters heaven on the same condition. How disastrous for the human race it was when Eve, the world's first mother, heeded the voice of the tempter! By her transgression, sin entered to mar God's handiwork.

In the Presbyterian Cemetery, Brighton, England, is a memorial stone to the memory of the "Four Infant Sons of George Sawyer, 1847 - 1850" and the following epitaph:

> Bold infidelity! turn pale and die;
> Near to this tone four infants' ashes lie.
> Say, are they lost or saved?
> If death's by sin, they sinned because they're here.
> If heaven's by works, in heaven they can't appeal;
> Reason, ah, how depraved!
> Revere the page, the knot's untied;
> They died, for Adam sinned.
> They live, for Jesus died.

The Provision of Restoration

Our finite minds cannot fully comprehend the truth about Jesus coming into our world as the Lamb slain *before* the foundation of the world (John 17:24; I Pet. 1:20; Rev. 13:8; 17:8). Calvary was no unpremeditated plan on the part of God to meet an emergency, but was conceived by Him in a past eternity. Before He created the universe and man, and before time began, because of His omniscience, God was able to foresee that man, after his creation, would sin and require a Saviour, and because of His love, gave His Son up to the work of the cross *before* He flung the worlds in space.

> "Twas great to call a world from nought,
> Twas greater to redeem."

The marvel and mystery of grace is that the plan of our redemption preceded creation, and that God knew before He created man in His own likeness how sin would deface such an image, and made provision accordingly. Thus we come to the first intimation in Scripture of God's redemptive purpose, namely, the sending of His only begotten Son to be the Saviour of a world of sinners lost and ruined by the Fall.

In Genesis 1 Jesus is seen as the Word of God by whom the worlds were framed (John 1:1; Heb. 11:3).

In Genesis 2 Jesus is foreshadowed by the Sabbath on which God rested, as the Giver of rest (Matt. 11:28-30; Heb. 4:3).

In Genesis 3 Jesus is anticipated as the One who would be manifested to destroy the works of the devil (I John 3:5, 8). This chapter tells the dark story of human guilt, and of how "sin entered into the world" (Rom. 5:12). Satan whispered to Eve "out of the dust" (Isa. 29:4), and in this calm of devilry the subtlety of the tempter is revealed. Eve was beguiled. With longing eyes she looked at the forbidden tree, and although she had heard the warning, "In the day that thou eatest thereof thou shalt surely die," there came a positive transgression of God's law for "she took of the fruit thereof" (I Tim. 2:14). Determined not to be alone in her guilt she "gave also unto her husband with her; and he did eat." And so, there are now two tempters—Satan tempted Eve; Eve tempted Adam, and thus both became fellow-sinners.

Made conscious of their guilt Adam blamed Eve, and Eve blamed the tempter. There came expulsion from the Garden with its calm peacefulness and high delight, and the world's first pair had to walk without the companionship of God, and from that tragic day to this the fruitless quest of man to find happiness without God has continued (Heb. 11:25). Before his fall Satan, because of his exalted position in the angelic hierarchy, doubtless became acquainted with God's plan to create a universe with earth as His special sphere of preparation, and of the creation of male and female for the propagation of a human race bearing the divine likeness. Cunning-like, Satan knew that if he could pollute the source of human life, the whole of its river would be tainted.

Was it not tricky of the tempter to beguile our first parents as he did? He had the wisdom to know that as parents and children would be one, the defection of Adam and Eve would give sin its terrible power in the world; that with their transgressions the whole of their posterity would be made subject at one blow to sin and death. It was thus that the Fall gave sin such universal empire to a thousand generations. Satan knew, only too well, that the family was sin's greatest stronghold, with children inheriting evil from their parents. The unity of parents and children has the strength of sin. But Satan was to learn that the parental relation was to have a nobler destiny, so we come to the revelation of the Promised Seed.

Satan had made a promise to Adam and Eve which found fulfillment in the ruin of sinners; now God makes a promise to Satan which was to find its fulfillment in the salvation of believing sinners. Titus spoke of "the hope of eternal life" as a blessing that was promised "before the world began." Now this promise given in a past eternity is publicly declared, and was received, not by the first sinners needing salvation but by the tempter, the source of sin. He was the first to learn of God's redeeming grace, and from Him, of his own doom.

"I will put enmity between thee and the woman, and between thy seed and her seed; it shall bruise thy head, and thou shalt bruise his heel" (Gen. 3:15. See Gal. 3:16, 19). The primary function of motherhood is indicated by the words, "her seed." Eve was to become the mother of all living, and from a woman a child was to come who would "destroy the works of the devil." In the fullness of time Jesus came as the seed of a woman for He was "made of a woman" (Gal. 4:4). If it was a woman who brought sin into the world, it was another woman who gave the world a child who became its Saviour. Her "seed . . . shall bruise thy head," and around this declaration of triumph over Satan's dominions, the rest of the Bible groups itself.

Ellicott has this suggestive comment on Genesis 3:15 –

> "Leave out these words, and all the inspiring teaching which follows would be an ever-widening river without a fountainhead. But necessarily with the Fall came the promise of restoration. Grace is no afterthought, but enters the world side by side with sin. Upon this foundation the rest of Holy Scripture is built, till revelation at last reaches its cornerstone in Christ."

Through Satan's evil machinations Jesus was bruised upon the cross (Isa. 53:5), but such a bruising was overruled for the accomplishment of God's saving purpose (Isa. 53:10). At Calvary Satan's head was bruised, which means that his power was dealt a decisive and destructive blow, and now in virtue of it we can overcome the enemy by the blood of the Lamb (Rev. 8:10). Satan is a defeated foe, and by faith we make the victory of the cross our own. Through Christ we are more than conquerors.

While God did not curse the woman as He did the serpent who deceived her, yet she was punished as being the next in guilt, and her retribution was to be twofold.

First, "her sorrow and conception" were to be greatly multiplied, meaning that her sorrow would be heaviest in bringing children into the world. With anguish and peril of life she would win the joy of bringing children into the world. Frequently a mother dies in giving birth to a child.

Second, "Thy desire shall be to thy husband." In the sin of rejecting God's command, Eve was the prime factor, and Adam yielded her too ready an obedience. Because of this, woman would live in subjection to man. Gradually, among the heathen, such a punishment became most bitter by the degradation women had to endure – and still do in some dark corners of the earth. Among the Jews of old, although the woman never became a mere chattel, she was liable to divorce at the husband's will, and was treated in all respects as his inferior.

The Primacy of Children

With the coming of the holy Child Jesus, the position of woman was elevated, and Christianity abrogated the penalty of cruel inferiority. In Christ there is neither male nor female – both are one in Him (Gal. 3:28). The Christian woman is no more inferior to the man than is the Gentile to the Jew under grace. Adam called his wife's name Eve because she was to be the mother of all living, or "life-producer." Although Adam received the condemnation of death because of sin, he knew that through Eve alone could human life be continued; and that through her seed would come the One who would be able to raise up man from his Fall. As Eve, then, was to be the first mother of children, and that the divine objective in the creation of Adam and herself was the ever-increasing number of children to populate the earth which God had prepared for them, we have come to one or two aspects of motherhood.

1. Childbearing

Paul, in his exhortation on the divine order of the sexes, refers to "the woman being deceived in the transgression," but that, "Notwithstanding she shall be saved in childbearing" (I Tim. 2:15). This phrase can be translated "she shall be saved through her childbearing" which can mean, she was to be saved by Him who would be born as the result of her childbearing. "God sent forth his Son, made of a woman" (Gal. 4:4). Expositors disagreeing with this interpretation affirm that the salvation mentioned by Paul cannot refer to salvation from sin, which is by grace through faith, but to safekeeping through the pain which came in childbirth as the result of the Fall (Gen. 3:16). "The reference is to the calling of a woman as wife and mother," says one writer, "as her ordinary lot in life, and to the anxieties, pains and perils of maternity, as the culmination and representation of the penalties woman has incurred because of the Fall."

2. Child-Values

Ancient Jews looked upon the coming of children into the home as a mark of divine favor and greatly to be desired. "Children are an heritage of the Lord; and the fruit of the womb is his reward. As arrows are in the hand of a mighty man; so are the children of the youth. Happy is the man that hath his quiver full of them" (Ps. 127:3-5). (See also Gen. 15:2; 30:1; I Sam. 1:11, 20; Luke 1:7, 28). The psalmist depicts a young father with his growing family around him as a vigorous warrior with his quiver full of arrows. If his was a family of sons, then the more defenders in the tribe the greater the victory over their enemies in the gates. Thus the birth of a male child was a special cause for rejoicing.

> Therefore men pray to have around their hearth,
> Obedient offspring, to require their foes
> With harm, and honour whom their father loves;
> But he whose issue is unprofitable,
> Begets what else but sorrow to himself,
> And store of laughter to his enemies.

But the Bible also reminds us that a baby girl can grow up and become a female-warrior able to route the enemies of the Lord, as Deborah did. What an idyllic picture the psalmist gives us of peace and happiness in "The Family Psalm" — Ps. 128:1. Here is a glimpse of that simple piety preserved through many generations under a humble roof. As Ellicott comments, "We see the father of the family, working hard no doubt, but recompensed for all his pains by an honorable competence, and the mother, instead of seeking distraction outside her home, finding all her pleasures in the happiness of her numerous children, who, fresh and healthy as young saplings, gather around the simple and ample board. Happy the family, poor or rich, whose annals tell such a tale! But the happiness could not be real or sincere which did not look beyond the home circle, to the prosperity of the larger circle of the nations of which it forms part."

Alas! in our modern permissive society we have all too few such homes as the saintly, happy one described by the Hebrew poet, or as the one portrayed by Robert Burns in his poem telling the story of a godly peasant's home life, *The Cotter's Saturday Night,* part of which reads —

> The sire turns o'er wi' patriarchal grace,

The big ha'-Bible, ance his father's
pride.
He wales a portion with judicious
care,
And "Let us worship God!" he says
with solemn air.

From scenes like these old Scotia's
grandeur springs,
That makes her loved at home, revered abroad:
Princes and lords are but the breath
of kings,
"An honest man's the noblest work
of God."

If there were no sons born to a household, that family or branch became lost. Often, if a wife proved childless, another wife or wives might be added to the family (Genesis 16). There was also the custom that if a man died childless his brother should marry his widow, the children of such union being considered as belonging to the brother whose name and line were thus preserved from extinction (Deut. 25:5; Matt. 22:24).

3. Childlessness

With the introduction of the Hebrew monarchy, it was the hope of each Jewish mother that a son of hers might prove to be the Messiah. Such an honor was reserved for Mary who in becoming the mother of our Lord was blessed among women (Luke 1:42). All through the Bible it extols the importance and joy related to the possession of children, and correspondingly the intense sorrow and disappointment of a childless home. Among Hebrew women barrenness was looked upon as a reproach, or as a punishment inflicted by God, and involving, for the wife, disgrace in the eyes of the world. It was thus that Sarah, the wife of Abraham, was despised by her more fortunate handmaid Hagar (Gen. 16:4). Rachel, taunted by the envy of Leah cried, "Give me children, or else I die" (Gen. 30:1). The scorn of Peninnah made Hannah fret because the Lord had shut up her womb (I Sam. 1:6). Elisabeth, the wife of Zacharias, rejoiced when the Lord took away her "reproach among men" (Luke 1:25). With many another barren wife, the mother of John the Baptist could join in the climax of the praise of the psalmist "He maketh the barren woman to keep house, and to be a joyful mother of children (Ps. 113:9). The husband who feared the Lord had the promised reward that his wife would be like a fruitful vine, and their children like olive branches about their table (Ps. 128:3).

Fatherhood and motherhood meant material prosperity as well as marital pleasure, for with children came the expansion of property and increase in prestige and wealth. A father of sons was deemed to be a rich man. Thus every married couple desired to be fruitful and multiply that the blessings of fruitfulness might be theirs – "Replenish the earth, and subdue it; and have dominion." Under the Mosaic Law, those who prostituted marital relationship were smitten with childlessness (Lev. 20:20, 21). The sword made other women childless (I Sam. 15:33). Michal had no child because of the way she despised David (II Sam. 6:23). There were, of course, natural reasons for a barren condition (II Kings 4:14). Sometimes sin and idolatry were punished with childlessness (Jer. 22:30; Hos. 9:14). The divine ideal in a past eternity, however, was to "set the solitary in families" (Ps. 68:6).

4. Child Customs and Care

Ancient Hebrews were meticulous in the attention given to their children who were surrounded, not only with the love of home, but also with the religious influence of succeeding generations. Every child was taught to revere the God of their fathers. The first-born in a home belonged to God, and the ceremony of redeeming the child occurred on the thirtieth day following his birth. Friends of the family were invited to a feast, and the child was placed in the hands of a priest. The father carried some gold or silver in a utensil. The priest asked the mother whether the child was her first-born and, on being assured that it was, the priest pronounced the child as belonging to God. Then the father would offer the redemption money, which was accepted in exchange for the child (Num. 3:40-50; I Pet. 1:18).

Fitting ceremonies were celebrated at other stages in the life of a child. Among Palestine Jews, in the fourth year of a son, on the second day of the Passover there was the ceremony of the first cutting of his hair, with friends of the family sharing the privilege. Often, in the case of the wealthy, the weight of the child in currency was given as a donation to the poor. Then there was the further custom of circumcision which the Jews and other Eastern peoples observed. This rite was carried out on male children on the eighth day after birth (Gen. 17:12), and such cutting of the flesh was a sign of the Abrahamic Covenant (Gen. 17:7-14; Josh. 5:2-10).

Under the law of motherhood, there was the observance of purification on the part of the mother following the birth of a child. After thirty-three days her purification was fulfilled (Lev. 12; Luke 2:22). The concept of purity was graven deep in the conscience of an Israelite. When it came to the weaning of a child, such a custom was accompanied by great feasting (Gen. 21:8). In Bible times, all babies were breast-fed. Synthetic baby milk and foods were unknown. A child is born with a sucking instinct, and life depends upon it. How wonderful it is to watch a tiny baby grow on the nourishing milk which its mother supplies. This is why the Bible has much to say about the function of sucking and of its duration until weaning (Num. 11:12; Job 3:12; S. of S. 8:1; Isa. 49:15-23; Luke 11:27).

The handling of children is another practical matter the Bible mentions. Isaiah speaks of boys being carried in the arms, and girls being carried on the shoulders (49:22). Lane, in *Modern Egyptians*, records the observation, "The children of both sexes are usually carried by their mothers and nurses, not in the arms, but on the shoulders, seated astride, and sometimes, for a short distance, on the hip." The prophet has the expressions, "Ye shall be borne upon her sides," and "dandled upon her knees" (Isa. 66:12). Hebrew women exhibited great dexterity in the carrying of their children as well as their water-pots.

Sleep is most essential to young children. We have a saying that "they grow as they sleep." Sufficiency of sleep is as essential to life as a sufficiency of food, not only for children but also for adults. Infants sleep all the time except when feeding. It is figured that a child of two or three years of age should sleep for twelve or thirteen hours out of the twenty-four. Gehazi said to Elisha, of the Shunammite's little boy, "The child is not awaked" (II Kings 4:31). It is always a pity to rouse a child from a peaceful sleep, but Elisha found that the child was not in a natural sleep, but dead, and Jesus used the figure of sleep to describe the condition of the ruler's small child when

He said, "The maid is not dead but sleepeth" (Matt. 9:24).

Further, it is interesting to notice how early in life children learn and love to play. In His references to children, Jesus drew attention to their delight in play (Matt. 11:17). How glad the heart of Zechariah was as he saw in vision, "the streets of the city full of boys and girls playing in the streets thereof" (Zech. 8:5). In heaven there shall be a mighty multitude of happy children. Joyous children had a large place in the thoughts of Wordsworth as well as in the glorious vision of the prophet. The poet, according to a tradition common in pagan lands, depicts mortals being carried to earth from a heavenly island by an immortal sea, and so wrote –

> "And see the children sport
> upon the shore,
> And hear the mighty waters
> rolling evermore."

If, in the millennium, "the child shall die an hundred years old" (Isa. 65:20), then they will have unlimited playtime. Jesus noticed children at play. When He came to a market place in a town near the shores of the Sea of Galilee, amid the busy scene He came upon a group of children playing at marriages and funerals. As now, so then, children love to imitate their elders, and Jesus, in teaching those around Him, compared the Jews who would not listen either to Him or to John the Baptist, as being like the discontented children in the market place who would not play at marriages or funerals.

"Whereunto shall I liken this generation? It is like unto children sitting in the markets, and calling unto their fellows, And saying, We have piped unto you, and ye have not danced; we have mourned unto you, and ye have not lamented" (Matt. 11:16, 17).

Jesus thus used children at play as a lesson to adults. What interested Him in the games of Jewish children was not so much the games themselves as the spirit of those who played them. His heart was glad, as He marked the contented, unselfish spirit of some, but grieved when He saw others cross and pettish and disagreeable. Children should be taught to show the right spirit in their playing, and that they can serve Jesus even in their games. Toys and games are quite natural for children, as Paul reminds, but when they reach maturity, playthings are put aside. "When I became a man," says the apostle, "I put away *childish* things" (I Cor. 13:11). But he was always careful to remain childlike in humility and trust.

As for the early education of children, it was undertaken at home, principally by the mother (Prov. 6:20; 31:1; II Tim. 1:5; 3:14, 15). The girls remained under their mother's charge until the time of their marriage, but the boys received their instruction from their father, or, as in the case of the wealthy, from tutors engaged for their education (I Chron. 27:32). These hired teachers are referred to as "the bringers up of the children" (II Kings 10:5). Paul speaks about a child being "under tutors and governors until the time appointed of the father" (Gal. 4:2). Among the Persians there was a similar position in the households of wealthier families. Morier in his *Second Journey Through Persia* observed –

> If a boy, the father appoints a steady man from the age of two years to be his *laleh,* who, I conjecture, must stand in the same capacity as *the bringers up of children* . . . but if it be a daughter, the tutoress was a woman called *gees sefeed,* or *white head,* attached to her for the same purpose as the *laleh.*

The Melzar was the name given to the officer in the Persian Court responsible for the education and welfare of Daniel and his friends (Dan. 1:11).

The religious training of children began early, with all of the children taking part in the Sabbath and Passover festivals. Boys would attend the synagogues and schools regularly. Josephus, the Jewish historian is the first to mention schools for children. According to the Talmud, the first school for children was established about 100 B.C. By the time of Christ, such schools were common. Reading and writing were practiced from early times (Isa. 8:1; 10:19). As soon as the children could speak distinctly religious training began with great stress being laid on the Torah, or the Law of Moses. The boys in a family were also trained in agriculture or trades. As a boy, Christ learned carpentry.

As children grew up they retained a strong love for their parents, particularly, the mother. There was no insult that could be worse in the eyes of Orientals than that of any slur cast upon their mother's character. It is here that we can understand the taunt of Saul against Jonathan his son – "Thou son of the perverse rebellious woman." Saul did not intend to reproach his wife personally, but to intimate his wrath against her son. Such treatment was acutely felt by children, for in every Eastern family the great object of respect and devotion is the mother. When the Eastern people were angry with anyone, they would abuse and vilify his parents. "Strike me," said a traveler's servant to his master, "but do not curse my mother."

When a child reached the age of twelve it was usual to present him in the Temple. The present confirmation of youth in the Anglican Church is akin to the Jewish custom. Thus we read of Christ that, "When he was twelve years old, they went up to Jerusalem" (Luke 2:27, 42-52). Jewish boys today go through a similar ceremony. The lamentable lack of the religious training of children in our modern age is largely responsible for the way young folk seem to have so little regard for Christianity, morals, discipline and authority. They fail to remember God in the days of their youth (Eccl. 12:1). Did the prophet have in mind the petulance of youth deriding the experience of age in mind when he wrote, "The child shall behave himself proudly against the ancient, and the base against the honourable" (Isa. 3:5)? At any time, of course, "Better is a poor and a wise child than an old and foolish king, who will no more be admonished" (Eccl. 4:13). How true is the further word of Solomon about the manners of children: "Even a child is known by his doings, whether his work be pure, and whether it be right" (Prov. 20:11).

5. Child Worth and Influence

When Jesus requested children to come to Him, He recognized their value in His world and work as they came to play their part in them. He knew, as no other, that the moral quality of a generation was dependent upon the environment of home, school, and church of children coming into it from the previous generation. J. Edgar Hoover, head of the F.B.I. of America, who often stresses the importance of right child-training in the building of society, has reminded us that, "Today's unchurched child is tomorrow's criminal." Whether a boy is to become a John Wesley or Adolph Hitler in the next decade depends much on those who have his character training in hand. It is child by child that we create our communities and countries. Our concern for children must not cover only their early days but also what they may become tomorrow.

The Roman Catholic Church thoroughly believes in the dictum of Xavier, "Give me the children until they are seven and anyone may have them afterwards." Gardeners know that if they want a garden of good fruit, they must get their trees young and care for them. Is this not the thought enshrined in the following anonymous lines –

> An angel passed in his onward flight,
> With a seed of love and truth and light.
> And cried, "O where shall the seed be sown
> That it yield most fruit when fully grown?"
> The Saviour heard and He said, as He smiled –
> "Place it for Me in the heart of a child."

The value and potency of children are constantly enforced in Scripture. Think of who and what one Child became –

"Unto us a child is born, unto us a son is given: and the government shall be upon his shoulders: and his name shall be called

> Wonderful,
> Counsellor,
> The mighty God,
> The everlasting Father,
> The Prince of Peace." (Isa. 9:6)

"She brought forth a man child, who was to rule all nations with a rod of iron" (Rev. 12:5).

A striking estimation of the influence of a child is given by Isaiah in his peaceful description of the millennium, "A little child shall lead them" (Isa. 11:6). We read of one who said, "I am but a little child: I know not how to go out or come in," but it was no child who uttered these words. They came from the lips of a full-grown man who became a king renowned for his wisdom (I Kings 3:5). Solomon prayed that he might have wisdom above everything else, and God gave it to him in abundant measure. Does not God offer His treasures to all children and to all who trust Him in childlike simplicity? If children are taught to seek "the understanding heart," then a childhood of joy, a youth of success, a manhood of influence, an old age of tranquility will be theirs.

Often a child is used by God to lead adults into the way of peace. We have known of children going home from Sunday school excited about the truths of Jesus they were taught, and for parents to become convicted and ultimately led to church and to Christ. The simple faith of a little child is not only precious in the sight of Him who is "the Friend of little children," but also influential in the extension of His cause. Every little child is first of all God's child, for He it was who conceived the plan of filling this world with children. Does not such a thought clothe a child with dignity?

The story is told of a famous painter who was unique in the beautiful cherub and angel faces he painted. One day a friend came into his studio and asked him where he got models for his angels. In answer the artist pointed to a little ragged boy who was standing in the corner. "What?" said the visitor, "how can a boy like that be your model?" "Because," replied the artist, "every time that I look at him, I seem to see angels' wings sprouting beneath his rags." What he meant was that he could not look at that poor boy without remembering that, in spite of his rags, he was still God's boy and one He wanted to find a place for in His kingdom if only he sought to live as God's child, obedient to Him and to his parents.

One of the most beautiful things noticed concerning the great day of Jesus' entrance into Jerusalem was the presence of children in the Temple waiting for their King and then in gladsome chorus sing, "Hosanna to the Son of David." The bigoted priests and scribes sneered at "the children crying in the Temple" (Matt. 21:15), but the heart of Jesus was thrilled at the sight of boys and girls in the sanctuary and that they saw in Him One who had every right to the title of royalty. Those appreciative children teach us three lessons –

a. *Those Children Saw What Others Were Blind to.* Priests and scribes with their knowledge of Scripture and learning should have seen in Jesus the promised Son of David, but the children with their single eye saw what the religious leaders missed. That day in the Temple centuries ago taught that none can understand Jesus and His love better than a little child. "The child sees the childlike; and the heart of Jesus is the heart of the most childlike." Did He not say of Himself, "Learn of me, for I am meek and lowly in heart"?

b. *Those Children Sang While Others Remained Silent.* That day in the Temple the children led the praise of people. The word "cry" used of them means the lifting up of the voice with strength; a bold, full, hearty song which Christ declared the perfection of praise. From priest and scribe Jesus received rebuke, but from the children, rejoicing. Hymns from the lips of innocent children have often influenced parents for good. The music of which Martin Luther spoke, when he said that Satan was its bitter enemy, was the heartfelt music Jesus heard as He was greeted by the children with a glad "Hosanna"!

c. *Those Children Received a Blessing Which Others Lost.* How Jesus must have smiled at those little songsters for their greeting was sweetest praise to His ear! No wonder Jesus drew attention to His delight in the children's songs of praise and of how willing He was to open wide His arms to them. Sore displeased the chief priests and scribes said to Jesus, "Hearest thou what *these* say?" Back came the reply of Jesus. "Yea; have ye never read, Out of the mouth of babes and sucklings thou hast perfected praise?" (Ps. 8:2; Matt. 21:16). What a rebuke that was for those who should have been the first to recognize in Jesus, the Son of David, and bless His holy name!

A further tribute to the unconscious, effective power of a child appeared in *The British Weekly* issue of 15 July 1912 which contained a true story from Devonshire. It concerned a very sick child in a country cottage whose younger sister heard the doctor say when he was leaving, "Nothing but a miracle can save her." The anxious girl went to her bank, took out the few coins it contained, and in perfect simplicity of heart went to shop after shop in the village and said, "Please, I want to buy a miracle." She was always disappointed, and moreso when the local chemist could not help her. "My dear," he said, "we don't sell miracles here." Outside the door two gentlemen heard the girl's request, and one of them, a famous doctor from a London hospital, asked for and received an explanation for the desired miracle. He hurried to her cottage and examined her sick sister. The doctor told the mother it was only a "miracle" that could save her child, and that it must take place at once.

With his instruments at hand, he performed the operation, and the dear girl's life was saved. What simple trust and confidence are given unto babes!

A further illustration of the usefulness of children is seen in the expressive emblem the Bible employs to describe their worth, namely, arrows! "As arrows are in the hand of a mighty man (giant); so are children of the youth. Happy is the man that hath his quiver full of them: they shall not be ashamed, but they shall speak with the enemies in the gate" (Ps. 127:4, 5). If you are fortunate enough to have a family of healthy, happy children in your home, do you look upon them as a quiver of arrows? If this psalm was written by King Solomon then he knew all about the effectiveness of arrows, for he had often watched a mighty archer shoot them far into the distance and the darkness to strike a target that could hardly be seen. Happy is the home and the country which have their quiver full of good, strong, active, Christian children. They shall not be afraid when they speak with the enemies in the gate. Children, if rightly trained and nurtured, can be a blessing while they are yet children, and be more wonderfully used as they reach maturity by the divine Archer to pierce many dark hearts at home and abroad.

The poet Howell would have us know that –

> "Children are God's Apostles,
> day by day
> Sent forth to preach of love,
> and hope, and peace."

John Milton, the blind bard observes –

> "The childhood shows the man
> As morning shows the day."

EXHORTATIONS

Children and God

Children and Christ

Children and Scripture

Children and Parents

Children and Tragedy and Death

EXHORTATIONS

Children and God

The words "son" and "daughter" are from an original root meaning "to build," and suggest what David had in mind when he wrote about being "made in secret, and curiously wrought" in his "mother's womb" (Ps. 139:13-16). Today, as we shall see, women are taught how to prevent or destroy such a divinely designed structure. The Bible teaches us that children are to be regarded as divine gifts, pledges of God's favor, and as His heritage (Gen. 4:1; 33:5; Ps. 127:3), but we live in a degenerate age in which rulers, legislators and parents fail to observe the value God places upon children, and also the injunctions given to equip them for life in the home and in society.

Hell is intensifying its efforts to destroy children both before their birth and after. Marriage was ordained for the procreation of children, but an ever-increasing variety of drugs, pills and contraceptive devices are designed to prevent such a purpose. Further, we now have legalized abortion, so that if conception takes place, in or out of wedlock, babes in the process of creation can be murdered before they enter the world as unwanted creatures. Surely these unnatural practices and perversion of the divine order deserves the righteous judgment of the Creator Himself?

Then the widespread tragedy of broken homes and of the evermounting numbers of divorces and remarriages with many children having a succession of fathers or mothers who, without compunction of conscience indulge in a kind of progressive polygamy, are largely responsible for the lamentable increase of juvenile delinquency. The fact of the matter is that juvenile delinquency would not be so rampant if it were not for so much parental delinquency. Too many children are blighted during their impressionable years and grow up in an atmosphere of instability. Is it any wonder that our children's courts are so full of wayward youngsters, and our prevention and corrective centers are so overcrowded?

Those who have anything to do with children know only too well that our sex-ridden society is responsible for the birth of so many unloved and unwanted babies. Some of our educators and psychologists will have much to answer for at the bar of God for the advocacy of what is known as permissiveness, which teaches the abandonment of moral restraint. And so in our permissive society school girls are taught the use of contraceptives because of the increase of pregnancy among them. What chance have boys and girls of becoming men and women of character in the corrupt atmosphere surrounding them?

Then, what can we say about rulers waging war for power, prestige and possessions, and in their struggle, allow multitudes of babies and children to die slowly of starvation? How shocked we were over those horrible, heartrending pictures of precious Biafrans, emaciated children taken out into the bush and left to die! While food and clothing and medical supplies were rushed to their relief, we think of the countless thousands of those dear children who died a terrible death, and were robbed, therefore, of God's purpose in their creation. Because the hope of a better world rests with the children of the world, it is essential to get back to what the Bible has to say about their management and ministry. As we are now to see, the Bible has some pertinent things to say about the care, conduct, character and cultivation of the children we bring into the world.

1. Asked of God

Because the birth of a child was always a joyful event in a family, especially if the baby was a boy, a childless home was a source of great distress to the wife. This is why Scripture records the vehement desire of the barren to become the mother of children. In the case of Rebekah, it was her husband, Isaac, who "entreated the Lord for his wife, because she was barren: and the Lord was entreated of him, and Rebekah his wife conceived" (Gen. 25:21-26). Husband and wife received a double answer to their prayer for Rebekah bore twins, Esau and Jacob.

Rachel was another wife who longed for a child, and, in desperation cried to Jacob her husband, "Give me children, or else I die" (Gen. 30:1). Her desire was satisfied, her reproach as a barren wife was removed, and she bore a son who was to become one of the most illustrious figures in Jewish history, namely, Joseph. Then we have the well-known record of the wife in Shiloh who, in bitterness of soul, wept sore, and made a vow unto the Lord that if He would but open her womb and give her a son, she would dedicate him without any reserve to His service. It was not enough for Hannah that her husband, Elkanah, was "better to her than ten sons," she wanted a man child of her own that she could "give to the Lord all the days of his life." God heard her prayer and gave her a son whom Hannah called Samuel, which means, "Asked of God" (I Sam. 1).

At this point a word or two is necessary about the problem of barrenness. As woman was created to bear children, what were the causes of her sterility or infertility? Gynecologists attribute the lack of reproduction to some congenital disorder or malformation on the part of husband or wife or both. But the Bible declares that the giving or withholding of children is God's prerogative. In the case of Michal, David's wife, her barrenness was divine chastisement for her ridicule of her husband. "The five sons" she is said to have had were her nephews, the sons of her sister, Merab, wife of Adriel, whom Michal brought up for the widower, Adriel as her own sons (II Sam. 6:23; 21:8). (See under *Childlessness*). In other cases, in the secret counsels of God, children were withheld from those who desired them. It was so with Rachel, but in His own time, "God opened her womb" (Gen. 30:22). While Peninnah had several children, the other wife of Elkanah, Hannah, "had no children," for the reason given, "The Lord had shut up her womb" (I Sam. 1:5, 6). But "the Lord remembered her . . . she bare a son" (I Sam. 1:19, 20).

Hannah prayed for a son, and when her heartfelt petition was granted, she said, "The Lord hath given me my petition which I asked of him." Whether she asked for three boys and two daughters who followed Samuel, we are not told. It is said, however, that her ability to produce further children was of God – "The Lord visited Hannah, so that she conceived, and bare three sons and two daughters" (I Sam. 1:27; 2:21). When a young Christian couple sets up home and the bearing and possession of children are considered, husband and wife are much in prayer over such a solemn matter, and when babies appear they are received as answers to prayer.

But the fact must be faced that when God fashioned Adam and Eve He endowed them with ability to propagate the human race, and children, therefore, are the natural result. The vast majority of children born daily into the world are born of heathen or godless parents who are absolute strangers to prayer as we understand it. They did not ask, as Hannah did, for a child or children, yet they came because of man's God-given power to bring forth children. Blessed is the child prayed and longed for, and then prayed over after its arrival and through the years of childhood!

2. Given of God

Arising out of the above is the truth that the gift of a child was the height of joy, just as the death of a child marked the depths of woe. When Esau ran to meet Jacob on his return home and saw all the children, he asked, "Who are these with thee?" Jacob answered his brother, "The children which God hath graciously given thy servant" (Gen. 33:5). Learning of the tragic death of his sons, Job said, "The Lord gave, and the Lord hath taken away" (Job 1:19, 21). The first mother in the world said of the first child to be born in the world, "I have gotten (or received) a man from the Lord" (Gen. 4:1). Christ came as God's unspeakable gift to a sinful world, "He gave his only begotten Son" (John 3:16).

The question we want to ask at this juncture is, although male and female are able, through natural processes, to fashion the body of a child, are they able to transmit life to it making it, thereby, a living organism? The Bible teaches that God is the Source of Life, "In him was life: and the life was the light of men." "I am the . . . Life" (John 1:4; 14:6). The Lord not only stretched forth the heavens and laid the foundation of the earth, but "formeth the spirit of man within him" (Zech. 12:1). Does not Solomon remind us that when the body as dust "returns to the earth as it was," but the spirit, or life, within the body "shall return unto God who *gave* it" (Eccl. 12:7, See 3:21; Num. 16:22)? It is our firm conviction that man has never created life nor is he able to create it. This is God's prerogative alone.

Not so long ago universal coverage was given to the dramatic news from Cambridge, England, that it is now possible to cultivate human life in a test tube, and for childless wives to have a baby apart from the God-ordained method of sexual contact.

Without going fully into this first step of producing "test tube babies" which, it is affirmed, will bring new hope to infertile women throughout the world, what the scientists have done is this. From female volunteers eggs were removed and then mixed with the fluid containing male sperm. Once fertilized these eggs could be implanted back into the womb where they could mature naturally. The reaction to this alien way of producing life was rightly condemned by the Roman Catholic Church in the statement that "Only when the creation of life is carried out according to the will and plan of God, does the actual procreating of new life achieve the ends sought by it."

We cannot but heartily agree with Rome on this issue that it is a travesty of the natural way in which a child should be born, and that creating human life in this way is immoral. The sentiment expressed by a forceful writer, Mrs. Kathren Plummer, who, for over eight years has hoped for a child of her own, thinks that the idea of test tube life is appalling — "If it's not my baby then let it grow in its rightful place. I'd certainly take it over when it was born but I could not contemplate actually giving birth. I'd feel it was a parasite. The thought of having a complete alien entity in one's womb is sinister."

Another fearful aspect of scientific discoveries at Cambridge is the cracking of the secret of the structure of "the chemical of life" — DNA, which American scientists can now create artificially. This is the chemical storing the genetic codes which color the eyes and hair, and in all probability are passed on. Thus, by tinkering with this genetic code characteristics can be changed. Further, it is possible to tell the sex before a child is born by examining the egg outside the body. Researchers say that by their efforts sex-linked diseases, such as hemophilia — a serious disease in boys, and the birth of mongoloid children can be prevented.

The problem is, Where are these shattering possibilities to end? Mary Shelley's *Frankenstein* concerns a human being that began life in a laboratory. But her black hero went out at his task with a clumsiness that produced only a pathetic shambling monster, alien to society. Scientist Edwards, interviewed about the Cambridge discovery, said: "We don't want to produce monstrosities in a test tube. We would stop at the stage where these eggs are still microscopic."

Scientists regard it as a distinct practical possibility to produce human beings, as both British and American scientists are doing with carrots and other vegetables. Carrot cells from a single plant can be grown in a special broth to produce some 10,000 new, growing carrots. Ultimately, those who think they can create life, hope to have the know-how of breeding groups of human beings, called "clones" after the Greek word for a "throng." The vision is that of the production of a cohort of super-astronauts, or soldiers or statesmen, each with identical physical and mental characteristics suited to the job they have to do.

As Christians, we condemn all efforts to bring children into the world without the divinely prescribed, essential personal relationship of the family. Much is made of the fact that by the test tube life, no woman need to be without a baby if she wants one. Childless wives have our sympathy, but yielding to the technique now possible, may give them the kind of children they would be better without.

In his pride of achievement, the scientist may now think of himself as being on a par with the Creator Himself, seeing he is now able to produce a "virgin birth." Although scientist Edwards said, "We have produced a test tube baby — that is, if you define a baby as a baby at the moment of fertilization," he, or any other scientist cannot produce *life* within the egg. The bestowal of life is God's prerogative alone.

When the Lord God formed Adam out of the dust of the earth, He gave him a perfect body with all necessary blood vessels, but in order for him to become a living soul, God had to breathe into Adam's nostrils "the breath of life" (Gen. 2:6). In that divine act something left God and became an integral part of Adam. Life came to his body, not as the result of any inward bodily organization, nor was it derived by evolution from any other creature, but as a gift direct from God. We read a great deal about apparently dead people receiving "the kiss of life" and experiencing the recovery of consciousness and activity. But life is not imparted by such a kiss – which is a kind of imitation of God's act in giving Adam life.

What actually happens if a person for some reason or another suddenly expires, and one is near to give the supposed kiss, is that the mouth of the lifeless-looking one is opened and the living person breathes air or wind into the still body on the ground and simply sets the lungs in motion again. The one receiving the breath is not dead – if he is, then resurrection is impossible – but if life is still in the blood, then sometimes a quickening into visible life takes place. Natural life can be revived and maintained only by the extracting of oxygen from the atmospheric air. Further, if, during an operation the patient's pulse fails, and the heart is swiftly massaged by the surgeon, no massage can restore normality if life has left the blood.

It is these facts that cause us to consider the remarkable words of Moses in the blessing of God upon Noah and his sons as they went forth from the Ark to replenish the earth with children, "But flesh with the life thereof, which is the blood thereof, shall ye not eat" (Gen 9:4).

Here, the principle of animation, causing both man and animal to live is "God's special gift: for He alone can bestow upon that aggregation of solids and fluids which we call a body, the secret principle of life. Of this hidden life the blood is the representative, and while man is permitted to have the body for his food, as being the mere vessels which contain this life, the gift itself must go back to God, and the blood as its symbol be treated with reverence."

When Moses came to the setting forth of dietary laws for the physical well-being of the Israelites, he used a phrase similar to that above, "The life of all flesh is the blood thereof. It [the blood] is the life of all flesh; the blood of it is for the life thereof" (Lev. 17:14). This declaration can be made to mean, "The soul of all flesh is its blood, in, or through its soul," and implies that the sacredness of the blood arises from the fact that it contains the vital principle of life. The clauses can also be rendered, "The life of all flesh is its blood in, or during, its life," meaning that the life of all creatures consists in its blood; but only as long as the blood contains this life. All the time life is in the blood, a person is not dead. Just when the life leaves the blood is one of the secrets of God. What we do know is that if the blood is dried up, or coagulated, then life has passed away from it. Life, then, beginning to possess the blood of the small developing body of the unborn child at a set time, is the gift of God.

3. Promised of God

While it is true that God created man for the purpose of multiplying himself, and created the earth as the dwelling place for all the children springing from our first parents, there were occasions when He gave specific promises concerning certain children who would be born to accomplish specific purposes. From the first woman would come the seed, that is, a Child and children, to thwart the seed of Satan, meaning not only Satan himself, but all his children or emissaries (Gen. 3:15).

When God established His covenant with Abraham, the first Hebrew, He promised him that his wife Sarah would become "a mother of nations; kings of people shall be of her," and, by a miracle, God made her the mother of Isaac, the promised son in whom the line of Christ was to run (Gen. 17:15-19; 18:10). Abraham, the friend of God was not only richly blessed of his divine Friend, but received this commendation from Him, "I know him [Abraham], that he will command his children and his household after him, and they shall keep the way of the Lord, to do justice and judgment" (Gen. 18:19). As every child comes into the world full of promise, the parents of that child are thrice blessed if God knows that they will command their offspring aright, and constantly strive to keep them in the way of the Lord.

Another who received the promise of a child was the "great woman of Shunem" who had been so kind to Elisha the prophet and his servant Gehazi. Eager to reward her for her gracious hospitality, Elisha told Gehazi to find out if there was anything she needed. "Thou hast been careful for us with all this care; what is to be done for thee?" A true patriot, this wife of high estate desired nothing save peace to dwell among her own people (II Kings 4:8-13). But Gehazi learning that she had no child, probably owing to the advanced age of her husband (4:14), said to Elisha, "She hath no child." Calling her, Elisha told her that about that time next year she would embrace a son, which she did (4:16, 17). Tragedy, however, was to overcome the parents' most welcome child, as we shall explain under the aspect of *Children and Death.*

Righteous and blameless before God as Zacharias and Elisabeth were "they had no child, because that Elisabeth was barren." Why, we are not told. But although this godly man and wife were well stricken in years, and too old to have children (Luke 1:7, 18), the divine messenger came with the glad tidings that they were to have a son who would be filled with the Holy Spirit from his mother's womb. Although far beyond the child-bearing stage, the God who created the body and can reverse its laws, took away the reproach of Elisabeth among men, and made her the glad and honored mother of John the Baptist, the dynamic forerunner of the Lord Jesus. The promise to praying Zacharias was redeemed, and although stricken dumb as an evidence that God meant what He had promised, he recovered his speech at the birth of his son and named him according to divine instructions, John (Luke 1:3-25, 57-80).

Promises abound as to the coming of the greatest Child this earth has ever known. In the fullness of time God sent His promised Son into the world, and with the announcement of Gabriel to Mary that she had been chosen to become the mother of Jesus, Zacharias magnified God for His faithfulness in redeeming His promise to the fathers of Israel, to Abraham and to his seed for ever (Luke 1:55, 68-75). As a child Jesus was *born,* but as a Son He was *given,* indicating the union of deity and humanity in the holy One born of Mary, called the Son of God (Isa. 9:6; Luke 1:26-38, 46-56).

All of these godly hearts experienced that what God promised, He graciously performed. "According to all that he promised: there hath not failed one word of all his good promise, which he promised" (I Kings 8:56).

4. Belonging to God

By creation, all children are God's, seeing that He was the One who had designed family life in a past eternity, and in the Garden began the unending entrance of children into the world He created for them. God had every right, therefore, to claim the first-born of the children of Israel for Himself (Num. 3:12, 40, 45). The ceremony of redeeming the first-born occurred on the thirtieth day after birth, when friends of the family were invited to a feast, and the child was placed in the hands of the priest. Then the priest, asking the mother whether the child he held was her first-born, and receiving an answer in the affirmative, claimed the child as God's. The father then offered the redemption money of five shekels, which was accepted in exchange for the child. (See I Pet. 1: 18).

Israel was taught that the first-born of animals, the first fruits of the produce of the earth, as well as the first-born of human beings belonged to God (Exod. 11:5; 23:16; 34:19). The first-born possessed definite privileges which were denied to other members of the family. The Law forbade the disinheriting of the first-born (Deut. 21:15-17). Our Lord Jesus Christ is referred to as the First-born among many brethren, and of every creature (Rom. 8:29; Col. 1:15, 16; Heb. 1:6). The application of this term to the Saviour may be traced back to the psalmist where the Davidic ruler, or perhaps the Jewish nation, is alluded to as the first-born of Jehovah (Ps. 89:27). The custom of redeeming the first-born son is preserved among Jews to this day.

In a Christian home, all children born into it are received on trust as belonging, first of all, to God. Thus they are dedicated to Him to use as He deems best. As His property, but loaned to godly parents to love and care for, children should be taught that they belong to God, as well as to their home, and must, therefore, grow up and live as those who are His children. Dedicatory services for infants in the house of God are a recognition of God's proprietorship. How impressive are the lines of H. Coleridge on the Ordinance of Dedication!

> I stood beside thee in the holy place,
> And saw the Holy Sprinkling on thy brow
> And was both bond and witness to the vow,
> Which own'd thy need, confirm'd thy claims of grace;
> That sacred sign which time shall not efface,
> *Declared thee His* to whom all angels bow —
> Who bade the herald saint the rite allow
> To the sole sinless of all Adam's race.
> That was indeed an awful sight to see;
> And oft I fear for what my love hath done,
> As voucher of thy sweet Communion
> In thy sweet Saviour's blessed mystery.
> Would I might give thee back, my little one,
> But half the good that I have got from thee!

Parents who take this consecration of children lightly should remember the condemnation of Wordsworth —

> "Shame if the consecrated vow
> be found
> An idle form, the Word an
> empty sound!"

5. Favored of God

When the angel Gabriel was sent from God to the virgin whose name was Mary to inform her of the divine choice of her as the mother of our Lord, he greeted Mary by saying, "Hail, thou that art highly favoured, the Lord is with thee: blessed art thou among women" (Luke 1:28). The words "highly favoured," are given in the margin as "graciously accepted" or "much grace." "Endued with grace" is the thought implied and covers not only grace, or consciousness in a person, but also grace on the part of the giver of a favor to that person. Mary had "found favour with God" (Luke 1:30), and was now to be favored by Him. In the course of time, the Holy Child whom Mary was privileged by God to bear, was to increase "in favour with God and man" (Luke 2:52).

Sarah likewise felt that God had highly favored her in the reversal of her long barren condition making her the mother of Isaac when she was far past the child-bearing period. "She [Sarah] said, Who would have said unto Abraham, that Sarah should have given children suck? for I have born him a son in his old age" (Gen. 21:7).

Many other ancient, saintly mothers magnified God for His grace and favor in the children born to them. "He [God] hath blessed thy children within thee" (Ps. 147:13). Would that all parents could look upon the infants coming to grace their homes as a divine favor! How apropos are the anonymous lines written for parents! –

"I'll lend you for a little time
A child of Mine," He said,
"For you to love the while she lives
And mourn for when she's dead.
I cannot promise she will stay,
Since all from life return,
But there are lessons taught down there
I want this child to learn.

I've looked the wide world over
In My search for teachers true,
And from the throngs that crowd life's lanes
I have selected you.
Now, will you give her all your love,
Nor think the labour vain,
Nor hate Me when I come to call
To take her back again?"

6. Capable of Glorifying God

In one of his wonderful Hallelujah psalms, the psalmist exhorts all the angels, all the starry hosts and all aspects of nature to praise the Lord. Those on earth – kings, princes, judges, young men and maidens, old men, and children – are likewise exhorted to swell the chorus and praise the name of the Lord (Ps. 148:12, 14). He who made us with the gift and power of song loves to hear the little ones sing. Already, we have drawn attention to the children who sang praises to the Lord in the Temple, and how, when they shouted, the priests and scribes were surprised and asked Christ whether He accepted their praise of Him as "the Son of David." Did He approve of the interruption of the order and quiet of the Temple by those junior, lusty voices? In reply, He quoted from one of David's psalms: "Out of the mouth of babes and sucklings thou hast perfected praise" (Ps. 8:2; Matt. 21:16).

Yes, the Hosanna of those children contained the truth which the supposed interpreters of the Law had rejected. What was hidden from the professed wise men had been revealed unto babes. So, to Jesus, the innocent brightness of childhood was a joy, and far more acceptable than the hypocritical, half-hearted, self-seeking homage of those religious leaders.

Parents cannot begin too early to teach their children to lisp the name of Jesus. They should grow up with their minds stored with the truth of good hymns, for their influence can be far-reaching.

People and realms of every tongue
Dwell on His love with sweetest song,
And *infant voices* shall proclaim
Their early blessings on His name.

7. Obedience to God

Under divine inspiration, Moses commanded the Israelites saying, "Thou shalt obey his voice according to all that I command thee this day, thou *and thy children,* with all thine heart, and with all thy soul" (Deut. 30:2). One of the most wonderful powers God endows us with as we come into the world, is that of the *will* — the power of determining what we are to be and do. This most delicate instrument, on which the future life of a child depends, must be directed and strengthened by its parents, so that the child is trained all unconsciously to hold and to exercise the will to the glory of the God who gave it. Unless the parents themselves strive to be obedient to God in all things, they cannot expect to succeed in the solemn task of teaching their children to obey the divine voice.

A child's first virtue is obedience. The little one may not be able to understand or approve what it is asked to do, but does it because the parent lovingly commands. Learning to submit to a higher authority in the home, the child comes to understand parental instruction as to the necessity of obeying God's commands. Andrew Murray reminds us that, "Obedience from this principle will thus secure a double good; while guiding the will into right habits it strengthens the command the child has over it. *Before the child knows* to 'refuse the evil, and choose the good,' in this first stage of childhood, simple obedience is the law." The constant prayer of parents must be for grace, wisdom and patience as they seek to train the will of the child to become obedient to the will of God. To quote Coleridge again —

> Ere thou wert born into this breathing world
> God wrote some characters upon thy heart.
> Oh, let them not like beads of dew impearl'd
> On morning blades before the noon depart!
> But morning drops before the noon exhale,
> And yet those drops appear again at even,
> So childish innocence on earth must fail
> Yet may return to usher thee to Heaven.

Surely one of these characters engraved upon the heart of a child is that of obedience to God and to parents. The holy Child Jesus learned this priceless lesson. He was subject to His parents (Luke 2:41, 51). And so —

> Christian children all must be
> Mild, obedient, good as He.

8. Remembrance of God as Creator

In his remarkable portrayal of the trials and tribulations of old age, Solomon sets out with an exhortation to the young, to remember God as their Creator as they enter life (Eccl. 12). It is interesting to note that the term "Creator" is used as a divine name by Isaiah (40:28; 43:15), and that like another divine name, "Elohim," it is in the plural suggesting the three Persons of the blessed Trinity. Thus it should read "Remember thy Creators." At the beginning God said, "Let *us* make man in *our* image." Father, Son, and Holy Spirit were all united in the creation of man, and all born of God must remember that they owe their wonderful body, with all its powers, to the Trinity. The word "remember" means "ever to be mindful of," and we should never forget that we have been fearfully and wonderfully made. It was Elohim who made us, and not we ourselves.

"Begin in the beginnings of thy days to remember Him from whom thou hadst thy being. Call Him to mind through all the days of childhood and youth, and never forget Him. Guard against the temptations of youth, and thus improve the advantage of it."

As a child's mind develops and it becomes fascinated by the wonders of the universe around, as well as the marvels of their own body, the parents have a great opportunity of leading those in the cream and flower of their days to Him whose hands fashioned them, and also into the necessity of yielding their bodies to the Creator for use in His service. Linked to Solomon's exhortation is that of Paul's, "Remember Jesus Christ." The young must be taught that the recognition of God as the Creator is not sufficient. In order to become His, Jesus must be received as the only Saviour from sin. Then, by creation and redemption, they become doubly His.

9. Fearing God

When Moses came to the Israelites with the statutes and judgments he had received directly from God, he urged the people to hear and fear, and to teach their children to fear the Lord. "Hear my words, that they may learn to fear me all the days that they shall live upon the earth, and that they may teach their children" (Deut. 4:10).

Although the word "fear" occurs hundreds of times in the Bible, it does not mean the same emotion in every case. At times, it means "dread" or "terror," as in the repeated phrase, "Fear, and the pit, and the snare" (Isa. 24:17). But the oft-recurring phrase, "The fear of the Lord," does not mean a fear of Him as if we would crawl and cringe before a tyrant. The words imply a reverential trust, with hatred of evil. This is the significance of David's statement, "The fear of the Lord is clean" (Ps. 19:9).

The homes of today, in which children are taught to love and reverence the Lord, are few and far between. Too often they grow up hearing His name taken in vain. If a home is shadowed by morbid fears and frictions because of overcrowding, constant bickerings, nervous tensions, anxieties over shortage of money, lack of patience, love and understanding among the members of the family, how can we expect children to be taught to fear the Lord in such a tense atmosphere? Fears, whether real or imaginary, destroy peace of home and heart. The prophet could say, "I will trust, and not be afraid" (Isa. 12:2). Faith and the wrong kind of fear cannot exist together. In a home where trust in God prevails, children, whom God made to worship, have no difficulty in growing up, reverencing His holy name.

10. Dedicated to the Service of God

One of the most beautiful, touching and instructive child's record in the Bible is that of the surrender of the young Samuel to the house and service of the Lord. He had been eagerly longed and prayed for, so as soon as he was born his mother gave him back to the Lord for "all the days of his life" (I Sam. 1:11). Without hesitation she offered him as a sacrifice unto the divine Giver (I Sam. 2:1, 11). Samson was another who was committed to God before and at birth (Judg. 13). Job, being a perfect and upright man, one who feared God and hated evil, must have dedicated his seven sons and three daughters to

God as they were born into his home (Job 1:1, 2).

Because of the godliness of Zacharias and Elisabeth, they willingly gave up their son. Filled with the Holy Spirit from his mother's womb, John the Baptist never stained the vow of consecration taken by his parents at his birth (Luke 1:13-17, 57-80). As soon as she was able, Mary brought her illustrious Child and presented Him to the Lord, in obedience to the divine law, "Every male that openeth the womb shall be called holy to the Lord" (Luke 2:21-24). Such dedication of infants was a recognition of divine right of ownership. Is it not this thought Bishop Heber enshrined in those impressive lines of his?

> O Thou, whose infant feet were found
> Within Thy Father's shrine,
> Whose years, with changeless virtue crowned,
> Were all alike divine;
>
> Dependent on Thy bounteous breath,
> We seek Thy grace alone,
> In Childhood, Manhood, Age and Death,
> To keep us still Thine own!

When Christian parents bring their "earthly darlings to the cross for life or death," as John Keble put it, they reflect although dimly, the surrender of God when He gave His dearly beloved Son to be born as the Saviour of the world. As our children are the only earthly possessions we can take with us into eternity, it is incumbent upon us to see that as "heirs of immortality" they share the glory awaiting us. If dedicated to God from birth, and constantly surrounded by the consecrated life and living of a Christian home, there is not much fear of children thus blessed and protected, straying from its holy atmosphere.

What a saintly soul Susannah Wesley was! The mother of nineteen children, including John and Charles Wesley, she dedicated her large brood to God, and did not consult child guidance textbooks for guidance as to the preservation from evil in the lives of her children. Here are the *Sixteen Rules* she laid down, over 200 years ago, for keeping her many sons and daughters in the paths of righteousness.

1. Eating between meals not allowed.
2. As children they are to be in bed by eight p.m.
3. They are required to take medicine without complaining.
4. Subdue self-will in a child, and thus work together with God to save the child's soul.
5. Teach a child to pray as soon as he can speak.
6. Require all to be still during Family Worship.
7. Give them nothing that they cry for, and only that which they ask for politely.
8. To prevent lying, punish no fault which is first confessed and repented of.
9. Never allow a sinful act to go unpunished.
10. Never punish a child twice for a single offense.
11. Commend and reward good behavior.
12. Any attempt to please, even if poorly performed, should be commended.
13. Preserve property rights, even in smallest matters.
14. Strictly observe all promises.
15. Require no daughter to work before she can read well.
16. Teach children to fear the rod.

In our modern age when even young children are given latitude undreamed of a century or so ago, the rules of Susannah Wesley may seem antiquated and too strict, but society would not be as corrupt as it is if only these same rules could be enforced in family life. If they could produce consecrated men like the Wesleys, then, by all means let us return to their godly mother's most spiritual and practical advice for the safeguard of childhood. Both the church and the nation cannot rise spiritually unless the children within their borders represent godly homes, and grow up passing out into the world as children of God through faith in Jesus Christ. From earliest years children should be taught to pray –

> Saviour, while my heart is tender,
> I would yield that heart to Thee,
> All my powers to Thee surrender,
> Thine, and only Thine, to be.

11. Contact With the House of God

While the provision and advantages of a truly Christian home are of inestimable value in the shaping of the character of children, there are also the additional influences of church, Sunday school, and all the activities of child evangelism groups. Countless numbers of boys and girls have been won for the Saviour through summer camps convened both for their enjoyment and salvation. Although Samuel was "a young child," his mother "brought him unto the house of the Lord" (I Sam. 1:24), and all Samuel heard from, and about, the Lord he retained. "He did let none of his words fall to the ground" (I Sam. 3: 19).

Parents who seldom darken a church door, and have little interest in the spiritual benefits to be derived from contact with a house of worship, cannot expect their children to grow up with an appetite for all that is Christian, even though they may send them to a Sunday school – in many cases to get rid of them for an hour or so. There is no more impressive sight than that of mother and father and children seated together in the Lord's house on His day. The joy and satisfaction of parents in the things of God are contagious, as they experience, as they see their children developing under the impact of the Word of God. On the Jewish Sabbath, the holy Child Jesus was always to be found in the synagogue – a custom He maintained throughout His life. For their spiritual welfare and safeguard the children of our homes must grow up accustomed to contact with all that a God-honoring church in their community offers for their profit and pleasure. How captivating are the lines of Margaret Sangster in *Children in Church!*

> The little children in each pew are like enchanted flowers.
> They nod and sway – and yet, they plan – across the quiet hours.
> And some of them drift into sleep, against a mother's breast,
> And some of them in singing hymns, find stimulating rest!
> Their parents smile and sometimes nod, above each curly head,
> But, oh, they listen carefully as lesson texts are read –
> And feeling fingers touch their own, like drifting butterflies,
> They peer, with heightened tenderness, into each others' eyes.

In the Anglican handbook on "Christian Seasons" there is the following prayer to be used on the day of "The Consecration of Childhood" –

> Grant, we beseech Thee, O Lord, that this Child may hereafter not be ashamed to confess the faith of Christ crucified, and manfully to fight under His banner against sin, the world, and the devil, and to continue Christ's faithful soldier and servant unto his life's end.

12. Ignorant of God

What a great gulf there was between the godly child of Hannah and the two children of Eli, the priest. Samuel was cared for in the house of the Lord. "The sons of Eli were sons of Belial: they knew not the Lord" (I Sam. 2:12, 26). What a heartbreak those godless boys must have been to their godly father, especially as he contrasted them with little Samuel who had God's favor! Hophni and Phinehas, who both perished in one day for their sacrilege, were children who behaved themselves proudly against their honorable father (Isa 3: 5). Solomon reminds us that children left to themselves bring shame to their parents (Prov. 29:15). What a sad sight it is to see children left to themselves! In our highly industrialized age, when both father and mother go out to work, children are farmed out to others, or left to fend for themselves — often with dire consequences.

It is indeed a grievous sin to leave the young to themselves, neglect personal care of them, or give them too much money to spend, or liberty to do as they like; but sadder still for a child's soul to be left to itself — a child who has never heard of Jesus the Saviour from the lips of those of whom he is part. Both the Bible and human experience indicate that the most sincere Christian parents can have the most godless children, in spite of a religious upbringing; and that the most sinful parents can have a child who becomes a saint. In the main, however, where mothers "love their husbands, love their children, are discreet, chaste, keepers at home," the children themselves are "faithful children not accused of riot or unruly" (Tit. 1:6; 2:4, 5). Children of believing parents should always strive to follow their example and counsels.

Unwanted children, given over to others to adopt; children turned out into the streets with indifference to evil associations that may be formed; children of Christless homes, who grow up without contact with church or Sunday school, should be the deep concern of all who have the spiritual welfare of the young at heart. To claim them for God is a hard task. Lack of a religious upbringing, crime, violence and sin they see on TV and on films, are responsible for the widespread decline in Sunday school attendance. All who have a passion for the salvation of the boys and girls in their own neighborhood need much patience, understanding, tact and love; and come to prove that often "the choicest wreaths are wet with tears." But child evangelism is always rewarding, for in the winning of a child for Christ there is a double salvation — the soul is saved from sin and the life secured for the service of the Saviour, so that, even in later years, this child of God can say with Browning, "I love thee . . . with my childhood's faith."

Children and Christ

The gospels portray Jesus as a lover of children. Having entered the world as a child, He knew the child heart, and thus childhood was always sacred in His eyes. What strong condemnation He had for those who outraged the rights of children, and how warmly He welcomed the little ones whom He presented as models to those aspiring to the Kingdom of Heaven! How the lusty voices of the young love to sing! —

> I'm glad my blessed Saviour was once a child like me.
> To show how pure and holy His little ones might be;

And if I try to follow His footsteps here below,
He never will forget me, because He loves me so!

Some writers have made much of the fact that Jesus is nowhere depicted as laughing, the implication being that as the Man of sorrows life was far to solemn for Him who trod the winepress alone. But while it is true that there was never any sorrow like unto His sorrow, yet it must not be forgotten that it is also said of Him that He was "anointed with gladness *above* his fellows" (Heb. 1:9). "Above His fellows" means that He was the "gladdest," as well as the "saddest" Man of His time. The gospels reveal that He had much to say about peace and joy and happiness, and it would have been unnatural if Jesus did not have a countenance bearing the smile of an inner contentment. Further, if He had had a face that was severe and serious-looking, the little children who learn to smile before almost anything else would not have been attracted to Him as they were. When He took them up in His arms and blessed them there must have been a smile on His holy face, evoking smiles of appreciation on the fresh faces of those He blessed.

All who have the highest interests of children at heart can learn much from the Master's association with them as they gathered around Him. Here is a brief summary of His treatment of the little ones and of His teaching concerning them.

1. They Were to Be Fashioned After Christ

Not only adult believers but children as well were left an example by Jesus that they should follow His steps (I Pet. 2:21). Their conception differs from that of Christ, seeing He was "conceived of the Holy Spirit," and born into the world without sin (Luke 1:35). But as a child He left all children an example to emulate. Luke the beloved physician, who doubtless learned a good deal from Mary in confidential conversations about the birth and childhood of Jesus, has given us an intimate sketch of His early days. "The child grew, and waxed strong in spirit, filled with wisdom: and the grace of God was upon him. He went down with them [his parents] . . . and was subject unto them: . . . and Jesus increased in wisdom and stature, and in favour with God and man" (Luke 2:40, 51, 52).

The mother of Jesus was mystified over many of the sayings of her Child, and kept them stored in her heart. Always close to His honored mother, Christ had her uppermost in His thought as He came to die (John 19: 26, 27). The characteristic features which Luke gives us of the childhood of Jesus serve as an ideal which all godly parents should train their children to reach. Another hymn suggests:

I loved to think, though I am young,
My Saviour was a Child;
That Jesus walked this earth along,
With feet all undefiled.

He kept His Father's word of truth,
As I am taught to do;
And while He walked the paths of youth,
He walked in wisdom too.

2. They Were Wanted by Christ

When the disciples frowned on the parents for troubling their Master with their children, He said, You must let little children come to Me, and you must never stop them. The kingdom of heaven belongs to little children like these (Matt. 19:14). Does this rebuke not teach us that the salvation of children must not be neglected, that they must be received as Himself, that it was not His will that one of these little ones should grow up and perish in sin? (Matt. 18:11-14). How His tender heart must be grieved as He looks down on the countless number of dear children who are either unwanted and neglected, or born into and brought up in godless homes, or left to die terrible deaths in the starvation areas of the world!

Jesus yearns over all the children of the world, irrespective of their color and race, and we should share His love for them. We must seek to bring them to Him because they need Him as Saviour, Teacher and Friend. Satan, who knows only too well the value of a child, concentrates his efforts on the destruction of its purity. The subtle enemy understands that every child is born close to heaven's gate, and thus when we speak of innocent childhood the destroyer is alert to blight that innocence as he did in the lives of Adam and Eve. Children's consciences are tender, and their hearts have fresh affections that turn as readily to Jesus as buds of a plant to the morning sun.

The question may be asked, At what age should a child be brought to Jesus? If he was dedicated to Him before he was born, and the dedication was reaffirmed at his birth, Christian parents find it easy to lead the child to the Saviour. What He made clear in His criticism of the disciples was that they were not to forbid or hinder children of any age coming to Him. Josiah began to seek the God of David when he was only eight years of age. Jesus did not teach that children, as such, are all His and do not need to be brought to Him. What He did teach was that the distinctive characteristics of a child – humility, dependence, and faith – are the attitude that every sinner must take toward Him in order to be saved.

It has been said that, "Children may act grace as soon as they can act reason, may be made to know their heavenly Father as soon as they do their natural parents." Their tender age is no bar to their acceptance of Christ. Some of the most consecrated Christian workers cannot give the date of their conversion. Under the guidance of godly parents, they seem to grow up in the Lord, and cannot remember a time when they did not love Him. This is the ideal that parents should pray for and aspire to with their children, leading them to pray for themselves –

In the glad morning of my day,
My life to give, my vows to pay,
With no reserve, and no delay,
With all my heart, I come.

3. They Were Brought to Christ

How delightful it is to read of the way parents, seeking Christ's benediction upon their children, brought them to Him that He should teach them, and how He took them up in His arms, and put His hands in blessing upon their heads (Mark 10:14, 16). Matthew adds that He also prayed for "the little children" as His hands rested on their heads (19:13, 15). Luke says that "infants" were brought to Him, to receive His "touch" (18:15). The disciples could not be bothered with having children around, but Jesus rewarded their loving parents who desired His benediction upon their offspring.

As Jesus fondled those little ones and smiled upon them, as we have just observed, He would not have been human if His brow had never relaxed, His eyes had not brightened, and His lips had not moved in pure gaiety and laughter. His outward gestures declared His good will toward them, and His enjoyment of their company. A sweet child once said to a friend, "When I am well I like to be carried by my father, but when I am sick I like my mother to carry me." When asked the reason, he replied, "When I am well my father carries me on his back, and it is great fun; but when I am unwell, my mother carries me in her arms, and it makes me feel better." With a father-mother heart, for He created both, the Lord carried those children in His arms, and upon His shoulders (Isa. 46:7; 49:22; Ezek. 12:7).

What a sweet picture this is, then, of children with their fears soothed by the comforting voice of Jesus. Even little boys and girls want friends, and in the One who nestled them to His side there is indeed "A Friend for Little Children," not only, "above the bright, blue sky," but here on earth where, so often, children need such a Friend who loves to carry the lambs in His bosom (Isa. 40:11). Why did those mothers bring their little ones to Jesus? What was their object? The children were not sick, or diseased, or lame, and because they were so young they would not be pressing so closely to Him merely to listen to His words. No! all those loving mothers wanted for their children were the prayers and blessing of the great Teacher. Responding swiftly to their desire He took them up in His arms of love saying, "Suffer the little ones to come to me." Is it any wonder that children love to sing today?

> I wish that His hands had been placed
> on my head,
> That His arms had been thrown
> around me,
> And that I might have seen His kind
> look when he said,
> "Let the little ones come unto Me."

The primary responsibility of parents is not to bring up their children and give them a good education, but to bring them to Jesus for salvation and blessing. Is there not a deep significance in the word "*Suffer* little children to come unto me"? We "suffer," or allow, or permit that which we are not naturally inclined for, which we would prefer otherwise. It was against the inclination of the disciples to understand that little children should have anything to do with their Master, and so received His command, "Forbid them not; allow them to come unto me." They could not fathom any connection children had with the kingdom of heaven, and Jesus revealed how they were nearest the kingdom, and the most fit for it. Andrew Murray observes – "It is only as it were by *sufferance* that the religion and the faith of a child is borne with; a thing not to be too much trusted or rejoiced in. No wonder that with such a spirit in parents or the church the youthful grace is quenched, and that the child's religion becomes very much as that of the majority of older people. Let us hear the words of the Master today. If you cannot understand or fully approve, still do not forbid nor hinder the children coming to Jesus; just bear with it, until you see how He can bless them, until His word, 'of such is the Kingdom,' has entered your heart, and you learn to receive them as He did."

If only the mass of children growing up today without any contact with Christian influences had parents recognizing that God gave the religious training of children into their hands, what a different preparation for life they would have. Alas! the natural, simple faith and sense of love and duty of a child to Jesus is so often terribly checked or choked by the irreligious example and conduct of those around. With Christian parents it is different for they know that they are likewise guardians of their children and are to watch and foster their spiritual growth. What judgment rests upon any parent who hinders his child from coming to Jesus, or who comes between his child and Jesus! How richly blessed children are when the warmth of their parents' love for Jesus, fosters a like love in their little hearts for Him! Yes, and happy are those parents who have brought their children to the Saviour as their Teacher in the revelation of the mysteries of divine love.

All who have any responsibility for the welfare of children should constantly pray for open eyes to see in the little ones all that Jesus sees, to think of them as He does; and for heavenly wisdom to guide their feet to Him whose possessions are for parents and children alike (Acts 2:39). The Lord is the Friend of both parent and child, and He has only one call for all, "Come unto me." Paul reminds us that the kingdom of God consists of "righteousness, and peace, and joy in the Holy Ghost" (Rom. 14:17), and these virtues can be experienced by children in their simple and childlike way. When Jesus said, "Little ones which believe in Me," He recognized child salvation by faith.

4. They Were Defended by Christ

What solemn things He had to say about those who offend the little ones believing in Him! It would be better for them, He said, if a millstone was fixed to their neck, and they were drowned in the depth of the sea (Matt. 18:5, 6). Heed must be given lest we despise *one* of these little ones. The word "offend" means, "cause to stumble," and is the same term used concerning Judas (Matt. 26:24). The stumbling or betrayal of children is more sternly rebuked by Jesus than anything else. Here are some of the ways we cause children to stumble today —

By teaching them to do evil things.
By mocking at their early piety and childlike faith.
By living inconsistently before them.
By taking them to places where holy things are ridiculed.
By allowing them to read the wrong books and magazines.
By neglecting to take them to church and Sunday school.
By failing to teach them to read the Bible.
By disregarding their childlike desire to pray.
By never speaking to them simply and lovingly of their need of Jesus as Saviour.

Too often parents forget that their life is the child's copybook. John Locke wrote that, "Parents wonder why the streams are bitter when they themselves have poisoned the fountain." How telling are the lines of Dorothy Law Nolte on, "Children Learn What They Live."

If a child lives with criticism he learns to condemn . . .
If a child lives with hostility he learns to fight . . .
If a child lives with fear he learns to be apprehensive . . .
If a child lives with pity he learns to feel sorry for himself . . .
If a child lives with ridicule he learns to be shy . . .
If a child lives with jealousy he learns what envy is . . .
If a child lives with shame he learns to feel guilty . . .
If a child lives with encouragement he learns to be confident . . .

If a child lives with tolerance he learns to be patient . . .
If a child lives with praise he learns to be appreciative . . .
If a child lives with acceptance he learns to love . . .
If a child lives with approval he learns to like himself . . .
If a child lives with recognition he learns that it is good to have a goal . . .
If a child lives with sharing he learns about generosity . . .
If a child lives with honesty and fairness he learns what truth and justice are . . .
If a child lives with security he learns to have faith in himself and those about him . . .
If a child lives with friendliness he learns that the world is a nice place in which to live . . .
If you live with serenity your child will live with peace of mind . . .

5. They Were Used as Models by Christ

William Paley, a renowned English theologian and philosopher (1743-1805), was wont to say that of all proofs that the world gave him of the benevolence, the good will of God, our Creator, the chief was the pleasures of little children. In the innocent, radiant happiness of children without care and without sorrow, the wise man saw what God intended mankind to be. Was it not this same observation of children that led Jesus to take the little child and sit him down in the midst of His disciples when they were quarreling over who should be the greatest among them? How skillfully and forcefully Jesus used that child as an object lesson! Grown men – and His followers too – had to learn what it was to be childlike, in emulating a child's –

Lowliness of Mind
Willingness to Learn
Simplicity of Faith
Freedom From Carefulness
Contentment in the Enjoyment of Life
Confidence in Love
Dependence on the Father

a. *The Lesson on Conversion.* What did Jesus actually mean when He said, as He pointed to the little child sitting in the midst of the disciples – "Except ye be converted, and become as little children, ye shall not enter into the kingdom of heaven" (Matt. 18:3)? It is clearly evident that the conversion spoken of was not the aspect we commonly think of as a religious experience involving a deep conviction of sin, a repentant heart and acceptance of Christ as Saviour. Those whom Jesus was seeking to rebuke and instruct were already His. As disciples, theirs had been the committal to His claims. The word conversion means "to turn about," or "again," and is used in this sense in the experience of Peter, when being forewarned of his coming denial of Jesus. He said to Peter, a conspicuous disciple, "When thou art *converted,* strengthen thy brethren" (Luke 22: 32). Peter was going to turn from his Master, but when turned back again, he would be able to safeguard others from his own desertion of Jesus.

What the self-seeking disciples had to learn was the necessity of turning from their obsession of ambition, position, and prestige, and regain the lowliness and relative blamelessness of children. Egotism and rivalry are not of the kingdom of heaven. Argument over precedence in such a kingdom revealed that they were not fully in it. Such a kingdom is, first of all, spiritual, and its first condition was abnegation of self. The conversion, then, which the disciples sadly needed, was the understanding that "the secret of true greatness lay in that unconsciousness of being great, which takes the lowest position as that which of right belongs to it." Phillips' *New Testament in Modern English* clarifies the passage from Matthew, "Believe me," Jesus said, "unless you change your whole outlook and become like little children you will never enter the kingdom of Heaven" (18:3).

b. *The Lesson on Simplicity.* The transition from the plural, "become as little children" to the singular, "this little child," gives an almost dramatic vividness to the form of our Lord's teaching, comments Ellicott, who also suggests that the house in which this incident took place was "probably Peter's, and the child may have been one of his." Whoever the privileged child was whom Jesus chose as a model of the special beauty of childhood, as His loving, smiling eyes looked upon "this little child," we can imagine how "with blushing face and downcast eyes" the child would shrink from the notice drawn to him by Jesus.

From this innocent child sitting in the center of the circle of the disciples and parents, Jesus drew attention to his simple faith, obedience, simplicity, and lowliness. These were the lessons they were to learn, and were what Solomon earnestly desired as he faced tremendous responsibilities and said, "I am but a little child" (I Kings 3:7). Crowned as king, he prayed to be humble, thoughtful and distrustful of himself, but somehow when he reached such glory and dominion in his reign the wise man forgot his prayer for childlikeness. Jesus would have us know that the greatest in His kingdom are those who emulate the humility and simplicity of children, and who, in receiving little ones for His name's sake, receive Him who was meek and lowly in heart (Matt. 18:4, 5). Wordsworth in *The Prelude* exclaims –

> Oh! mystery of man, from what a depth
> Proceed thy honours. I am lost, but see
> In simple childhood something of the base
> On which thy greatness stands.

c. *The Lesson on the Teachable Spirit.* What a wonderful model of the life of faith a simple child is! How utterly dependent it is upon its parents for everything – food, clothes, home, love, and all else. To its expanding mind the world is full of wonder; and in its necessary training becomes teachable in spirit. Thus, when Jesus spoke about "becoming as a little child," He implied that our attitude must be that of simple reliance upon God, and confidence in what He pleases. Further, we must become more childlike in our eagerness to know His mind and will. Expounding the brief prayer of Jesus about the child-like mind, Dr. R. A. Torrey referred to "The Baby Method," in our quest for truth – "I thank thee, O Father, Lord of heaven and earth, because thou hast hid these things from the wise and prudent, and hast revealed them unto babes. Even so, Father: for so it seemed good in thy sight" (Matt. 11:25, 26). While "the wise and prudent" here may have been the Scribes and Pharisees who were wise in their own conceit, and the "babes" may have been the disciples who received truth in the spirit of a little child, we must have the simpleheartedness of the child if we would enter into the secrets of the Lord. All truth is revelation, and the same always comes to those who are willing to be taught of the Spirit. Paul reminds us that those who exult in human wisdom merit the judgment of God, "I will destroy the wisdom of the wise, and will bring to nought the understanding of the prudent" (See I Cor. 1:18-31).

A child sees and appreciates the child-like, and the heart of Jesus is the heart of the most child-like, as those children observed when, seeing Him in the temple, their bold and hearty song filled its precincts with "Hosanna to the Son of David!" What was hid from the proud Pharisees that day was revealed unto the babes who were so eloquent in their praise of the One they discerned as their Friend and Saviour.

> Once on earth the children praised Him,
> And "Hosanna" was their cry;
> Now that God to Heaven has raised Him,
> Loud they praise Him in the sky:
> Shout, then, children, shout your praises,
> Loud let grateful anthems ring:
> Jesus is the children's Saviour,
> Jesus is the children's King.

Children and Scripture

While it is true that children dominate Scripture, it is likewise true that Scripture is closely associated with children. How grateful those parents are who share the great joy of John as they see their children "walking in truth" (III John 4). Parents and instructors of the young receive much advice from the Bible regarding the religious truths they should teach the young — truths that will stand the wear and tear of time as they grow up. Children must be told "the old, old story, softly, with earnest tones and grave," and how fascinated they are as Bible stories are read or retold to them! Solomon says, "Train up a child in the way he should go: and when he is old, he will not depart from it" (Prov. 22:6). But if he is not to depart from it when he is old, the truths of the Word must sink deep into the child's heart.

There is a proverb which declares that "Little pitchers have long ears," and means that little children often take in more than we think they do, and keep in their memory things which we feel they must have forgotten. Do you know that there is a remarkable chapter in the Bible which is unique seeing it contains the words a mother taught her son, and which he never forgot? "The words of king Lemuel, the prophecy that his mother taught him" (Prov. 31:1). Without doubt, the Bible, is the "Children's Book," and one which God intends them to read and remember. This is why He caused it to be written in a simple, clear, and attractive way with all kinds of stories to inspire even the youngest not yet able to read themselves, but who are held in wonder as they are read to them.

1. Observe the Law of God

Among the commandments God gave His people by the hands and lips of Moses were those concerning parental instruction of the young in divine truth. "Thou shalt teach them [these commandments] diligently unto thy children, and shalt talk of them when thou sittest in thine house, and when thou walkest by the way, and when thou liest down, and when thou risest up" (Deut. 6:1, 2, 5-7. See also 31:11-13). Here we have the law of individual duty, for parents receiving the divine commandments were to strive not only to keep them themselves, but were held responsible for continuance in the commandments among their children. Further, parents are told how diligent and unceasing their tuition must be.

a. *Their Instruction of the Young Had to Be From the Heart.* The words taught had to be deep *in* the heart of the parent, and then he had to instruct his children *from* the heart. "With all your heart." Commands and instructions exercise little influence when given by a cold, listless or uninterested teacher. The heart alone can gain another heart, and parents and teachers must always remember that the loving warmth of interest and affection never fail to awaken corresponding emotions in the hearts of the children being taught. So we have the heart's secret love connected with the spoken word, "*Thou* shalt love the Lord thy God with all thy heart. And these words shall be *in thy heart* (the parent's heart). *And* thou shalt teach them to thy children." What a lack of this heart teaching there is today among those who try to teach the young!

b. *Their Instruction of the Young Had to Be Diligent.* Moses used a striking word when he said, "Thou shalt *diligently* teach them unto thy children." The original word for "diligently," as given in the margin, reads "Thou shalt *sharpen* them unto thy children." The word is associated with the sharpening of weapons, as arrows and spears, to make them penetrate deep in the flesh of victims. What is the use of an arrow although shot from the bow, if it has not been sharpened to pierce the heart of any enemy.

Godly parents know only too well that there must not be any cold declaration of the truth of God they seek to communicate to their children. A mere intellectual approach will be as an unsharpened arrow. Is not the Word "a sharp two-edged sword"? Therefore, if its truths are to become as nails fastened in a sure place in the hearts of the young, they must be driven home, not only by love but also by the confirmation of a consistent and holy life on the part of the instructor.

c. *Their Instruction of the Young Had to Be Persevering and Continuous.* Parents had to "talk of them" often. Training of child character is not attained by sudden, spasmodic, and isolated efforts, but by regular and unceasing repetition. "Thou shalt talk of them, when thou *sittest* in thine house, and when thou *walkest* by the way, and when thou *liest* down, and when thou *risest* up." Thus, the whole life, with all its duties, had to be interwoven with love for God's Word, Presence, and Service. Children were to be immersed in the words and ways of God, with the whole of the day and the whole of life characterized by uninterrupted fellowship with their Father in heaven. With so much in the world today clamoring for the attention of children, the command of God may seem to be too ideal and entirely unattainable. Parents, however, the first and highest teachers of their children, must strive to walk in the love and presence of God, that their whole life may have a holy influence educating their children for Him who gave them.

2. Knowledge of the Word of God

In one of the most descriptive expositions of the source and structure of the Holy Scriptures Paul gives us a brief biographical sketch of Timothy in the second letter he sent his son in the faith, in which he reminds him of childhood influences — "Continue thou in the things which thou hast learned and hast been assured of, knowing of whom thou hast learned them; And that from a child thou hast known the holy scriptures, which are able to make thee wise unto salvation through faith which is in Christ Jesus" (II Tim. 3:14, 15).

It was from his godly grandmother, Lois, and his saintly mother, Eunice, that the child Timothy was instructed in the genuine faith the Scriptures inspired (II Tim. 1:5). The word Paul used for "known" implies, "a knowledge that has a powerful influence on the knower," as he indicates when he reminds Timothy how from early childhood his mind had been familiar with Scripture which had opened his mind to a saving faith. What an advantage it must have been for young Timothy to have had a mind so fully stored with the truths of Holy Writ! It was so with King Lemuel, whose nameless mother taught him so many precious things that had an impact on his life (Proverbs 31:1).

The connecting link between those two Christian women and Timothy was Scripture which always needs believing parents as its messengers. As Andrew Murray expresses it in his chapter on "Children and Scripture" – "The believing parent needs Scripture as the vehicle for the communication of his faith. A parent's faith teaching the Word of faith may count upon the child's faith as the fruit of his labours."

There would be more children growing up as Timothy did, guarded by the truth he learned at home, if only parents would understand that one of the highest honors God has bestowed upon them is to become the first interpreters of His inspired Word to their children. Paul, of course, makes it clear that it is essential for the parents to have in their own hearts unfeigned, or genuine, faith in God and His Word, if they are to be used of Him to awaken faith in the hearts of their children.

a. *Parents Must Teach Their Children to Believe the Bible.* Ours is the age of doubt in which the authority, and inspiration, and veracity of Scripture are being assailed by religious leaders who should be foremost in the defense of the reliability of the Bible. As faith in God implies faith in what He says, how can any person claim to be a messenger of God if he denies what God says? Doubt in a parent's mind as to the Scriptures being inspired of God makes it impossible for him to cultivate in his child a trustful acceptance of all God has declared. A child is naturally trustful and wants to trust. The Bible waits to be trusted, and it is the solemn responsibility of parents to guide the young trust of their children to that Word which never fails.

b. *Parents Must Teach Their Children to Know the Bible.* The "unfeigned faith" Paul wrote about depends upon knowledge, and Timothy had known the sacred writings as being able to make him wise unto salvation. In order to know the Word, the child-mind must have a simple, clear, and easy-to-be-grasped presentation of Bible truths. The well-known children's hymn puts it –

> Tell me the story simply,
> As to a little child . . .
>
> Tell me the story often,
> For I forget so soon.

It is only by frequent repetition that truth is rooted in the mind in such a way that nothing can efface it. This was why young Timothy grew up to feel so much at home in the Scriptures.

c. *Parents Must Teach Their Children to Love the Bible.* Unless there is deep and ever-deepening love for the Word, there will not be the reverence for it that it demands. One may have an interest in it and give it the assent of faith without real love for it. The psalmist could say, "O how love I thy Law!" Children will never love and revere the Bible unless their parents desire it above much gold. The language of love is the one a child learns most easily, and it is because its heart is most susceptible to love that it can be won before it is able to give a reason for its hope. In the case of Timothy when he was a child it was his mother's love for the Scriptures that created his love for them. Children must be taught to love the Bible not only for its fascinating stories, but because it is, in its entirety, the heavenly Father's Word to His children.

d. *Parents Must Teach Their Children to Obey the Bible.* Believing, knowing, loving, are always connected with doing. "If ye *know* these things, happy are ye if ye *do* them (John 13:17). Even in his earliest years obedience is a quality a child is quickly taught to render to its parent's will. Children, therefore, must be educated into the belief that God's will is not grievous but good; and that true happiness comes in obeying His will and delighting in its performance even as His own Son could. When parents, as God's children, live in obedience to His will and Word, they will teach their children how to read the Bible and follow its instructions. It is because the Holy Scriptures are a child's heritage from the Father in heaven that its parents must endeavor to lead children into the knowledge, the love and the possession of their treasures.

Well might we ask, "Who is sufficient for these things?" It is the gracious God alone who can enable parents to give their children the privilege Timothy enjoyed, who from his earliest youth had the unfeigned faith of a loving parent as his interpreter of the Holy Scriptures. Grace, wisdom and patient faithfulness are necessary to sow the seeds of all holy thoughts in the minds of the young, and God is always ready to gird all guardians of His lambs with these virtues in order that they, too, may become partakers of the divine promises (Acts 2:39). How apropos are the anonymous lines —

> An angel passed in his onward flight,
> With a seed of love and truth and light,
> And cried, "O where shall the seed be sown —
> That it yield most fruit when fully grown?"
> The Saviour heard what he said, and He smiled,
> "Place it for Me in the heart of a child."

Children and Parents

In almost all the civilized countries of the world, the foundations of home and parenthood are being destroyed. Insidious forces are combined to ruin their ancient fabric. Love without marriage, marriage without love, easy divorces, incompatibility, clash of temperament, deplorable housing conditions, nervous tensions, friction over money matters, and our modern industrial setup, all add their quota to the breakup of home life as God meant it to be, and which is so detrimental to the well-being of children. And behind all the disastrous inroads in marital relationship is the sinister figure of Satan, the destroyer of the love and peace of earth's first home.

Wholesome family life is the secret of a noble society. No nation is better than its homes, for where their unity and harmony are tampered with national morals consequently suffer. How true the adage is that, "Only the home can find a state"! It is said that, "Home is where the mortgage is." But while, in many cases, there is a mortgage to care for, a true home is one regulated by Christian principles, and where unselfish love reigns supreme. John Keble would have us know that –

> Sweet is the smile of Home; the mutual look
> Where hearts are of each other sure;
> Sweet all the joys that crowd the household nook,
> The haunt of all affections pure.

J. Thomson suggests that there is no place like home when –

> Home is the resort
> Of love, of joy, of peace and plenty, where
> Supporting and supported, polished friends
> And dear relations mingle into bliss.

J.R. Lowell says that –

> The many make the household
> But only *One* the home.

When this One is God Himself, the Original Architect of family life (Eph. 3:15), then home becomes heaven's twin sister. It was John Howard Payne (1792 - 1852) who gave us the well-known lines –

> 'Mid pleasures and palaces though we may roam,
> Be it ever so humble, there's no place like home;
> A charm from the skies seems to hallow us there,
> Which sought through the world, is ne'er met with elsewhere.
> Home, home, sweet, sweet home!
> There's no place like home! there's no place like home!

But homes of this order are not as numerous as they used to be. Many young people find home life a restriction, and leave it for no home at all, or for accommodation where they can live unhampered by parental control or interference. There are some who seem to be unfeeling, dangerously independent and somewhat arrogant, who look upon their parents as morons, antiquated, behind the times, "not with it," as they say. They have an assumed air of knowing everything. Further they feel no obligation toward their parents for all their keep and cost through their earliest years. Their attitude is that they had no responsibility in being brought into the world, and that those who did produce them should care for them. Thus, so many parents are brokenhearted, lonely, and neglected because of unfeeling, unthankful children who have cast them away as old clothes for which there is no further use.

On the other hand, there are parents who have miserably failed in their God-given responsibility in respect to their children. They were too long on exhortation, too short in example; heavy on law, light on love; insistent on discipline, but negligent on sympathy; niggardly or overindulgent. Parents in the home should heed the advice of Sir Francis Bacon in his essay on *Of Parents and Children* –

> The illiberality of parents in allowance towards their children is an harmful error; makes them base; acquaints them with shifts; makes them sort with mean company; and make them surfeit when they come to plenty. And therefore the proof is best, when men keep their authority towards their children, but not their purse.

Disregard of religious influences, or cruelty, or lack of comradeship, or intemperate habits on the part of parents often result in juvenile delinquency – and disaster! Homelife can brand a child for good – or evil. As the root, so the branch. Many a child finds it hard to forgive a prostituted parentage. How many, we wonder, fall into the category Oscar Wilde wrote about? – "Children begin by loving their parents; after a time they judge them; rarely, if ever, do they forgive them." Happy are those parents who can take that cry of brutal execration at Calvary, "His blood be on us and on our children," and make it the sincere prayer of their own hearts, and for their little ones! It is with this desire to see His blood upon many more houses (Exod. 12:13) as the token of salvation and security of all within them that we now come to consider, more specifically, what the Bible says regarding the obligations of parenthood, and of the responsibility of childhood.

1. Obligations of Parents Toward Their Children

The most superficial reader of the Bible cannot fail to be impressed with the many features of the filial relationship between parents and children. Affection of parents for the children, and children for their parents; privileged parenthood, and the dependence of children upon their parents, as well as their subordination to them; tenderness toward child life, and appreciation of the simplicity and the helplessness of children – all of the aspects indicate an intensely strong sense of the filial bond making the home one, and a horror of any violation of such a bond of love.

While we believe the divine ideal to be that of monogamy, meaning, marriage with one person at a time, as opposed to bigamy, which implies the act of marrying one person when already legally married to another, and polygamy, a state suggesting a plurality of wives, or husbands, the Orientals saw nothing immoral in the practice of polygamy. Female slaves, obtained as booty in time of war, or bought from poverty-stricken parents, became the concubines of their masters (Gen. 16:2, 3; Exod. 21:7; Judg. 5:30). In addition to these slave-concubines a wealthy and important person, even men of God, could take more than one wife, as did Abraham, Jacob, David, Solomon, and others. But the Mosaic Law forbade kings multiplying wives (Deut. 17:17). Adam, the first founder of the human race, and Noah the second founder, both represent monogamy, and emphasize it as God's ordinance. Several of the prophets dwell upon the thought of a monogamous marriage as being a symbol of the union between God and His people; and denounce idolatry as unfaithfulness to this spiritual marriage tie, as does Paul.

It is in the line of Cain that bigamy first appears, and serves to enforce the consequences of the Fall. Reasons are given for the bigamy of Abraham and of Jacob (Gen. 16; 29:23). Polygamy cancels out the unity of a home and as we know from Old Testament cases results in jealousy, rivalry and friction. It also goes against the divine ideal of one father and one wife dwelling together with their children in one close and affectionate bond. In modern society we have the spectacle of those who are divorced and remarried several times, with children of different marriages, trying to live together. What a travesty this is of home as God meant it to be, and of family life as He created it!

We have dealt with the foregoing matter in order to show that by parents we mean one husband and one wife with children born to them, constituting together one bond. Well, now, what are some of the obligations toward children which parents must observe? Because of its importance, we begin with

a. *The Recognition of the Law of*

Heredity. Students of human beings and behavior have unraveled many interesting features of what we have come to know as "heredity" which is the law by which living beings – animal as well as human – tend to repeat their characteristics, physiologically and psychologically, in their offspring. Observance of this law acts as a signal to husband and wife as they prayerfully plan a family. As they are, so will their children be. The Bible is our textbook as to how children resemble not only the physical features of their parents, but also their virtues and vices. Giants had giant-like sons (Gen. 6:4; II Sam. 21:18-22; I Chron. 20:4-8). There are also hints of hereditary diseases and physical ailments (Deut. 28:59-61; II Kings 5:27). Inheritance of characteristics and also of mechanical dexterity are mentioned (Gen. 4:20-22; Isa. 19:11).

We have previously seen that as the result of the sin of Adam and Eve all inherit the evil tendency. We are sinners by birth, and then by practice. Particular forms of sin in ancestors continue in descendants, and qualities in parents are repeated in their children. This may be one reason why children of offenders were slain with their parents, thus preventing the perpetuation of their sin (Num. 16:11; II Sam. 21:1-9). Occasionally, national features are thought of as being hereditary, and are traced back to a single source (Gen. 9:22-27; 21:20, 21; 27; 49; Rom. 4:12; 11:26). But there are instances where this law of heredity is reversed for we read of godly fathers having ungodly sons, and of godly children coming from godless parents.

In the giving of the law to His people, God declared that He would visit "the iniquity of the fathers upon the children unto the third and fourth generation of them that hate me" (Exod. 20:5). But children are not condemned and punished for their inherited evil propensities – only for their practiced sinful desires (Ezek. 18:18-32). It is a fact, then, that under God's natural government of the world, the iniquity of parents is visited upon their children. As Ellicott in his comment on this divine law observes,

> Diseases caused by vicious courses are transmitted. The extravagance of parents leave their children beggars. To be the son of a felon is to be heavily handicapped in the race of life . . . We all inherit countless disadvantages on account of our first parents' sin. We each individually inherit special tendencies to this or that form of evil from the misconduct of our several progenitors.

While there are more deeply involved aspects of this law of heredity that we might touch upon, sufficient has been said that this is part of the scheme of divine government by which our world is governed; and that because of this, it is the solemn obligation of parents not to put their children at a disadvantage by not checking in themselves any evil tendency they have inherited. Always aware of original sin, parents must seek to live sanctified and separated lives so that their children may grow up "dead indeed unto sin, and alive unto God," thereby averting "the law unto sin." The birth of children can become the highest exercise of a faith giving glory to God, and the truest means of advancing the spiritual life of parents and children, as well as the interests of Christ's cause on earth.

b. *The Seal and Promise of the Covenant.* The faith of parents needs just what the faith of every believer does, namely, the willingness to understand, to get an insight into what God has undertaken to be and do. Does not the Bible say, "By faith we understand"? When faith grasps the truth of divine planning and undertaking then it is a simple exercise to rest and trust, to praise and act. Thus, when believing parents meditate upon the revelation of God as understood and acted upon; and believing, there is the joyous expectation of the fulfillment of the desire to have a home — holy to the Lord. Is this not the testimony of many of the families of ancient Israel; and is it not here that we can appreciate the divine covenant concerning children?

(1.) *Constitution of the Covenant.* Among the several covenants mentioned in Scripture is the prominent one associated with the children of believing parents. In order to comprehend the significance of such a covenant, it is necessary to carry with us an understanding of the nature of a covenant. Some authorities suggest that the word, "covenant," springs from the Assyrian root meaning "fetter" or "to bind," and implies a binding contract between parties, whether between God and man, or between men and men. It is affirmed that there are two shades of meaning, somewhat distinct, of the Hebrew word for covenant.

One is when it is properly a covenant, that is, a solemn mutual agreement.

The other word carries more of a command, that is, instead of an obligation imposed voluntarily assumed, it is an obligation imposed by a superior upon an inferior — which is the nature of all covenants between God and men.

A covenant, then, between contracting parties, is an agreement of a solemn and binding force. Among the early Semites, a covenant was primarily a "blood brotherhood" in which two men became brothers by drinking each other's blood. Such an act not only bound the two together but also brought them into a relationship with the god of the clan who was supposed to govern the community life of the clan. The Old Testament covenant related to children is sometimes expressed in the form of an oath, with promised blessing upon its keeping, or with a curse invoked if the oath or covenant is disregarded.

As used by David, the term is employed in a more general way of an alliance of friendship and confidence between God and those who are His — "The secret of the Lord is with them that fear him; and he will shew them his covenant" (Ps. 25:14).

(2.) *Children of the Covenant.* When Luke penned the phrase, "the children . . . of the covenant" (Acts 3:25), he traced such a contract back through the ages when God said to Abraham — "He that shall come forth out of thine own bowels shall be thine heir. And he believed in the Lord; and he counted it to him for righteousness" (Gen. 15:4, 6). The patriarch had poured out his complaint, "Behold, I go childless," but God made an agreement with Abraham that he would have an heir, whose descendants should be as "the sand of the seashore in multitude." Thus, the natural longing for a child became the channel of the most wonderful fellowship with God, and the natural seed became the heir of God's promise and spiritual blessing.

Although God had begun to acknowledge with Noah the validity of the oneness of parents and children in the dealings of grace — "Come thou and all thy house into the ark" (Gen. 7:1) — there was no previous covenant between God and Noah concerning the latter's children. But with Abraham it was different. From Abraham, in every Hebrew home, the child was to be taken up into the covenant with the promise that from its birth it would be the object of God's care and the parent's faith. In all that is involved in the contract between God and Abraham, concerning children, believing parents are taught that it is not only in their individual capacity, but especially as parents that from the first hope of having children, they are, themselves, in covenant relationship with God, and are called to exercise Abraham's faith.

Thereafter they must receive their children as coming from God's hands, and as being embraced in the covenant between Him and the parents. Being endowed with the wondrous power of bringing children into the world, consecrated parents must fully understand the promises connected with the birth of their offspring, and of how, by faith, they can claim their children for the Lord. Andrew Murray would have us know that this precious truth concentrates on one great lesson, namely –

> The fatherhood and the childhood of this earth hath a Divine and heavenly promise, and everything connected with it must with us be a matter of faith, a religious service holy to the Lord and well-pleasing in His sight. I must not only believe for myself; if I would fully honour God, my faith must reach forth and embrace my children, grasping the promises of God for them too. If I would "magnify the riches of God's grace," if I would with my whole nature and all my powers be consecrated to God's service, and if I would accomplish the utmost possible within my reach for the advancement of His Kingdom, it is especially as *parent* that I must believe and labour.

The promise is, "According to your faith be it unto you," and believing parents experience that there is nothing that so mightily quickens the growth of their faith as the reaching out after the divine blessing for their children. There is no limit to what God is able to accomplish through a believing parenthood, as the promise of God is embraced and the power of faith is exercised. It is in this way that "the natural seed becomes the heir of spiritual blessing, and the parental relationship one of the best schools for the life of faith." Our heavenly Father, who has taken into His covenant charge and keeping godly parenthood, has also contracted to sanctify and bless the seed of His people.

(3.) *Certainty of the Covenant.* Another aspect of the covenant God made with Abraham was the assurance that the same promise applied to parents and child alike; and that with the sanctification of the parents, God has a better opportunity of claiming possession of their children before sins get the mastery. Covenant faithfulness is expressed in the phrases – "I will establish my covenant between me and *thee and thy seed* after thee . . . I will be a God unto thee, and to thy seed after thee" (Gen. 17:7).

"A God unto thee, and to thy seed." What a blessed promise, so certain of fulfillment! Because God is true, He cannot go back upon His word, and if the condition of faith is met, He will see to it that the faith of parents for their children will not be disappointed. What must not be forgotten is the fact that God does not hold His promise in abeyance to wait for the child's faith, but the promise is given in response to the faith of the parents with the assurance that the child's faith will follow. Thus, venturing all upon God's faithfulness, and striving after personal holiness, parents, in the training of their children, have the joy of seeing them loving and serving the same Lord. This is the way that children of the covenant become the children of God. Fathers and mothers must believe, not only for themselves, but for their children.

(4.) *Command of the Covenant.* It is perfectly true, as James reminds us, that, "Faith without works is dead" – a truth that applies to parental faith as well as personal faith. Such parental faith is God's promise concerning children will be manifested by parental faithfulness to God's will in respect to conduct and action. As a parent, Abraham had the reputation of being obedient to the divine command –

> I know him [Abraham], that he will command his children and his household after him, and they shall keep the way of the LORD, to do justice and judgment; that the LORD may bring upon Abraham that which he hath spoken of him (Gen. 18:19).

Faithful parenthood is fully sympathetic with God's plans for the spiritual training of children. Helpless babes are committed to believing parents for them to influence for God, so that they, too, may become members of His family on earth. Emphasis in God's conception of Abraham's character is upon the word "command" – "To the end he may *command* his children." It is to be feared that far too many parents do not discern the heavenly harmony between authority and love, between obedience and liberty. They forget that as parents they have been clothed by God with a holy authority, to be lovingly exercised in leading their children into paths of righteousness.

There is a sense in which parents are potters, and their children the clay, waiting to be molded according to the divine plan. Their character waits to be influenced by the quiet, tender exercise of authority which, when strengthened by the silent testimony of example and life of those around never fails in its purpose. Alas! the spirit of modern permissiveness and liberty have penetrated our family life with disastrous results. Command is a missing element in parenthood, and one which children, who have been pampered to, and allowed to have their own way, have grown up to scorn. Thomas Carlyle could write, "I acknowledge to all – but omnipotence of early culture and nurture." Would that we had more homes today providing a similar upbringing of children! It was Sir H. Baker who gave us the lines –

> O ye who came that Babe to lay
> Within a Saviour's arms to-day,
> Watch well and guard with careful
> eye,
> The Heir of Immortality!

When, in due course, parents take their little ones to the house of God for a dedicatory service, the church unites with the home in a vow to care for the spiritual welfare of the child presented to God over whom the words are repeated –

> We receive *this child* into the congregation of Christ's flock, that *he* may be instructed and trained in the doctrines, privileges, and duties of the Christian religion, and that *he* may be Christ's faithful soldier and servant unto *his* life's end.

(5.) *Compensation of the Covenant.* The promised reward of parental faith and faithfulness is both sure and large. Confident that "Abraham would command his children and his household after him" the divine benediction followed – "That the Lord may bring upon Abraham that which he hath spoken of him." The rich blessings of the covenant came true in the experience of Abraham and Sarah, for linked together in the covenant were God's faithfulness and that the parents made. Is it any wonder that because of his performance of the covenant obligation Abraham was rewarded by being called, "the friend of God"?

The prophet Jeremiah would have us know that it is part of God's covenant that He will first teach parents to keep it, and then reward, in His own bountiful way, that keeping. "I will give them one heart, and one way, that they may fear me for ever, for the good of them, and of *their children after them*" (Jer. 32:39). That the psalmist agrees with the prophet as to the blessing accruing from a fulfilled covenant is evident from the words of David that "The mercy of the LORD is from everlasting to everlasting upon them that fear him, and his righteousness unto children's children" (Ps. 103:17). There are two sides to the coin of parental responsibility, namely, to be full of faith, and then to be faithful.

(a) Being full of faith implies implicit trust in the living God, in His covenant for parents and children alike, in His promises for a home ordered after His will, and in His faithfulness to undertake according to His Word.

(b) Being faithful is the other side of the coin. If we are full of faith, then, we shall be faith-full, taking the Bible as the measure of life for the whole family.

Parental faithfulness involves self-discipline and the constant exercise of faith, and results in the blessing of having children like olive plants about the table (Ps. 128). How parents – and all believers – have to pray for that ever-growing faith which is the root of an ever-growing faithfulness! Well might all believing parents pray as Andrew Murray suggests they should –

> O my God! hast Thou indeed taken me too into this wonderful covenant, in which Thou art the God of the seed of Thy saints, and makest them the ministers of Thy grace to their children? Open my eyes, I pray Thee, to see the full glory of this Thy covenant, that my faith may know all that Thou hast prepared for me to bestow, and may do all Thou hast prepared for me to perform. O my God! may Thy covenant-keeping faithfulness be the life and strength of my faith. May this faith make me faithful in keeping the covenant.

c. *The Folly of Favoritism.* We have already indicated that parents are under the obligation of exercising authority or rule in the home. Some are more naturally rulers than others and command obedience. Reluctance to rule, however, does not take away the responsibility of the parent. Failure to control can result in dire consequences for parent and child alike. One of the saddest rebukes administered to a godly parent for being too indulgent of his children was that which Eli received from God. The aged priest had been unceasingly faithful to God's house and was ready to die for the Ark of God, but he had proved unfaithful as a parent. He loved his sons too much to restrain them. Hophni and Phinehas "made themselves vile, and he [Eli] restrained them not," and such parental weakness brought severe judgment upon the house of Eli (I Sam. 3:13; 4:17).

Tenderhearted, good-natured parents may find it hard to reprove, to thwart, or to punish a child for wrongdoing. But such misnamed kindness is actually unkindness in that it has terrible consequences. When conscience or experience tells parents that they have been too easygoing and guilty of consulting the will and the feelings of their children more than the will and honor of God, they should ponder carefully how Eli and his home came under God's judgment. Parents are destined of God to bear in the home the likeness of His own Fatherly rule, but if they are weak in disciplinary rule, then the character of their children suffer. God-appointed parental rule in the family is the symbol of His own authority, in which parents and children alike are to honor Him: to dishonor Him is to lose His favor and blessing.

Another aspect of parental weakness is that of favoritism in a family; and because "the greatest favorites are in the most danger of falling," as a German proverb puts it, conspicuous preference should be avoided. How apparent this is in the tragic experiences overtaking the home-life of Isaac and Rebekah! While there are those who feel that Rebekah should not be blamed for her partiality, seeing she had a better right to the preference she cultivated than Isaac had to his preference for Esau, the fact remains that the harmony of that ancient home was destroyed through the parents taking sides. "Isaac loved Esau . . . Rebekah loved Jacob." No wonder Esau came to hate Jacob and caused his mother to become weary of her life (Gen. 25:28; 27:41, 46). If Esau and Jacob had been equally loved, the friction, jealousy, deception, sorrow, and separation overtaking the home would not have marred it.

As the two boys grew up, diverse characteristics appeared with Esau becoming "a cunning hunter, a man of the field," that is, one who loved to roam over the open, uncultivated wilderness in search of game. And Isaac, his father, loved Esau "because he did eat of his venison" which he caught. Thus it would seem that Isaac's love for his son originated in a very sensual cause. Esau had a body covered with hair as coarse as that of a kid in the field, which spoke of a strong and vigorous, but sensual nature which produced a carnal love. But with Jacob it was different. He was "a plain man," that is, one of general integrity or uprightness. Esau was more at home in a tent out in the wide open spaces, but Jacob preferred to stay at home and busy himself with domestic occupations, and, always around his mother, he became her favorite.

Commenting upon the difference of affection on the part of Isaac and Rebekah, Matthew Henry says that "they had but these two children, and, it seems, one was the father's darling and the other the mother's.

(1.) Isaac loved to have his son active. Esau knew how to please him, and showed a great respect for him, by treating him often with venison.

(2.) Rebekah was mindful of the oracle of God, which had given the preference to Jacob, and therefore she preferred him in her love."

While it is quite natural for children to reveal differing temperaments and characteristics as they grow, if all are equally loved then there is unity in the home in spite of diversity. The folly of Isaac and Rebekah was the way they allowed the varying characters of their two children to result in a divergence of feeling toward them. How true it is that as we sow so we reap for when one of the boys became a man and a father of many children he exhibited the favoritism of his old home, and experienced something of the hatred and agony following in its train. "Israel [Jacob] loved Joseph more than all his children, because he was the son of his old age" (Gen. 37:3). Favoring him above the others, Jacob made him a beautiful coat, with what result? "His brethren saw that their father loved him more than all his brethren, they hated him, and could not speak peacefully unto him." From then on they plotted his death, and we all know the story that follows.

Further, it would seem as if Jacob became a favorite of the Lord for we have the somewhat puzzling statement, "Jacob have I loved, but Esau have I hated" (Mal. 1:2, 3; Rom. 9:13). What the prophet Malachi implied was that God had taken Jacob into covenant, but had refused and rejected Esau. God reserves to Himself the decision to receive one and refuse another, as is seen by the examples of Moses and Pharaoh, and what He prefers should be our preference. As to the term "hated," we must not read into it the bitter animosity we connect with it. No personal enmity is implied, but simply a decisive rejection of a rival claim. Esau was not in the line of promise and was thus repudiated by God as an heir. Bishop Handley Moule would have us know that –

> Esau's *profanity* was the concurrent occasion, not the cause of the choice of Jacob. The reason of the choice lay in the depths of God, that World "dark with excess of bright." All is well there, but not the less all is unknown.

Amid the mystery of divine choice in respect to personalities we accept the declaration –

"Who maketh thee to differ?
Who hath fashioned thee to honour?"

Has not God the sovereign right to put down one, and set up another? (Ps. 75:7).

From the harmful influence of undue favoritism in a home, often causing it to become divided against itself, there is a justifiable favoritism we can heartily recommend. If a child is born mentally or physically deficient, after the initial shock it is often amazing how such an afflicted one becomes the chief one in the family to receive love, patience, care, and sacrifice. What devoted attention this unfortunate child receives from all the rest at home! One has known of homes in which there was a Mongoloid child receiving a wealth of affection that was simply overwhelming to witness. All praise to those parents who are able to favor a stricken child in the family circle!

d. *The Rod of Correction.* Among some present-day educators of the young, the abolition of punishment, restraint or discipline is stressed. Children must not be repressed or corrected, but given freedom to express themselves as they want to. The Bible, however, thinks differently and has a good deal to say about child correction, as well as God's correction of His children. "Happy is the man whom God correcteth" (Job 5:17; Prov. 3:12; Jer. 2:19; 10:24; 30:11). But think of these exhortations related to child discipline and punishment –

"Correct thy son, and he shall give thee rest; yea, he shall give delight unto thy soul" (Prov. 29:17).

"We have had fathers . . . which corrected us" (Heb. 12:9. See Prov. 3:11, 12).

"Foolishness is bound in the heart of a child; but the rod of correction shall drive it far from him" (Prov. 22:15).

"Withhold not correction from the child; for if thou beatest him with the rod, he shall not die" (Prov. 23:13).

"Your children . . . received no correction" (Jer. 2:30; 5:3).

"Train up a child in the way he should go" (Prov. 22:6).

"He that spareth his rod hateth his son" (Prov. 13:24).

Boswell in his monumental *Life of*

Johnson, quotes the saying of Samuel Johnson (1709 - 1784) – "The rod produces an effect which terminates in itself. A child is afraid of being whipped, and gets his task, and there's an end on 't."

It is from Samuel Butler's *Hudibras* that we have the phrase – "Spare the rod, and spoil the child." There are certainly a good many spoiled "brats" in home and school simply because the rod was spared on them. Thomas Hood (1799 - 1845), in *The Irish Schoolmaster* has the pertinent lines –

> "He never spoils the child
> and spares the rod,
> But spoils the rod and never
> spares the child."

Although the education of a Jewish child was stern, paternal and maternal affection for children who were worthy of it was never stinted. We read of Jacob that "all his sons and all his daughters rose up to comfort him" in the hour of his grief (Gen. 37:35). Another touching and vivid example of parental love is heard in Jacob's despairing cry when Benjamin, the child of his old age, was taken from him (Gen. 44:20).

It is to be regretted that we have come to a time when parental authority has become a joke, and discipline is a forgotten word. As for self-restraint, it hardly exists. Too many parents indulge their children in the delusion that they are being good to them, and so we have a young generation possessed by a mania for "a good time." Lord Mountbatten, the renowned British naval hero, had some pertinent things to say to a reporter who interviewed him in his vice-regal home in Hampshire. Talking of his life and times, and of being a stickler for discipline, this famous figure said –

> Discipline in general is anathema to youth. It has become a dirty word and youngsters believe it means square-bashing and half-a-dozen on the backside. But that's not the point of the word. It comes from the Latin and it means teaching, the instruction of disciples . . . I am trying not to be pompous, but being disciplined is being able to control yourself to your best advantage.
>
> Why is the new generation kicking over the traces? Because there has been a lack of discipline, a lack of teaching by their parents . . . and yet youth lacks belief in its parents. Young people should give their parents credit for what they have done.

It is therefore evident that in the purpose of God there must be parental correction as well as parental instruction. God loves children and desires their parents to train them for Himself, just as He wants those whom He loves, and chastizes, for Himself (Rev. 3:19). The latter make the best kind of parents, for being subject to divine rule they are fitted to rule their house well. Self-rule is the secret of all rule; as you honor the law yourself in self-command, others learn to honor it too. As God cannot suffer sin to go unpunished in Christian parents, they in turn learn how to administer correction to disobedient children.

Parents, seeking to live under the hand of God, are quick to learn the simplest laws in the art of ruling their children during their growth. All hard, harsh, loveless tones, and punishment beyond what is merited, must be avoided. Parents acting as despotic rulers only add to youthful rebellion. Any necessary rebuke must be given in a quiet deliberate tone with self-control; and if the rod is required it must be held with a hand of tender love. If done this way it will hurt the parent more than the child. It is because weakness can become wickedness, both in child and parent, that rebuke is necessary. Therefore, not to rule and restrain our children, never to repress them, but always to give them their own way implies that we honor them more than the God who commands parents to exercise authority in the ordering of their home.

Living in Britain as I do, I was amazed to read in the London daily press a report from Peter Younghusband, the prominent Washington reporter, entitled —

Is It All Spock's Fault?

Then followed this clear and caustic comment on the undisciplined children of today —

> Doctor Benjamin Spock's book, *Baby and Child Care,* was first published in 1946. By 1950 it rivaled the broom as an essential piece of equipment in American households.
>
> Today it is being said, sourly, that Dr. Spock's babies are the kids who are now raising hell in American universities.
>
> This is because Dr. Spock counseled against the good, old-fashioned clout over the ear when children are naughty, and advocated instead a broad permissiveness in child-rearing which has become an American way of life. One result has been that non-Americans quite frequently find American children undisciplined and objectionable.
>
> The case against Dr. Spock gathered momentum last year. Children who had been under his influence virtually from the womb found themselves even more affected by him when they got to college.
>
> The eminent doctor joined them in person in Left-Wing campus demonstrations, leading them in anti-war campaigns and urging them to burn their call-up papers.
>
> Young Americans have been raised to question discipline and to have their childhood whims indulged in the past 20 years.
>
> It is not surprising that when faced with authority on entering university, or the Army, they buck at their first taste of real discipline.
>
> But there is very definitely another side of the coin — and that is that a lamentably small proportion of American professors do full justice to their job.
>
> The average American professor is not a quiet, donnish type in a hairy jacket, puffing a pipe and prepared to give lavishly and dedicatedly of his time to tuition in and out of class.
>
> He is a much more ambitious type who tends to see his university tenure as a stepping stone to greater things — to a corporation directorship or to a high position in government, or simply to be an authority backed by lots of literature bearing his name.
>
> Thus professors are too busy to have much time for lectures.
>
> Students find themselves continually put on to teaching assistants. Understandably, they don't like it.
>
> So the students turn to rebellion for stimulation. Need we look further than that for the basis of the disorders?
>
> This does not, of course, take into account the disruptions that have occurred for racial reasons — or the excesses of the students for a democratic society who have harnessed obscenity and violence to their campaign.
>
> Here again the universities have been at fault. By failing to rectify the wrongs speedily on the one hand and to take firm action against the excesses on the other, they have shown weakness.
>
> So where do we go from here? First of all it must be accepted that the days of the silent generation are over. Then students did as they were told and confined themselves to the conventional campus frolics like the traditional pantie-stealing raids on the women's residences to mark the coming of spring.
>
> What has to be contended with now is the takeover generation — the baby boom of the immediate post-war

years who will form 41 percent of the 24 - 43 age group in the next ten years, and by this fact alone simply cannot be ignored.

They are more sophisticated and more intelligent than students ever were before. They must be given the benefits of a decent higher education and legitimate wrongs must be righted.

But those who persist in destruction without good cause must be restrained, even to the extent of a clip over the ear. With all due respect to Doctor Spock.

e. *The Divine Pattern of Parenthood.* Our heavenly Father has not left Himself without witness even in the human parenthood on earth. That the earthly relationship is a reflection of the heavenly is borne by our Lord's question to His own — "If ye then, being evil, know how to give good gifts unto your children, how much more shall your Father which is in heaven give good things to them that ask him?" (Matt. 7:11).

From the fatherliness of God we can learn a great deal about our parental obligations. As He created man in His image and after His likeness, so our children should be, not only objects of our love, but also a reflection of our Godward aspirations. The more the Father/Mother heart of God is understood, the truer and more joyful the parenthood on earth. This is one reason why home life is a school as much for training parents as children; the deepest mysteries of God's love are best studied by a parent in his own bosom. The truth Jesus stressed was that if we, who are so imperfect as parents, can do so much for our children, what greater things God the perfect Father, the Fountain of Love, can accomplish for us.

A further lesson to be learned as we compare the fatherhood of heaven with the fatherhood of earth, is that in creating us as parents, God meant us in a real and solemn sense to be His imagebearers, in every way copying Him as our Father so that with Him as our model, the fullest spiritual influence can be exercised upon our children. As He educates us as His children into His ways and purposes until they become our own, so we must, in turn, train our children in the life we seek to live in Christ. It is in this way that children naturally rise from the Christ reflected in the home, to the unseen Christ above, and the home become the gate to the Father's home in heaven. The bright, living, happy piety of the parents, a mingling of holy reverence to God with childlike love, shines on the children from their early youth, that the name of God as Father will become linked with all that is lovely and holy in the memory of the child.

Alas! the best of us as parents have to confess that we have come far short of such a divine ideal. Having failed in our obligation Godward, we failed to surround our children with those holy influences so necessary as a safeguard as they come to face the temptations in the world. Ludwig Helmbold, a poet who lived over 400 years ago, left on record these stanzas for the guidance of parents —

> Obey your Lord and let His truth
> Be taught your children in their youth.
> That they in church and school may dwell
> And learn their Saviour's praise to tell.
>
> For if you love Him as you ought,
> To Christ your children will be brought.
> If thus you place them in His care,
> You and your household well shall fare.

The Apostle Paul has some pointed things to say to parents, especially if they have any official association with church life and work. Whether elders or deacons, they were under the obligation of "ruling their own children and their own houses well," for unless they ruled well their own home, having "their children in subjection with all gravity," how could they expect to take care of the church of God? (I Tim. 3:4, 5, 12). Yet many of us have known godly preachers having children who, by lip and life, contradict the solemn truths they were brought up to revere. What a heartbreak it is for a pastor or evangelist to be used in the salvation of others, yet to have those of their own flesh and blood untouched by their influence and ministry! Generally speaking, however, godly homes produce godly heirs.

(1.) *Example Is Better Than Precept.*

Both example and precept are necessary in the moral and spiritual culture of children, but the truth lived out day by day in the home gives added force to the truth taught. How apt is the question of Paul as we think of personal, parental self-culture, "Thou therefore which teachest another, teachest thou not thyself?" (Rom. 2:21). The security of children for Christ depends far more upon the life of a parent than upon what he may say. There is no doubt whatever that the atmosphere of a truly Christian, well-regulated home, in which quiet thoughtfulness in speech and act, all unconsciously sets its mark on the children within it.

"Johnny," said a father to his child, who was hesitating about obeying his father's will, "whose will must you do, your own or papa's?"

"Papa's will," was the reluctant answer. But another question followed from child to parent.

"But whose will must papa do, then?"

At once, the father said, "God's will," and went on to explain that His will was a wiser and better will than his own.

To quote Andrew Murray again —

> The parent who can appeal to his daily life with his children, that they know how he in all things seeks to do the will of his God, and can in his prayers, in their presence, appeal to his God too, will find in the witness of such a life a mighty power to inculcate obedience in the child.

Parents who desire their children to grow up loving, kind, teachable and obedient, must always be on their guard for little eyes are always watching, and little ears are always listening. What hope have parents of reproving or restraining occasional outbursts of temper in their children if they themselves give way to impulse and anger? Inconsistency nullifies good advice. An old saying has it, "Be what you would make others." It is in the daily life of the parents that the children gain their most indelible impressions. To rightly fill their place as parents, they must daily pray that there may be deeply imprinted on their heart the solemn thought that they can only effectually teach their children as they themselves are taught of God; that the truth influencing their lives will influence those whom God has given them to train.

(2.) *Parents as Interpreters of Redemption.*

By a covenant of blood, God promised to be "the God of all the families of Israel." Was this not the message the sacrifice of the Lord's passover conveyed? Instructed of God, Moses exhorted Jewish parents to interpret to their children the origin of the Passover ordinance.

> "It shall come to pass, when your children shall say unto you, What mean ye by this service? That ye shall say, It is the sacrifice of the Lord's passover, who passed over the houses of the children of Israel in Egypt, when he smote the Egyptians, and delivered our houses" (Exod. 12: 26, 27).

Can you not imagine how the Jewish children would sit open-eyed and enthralled as the story of that great deliverance was repeated? As parents kept the Feast, and observed all its requirements, a twofold aspect would be recognized by those performing the service.

(a) The parents themselves dealt with God on behalf of their children, thus bringing down the blessing of heaven on them. The father of the home, as he sprinkled the blood of a lamb upon his house, secured God's protection for all beneath its roof.

(b) Then, in dealing with his children for God, the parent sought to lead them up to Him, and by instructing them in what God had done the parent would seek to lead his little ones to accept this mighty Deliverer as their own God. These two parts of parental instruction were closely and inseparably linked to each other, the first being the root and origin of the second – and the second being the full appropriation of the first. Like a *priest*, the parent would sprinkle the blood; and as a *prophet* he would instruct those sheltered by sacrifice.

As Jewish parents were under the obligation of interpreting the holy mystery of the Lord's Passover, so Christian parents have the solemn duty of explaining to their children the message of Christ dying on a cross for the sins of the world. Such interpretation involves the necessity of a personal salvation. The parent must know God, as the God of Redemption, if he is to convince his child of the true significance of the cross. Is this not the force of the injunction, "Thou shalt shew thy son in that day, saying, This is done because of that which the Lord did *unto me* when I came forth out of Egypt" (Exod. 13:8)?

Another thought to contemplate is that when the Jewish father sprinkled the blood upon the door of his house he preserved his child as well as himself from the destroying angel. What the helpless child could not do for himself, his father did for him, and God, who had honored the father so to act in behalf of the child, accepted the deed. Thus, initially the child was made a partaker of the blessing of that sprinkled blood. Thereafter as the father pleaded with God on behalf of his child, he would remind Jehovah of the blood and the oath of the covenant, and claim for his loved one the blessing of redemption. The fervent hope of the parent would be that his child would grow up to personally accept and ratify the covenant.

With the joy of a personal experience of God's redeeming grace in their hearts, and the unceasing guidance of the Holy Spirit to train their children aright, Christian parents, as they testify of a Saviour's love, often have the thrill of seeing their children opening the avenues of their being to Him who died to have them as His children. How happy is the heart of a child when, through home training, he can truly sing –

> I know 'twas all for love of me
> That He became a child,
> And left the heavens so fair to see,
> And trod earth's pathway wild.
> Then, Saviour, who wast once a child,
> A child may come to Thee:

And oh, in all Thy mercy mild,
Dear Saviour, come to me!

(3.) *Parents and Teachers as Shepherds.*

While it is perfectly true that our tender heavenly Shepherd carries the lambs in His bosom, He has committed their guardianship to parents, pastors, and to day and Sunday school teachers. These are the undershepherds little eyes can see and come to trust; and who, if they fail in their sacred trust, defeat the will and purpose of the Good Shepherd for His lambs. It is in this connection that we can understand the appeal of Jesus to Peter as He was about to ascend on high, leaving Peter to gather sheep and lambs into His fold. *Feed my lambs!* (John 21:15). What must not be lost sight of is the fact that this was our Lord's commission to His church of all time through Peter, and as such, reveals the place the rearing of little ones has in His loving heart!

Because the children of today will form His church of the morrow, heed must be given to Christ's special charge concerning them. As lambs children are weak and helpless. All who have the care of them must recognize their feebleness and nurture them in every way, seeing they are the hope of the future. Leaving a sheep farm in company with its master one evening, a friend heard him call to a shepherd, "Take great care of the lambs! There is a storm coming." Jesus knew what a terrific storm of persecution would overtake the infant church, and of how Peter himself would be martyred. Therefore we have the moving appeal of one of His last words before His Ascension, "Care for My lambs!"

Peter, as a fisherman, knew a good deal about fish, but *lambs,* well! they were outside his province. When Jesus called Peter to be an apostle, it was that he might become a "fisher of men" – his daily vocation becoming a symbol of his heavenly calling. Now, as the one-time fisherman stands on the threshold of the establishment of the church, his Lord announces that he is no longer a fisherman – catching men – but a shepherd – caring for lambs. Is there not a deep and significant meaning in such a change of occupation? What points of difference are there between fishing and lamb-rearing? Peter as a fisherman knew that what he caught in the sea he neither reared or fed, and once in his net only the full-grown, edible fish were retained, the little ones were cast back into the sea. Further, when caught, the fish were alive but quickly died and became fit for human consumption once dead.

But Peter is now to function as an undershepherd, exercising all possible care for the young and the feeble in Christ's church. If sheep are weak and helpless animals, how much more the little lambs who cannot look after themselves, and on whose growth the hope of the shepherd depends. Like lambs, children are endowed with potential that must be guarded and developed. For these frisky little creatures food is the condition of their growth so they must be fed with the pasture the shepherd provides. Can we not imagine how Peter, facing the future as an undershepherd, would weigh the significance of each word of the Great Shepherd of the sheep?

FEED

Lambs cannot seek necessary food for themselves – those responsible for their welfare must supply it, and all they eat comes from without to be assimilated into their bodies. With the feeding of Christ's lambs it is the same. Their small bodies grow and mature by food from the visible world – their minds are nourished by the thoughts entering the mind – their spirits are fed by the precious words of God taught by parent or teacher. So, as a mother studies what her child should eat for its body, so she will strive to feed her lamb with thoughts of divine wisdom and love.

It was to one that had a deep love for Jesus who heard His request, *Feed* My lambs! and only those inspired by the love of, and to, Jesus can truly take charge of the lambs in home and school. It is thus that the food feeding them will have the warmth of a divine love about it. The relationship between parents and children is, or should be, one of love, and where such love is purified and elevated by the love of God, shed abroad in the heart by the Spirit of love, then the tending of the lambs is looked upon as a service of love for Him whose love is ever inspiring.

MY

While parents may look upon their children as their own, seeing they are flesh of their flesh, Jesus reminded Peter that they were, primarily, *His* lambs – His property entrusted to parents and undershepherds to care for and nurture. It is because those He is to use for the spiritual and moral welfare of the next generation are the children of today that those who have their growth in their hand must grasp the possibilities of the future and train them as the coming flock.

Can we say that we look upon children with the eyes of Jesus, and endeavor to catch His spirit as He pleads Feed *My* lambs? They are His, and He loves them because of their childlike simplicity and heavenliness, and counts them of great worth, not only for what they are, but also for what they are to become. Further, because they are His, we must daily love, feed, and care for them, that they may grow up as the sheep of His pasture. In his pentecostal sermon, Peter the undershepherd reminded the people that the promise of God's salvation was not only for them, but their children as well (Acts 2:39. See Isa. 44:3-5). The daily experience of the heavenly Shepherd's love in his own heart was a daily lesson to Peter on how to feed Christ's little flock of lambs, as well as the grown sheep of His flock.

LAMBS

As already indicated, lambs are so dependent upon others. Left to themselves they are weak, feeble, and defenseless; and their very frailty and powerlessness compel shepherds to undertake their safety and provision. In using the figure of lambs, our Lord reminded Peter, and through him, all who have special charge of children, not only of their value but also of their need of all loving care because of their helplessness. It is because "but little children weak, Nor born in any high estate," that we must emulate the example of the divine Shepherd Himself who "gathers the lambs with his arm" (Isa. 40:11). The secret of influence as expressed by F. R. Havergal in the following lines can be adapted and applied to all who have the solemn charge of nourishing and rearing those who are tender in years –

> A Spirit whose power may touch and bind
> With unconscious influence every mind;
> Whose presence brings, like some fabled wand,
> The love which a monarch may not command; –

As the spring awakens from cold repose
The bloomless brier, the sweet wild rose —
Such would I be!

f. *The Necessity and Nature of Child Nurture.* In the family of believers, Paul exhorts parents to bring their children up "in the nurture and admonition of the Lord" (Eph. 6:4). There is an inference here that the children of a home belong not only to the parents, but also to the Lord, and that, consequently, undue severity in instruction must not be countenanced. In all Christian education of His little ones there must be gentleness, forbearance and love. Ellicott reminds us that "Christianity gradually softened the stern authority exemplified in the old Roman Law." As to the phrase Paul employs, Ellicott says that it covers the two elements of education —

Nurture is a word signifying generally "the treatment to a child, but by usage appropriated to practical training, or teaching by discipline." This is the same word given as "chastening" in Hebrews 12:4-11.

Admonition implies the "putting children in mind" by word of instruction and is the same word translated "rebuke" in Tit. 3:10, inasmuch as it implies warning, being distinguished from teaching (Col. 3:16).

If the principle of all child cultivation and discipline is the development of child faculties, until they reach the perfection of which a child is capable, and the preparation of the child to fulfill its destiny, then the parents' labor will not be in vain if it is *in the Lord.* It is only a full understanding of Solomon's pregnant phrase that is vastly important in all child nurture — "The way in which he should go" (Prov. 22:6), which, if followed, will not be departed from. "When he is old, he will not depart from it." The principle laid down here is universally true. In his exposition of Solomon's dictum, Andrew Murray stresses two points as to failures in the spiritual and moral failures in child-training —

(1.) Either the parent did not make "'the way in which he should go' his one aim in the child's training . . . As to the way in which he should go," we need be in no doubt. "The way of the Lord" God calls it, when He speaks of Abraham training his children. Other designations of "the way in which he should go" come to mind —

"Walking in His ways"
"The way of His footsteps"
"The way of His commandments"
"The way of holiness"
"The way of peace"
"The way of life"
"The new and living way"
"Walk in Him"

Christ, who calls young and old alike to walk in His footsteps, says of Himself, "I am the way." The early, persecuted saints were those whom Saul found and bound of "this way" (Acts 9:2). If parents desire to see their children saved, and growing up in the fear of the Lord, they must from the beginning of their children's understanding guide their thoughts to the way they should go.

(2.) Further, they must be "trained up," and the word for "train" is one of deep importance for parents and teachers to understand. Such essential training is not teaching, not commanding, but something beyond these aspects of tuition. What is involved is "not merely telling the child what to do, but showing him how to do it and seeing that it is done, taking care that the advice or the command given is put into practice and adopted as a habit." The illustration is used of the training of a young horse, and of how it is made to yield its will to its master's until at last it is in perfect sympathy with him, and yields to his slightest wish. It is carefully directed and accustomed to do the right thing until it becomes a habit, a second nature. When necessary, its own innate, wild tendencies are checked and restrained; and encouraged thus by a loving master, the young animal is helped to fully exercise its powers in subjection to the master's rule.

As those who train young horses, help with voice and hand and thoughtful care to nurture them, so parents should bestow similar care on the training of their children, seeking by voice and hand to accustom them to do easily and willingly what is asked of them. There are those who were brought up *at* a mother's knee – others were brought up *over* the knee. The habitual effort to bring the developing will of the child to obey the authority of love is a necessary element in training, seeing that success in training depends more on forming habits than inculcating rules. By repetition, a child learns to do certain things until they become so familiar and natural that it seems strange to him not to do them. Once the habit of obedience is formed, it becomes the root of other habits.

Parents, seeking by faith and prayer to mold, strengthen and guide the will of children in the way of the Lord can count upon His workings in their hearts. They can have the joy of seeing their children not only obeying their commands, but happy in the approval of all that is commanded, that is, obeying their parents, not because they have to, but because they delight to, knowing that what is asked of them is for their highest welfare. In a summary note at the end of his most illuminating work on *The Children for Christ,* Andrew Murray extends these points –

(1.) Training is more than teaching.

Teaching makes a child know what he is to do; training influences him, and sees he does it. The former deals with the mind; the latter with the will.

(2.) Prevention is better than cure.

Not to watch and correct mistakes, but to watch and *prevent mistakes,* is true training. The highest aim of true training is to lead the child to know he *can* obey and do right, and be happy in obedience.

(3.) Habits must precede principles.

With a child, the body grows for the first years of life while the mind is to a great extent dormant. Habits prepare the way for obedience from principle, not command.

(4.) The cultivation of the feelings precede that of judgment.

Early years of childhood are marked by the liveliness of the feelings and the susceptibility of impressions, and these are used by the parent to create feelings favorable to all that is good, making it attractive and desirable.

(5.) Example is better than precept.

The power of effective training lies, not in that which a parent might say and teach, but in what he *is* and *does.* We cannot teach children ideals we fail to live up to ourselves. When we *live* what we *teach,* we are able to *teach* others to *live.*

(6.) Love that draws is more than law that demands.

Love never seeks its own, and the love of parents for their children lives and gives itself for their full training. Parental love inspired by divine love exercises a mighty influence in the home and is always the inspiration in the secret of effective nurture.

g. *Handmaids of God's Redeeming Love.* In the Anglican *Book of Com-*

mon Prayer, an "Invocation of Blessing On The Child" there is the prayer – "Grant that the old Adam in this Child may be so buried, that the new man may be raised up in him." Then for children there is a ceremony relative to the appointment of Godparents, chosen from among the relatives or friends of the parents of the children. The question is asked in "The Catechism" –

"What did your Godfather and Godmother then do for you?" The reply is given, "They did promise and vow three things in my name.

(1.) That I should renounce the Devil and all his works, the pomp and vanity of this wicked world, and all the sinful lusts of the flesh.

(2.) That I should believe all the Articles of the Christian Faith.

(3.) That I should keep God's holy will and commandments, and walk in the same all the days of my life." Children of more mature years have to answer, "Yes, verily; and by God's help so I will."

It is to be doubted whether the majority of these sponsors for children at baptism or confirmation actually function in a God-like way toward those they vowed to oversee in spiritual matters. After all, the most effective guardians of children are not Godparents but *godly* parents, particularly the mother of the children. For such a task God created wonderful mother-love which, when directed into the right channel transforms a mother into a handmaid of God's redeeming love. When God sought to reveal His love to a lost world He chose a woman to give His eternal Son a human form. As Myers expresses it –

> Not to the rich He came and to the ruling
> Men full of meat whom wholly He abhors –
> Not to the fools grown insolent in fooling,
> Most, when the lost are dying at their doors;
> Nay, but to her who with a sweet thanksgiving
> Took in tranquility what God might bring,
> Blessed Him and waited, and within her living
> Felt the arousal of a Holy Thing.

One to whom the phrase of MacDonald applies – "The God-life at thy heart," was the saintly mother of Abraham Lincoln who, until his assassination in 1865, constantly extolled her benign influence over his life. More than once he testified, "All that I am or hope to be, I owe to my angel mother." Countless numbers agree with the sentiment expressed by Strickland Gillilan –

> You may have tangible wealth untold;
> Caskets of jewels and coffers of gold;
> Richer than I you can never be –
> I had a mother who read to me.

A mother is not only a child's first lover and constant babysitter, but a name for God in the lips and hearts of little children as W. M. Thackeray put it. Henry Ward Beecher adds the tribute, "The mother's heart is the child's schoolroom." We can gather many sweet eulogies to the value of mothers from ancient proverbial literature. A Jewish proverb says that, "God could not be everywhere, and so He made mothers." Among Persian proverbs we have, "Heaven is at the feet of mothers." From Spain we have the saying, "An ounce of mother is worth a pound of clergy." A child's first minister of holy things is a Christian mother and because of this, "Men are what their mothers make them," as Emerson expresses it. No other than Napoleon Bonaparte said, "The future destiny of the child is always the work of the mother."

What a shining light a true mother is to all her loved ones, day and night! Is she not the only one who can divide her love among several children, and for each child still to have all her love? To a child, the most wonderful face in all the world is that of mother. Does not the Bible give prominence to the sacredness of motherhood? At the opening of New Testament history we read of John the Baptist, "He shall be filled with the Holy Ghost, even from his mother's womb" (Luke 1: 15). Thus, a saintly woman's womb was "the work-place of the Holy Spirit." Apart from the divine enduement John received at his birth, he entered the world spiritually fortified because his mother was a Spirit-filled woman before his birth.

What higher commendation could any parents have than that which Luke gives to Elisabeth, and her priestly husband, Zacharias –

"They were both righteous before God, walking in all the commandments and ordinances of the Lord blameless."

Being "*without blame* before him in love," such holy parents could count upon the power of the Holy Spirit in their unborn child, whose conception was miraculous in that Elisabeth being "barren and well stricken in years," was beyond the period of childbearing. With "the sweet omnipotence of Love" at His command God is ready to work any miracle He pleases, but observing His own laws, desiring a holy child as the forerunner of His Son, He sought for holy parents. Thus, "it is the God of Nature, who in the world of cause and effect has ordered that like begets like, who is also the God of Grace."

It is to be feared that the majority of mothers – and fathers, too – do not seek after a life of blamelessness before God, and consequently beget children which are spiritually handicapped from their birth. If only all mothers cherished the highest and the brightest hope of holy motherhood, namely, to have children filled with the Holy Spirit from their birth, what a purer world ours would be! How saintly Elisabeth must have been overawed at the angel's message concerning her unborn child! Luke gives us three aspects of the child born under the covering of the Holy Spirit.

(1.) *A favor for John's parents.* "Thou shalt have joy and gladness." Disappointed through many long years at being childless, how Zacharias and Elisabeth must have been filled with the holy happiness of heaven. How sad that many parents have had reason to sigh in bitter agony, Would God my child had never been born!

(2.) *A favor for the world.* "Many shall rejoice at his birth." What mighty things were accomplished through the life and preaching of John the Baptist. Many of the disciples of Jesus, some of whom became apostles, were converted through the revival preaching of John. Blessed are those mothers who live to see their children greatly used for the salvation of lost souls.

(3.) *A favor for John himself.* "He shall be great in the sight of the Lord." John bore witness to Jesus, and Jesus said of him that "among them born of woman there hath not risen a greater than John the Baptist," but the crown of all prophecy concerning him was, "He shall be great in the sight of the Lord." So he was a joy to his parents, a blessing to his fellowmen, and an honored man in the sight of God. A man may not be known much among men, yet great in God's sight for He does not see as man sees. How mothers need to be aroused to understand what holy motherhood means in God's sight! If only all of them could live as Elisabeth did –

believe and receive what she did, their children would enter the world under the overshadowing of heavenly grace, and prove to be a blessing in it.

Another devout handmaid of the Lord was the Virgin Mary, cousin of Elisabeth, and the one of whom Gabriel could say, "Blessed art thou among women, and blessed is the fruit of the womb, and blessed is she that believed" (Luke 1:42,45). What would you say was the most conspicuous feature, from the human side of Mary's motherhood? Was it not the childlike simplicity of faith manifested in the surrender of herself to the Holy Spirit for the accomplishment of the divine purpose? Doubtless overwhelmed by the heavenly announcement, Mary immediately replied, "Behold the handmaid of the Lord; be it unto me according to thy word" (Luke 1:38). She became the Lord's bondwoman, and in quiet trust and expectancy waited for Him to do what He had said He would. And the miracle happened, for within the womb of the Virgin the Holy Spirit became the love-knot between our Lord's two natures, linking deity and humanity and fusing them into one. He made possible the One who came as the God-Man.

The surrender of Mary teaches every mother to yield herself to God, that in, and through her, His purpose and glory may be made manifest. A truth believing parents must not lose sight of is that each of their children under divine guardianship can be a link in the golden chain of the good pleasure of God's will. Over all the impulses of human love and the instincts of a God-given maternity there hovers a divine purpose using them for the carrying out of His plan. Thus children of a godly home can become as the stones of the great temple of which the holy Child Jesus is the cornerstone.

Twice over it is said of Mary that she "kept all these things, and pondered them in her heart." Such holy quiet of meditation and reflection fitted her for the blessed duties of motherhood. The truths she pondered over taught her to regard everything connected with the birth of her Child as being a matter of deepest interest to her heavenly Father, as well as of great importance in His redemptive plan for mankind. Before her Son saw the light of day, Mary claimed all the exceeding great and precious promises on His behalf. No wonder we read of her, "*Blessed* is she that believed."

If only there were more mothers like Mary, there would be more children like her Son, Jesus, His miraculous conception, deity and sinlessness excepted. One of the most remarkable illustrations of unity in the world is the unique oneness of mother and child, not only physically, before the umbilical cord is cut, but in her own life and character she imparts which determines, to a great extent, what her child is to be. When God gave His Son to be born of a woman, this law was not violated, and the mother He chose for His Son was doubtless all that grace could make her to be the fit vessel through whom He should receive His human nature and disposition. How necessary it is for all respective mothers to prepare themselves spiritually, to receive their children according to God's Word; and after their birth, to train them in harmony with that Word, so that they can enter into the full enjoyment of all the promises of the Word.

In these days of sexual liberty far too many young women enter into unwanted motherhood, and try to prevent it by abortion. But all God-fearing, rightly married wives, entering motherhood, join in Mary's thanksgiving over her Child, as their children are born – "My soul doth magnify the Lord, and my spirit hath rejoiced in God my Saviour." Birth-pangs give way to exquisite joy as a woman realizes that she has become the living mother of a living child. "She remembereth no more the anguish, for the joy that a man is born into the world." Looking at the precious little treasure God has given her, the mother is stirred to praise Him, and dedicate both herself and her child to Him, so that as an immortal being the child may be fitted to show forth God's salvation among men. With a true and grateful heart she not only rejoices but prays –

> Here am I and this precious child Thou hast given me, the witness of Thy power and Thy goodness; may our lives, all our days devoted to Thee, be the sacrifice of thanksgiving we bring Thee.

h. *The Double Surety of Children.* The Greek word for "surety" is "bail," that is, one who personally answers for anyone, whether his life or property, and is to be distinguished from a "mediator." As our Surety, Jesus is the personal guarantee of the terms of the new and better covenant secured on the ground of His perfect sacrifice (Heb. 7:22, 27). As the context makes clear, His is an abiding and unchanging Priesthood. *Bail,* the person providing security is from the Latin, *bailus,* meaning "burden bearer." When Joseph and Mary brought Jesus to Jerusalem, and in the Temple presented Him to the Lord, although a helpless infant He was yet a pleasing sacrifice, a sweet-smelling savor (Luke 2:22-24).

Jesus was not only Mary's first-born, but also the Father's first-born among many brethren. He became the Forerunner through whom all little ones can be made acceptable to God. Jesus was made like our children, that they might be made like Him and have Him as their Surety. In respect to His humanity, He was made like us that through grace we might be made like Him. The object of the presentation in the Temple was an acknowledgement of God's claim upon the children presented, and of the necessity of devoting them to God as His property. Then, as the child can understand it, he must be taught that he was presented with Jesus, like Jesus, in Jesus, to the Father, and of his fellowship in the life and spirit of Him who became the Surety of children. It is in this way that the holy childhood of Jesus overshadows and sanctifies the children of a godly home.

When parents dedicate a child to the Lord in an intelligent, childlike, heartfelt faith, such an act greatly influences the daily treatment of the child because he is thought of as God's devoted and accepted property. As for the parents themselves, they see their responsibility as trustees to whom has been committed the keeping and training of their child; his guardians and guides as they seek to make the holy childhood of Jesus the protection of the childhood of their child. What a wonderful safeguard for children is a sanctified home! Happy is a consecrated home in which all can say, "We will serve the Lord" (Josh. 24: 15).

As to the heritage of holiness, is it not another surety for children? Paul gives us the precious, arresting sentence, "Now are they [your children] holy" (I Cor. 7:14), which seems to imply that "God's holiness and our children are meant for each other; as parents we are the God-ordained links for bringing them into perfect union."

It was to sanctified parents that Paul wrote "Your children are holy." There has been secured for every child that treasure of sanctification prepared in Christ and which the Spirit of sanctification makes a personal possession as the child is trained in the way of holiness by holy parents.

If "Holiness" is written upon the doorposts of our home, and the home and family are looked upon as God's home, the dwelling place of His holiness, then all that is contrary to holiness will be kept outside the home. Parental holiness is an indispensable condition for educating a holy child and training him to show forth the glory of His holiness. The word holy, not only signifies a relation — a destiny — a pledge of a divine life-power, it also describes a character, for God *is* holy, and so urges us to be like Him. It is therefore the solemn task of Christian parents to train their children in such "dispositions and habits, such ways of thinking and feeling and acting, as shall be in harmony with the Faith, that they are holy in Christ and belong to the Spirit, as shall be a preparation for His dwelling in them and using them as His temple." How rewarded are parents who are separated unto God, when they see the young child-life in their home separated from the world, its spirit and its service; and consecrated to God and the fulfillment of His will.

From an unknown source we have the lines —

> The family is like a book,
> The children are the leaves,
> The parents are the covers
> That protective beauty gives.
> At the first pages of the book
> Are blanks and purely fair,
> But time soon writes its memories
> And paints its pictures there.
> Love is the little golden clasp
> That bindeth up the trust.
> Oh, break it not, lest all the leaves
> Shall scatter and be lost.

2. Obligations of Children Toward Their Parents

Having fully considered parental obligation we now turn to the other side of the coin and discover what the Bible has to say regarding the obligation of children toward their parents — an aspect many present-day children seem to be ignorant of. In ancient times public opinion stoutly upheld respect for, and obedience to, parents. Everywhere in the Bible we have abundant evidence of the bond that bound Jewish families together. In our day the disintegration of family is largely related to Gentile homes. Very few Jewish families, in comparison, fall apart. The characteristic unity of the home circle has been wonderfully maintained through the centuries. Here are a few illustrations of the Biblical affinity between parents and children —

When Hagar the outcast knew there was no more water in her bottle to keep her child alive, she laid him under the shrubs and said, "Let me not see the death of the child. And she sat over against him, and lift up her voice, and wept" (Gen. 21:16).

A benediction was pronounced upon those who lovingly honored their parents — a benediction both Jews and Gentiles can enjoy — "That thy days may be long upon the land which the Lord thy God giveth thee" (Exod. 20:12. See Deut. 5:16). Under the same Mosaic Law we have the solemn judgment, "He that smiteth his father, or his mother, shall be surely put to death" (Exod. 21:15).

When King David heard of the tragic death of his son, Absalom, we read that he was much moved, and retiring to his private chamber, cried,

"O my son Absalom, my son, my son Absalom! would God I had died for thee, O Absalom, my son, my son!" (II Sam. 18:33).

Stripped bare of all the comforts and amenities of his large and hitherto happy, holy home, Job sighed for the old days, "Oh that I were as in months past . . . When the Almighty was with me, when my children were about me" (Job 29:2, 5).

Solomon, as we have already indicated, had much to say about obligations of children toward parents, as well as parental obligation. Children were taught to hold precious the spiritual instruction received, "My son, keep thy father's commandment, and forsake not the law of thy mother: Bind them continually upon thy heart, and tie them about thy neck. When thou goest, it shall lead thee: when thou sleepest, it shall keep thee; and when thou wakest, it shall talk with thee" (Prov. 6:20-22).

In his prediction of the Assyrian invasion, Isaiah was inspired to make the prophecy concerning his child, "Before the child shall have knowledge to cry, My father, and my mother, the riches of Damascus and the spoil of Samaria shall be taken away before the King of Assyria" (8:4).

Micah, dejected that one aspect of national apostasy would be, "The son dishonoureth the father, the daughter riseth up against her mother" (7:6). What a tragic situation it is when a man's foes are those of his own household!

When the wife of Zebedee came to worship Jesus she brought her sons with her. (Matt. 20:20).

A father's heartfelt concern for his child, possessed by a dumb and dangerous spirit, is expressed in the words, "Straightway the father of the child cried out, and said with tears, Lord, I believe; help thou mine unbelief" (Mark 9:24).

In like manner, the nobleman of Capernaum, distressed over his sick son, besought Jesus, "Sir, come down ere my child die" (John 4:49).

Paul wanted young Timothy to know that the reward or recompense of parents by children was "good and acceptable before God" (I Tim. 5:4).

That the home is a closely-knit fellowship is implied in the exclamation, "Behold I and the children which God hath given me" (Heb. 2:13).

While one could gather out further instances of the unity of home life in Israel, and of the concern of one for the other within the home, sufficient has been cited to prove its noble estimation recognized both by parents and children alike. Now let us seek to classify more particularly what the Bible says regarding the accountability of children to parents.

a. *Attendant Upon Parental Instruction.* Early education was primarily in the home. We have already seen that it was the parents' responsibility to rear children in the way of the Lord, also the children's responsibility to accept home teaching and obey parents as a preparatory discipline for the higher relationship to God (Gen. 18:19; Deut. 6:7; 11:19). While a boy at twelve years of age became a "son of the law," or became a subject to the law advancing to fuller instruction, at five years of age he was already under his father's tuition. The children, however, grew up more or less under their mother's care, the girl usually continuing with her mother until her marriage (Prov. 6:20; 31:1; II Tim. 1:5; 3:14, 15). Sometimes wealthier families employed tutors (I Chron. 27:32). Schools for children are first mentioned by Josephus, the Jewish historian. From *The Talmud* we learn that the first school for children was instituted about 100 B.C., and by the time of Christ were fairly common.

From early times children were taught to read and write even in the poorer families (Isa. 8:1; 10:19). Solomon, in the Book of Proverbs urges care, even to severity in the training and teaching of children. (See 3:12; 13:24; 15:5; 22:6; 29:15.) Explicit are the exhortations — "My son, hear the instructions of thy father, and forsake not the law of thy mother" (Prov. 1:8) and "A wise son heareth his father's instruction" (Prov. 13:1).

The significance of religious feasts and ordinances had to be taught the children (Exod. 12:26, 27). The acceptance and understanding of the truths taught by parents became as an ornament of grace upon the children's heads and as chains about their necks (Prov. 31:1). Truth lived out in the lives of parents adds reality and power to lip instruction. Too often how they live speaks so loudly that their children cannot hear, or fail to follow, what they say. Timothy became the faithful companion of the greatest of the apostles, because the Scriptural instruction he received from his devoted mother had passed through the crucible of her own heart. Timothy but emulated his mother Eunice's unfeigned faith (II Tim. 1:5).

b. *Careful About Honoring Parents.* The ancient commandment has never been withdrawn, "Honour thy father and thy mother." No string is attached saying that they should be honored if they are worthy of it. Parents, no matter how undeserving of respect, should always be revered seeing that under God they gave us life. Wise rulers make good subjects, and firm and considerate commanders have faithful soldiers. In like manner, parents honoring God in all their ways make it easy for their children to honor them. It is on the character of father and mother that their children's fulfillment of "The Children's Commandment" — Honour thy father and thy mother — will depend.

A child can only honor what he sees and knows to be worthy of honor, and it is the high calling of parents so to speak and act and live in the presence of children that honor may spontaneously and unconsciously flow out from them to their parents. Kings receive honor, and if parents reign and rule in love and the fear of God, honor will be given them. As a child's first virtue is the honoring and obeying of his parents, how essential it is for them to honor God in the eyes of the child. Andrew Murray observes that —

> The sentiment of honour, reverence, is one of the noblest and purest our nature is capable of. The power of perceiving what is worthy of honour, the willingness to acknowledge it, the unselfishness that feels it no degradation, but a pleasure, to render it — all this is itself honourable and ennobling; nothing brings more true honour than giving honour to others. This disposition ought to be cultivated most carefully in the child, as an important part of his education. It is one of the chief elements of a noble character and a preparation for rendering to God the honour due to Him.

c. *Observance of Filial Fear.* It is necessary to observe the contrast between reverent awe and slavish terror. The words the Bible uses for "fear" have two principal meanings, as the *Zondervan Pictorial Bible Dictionary,* points out —

1. That apprehension of evil which normally leads one either to flee or fight.
2. That awe and reverence which a man of sense feels in the presence of God, and to a less extent in

the presence of a king or other dread authority.

When the disciples cried out for fear thinking they saw a ghost they were afraid, terrified (Matt. 14:26); but when Paul speaks of those who have no "fear of God before their eyes" (Rom. 3:18), the second meaning is implied. The word "reverend" occurring only once in Scripture (Ps. 111:9), means "to be feared," or reverenced. In the Old Testament some fifteen different Hebrew nouns are rendered "fear." The two implications of the word can be found in Psalm 31:13, "Fear was on every side"; and Proverbs 9:10, "The fear of the Lord is the beginning of wisdom."

When Moses explained the earthly relationship and walk of God's earthly people, he wrote, "Ye shall fear every man his mother, and his father" (Lev. 19:3), which is equivalent to the exposition on chastening in the epistle to the Hebrews – "We have had fathers of our flesh which corrected us, and we gave them *reverence*" (12:9). Parents fail in their responsibility when they are cruel, or too demanding, exacting, or inconsiderate in their treatment of the children God gave them. Boys and girls should never be scared, terror stricken, or afraid of their parents. Alas! too many are, and often run away from a house of loveless, harsh atmosphere.

The sort of fear that Moses urges on the part of children for their fathers and mothers is that of loving respect and reverence, because of their godliness, love, sympathy and patience. It was this aspect of fear that Jesus, as a child, manifested toward Mary and Joseph. If "the fear of the Lord" is a definition of piety, then the fear of, or reverence for, parents will enable children to understand more fully what it means for them to look upon the God their parents love and serve as One who is "holy and to be feared" (Ps. 111:9). Such fear is the fundamental principle upon which true religion and a happy home rest, (Prov. 29:17). Irreverence on the part of children toward an older person is visited by a signal instance of divine judgment (II Kings 2:23, 24).

d. *Obedience to Parents.* That the Bible has much to say about obedience is evidenced by the fact that the word occurs more than 150 times throughout its pages. God demands obedience from the army of heaven and from the inhabitants of earth, and Jesus is always the model of obedience to God. Then obedience to those who are over us, and to parents by their children, likewise occupies space in Holy Writ. Here are some instances of obedience to parents –

"Jacob obeyed his father, and his mother (Gen. 28:7).

"Jacob called his son Joseph . . . thou shalt carry me out of Egypt, and bury me in their buryingplace. And he [Joseph] said, I will do as thou hast said" (Gen. 47:29, 30).

"Children, obey your parents in the Lord: for this is right" (Eph. 6:1).

Obedience is to be "in the Lord," implying that both parents and children, recognizing the Saviour as Lord of their life, find loving submission pleasant. This is the right and only source of delight. Obedience is never irksome, unpleasant or feigned when it is "in the Lord." What should be the action of a Christian toward obeying the demands of an unchristian parent, especially if they are in conflict with the child's faith in God? The apostolic principle should be observed, "We ought to obey God, rather than men" (Acts 5:29, 32).

"Children, obey your parents in all things: for this is well pleasing unto the Lord" (Col. 3:20).

Obedience in some "things" not of the Lord is never well-pleasing to Him. It has been pointed out that the position of children was one of complete subordination to their parents (Gen. 22; Judg. 11:39), and the sacrifices to Molech of children by parents, indicate that the father had powers of life and death over their children, but these powers were limited (Lev. 18:21; 20:2-5; Deut. 21: 18-21; II Kings 23:10; Jer. 32:35). Reverence and obedience on the part of children toward their parents were strongly enjoined (Exod. 20:12; Lev. 19:3; Deut. 17:16).

Christian parents, living in obedience to God's will, are never in danger of repressing the healthy development of a child's moral powers by demanding implicit obedience to their will. Such a child is trained to believe that because of the superior wisdom of his parents, they know what is best for him, and so command him accordingly. When Paul said that children must obey their parents for *this is right,* it is so, not because the child approves or agrees, but because the command is given by a parent, the one in authority. Children who thus obey, honor their parents.

All parents, who are the Lord's, as well as bishops and deacons, must rule well their own house, having their children in subjection with all gravity (I Tim. 3:4, 5-12). This is the "home rule" that magnifies the Lord, and keeps the home as His sacred dwelling place. The lives of obedient children are a hymn of praise to the glory of God, especially if they obey His voice. Obedient children are those who obey the Lord because they love Him – obey Him in all things – find in obedience its own reward. In the keeping of God's commandments, "there is great reward." It was Benjamin Franklin who said, "Let thy child's first lesson be obedience, and the second will be what thou wilt." Further, a truism that must never be lost sight of is that, "a child has to learn obedience in the home or he will never learn obedience to the heavenly Father." Whether young or old, we must walk or learn to walk on the two feet, trust and obey.

e. *Growing Love for Parents.* Perhaps the most touching episode in the Bible of a son's love for his father was Joseph's action when he met his father after a long absence. Jacob had mourned his son as being dead. When they ultimately met, Joseph fell on his father's neck, and "wept on his neck a good while" (Gen. 46:29). How Jesus felt toward His mother is seen in the provision of her future as He died upon the cross (John 19:26, 27). If heaven gave Him, as the divine Son, a Father's love, earth provided for Him, as the Child Jesus, a mother's love and care so that "in all things he might be made like unto his brethren." How true are the lines of the old melody –

> "There is beauty all around,
> When there's love at home."

Love for God on the part of all the members of the family, and love for each other in the home circle, transforms any home into a palace beautiful. The song of the ideal home goes like this –

> "Now abideth love, comfort, sufficiency, these three, but the greatest of these is LOVE."

As the Apostle Paul in his extensive missionary ministry often visited and stayed in homes of believers, one wonders if he had had experience of some of them suffering from a lack of love. Gathering together a few relevant references it would seem as if he warned against three aspects of home education –

1. Children can be often very irksome and provoking.
2. Parents are in danger of allowing themselves to be provoked.
3. The general result is that parents again provoke their children to wrath.

Paul's warnings and exhortations open up the vexed question of the difficulty of giving reproof or punishment in the right spirit, or in keeping with one's Christian testimony. It is when a child least deserves love that he needs it more. Certainly the best of parents have need of patience, wisdom and self-control, if the rule of parents is looked upon as a reign of love.

"Love suffereth long, and is kind; . . . seeketh not her own, is not easily provoked" (I Cor. 13:4, 5).

"Ye fathers, provoke not your children to wrath" (Eph. 6:4).

"Fathers, provoke not your children to anger, lest they be discouraged" (Col. 3:21).

"Teach the young women . . . to love their children" (Tit. 2:4).

From the above Scriptures we observe that both mothers and fathers share the responsibility of the management of their children. Such a care is not to be thrown upon one or the other but is to be borne together. After a hard and exacting day at work, a father may feel that he cannot be bothered with the children, and their clamor for loving attention may be regarded more as a burden and weariness than as a charge from the Lord to be met in the spirit of love and gladness. It is because "God has joined to the weakness and gentleness of the mother the firmness and strength of the father" that each must take his or her part in the creation of an atmosphere of love in the home. When they are helpers together in such a fruitful task, their little ones grow up loving them, and never fail to show their affection even when the parents are old and gray-headed.

Observation had led the Apostle Paul to exhort fathers, in particular, not to provoke their children to wrath for he knew that a parent giving way to anger or temper slays love in the heart of his child. It is hard for a child to believe in love if it has a scowling face. To inspire a child to love God and his parents it is essential to have a home reflecting the life of love the heavenly Father manifests in the guidance and tuition of His children.

> Beloved, let us love:
> For only thus
> Shall we behold that God
> Who lovest us.

We readily concede that all children are not alike; that while one in a home may be loving and obedient, another may be the reverse and the constant source of annoyance. But if the child provokes the parents, the latter must be careful how to react to such provocation. Love and patience are necessary to bear with waywardness in children for if the parents are taken up unawares by what is so trying to temper and longsuffering, and give way to angry feelings, the effort to foster love becomes more difficult. A father's hasty temper often inflames a child's passion and he becomes his provocation to wrath. It is because God meant the rule of the family to be like His own – a reign of law inspired by love – that a father needs a love that is not easily provoked, even when there are sudden outbreaks of temper in his children and the little vexations arising from childish mistakes, naughtiness and little quarrels.

In child training, lovingness, tenderness, gentleness and forbearance are so necessary if a child is to be encouraged into goodness. Parental tranquility and kindness pay rich dividends in the love and confidence children come to manifest, for it will not take them long to reciprocate the love which is a principle of action as well as an evidence of natural instinct. At all times parents must be, by the grace and power of God, models of a holy, patient love, inspiring by it the ever-growing affection of their children. It is only thus that they can be trained after the divine mind and become a joy both to God and their parents.

f. *Filial Care of Parents.* While the Bible has much to say about the parental care of children, it speaks with equal voice about the filial care of parents. In so much of our home life today there is little love and long-suffering and children grow up without much respect for their parents, and leave them as soon as they can. What heartbreaks parental negligence produces! Too many forget the sacrifice of those who fed, clothed and educated them. God called upon the heavens and the earth to hear His heart-moan over the cruel treatment He received from the children for whom He had done so much — "I have nourished and brought up children, and they have rebelled against me. The ox knoweth his owner, and the ass his master's crib: but Israel doth not know, my people doth not consider" (Isa. 1:2, 3).

Shakespeare, in *King Lear,* expresses the thought —

> How sharper than a serpent's tooth it is
> To have a thankless child!

The increasing number of lonely old people in a room or two of their home, or in institutions for the aged, testify, in many cases, to thankless, heartless and forgetting children. But divine instructions as to the care of parents are most explicit.

"Thou shalt . . . honour the face of the old man" (Lev. 19:32).

". . . go up to my father, and say unto him, Thus saith thy son Joseph . . . I will nourish thee" (Gen. 45:9-11; 47:12).

"Whosoever shall say to his father or his mother, It is a gift" (Matt. 15:5).

"[Children] requite (reward) their parents: for that is good and acceptable before God" (I Tim. 5:4).

In writing to the Corinthians, Paul made it clear that "The children ought not to lay up for the parents, but the parents for the children" (II Cor. 12:14).

Then in his first letter to Timothy there was the apostle's declaration that, "If any provide not for his own, and especially for those of his own house, he hath denied the faith, and is worse than an infidel" (I Tim. 5:8).

Strong words these! Would that parents who do not provide for their children, and children who fail to provide for their needy parents in their old age would heed them! Behind the statement — "worse than an infidel" — is the thought that the rules even of the nobler pagan moralists forbid such heartless neglect and selfishness. So, for a professing Christian to deliberately fail in the observance of his plain duties to his nearest relatives, brings shame and disgrace on the cause of the loving Christ who made full provision for His mother before He left her.

g. *Penalties for Dishonoring Parents.* The world has always had dishonorable parents, and God has some solemn advice for their children not to imitate them in their wickedness. "I said unto their children . . . Walk ye not in the statutes of your fathers, neither observe their judgments, nor defile yourselves with their idols" (Ezek. 20:18).

But He has far more to say about children who dishonor their parents. In no uncertain way He describes such shameful behavior and the judgment it truly deserves.

Anyone who is disrespectful to his parents is accursed (Deut. 27:16).

Irreverence on the part of children toward an older person is visited by a signal instance of divine judgment (II Kings 2:23, 24).

Condemnation follows the despising of parents (Deut. 27:16; Job 19:18).

The just punishment of a prodigal son (Deut. 21:18-23; Prov. 15:5, 20; 19:26).

Mockery of parents results in severe penalty (Prov. 30:17).

Parents cursed by their children are requited (Exod. 21:15, 17; Mark 7: 10-12).

Death was meted out to those who smote their parents (Exod. 21:15).

The false premise of parental robbery (Prov. 28:24).

The calamity of children who are foolish (Prov. 19:13).

Divine action against children who spurn parental advice (I Sam. 2:25).

Advocacy of firm discipline with corporal punishment (Prov. 22:15; 23: 13; 29:15).

If, "Virtue is the fount whence honour springs," then the dishonorable, unworthy treatment of some parents by their children is an evidence of the latter's lack of the virtues of love, gratitude and thoughtfulness. "Render honour to whom honour is due" is a dictum of the Bible which children in particular should remember (Rom. 13:7).

Children and Tragedy and Death

Shakespeare makes Lady Macbeth say –

. . . " 'Tis the eye of childhood
That fears a painted devil

To the mind of a child, fears are usually imaginary. The most trivial, insignificant things can cause alarm and make him afraid. Wise parents are always careful never to frighten or scare their children. Often a fright has dire effects. What concerns us in this section of our study are the tragedies, afflictions and death overtaking even children and which often raises the question, Why do the innocent suffer? When babies enter the world blind, or deaf and mute, or all three, as in the case of the remarkable Helen Keller, or mentally or physically deformed, our finite minds often question the love of God. As for babies born dead, or who die soon after birth, what anguish they bring to parents whose hopes are crushed. Two friends eagerly anticipated the coming of their first, and only child. He came, but died a day after his birth, and his father told me that the babe in his tiny coffin was the heaviest weight he had ever carried. No wonder! In that small casket were two broken hearts. Although God sanctified such a grief to those two sincere believers, the scar remained throughout their long childless life together.

Andrew Murray suggests that in God's great school of tribulation there are many classes. In the department where God trains parents, there is one room which all greatly fear to enter. Many struggle and murmur as they are let into it. As darkness closes in over them, faith in God's love and wisdom is shaken, if, for instance, a child prayed and longed for is born a mongoloid. What a vivid picture of parental despair we have in Jacob who refused to be comforted by his sons and daughters over the loss of Joseph, "If I be bereaved of my children, I am bereaved." We also hear his despairing cry when Benjamin is taken from him — Benjamin, "a child of his old age, a little one . . . and his father loveth him" (Gen. 43:14; 44:20).

It may come as a surprise to many Bible readers to learn how full the Bible is of sick, deformed, persecuted, demon-possessed, and martyred children. Here is a catalog of such children, some of whom we will deal with more fully in our next chapter.

1. Born Deformed

Babies born with a congenital deformity, that is, some kind of malformation acquired during pregnancy, bring with their misshapen or defective bodies a good deal of disappointment and anxiety for their parents. One has seen some horrible monstrosities in hospitals designed to care for such unfortunate babies. Modern science, through drugs designed to assist women while bearing children is responsible for the terribly marred children known as "thalidomide babies." Legless, armless, and twisted frames, pictures of these twisted bodies shocked the civilized world. The senior executives of the Gruenenthal Chemie, the German firm responsible for putting the thalidomide drug on the market have been forced to pay heavy damages to the parents of "thalidomide children," as they are known, because of the rudimentary limbs and malformations they were born with. In West Germany alone it is estimated that there are some 2,000 of these terribly deformed children. The Bible records instances of those who were born disfigured, but not as the result of drugs.

The man whom Peter and John saw at the Beautiful Gate of the Temple, whom friends laid daily in a conspicuous place for worshipers to see and help, had been "lame from his mother's womb." What badly formed legs he must have had to have warranted being "carried" by strong arms of sympathizers! (Acts 3:1-11). But the Lord who came that the lame might walk (Matt. 11:5), empowered the apostles to perform the first apostolic miracle. The people marveled when they saw this man afflicted from birth "walking, and *leaping*, and praising God."

Then there is the further miracle of the impotent man at Lystra, who had been "a cripple from his mother's womb" (Acts 14:8). As this helpless man sat and listened to Paul, the apostle perceived that he had faith to be healed of his crippled condition, and commanded him to stand on his feet — something he had not been able to do since he left his mother's womb — and "he leaped and walked." Such a miracle constrained the Lycaonians to say that the gods had come down to them in the likeness of men (Acts 14:6-18).

Another record of a man pitifully lame is that of Mephiboseth who was not born crippled, but became so when only five years of age. This son of Jonathan, Saul's son, was dropped by his nurse as she picked him up and fled in haste from enemies, stumbled, and let her "precious burden fall." King David, for Jonathan's sake, showed much consideration for his son so badly lamed in both feet (II Sam. 9:1-13; 21:7). Deformed Mephiboseth "did eat continually at the king's table."

In the Chapel of St. Nicholas, Westminster Abbey, London, is the tomb of a little child who died because of a mistake of its nurse. In the nurse's will it was discovered that she never ceased to lament the little girl, and begged urgently, if possible, to be buried beside it — which she was.

2. Born Blind

Only those parents who have had a sightless child can enter into the feelings of those in the gospels who had a son "born blind" (John 9:19, 20, 32). In those far-off days, children who were blind from their birth were indeed helpless. If their parents were poor, all that a blind person could do was to sit and beg, as did the blind beggar at the pool of Siloam (John 9: 1-41). Through the centuries the condition of the blind has vastly improved. Now blind children, or those who go blind, or who are blinded through one cause or another, have schools and institutions where they are taught to read and write and type, and to learn useful occupations, thereby making them self-supporting. Blind persons are also granted pensions and given specially-trained dogs to lead them around. Job speaks about being "eyes to the blind" (29:15), and this is what these seeing eye dogs are. (See Rom. 2:19).

In His rebuke of Moses for his hesitancy in confronting Pharaoh through lack of faculty of speech, God reminded Moses that the perfection of all our faculties is His work. "The Lord said unto him, . . . who maketh the dumb, or deaf, or the seeing, or the blind? Have not I the Lord?" (Exod. 4:11). Some parents might think God cruel and unjust who have a deaf and dumb, or blind, child as they read that latter phrase, "Have not I the Lord?" Why should He as the God of love permit such defects and deformities of human nature? As the omniscient Lord, He knows what is best for His own, and what He permits in their lives must be for their good and His glory. As the perfect One, He never makes a mistake, as a woman born deaf, mute and blind, Helen Keller, came to learn. (See Rom. 9:20, 21).

In some ways it may be worse for a child to be born with full sight and then to become blind later on, than for the child born blind. The latter having never seen the world, does not have the pain and problem of adjusting himself to it, as do those who have to when vision leaves them, or is taken from them as in the case of Samson when the Philistines gouged out his eyes (Judg. 16:21; Acts 13:11). Frequently the Scripture uses blindness as a symbol, as when Isaiah spoke about bringing forth "the blind people that have eyes, and the deaf that have ears" (43:8). The implication is that Israel had eyes but did not observe, had ears and did not hear. The blind and deaf were those who had succumbed to heathenism, but are spoken of as having capacities for sight and hearing which will one day be developed. (See also Isa. 29:18; 59:10; Matt. 15:14; 23:16; John 12:40; II Cor. 3:14; 4:4; II Pet. 1:9; I John 2:11).

3. Born Deaf and Mute

It is more than likely that the mute people we read of in the gospels, like the demoniac who was both blind and mute, were born with such an affliction (Matt. 9:32; 12:22; 15:30). There are others who lost their power of speech temporarily. (See Isa. 53:7; Dan. 10:15; Luke 1:20). Many children are born with such a disadvantage. Tragic though such a lack of verbal communication is, schools for the deaf and mute teach a remarkable finger language, enabling their students to converse among themselves, or to write out what they would like to say. If the deaf and mute man who Jesus healed had been born that way is there any wonder that he published abroad the miracle experienced

(Mark 7:31-37)? See also the miracle of the child cured of a destructive, mute spirit (Mark 9:14-29). With this child's liberation from Satan's power to rob the body of its normal facilities, a father's tears had much influence.

4. Born to Be Murdered

What wanton destruction of multitudes of precious babies the Scripture records! They perished before they had the opportunity of living the life they entered upon. How bereft of human feeling men must be when they can sink so low as to be responsible for the murder of little, innocent children! The sacrifices of children to Molech by their parents indicates how a father had powers of life and death over his children, although such powers were limited (Lev. 18:21; 20: 2-5; Deut. 21:18-21; II Kings 23:10; Jer. 32:35). Molech, or Moleck, was a deity worshiped by the Israelites, especially by the people of Judah toward the close of the monarchy. The chief feature of this worship was the sacrifice of children. This cruel cult was evidently introduced by King Solomon who, turning from God, sponsored various heathen religions. Prophetic denunciation of this brutal destruction of babies is most emphatic, revealing the mind of God (Ezek. 20: 25, 31), who claimed the first-born in right ways.

Mass annihilation of newborn babes was planned by Pharaoh to decrease the fast-growing population of Israelites in Egypt. Instructions to Hebrew midwives were to kill all the baby boys, but allow the baby girls to live. But the godly midwives would not participate in such wholesale slaughter, and "saved the men children alive" (Exod. 1:16-22; Acts 7:19). Pharaoh had charged that every baby boy should be cast into the river, and one was placed in the river who became Moses, meaning, "drawn out of the water" (Exod. 2:1-10). Later on, we will have more to say about this baby boy who became the deliverer of the people whom Pharaoh sought to destroy.

Akin to the Egyptian ruler's evil intention to mass murder all Hebrew male children was the edict of the Roman tyrant, Herod, who was more diabolical still in that he ordered *all* children up to two years of age, both boys and girls, in and around Bethlehem to be slain (Matt. 2:16-18). What an ocean of tears the parents of these first baby martyrs for Christ's sake must have been shed! It was because Herod had heard that the Babe born in Bethlehem was a King that he trembled for his throne. He thought that by killing all the children in the city Jesus would also be slain. But before the wholesale martyrdom began, Jesus was delivered (Matt. 2: 13-15).

In the Anglican calendar of events is the "Day of the Holy Innocents," designed to remember the death of those little children, slain at the time of the birth of Jesus, when He also was a baby child like them. It was on an Holy Innocents Day, almost 900 years ago, that Westminster Abbey was finished and dedicated by its first founder, King Edward the Confessor, who was himself an innocent, guileless man, almost like a little child. As the result of brutal, senseless wars through the ages, a vast company of innocent babes have perished, right down to Biafra where hundreds of little ones starved to death. What a happy place heaven must be with myriads of these child martyrs, singing,

Glory! Glory! Glory!

Then, going back to Pharaoh, there was the tragic day when Egypt became a nation with drawn blinds because there was not an Egyptian house in which there was not one dead (Exod. 12:30). The final judgment upon Pharaoh for his unwillingness to give the people of God their freedom from bondage was the death of the first-born from the king on his throne to the first-born of the captive in the dungeon, and also all the first-born of cattle. What a holocaust of destruction that must have been, particularly among children! It wiped out a whole generation of Egyptians, and forced stubborn Pharaoh to let the people go. Calling for Moses and Aaron at the midnight hour of tragedy, Pharaoh said, "Be gone; and bless me also" (Exod. 12:32). But what kind of blessing could such a cruel despot expect?

In Jewish literature there is a touching story in connection with that dreadful night. A Jewish father had one little girl, about ten years of age. She was his only child, and he was very proud of her. As the first-born child in that family, she would be the one to die if the angel's stroke should fall on their dwelling. Before going to sleep, she asked her father if the blood had been sprinkled on their doorposts. He said it was, and she fell asleep. But her sleep was disturbed. She awoke several times during the night, and each time she asked anxiously if it was all right about the blood. Assured that it was, she tried to sleep on, but it was in vain.

A little while before midnight she woke again, in great alarm. She asked her father to take her in his arms and carry her to the door, that she might see the blood. He did so; but found to his terror that there was no blood on the doorposts! It had been left to a servant to attend to it, and he had neglected it. Her father ran to get the blood, and then sprinkled it on the doorposts with his own hand. His dear child saw the blood there. Then she knew that they were safe and she went sweetly to sleep. That blood protected them when the destroying angel passed over.

That children often suffer for their parents' sins is evidenced by the apostasy of Korah, Dathan and Abiram, and who consequently were consumed in all their sins. These men with all their families, including their little children, were made to stand at the door of their tents (Num. 16:27), to learn the terrible news that not one of them would "die the common death of all men." As Moses ended his God-given message, the ground split open, and swallowed up all the families and everything belonging to them. It was better that the little children should die thus in their innocency than grow up to emulate the sacrilege of Korah, the leader of the rebellious princes (Num. 16:1, 2. See also Ezek. 9:6).

Haman was another with a treacherous heart for he conspired to destroy "all Jews, both young and old, little children and women, in one day" (Esth. 3:13). Had this enemy of God's people succeeded what a horrible act of genocide it would have been! But He whose eye is on the sparrow was watching over the nation His love had brought into being. In His eternal counsel He saw that a little girl born into a Jewish home would grow up to become the queen of Persia and Media, and that she would be perpetually remembered as the deliverer of her people. Had Haman brought off his evil conspiracy Esther herself would have perished. The tables however were turned against Haman, and the day he was hanged on the gallows he had prepared for the faithful Jew, Mordecai, turned the sorrow of all the Jews into joy. There was a Christmas-like celebration with feasting and joy, and the sending of gifts to one another (Esth. 9:22). The Feast of Purim was instituted which the Jews down to the present day have scrupulously observed.

5. Born to Die

While it is true that as soon as a baby is born, he begins his journey to the grave, if he is born with a healthy body and all his faculties, life, and not death, is hoped for. But in Scripture there are those who had the anguish of seeing their children, some of them newly-born, die. We are not mystified when the aged pass on. We expect the call to reach them at any time, and for many elderly people death is a happy release if they can read their title clear to a mansion in the sky. It is a different matter though, when a child prayed and planned for arrives to fill the home with joy, and then is taken to heaven a few hours or days after its arrival in this world. Although there may be a worse experience than that of having a baby in heaven, hearts bereaved in such a way are often mystified over God's providential dealings. Browning could write —

> I am young, happy, and free!
> I can devote myself; I have a life
> To give.

Yet many are born to live, then death robs them of giving a life for the service of God and of humanity. Those whose parenthood is so soon thwarted may, with Christian resignation, say with Job, "The Lord gave, and the Lord hath taken away," but sorrow is deep. Yet consolation is gathered from the fact that the little one called so soon to see the King in His beauty, experienced no pain or sin or the griefs and dark crimes of our cruel world. It was Alonzo Rice who gave us the appealing lines —

> How brief the stay, as beautiful as fleeting,
> The time that baby came with us to dwell,
> Just long enough to give a happy greeting,
> Just long enough to bid us all farewell.
>
> Death travels down the thickly settled highway,
> At shining marks they say he loves to aim;
> How did he find, far down our lonely byway,
> Our little one who died without a name.

Some time ago a most heart-moving article appeared in *The Reader's Digest,* under the title, "Death of a Son," which was the record of the most agonizing decision of his life which the Reverend David Sholin had to make. A baby boy was born to his wife Norma and him, whom they called Edward Allen, names chosen for him before he was born. But he was born severely retarded. Somehow the umbilical cord was pinched, cutting off the supply of oxygen, thereby damaging the brain. Doctors confirmed that the baby was mentally retarded and physically frail; that if he lived he would be an inanimate object. How hard it was to give up the many plans the parents had designed for their child!

The baby, although kept in an oxygen tent, failed to respond to any treatment. When the doctor suggested that the child should be taken out of the tent for periods of time, the anxious, distressed father sensed what was in the doctor's mind — "If he cannot survive on his own, he should not live at all." What should the father do — acquiesce in allowing the poor baby to die? Knowing that his child would never be the kind of loving human being that God had planned, permission was given to remove little Edward from the tent. He slept peacefully, and three days later died in the same deep sleep. Although the Sholin family grew to six children, baby Edward Allen had always had a special place in the parents' hearts, because he was not allowed to linger in a state of unknowing and uncaring existence, which both father and mother felt would be a denial of life.

The question of the morality of preserving life, artificially, in those who are born so tragically incapable of living a normal life, or in the case of the very aged so severely incapacitated, is one of grave concern. The Reverend Sholin has reached the conclusion that "God expects us to use wisely our knowledge and reason to exercise increasing control over human life, and death."

a. *Death of David's Child* (II Sam. 12:14-23). The death of the baby boy whom Bathsheba bore David was an act of divine judgment. Because David lusted after another man's wife, seduced her, then planned the murder of her husband, God declared that the child of shame would not live. "The child also that is born unto thee shall surely die" (II Sam. 12:14). Truly repentant for lust, deceit and crime, David besought God for the life of the child, but stricken of God, he was very sick at birth and after seven days he died. During the whole week David prayed and fasted, but when the baby was dead the king knew that grief could not bring him back, and so rose from his fast and ate. Resigning himself to the will of God, he uttered these words, so full of the hope of immortality, "Now he is dead, wherefore should I fast? can I bring him back again? I shall go to him, but he shall not return to me" (II Sam. 12:23).

Two thoughts emerge from this remarkable statement. The first is that of union beyond the grave. "I shall go to him." David was consoled by the fact that the separation was only for a little while. Father and child would meet again in the land where there is no death, no separation. The second thought is that David believed his child was in heaven. The king himself, although he had grievously sinned and was abundantly pardoned, knew that he would dwell in the house of the Lord forever (Ps. 23:6); and had the assurance that his child, dying a week old, and without practiced sin, would be there to greet his father – "I shall go to him in glory." Children, dying, knowing nothing of moral choice or of the power to discern right from wrong, go to heaven in virtue of the atoning work of Jesus at Calvary. It was Lord Byron who remarked that – "Heaven gives its favourites early death."

How touching is the poem of Moultrie on "The Three Sons." Two were living, but the third was dead, and the father is made to speak of him thus –

> I have a son – a third sweet son, his age I cannot tell,
> For they reckon not by years and months where he is gone to dwell . . .
> I cannot tell what form is his, what looks he weareth now,
> Nor guess how bright a glory crowns his shining seraph brow. . . .
>
> But I know, for God doth tell me this, that he is now at rest,
> Where other blessed infants be, on their Saviour's loving breast . . .
> What e'er befall his brethren twain, his bliss can never cease;
> Their lot may here be grief and fear, but his is certain peace.

b. *Death of Jeroboam's Child* (I Kings 14:1-18). Abijah the son of ungodly Jeroboam is referred to in the narrative as a "child," but several commentators believe that he was a young man of age and as heir-apparent to the throne, conducted himself decorously, being the only one of the house of Jeroboam who had "some good thing toward the Lord God of Israel." It would seem that Abijah was in his childhood days, however, for when he fell sick his troubled father sent his wife to Ahijah the prophet saying, "He shall tell thee what shall become of the child." The prophet foretold the child's immediate death at the moment his mother crossed the threshold of the home. "When thy feet enter into the city, the child shall die" – and die he did. All Israel mourned for him and he came "to the grave" – a significant phrase for Abijah was the only one in the family of Jeroboam to have a grave. The rest of the family had an ignominious death and end, being cast to the dogs to eat.

The reason given for his decent burial is "because in him there is found some good thing toward the Lord God of Israel in the house of Jeroboam." Had he lived, Abijah might have been infected with the terrible sin of his father, and so be involved in his ruin. Thus, in mercy, he was taken while he was good. He only, of the family, died in honor, and was buried and lamented. Matthew Henry observes that, "This hopeful child dies first of all the family, for God often takes those soonest whom He loves best. Heaven is the fittest place for them; this earth is not worthy of them." Herodotus, in his celebrated story of Cleobis and Bito, implies that at all times early death is heaven's choicest blessing. "Why died I not from the womb . . . then had I been at rest" (Job 3:11, 13. See Eccl. 14:1-3).

There is something singularly pathetic, then, in the declaration of Abijah's early death as the only reward which can be given to piety in the time of coming judgment. His death was a sign to a godless family that it would be ruined when he was taken by whom it might have been reformed. But as it was, Jeroboam himself died soon after his child, and left his crown to a son who lost it, and his life, too, and all the lives of his family within two years after, for such is the tragic record of Nabad who reigned after Jeroboam.

c. *Death of the Widow's Child* (I Kings 17:8-24). Bishop J.B. Lightfoot contends that Elijah was "the first prophet of the Gentiles." Hated and driven out by his own countrymen, Elijah turned to the Gentiles as the apostles were later ordered to do (Acts 18:6). Sidon, to which the prophet had been sent, was a Gentile city where the worship of Baal had flourished, and our Lord took notice of this as an early and ancient indication of the favor of God designed for the outcast Gentiles in the fullness of time (Luke 4:25, 26). Although many widows were in Israel in the days of Elijah, yet the prophet was sent to a poor, Gentile widow woman for shelter and food. But he found the widow so destitute and, along with her child, facing death by starvation. It was to this poverty-stricken widow that Elijah came that "he might still live upon Providence as much as he did when the ravens fed him."

We are all familiar with the double miracle Elijah performed in the most humble dwelling of the widow – a double miracle proving God's sovereignty both in the physical and material realms. In the first miracle God took care of the poor woman, her child, and her godly guest. "The barrel of meal wasted not, nor did the cruse of oil fail." The more the woman took from the barrel, the more was added to it by divine power.

God always hears the scraping of the barrel. A feature that must not be forgotten is that the meal and oil multiplied not in hoarding, but in the spending. For her willingness to feed the prophet first, the widow received ample recompense for her child and herself. She proved that in the days of famine God is able to feed His children (Ps. 37:19).

Ellicott, in his most valuable commentary, suggests that this miracle was in itself doubly miraculous. First, we see that God's higher laws of miracle, like the ordinary laws of His providence, admit within their scope the supply of homely and trivial needs. Second, there is the miracle of multiplication. Both the meal and the oil were multiplied, doing rapidly and directly what, under ordinary laws, has to be done slowly and by indirect processes. That God is able to furnish a table in the wilderness is seen in the experience of the Jews as they journeyed from Egypt to Canaan.

The second miracle was that of the resurrection of the widow's child who fell sick and died. Grief-stricken, the mother turned to Elijah for succor and help, for she recognized in him a holy man having power with God. In her deep, sudden and unexpected affliction she blamed Elijah for the death of her child, feeling that this was an act of divine judgment because of her former worship of Baal, the god of the Sidonians. The prophet never answered the widow's complaint but brought the matter before God. It was more than likely that the prophet had become attached to the child and was also sorrowful at his early death.

Taking the lifeless form of the child to his own small chamber, Elijah humbly reasoned with God concerning the child's death and supplicated God to restore the child to life again. Then he stretched himself upon the child three times, and perhaps gave him the kiss of life, effecting, if he could by his own warmth and breath, the restoration of the child. God heard the plea of the prophet, and Elijah became the first person in the Bible to raise the dead. When he prayed, "Let this child's soul come into him again," Elijah indicated that the child was actually dead and that his soul had left his body. What a thrill it must have been when the distraught mother saw Elijah carrying the child down the stairs and saying, "See, thy son liveth." She could scarcely believe her own eyes, but quickly confessed to the power and goodness of the man of God, and that the death and resurrection of her dear child was for the glory of God and for the honor of His prophet, Elijah the Tishbite. Legend has it that in later years that child which was raised from the dead became a servant of Elijah and later on of Jonah.

d. *Death of the Shunammite's Child* (II Kings 4:8-37). There are a few similarities between the double miracle Elijah performed at Sidon, and the double miracle his successor, Elisha, performed at Shunem. First there was the miraculous increase of the widow's oil resulting in the prevention of her two sons being taken as slaves to pay the debts of the home which her husband's death had incurred (II Kings 4:1-7). Then there is the second miracle which is actually a double miracle covering the Shunammite's barrenness and consequent motherhood, and also the resurrection of her child from the dead. Do you never wonder what the name of this commendable lady was? It seems a pity that so many fine women in the Bible are nameless.

(1.) *Her Affluence*

The Shunammite is described as a "great woman," implying that she was rich, influential, and well-known in the community for her character and good deeds. Nabal is spoken of as being "very great" because of the thousands of sheep and goats he posesssed (I Sam. 25:2). Evidently this woman of Shunem was not only of high rank but had considerable means because after the seven years' famine during which she sojourned in the land of the Philistines, she returned with "her household" to "her house and her land," and to "the fruits of her field" (II Kings 8:1-6). That she spent her money for the benefits of God's children is seen in the room she added to her house, and furnished for Elisha, and in the hospitality afforded him.

(2.) *Her Attentiveness*

In his constant journeyings between Carmel and Shunem, Elisha, who impressed the Shunammite with his holy demeanor, was invited in by the Shunammite for a meal. Whenever he passed by he "turned into the house to eat bread," then went on his way grateful for the kindness of the woman and her husband. But the pair of them felt they should do more for the tired prophet who passed their way continually. They built on an extra room to their house, and furnished it in Oriental style with the essential items of a bed, a table, a stool or chair, and a candlestick or lamp. What a boon this provision was for the weary prophet! How he must have appreciated this prophet's chamber, offering him security from all interruption or intrusion on his journey! Such a welcome lodging also meant that he could honor the hospitable home longer with his benign presence. Evidently provision was also made for Gehazi, Elisha's servant.

(3.) *Her Affliction*

Elisha felt that some recognition was due for the ungrudging hospitality (I Pet. 4:9) shown by this husband and wife in their Shunem home, and thus asked Gehazi, to whom the hostess would express her wishes more freely, to ascertain how she could be rewarded for all her care. She spurned court and courtly interests and favors, preferring as a commoner to live quietly where she was. Then Gehazi suggested that seeing she had the misfortune of being childless, and consequently had no heir to leave her estate to, that a child would be a coveted reward. Being well off they required no royal preferment, but a child after barren years would indeed be a joy.

Confronting Elisha, the woman heard the pronouncement which she could scarcely believe, "About this time next year, according to the time of life, thou shalt embrace a son." The woman, astounded, replied, "No, my lord, do not lie unto thy handmaid." We can imagine with what emotion she answered this way for perhaps she was past the child-bearing period. At least her husband was old and incontinent. But at the prescribed time the miracle happened, and the woman's reproach rolled away. After so long an absence of any child's voice in the home, what a change that son must have brought about! We can imagine that after this the prophet was doubly welcome in that hitherto childless house. Elisha had thought of himself in debt to the woman for all her bountiful hospitality, but now as long as she lives, she will think of herself as being deep in the prophet's debt and never able to do too much for him. Further, although that son became dear to his parents, as the son of their old age, we may also suppose that he became dear to Elisha, as the son of his prayers and faith.

(4.) *Her Anguish*

When the child was able to walk, he went out to his father who was with his reapers in the fields, but because his little head was uncovered in the hot season of harvest, he had a sunstroke. A servant carried the stricken child in to his mother, but he died soon after on her knees. What anguish the sudden death of a dear child causes! Here was a child of promise, a child of prayer, given in love, yet tragically taken. But the prudent, pious mother acted admirably. There was no panic, no outburst of angry complaint. She laid the corpse of her child on the bed Elisha used when staying in the home, and keeping the death a secret, she hurried as fast as she could to Elisha's base at the Mount of Carmel. With confidence in God's goodness, she believed that what He had taken away, He was able to restore. In such a faith she made no preparation of the burial of her much-loved son, but for his resurrection. So, of her, too, it can be said, "O woman! great is thy faith."

From a distance, Elisha recognized the Shunammite hurrying toward his abode, and sent his servant out to meet her and inquire if all was well with herself, her husband and her child. When she replied to Gehazi, "It is well," she was merely avoiding further explanation. "She would open her grief to the prophet's ear, and to none other." As Elisha had not heard from God about the death of the child, he listened to the mother's appeal. She did not desire a son, or beg for one as Rachel had. Her questions seem to imply that it would have been better to have had no son, than to have had one for death to claim so soon. The spontaneous outflow of the poignant sorrow of her mother-heart was adverse to the poet's sentiment that –

"'Tis better to have loved and lost,
Than never to have loved at all."

As the woman had given the prophet an explicit account of the child's death, so Elisha gave the mother of the child an explicit promise of the boy's resurrection. Gehazi was sent to lay the staff of Elisha upon the face of the dead child, but there is no life in a dead stick. As for the mother, she didn't follow Gehazi back to her home, but vowed never to leave Elisha until he himself went to the house of death. Why was Elisha's staff of authority ineffective in the raising of the child? Keil, the commentator, suggests that, "the prophet foresaw the failure of this expedient, and sought to teach the distressed parents and his followers generally, that the power of miracles was not *magically* inherent in himself, or in his staff, as they might imagine, but only in Jehovah, who granted the temporary use of that power to faith and prayer."

Yet another writer indicates that Elisha did not censure Gehazi for his failure to raise the dead child because he himself was at fault in supposing he could transfer the spirit and power of a prophet to his servant; and acted in haste without a divine incentive (See II Sam. 7:3). Is it possible that the Shunammite herself, with a woman's intuition, felt that the staff would fail to raise the dead, and thus refused to leave the prophet until he himself performed the miracle? Anyhow, Elisha was not long in making the journey, and reaching the house of mourning found the dead child laid upon *his* bed – the bed the grief-stricken mother had provided the prophet with.

(5.) *Her Adoration*

Elisha, left alone with the dead, prayed to the Lord, perhaps using the language of Elijah before him, "Let this child's soul come into him again." The process of resurrection was somewhat dramatic for Elisha laid upon the corpse, with his mouth to the cold lips, and his eyes to the glazed eyes, and his warm hands upon the death-stiffened hands of the child, and gradually "the life of the Divine Spirit which was in Elisha, was miraculously imparted by contact to the lifeless body," and the flesh of the child became warm. Then the prophet got up and walked to and fro in his room, stretched himself upon the child again, and as he did so the boy sneezed seven times, the repeated sneezing being a sign of restored respiration – an indication, not only of life, but liveliness.

What a thrilling moment it must have been when Elisha called the Shunammite and said, "Take up thy son!" It was in like manner that Jesus "delivered to his mother," the lad whom He raised from death by His word (Luke 7:15). Seeing her dear child wide-eyed and smiling, the overjoyed mother fell at the prophet's feet and in deep veneration recognized in him the agent of divine power. Can we not imagine how, as she clasped her resurrected child to her breast, she rained kisses upon that once dead face? Later on, we read of Naaman who, as he washed himself in the waters of Jordan, found himself cleansed of his foul leprosy and his flesh "like unto the flesh of a little child" (II Kings 5:14). Such was the healthy look of the child of the wealthy and influential Gentile believer of Shunem whom she held in her loving arms after he had returned from the dead.

e. *Death of the Child of Jairus* (Mark 5:21-43). The "little daughter" of Jairus, one of the rulers of the synagogue, was but twelve years of age when she became ill and died. In response to the plea and faith of the distressed father, Jesus was interrupted by another claim upon His miraculous power – a woman who had had a hemorrhage for twelve years – the age of the little girl (Mark 5:25). So here we have a miracle out of a miracle. Continuing His journey to the home of Jairus, He was met by a messenger who said there was no need for Jesus to go any further for the girl was dead. But He comforted the heart of the father by saying, "Be not afraid, only believe." In the word of such a King there was power. At twelve years of age, a child has had time to endear itself to its parents, and is about the time its character first comes to be seen and known. And this was one reason why that little life in the well-known house in Capernaum was precious in the Master's sight.

Reaching the home of sorrow, Jesus found the hired mourners of Eastern countries already there, wailing and shrieking as they were paid to do. Expelling them, He allowed only Peter, James, and John, and the parents of the dead damsel to follow Him into the chamber of death. The hired mourners laughed Jesus to scorn when He said, "The damsel is not dead, but sleepeth" – words that often brought consolation to bereaved parents while looking on the face of their dead child in the glorious hope of resurrection. Touching the hand of the girl, as she lay on her couch in the sleep of death, He addressed her in the Syrian words,

Talitha cumi, meaning, "My little lamb, my little pet lamb, rise up!" With such an endearing appellation He roused her from the sleep of death.

By His action and words, Jesus revealed to those once grief-stricken, but now joyous parents, that He was one with them in their parental love, in their domestic joy as well as in their domestic sorrow. His, "Fear not, only believe," is for all anxious mourners who will see their precious dead again in the land where there is no more death. Parents, whom death has robbed of a lovely child, must believe that He who makes the flowers to spring and the buds to come forth again, will raise the little flower once growing in the garden of the home, and grace it with eternal life, fragrance, and beauty. How apt is the experience of Martin Luther, one of the fiercest and most courageous men that ever lived. Toward his children, especially his little daughter, the monk was as gentle and kind as any woman.

But Luther's daughter Magdalen died when she was only thirteen years of age, and it is most affecting to read his grief, and, at the same time, his resignation to the will of God. "Magdalen, my little daughter, thou wouldst gladly stay with thy father here, and thou wouldst also gladly go to thy Father yonder. Ah! thou dear little thing, thou shalt rise again, and shine like a star; yea, like the sun." Luther, in his diary went on to say, "Her face, her words cleave to our hearts, remain fixed in its depths, living and dying — the words and looks of that most dutiful child. Blessed be the Lord Jesus Christ, who called, chose, and magnified her. I would for myself, and all of us, that we might attain to such a death; yea, rather, to such a life."

When Jesus said to the parents of the little daughter "weep not!" He was not condemning weeping. He Himself wept; and genuine weeping always touched His heart. His tears sanctify our tears. His first resurrection word was, "Woman, why weepest thou?" Those who weep over their dead are not to sorrow as others who have no hope (I Thess. 4:13, 14). As His redeemed, He is able to dry their tears and direct their gaze to His Father's home where all tears are wiped away. It was not enough for those wailing mourners to be expelled from the house of Jairus that there might be silence in the room of death; tumult of thought and feeling must be hushed too, so that within the soul, silence reigns.

Too often, "weeping is self-indulgence, a nursing of our grief, the fruit of being too absorbed in ourselves, the object we mourn, or the suffering we endure," says Andrew Murray. "Weeping often hinders the voice of God being heard, hinders altogether the blessing the affliction was meant to bring. We are only occupied with what we suffer, and God would have us think of the cause of the suffering, the sin with which we made Him suffer. By taking away a child, God meant to take us away from ourselves, and to make room in the heart for Himself. Weeping often only fills us with ourselves. God would have us, in the affliction we learn to bear, and love, and worship His will. Weeping is often the homage, yea, the adoration, of our own will."

The psalmist speaks of God as putting our tears in His bottle, which is but another way of saying that, even in the chamber of death, He is ever present, the true Friend, and as "the Resurrection and the Life" well able to comfort all who mourn. When He says to bereaved parents, "Thy little one is not dead," He is not mocking the deepseated sorrow of the heart. There may be the aspect of death, but we must not judge by sight. There is a better, more glorious life than the life of this earth, namely, the eternal life in which the undying God Himself dwells. Sleep of body is provided for all those who are in Him. Such is the blessed waiting time until He comes to gather all His own to Himself in glory. Weeping may endure for a night, but joy comes with the eternal morning.

> For e'en the tiniest jewel
> Shall shine in Jesus' crown,
> And sparkle there for ever
> When time itself has flown.

While it is true that "the increase of our house dies in the flower of their age" (I Sam. 2:33), there are some dead flowers that never lose their fragrance. Is not Christ the first fruits of all who sleep in Him (I Cor. 15: 20)? Children are His jewels and take on a brilliant luster in heaven. They are likewise His lilies, and He knows best when to transplant them to heaven before their purity is sullied (S. of S. 6:2). It is because death claims the young, as well as the aged, that parents must strive in every possible way to lead their children to Him who died for their salvation. The boys and girls of our home must be urged to secure the heavenly treasure – the precious pearl of truth – in life's fair morning, realizing that in the salvation of a child there is a double salvation. Not only is the soul saved, but the life secured for the Saviour to use.

> We want the young for Jesus:
> Be this our best employ:
> No mission could be nobler,
> Or fraught with sweeter joy.

When Augustine was but a boy his prayer used to be, so he recorded, "Make me holy, O God, but not yet, not yet." He desired to be good, but wished first to enjoy the pleasures of sin. In his sad volume, *Confessions,* the great man tells us what suffering and sorrow he would have been spared had he begun to follow God when he was young. The happiest people in the world are those who gave themselves to God as children, and who grew up, not only in years, but also in His knowledge and love, and sought to serve Him all their lives through. Blessed are all those godly parents who have "children that believe, not unruly" (Tit. 1:6). If God expects the children of believers to be believers too, then it is the responsibility of parents and teachers to help the children to believe. All the promises of God are "to you . . . and to your children (Acts 2:39).

EXAMPLES

Old Testament Children

New Testament Children

3
EXAMPLES

It is said that among the ancient Romans it was the custom among the wealthy fathers to display in the halls of their palatial homes, busts and statues of the great and noble sons of Rome. The object of placing them there was to give their children an opportunity to become acquainted with the history of these nobilities, and inspired thereby to imitate the commendable points of their characters. Without doubt, this was a wise custom to follow, for we can imagine how many of those Roman boys and girls were fascinated with the famous men in the past history of their nation, then the mistress of the world, and determined to try and become like them.

God has done something like this in the preparation of the Bible, which He has filled with interesting sketches of the lives and characters of renowned and also inconspicuous faithful men and women who were His servants in their own day and generation. The Apostle James reminds us of the use God intends we should make of the accounts of the lives recorded in His Word when he says, "Take my brethren, the prophets . . . *for an example*" (5:10). Does this not imply that we should meditate on the records of those we read about in the Bible, until we discern the model points of their lives, and then, by divine grace and power, seek to follow them as they followed the Lord. Paul reminds us that "whatsoever things were written aforetime were written for our learning" (Rom. 15:4). In one of the Collects of the Anglican Church is the prayer all of us may offer. It asks that –

> God would give us grace to follow His blessed saints in all virtuous and godly living, that we may come to the unspeakable joys which He has prepared for those who unfeignedly love Him.

Seeing that this volume is specifically about children, it is our purpose in this section to parade the named and unnamed persons whose childhood is mentioned, or whose birth merits attention. And, as we hope to indicate, many of them are examples or models which the children of today can shape their lives after. In his *Psalm of Life*, Longfellow reminds us that the

> Lives of great men all remind us
> We can make our lives sublime,
> And, departing, leave behind us
> Footprints on the sands of time.

In his speech on "American Taxation," delivered in 1774, Edmund Burke said that, "Great men are the guideposts and landmarks in the State." Let us see, then, how the young of this present age can be won over to high ideals, and yet warned by the failures of the young of past ages. (See II Pet. 2:6, 14, "cursed children.")

We have already pointed out that the purpose of creation was procreation, or self-propagation. After God created Adam and Eve, He said to them, "Be fruitful, and multiply, and replenish the earth" (Gen. 1:28). "Thou shalt bring forth children" (Gen. 3:16). After the Flood, when God made a fresh start to populate the earth He commanded Noah, "Be fruitful, and multiply, and replenish the earth" (Gen. 9:1). What must be remembered is the fact that Adam and Eve had no children until *after* their transgression, just as the three sons of Noah, who married before the Flood, had no children until after the universal catastrophe (Gen. 10:1). Adam and Eve had no birth, no childhood, no youth, but appeared as perfect, fully-developed adults. But since their far-off day, the millions entering the world were born as babies. The three billion of earth's population today all came into existence as, "a little baby thing, That made a woman cry."

Old Testament Children

It is a most profitable exercise to gather together the pictures of childhood found in the Bible, and endeavor to interpret them in the light of our own age when children seem to mature more quickly than they used to. The records of Bible children may appear as dry bones but they can be clothed with flesh, and made to live before us, so that although they are separated from us by thousands of years, we can embrace them and love them as if we had actually known them. As we come to know their stories we are alive with interest, grieved over their wrongs and grateful for their deliverances.

Let it be remembered that all the Bible children were real boys and girls, in whom the heart blood was red, and the same eager desires dwelt. Color of skin, language, dress and customs may have differed, but in each child there was the same beating heart, making them all of one kith and kin. None of these children can be counted as foreigner, for children are just children in every age and nation. A teacher of the ancient world used to give his children a simple object lesson. On the sand he would draw a large Y, to explain virtue and vice. Starting from the bottom of the letter, he showed that there was only one single path up to the point where the two limbs parted. At the point where the two limbs begin, the young person stands debating which of the two ways he should take – the way of virtue on the right, or the way of vice on the left.

Is this not where the Bible begins in the record of the first two children to be born in the world? Do we not have in Cain and Abel two living pictures of child nature, sketched by the divine artist, and hung up at the door of Revelation, to be gazed upon by children of all ages? The first two children to be born of Adam and Eve say to us every one is a Cain or an Abel – a child of darkness, or a child of light. The New Testament opens with a more pleasing pair of brothers – Andrew and Peter coming to Jesus, and remaining in heart and history, true brothers. When they came to the fork on the road of life they both followed the Saviour. But with the first pair of brothers on the opening pages of the Bible it was different.

1. The Child Cain

The initial book of the Bible is called Genesis, meaning, "first" or "beginning," not only because it is the magnificent portal of the divine library, as Jerome called the Scriptures, but owing to the fact that it contains many "geneses," or "firsts." In the opening chapters of the book we have the first man, first woman, first sin, first motherhood, first family, first quarrel, first murder, first grave, first indications of human development, and the first conflict between the two seeds – seed of the woman and seed of the serpent. As there cannot be a family without children, the birth of the first child, Cain, gives us the first picture of family life, and what a somber light it casts on home life since the coming of earth's first baby.

Cain was born *after* the transgression of his parents, and was therefore "born in sin and shapen in iniquity," meaning that he inherited their defiance of God and disobedience. Often parents can trace in the sins and evil tempers of their children their own shortcomings and sins, and how such an inheritance ought to humble the parents, making them patient and gentle, as well as earnest and wise in dealing with their sinning children. The solemn truth that God visits the sins of parents on their children ought to encourage them to believe that He will also remember to be merciful to the parents, and make the children recipients of the same mercy as well. It must further be noticed that in the first child's sin we have the root and type of all children's sins.

In an earlier chapter we discussed the reason why God planned family life. He destined it to be an image of the bliss of His home above, the mirror of the serene life that reigns there. But Adam and Eve sinned, and consequently the first family on earth, instead of being the symbol and gate of heaven, became the type and portal of hell. "Instead of the love and help and happiness for which God had appointed our social relation, envy and anger and hatred and murder render it a scene of terrible desolation." The root of all sin is selfishness. The middle letter of S I N is *I* – the big I – and pride of self separated man from God, and man from man in the Bible's first home circle.

Eve called her first-born son, and earth's first child, Cain, which implies "acquisition" or "possession." Although expelled from the garden the first father and first mother carried with them the revelation of a divine promise of a seed (Gen. 3:15), and it may be that Eve so named her baby, thinking that in him would be fulfilled the promise to her seed. If her statement implies, "I have gotten a man, *even Jehovah,*" as some scholars translate her saying, the same suggests a more definite belief and knowledge than are warranted. To render the words, "I have gotten a man with the help of the Lord," would seem to weaken the phrase as given in the Hebrew. It would be as if Eve's saying means, "I have gotten a man in relation to Jehovah," which would point definitely to a conviction that somehow or other this newborn, and first-born son was related to the divine promise and purpose. W. H. Griffith Thomas observes –

> Eve must have been quickly undeceived in this respect, for when her second child, Abel, was born there was no reference to the Lord, and the fact of his name meaning, Vanity, seems to show clearly that the mother had already become disappointed in her hopes of her first-born son.

Have you ever paused to imagine how Eve must have felt at being earth's first mother, and of how her heart must have stirred as her baby fed at her breast? Remember Eve had not had a mother, and had had no childhood. Being perfectly formed as an adult by the power of God, He endowed her with all the instincts and intuitions of motherhood, and likewise with the potential of mother love, so that when Cain was born – the first to be born of a woman – Eve knew instinctively how to care for her unique child. Adam called the woman God gave him Eve, meaning "Life," because she was to be "the mother of all the living," and as Cain was the first living being to come from her, there could not have been any living beings before or at that time on the earth. There is not a shred of evidence in the Bible for a pre-Adamite race.

Further, the phrase, "mother of all living" is an undeniable proof that all mankind, in all its different races, tongues, colors and types, proceed from one and the same stock. Paul had no hesitation in calling Adam "the first man" (I Cor. 15:45, 47), and "Adam was first formed" (I Tim. 2: 13). Some theologians dismiss Adam and Eve as mythical beings, but living children do not come from myths. If Adam is a mythical person, so is Christ, for in "Adam we die: in Christ we are made alive." Not only so, Adam did not develop through millenniums from a protoplasm or jellyfish, until he became an ape and then after further millenniums a man. God made everything "after his kind." When He made a monkey, He made a monkey to breed monkeys. When He created man, He fashioned him in one action, "after his kind," or in His own image and likeness.

When Adam begat Cain, it was "in his own image, and after his likeness," which implies the influence of a parent's life upon his children. The tragic life of Cain testifies to the blessing his parents lost in Paradise and of the curse accompanying sin. Grace, however, can renew again after the image of God, all who willingly repent and believe the Gospel. The narrative tells the tragic story how the first child became the first murderer, and gave earth its first grave and first martyr. As a tiller of the ground, and having an abundance of fruit, Cain thought within himself that an offering of his own efforts would be just as good as an offering by blood, such as his brother Abel presented to God.

Cain's sin was an echo of his parents' sin, namely, disobedience, for he sacrificed what *he* liked – not what God had commanded. Seeing that his offering was rejected, and his brother's was accepted, Cain "rose up against his brother Abel and slew him." Thus, he became a murderer, and, branded by God, was made to wander abroad, shunned and despised by men and condemned by Almighty God. The blood of righteous Abel cried out from the ground for revenge, but the blood of Jesus cries out for mercy. "Whosoever hateth his brother is a murderer, and ye know that no murderer hath eternal life abiding in him" (I John 3:15).

All who have the spiritual training of children at heart should be at pains to explain to them what is meant by "the way of Cain," the world's first child (Jude 11). It was the way of the formalist, who is one having the form of Christianity without its power – one who seeks to serve and worship God after his own will and way. "The way of Cain" was also one of utter selfishness. How envious Eve's first child was, and he saw that his brother's offering had been accepted and his own was not. God reasoned with Cain, and warned him (Gen. 4: 6, 7), but all to no avail. Even after he had slain Abel, Cain's foul act did not slay his own selfishness for he replied to God's quesetion, "Where is Abel, thy brother?" in sullen scorn, "Am I my brother's keeper?" John, the "apostle of love," warned his friends against becoming murderers in heart like Cain. The "way of Cain" is the way of the godless among the godly. Although bound to God's throne by all the ties of blood and brotherhood, Cain became the first model of all rebels who say, "Let us break their bands asunder, and cast their cords from us." Children of godly parents sometimes turn out to be profligates. From the door of a Christian home they drift to a Christless eternity. Later on, in the books of

Moses, we read of how God claims the first-born in the family for Himself (Exod. 13:1, 13-15). He has, of course, the first claim upon every child coming into a family for His own direct and immediate use. When Cain's parents received the first promise of redemption from sin, they doubtless did not understand that such a deliverance would involve God giving His First-born, His only begotten Son for their sin and for the sin of all succeeding generations of children springing from them.

2. The Child Abel

Apart from the bare statement, "She [Eve] again bare his brother Abel" (Gen. 4:2), we have no knowledge of how much younger he was than Cain. What we do know is that Abel was the first child in the world to become a victim of jealousy and murder. Death and the grave began with Eve's second son. A feature worth noticing is that with Cain and Seth, the meaning of their names is given but not so with Abel. The occupations of both sons is given. "Abel was a keeper of sheep, but Cain was a tiller of the ground." Abel's name, given at birth, carries no reference to its origin. But W. F. Wilkinson points out in his *Personal Names in the Bible* –

> Since the names of both the first son, Cain, and the third son, Seth, are representative of facts apprehended, or sentiments predominant, in the mind of their mother at the time of their birth, it is most reasonable to suppose that the name of the second son, Abel, had a similar character. It is difficult, however, to form a feasible conjecture as to the circumstances and feelings which gave rise to the name. It is *the first example of an ill-omened name.*

Then Wilkinson elaborates on the fact that the word "Abel," or rather "Hebel," is almost always translated "vanity," as in the frequently recurring declaration in Ecclesiastes, "All is vanity." Such a sense is derived from the original meaning "breath" or "vapor," and denotes that which is unsubstantial, transcient, fleeting. Now why did Eve give her son such a name at his birth? Some answer that it marked the mother's disappointment of the hope she had entertained with regard to Cain, both hers and the world's first child.

We lean to the view, however, that Abel was chosen as a name as the result of a prophetic insight or presentiment, as to his early and tragic death. By this time Eve understood something of the meaning of the curse pronounced upon Adam and herself. The outcast pair faced daily trials, and perhaps the sense of worthlessness of belonging to a race under the curse, and the uncertainty of things found expression in the name chosen for the newborn child. Thus the thoughts and feelings of the world's first two sinners were condensed in one word "Abel" – the name which is inscribed on the Book of Ecclesiastes as its motto and message – "Who knoweth what is good for man in this life, all the days of his vain life which he spendeth as a shadow" (6:12).

The word Hebel occurs nowhere else in the Bible as a proper name. The word Abel, has, in the LXX Version, the same spelling and forms in combination with other words. We see this in the names of several places, as from a totally different root, and means a "meadow" or "grassy plain," or in one instance "lamentation," as in Abel – *mizraim*, the mourning of the Egyptians (Gen. 50:11).

As a shepherd, did Abel have any divine intuition as to the Good Shepherd being "the seed of the woman"? The Bible takes cognizance of the fact that the short life of Abel was a pious one. Think of how John describes the one whose offering of blood God accepted, "We should love one another. Not as Cain, who was of that wicked one, and slew his brother. And wherefore slew he him? Because his own works were evil, and his brother's righteous" (I John 3:11, 12).

Sacred testimony to Abel's righteousness is also found in the "roll of martyrs," and likewise the fact that Abel's offering was accepted by God, not for his holiness, but for his faith, (Heb. 11:4). On the other hand, Cain was rejected as sinner because of his entire lack of faith for "without faith it is impossible to please God" (Heb. 11:6).

Earth's second child had an untimely and unlooked-for death, and as the first of the human race to die, what was the object of Abel's faith and his hope? Was the expectation of dying and going home to heaven a part of his faith? What faith in God that Abel had was founded on that sure first promise of "the seed of the woman" given to the serpent who had deceived Abel's mother. His faith, then, was set on God as his Redeemer, and on His promises. If, by faith, Abel saw Christ's day and rejoiced, then by virtue of such faith, Abel was the first one of earth to enter heaven. The writer to the Hebrews, in speaking of the better sacrifice Abel offered than his brother says, "By it he being dead yet speaketh (11:4).

Abel will always speak to our hearts for he was the first to offer a sacrifice involving death. His action is the first time we find anything said about a sacrifice in the Bible. The blood of the lamb shed, and its body offered as a burnt sacrifice upon a crude altar was a symbol of, and pointed to, Him who was to come as "the Lamb slain from the foundation of the world." Abel was indeed a modern speaker because his righteous life was in full harmony with the offering he presented to God, even though his revelation of Him was not as complete as ours is. By being righteous and acting righteously, dying at the cradle of humanity he still speaks to our hearts.

3. The Child Enoch I

The part of Africa known as Rhodesia received its name from Cecil Rhodes, who developed the area and added it to Britain when it was an empire. Enoch, Cain's son, born in the land of Nod, was the first child in the history of the world to have a city called after him. "He [Cain] builded a city and called the name of the city after the name of his son, Enoch" (Gen. 4:17). Thus, with the grandson of Adam and Eve the first civilization began. We must not confuse this Enoch with the Enoch, son of Jared, mentioned in the next chapter, as we shall presently see. While it is likely that Cain had many other children, only Enoch is mentioned. And the children Cain and his wife had were unique in that their mother and father were brother and sister. At the beginning of the race it was necessary for those in Adam's family to marry each other, seeing there were no other humans on earth to choose from.

We are told that Adam begat sons and daughters. Although only three of the former are named, none of the latter are named. The first daughter born to Adam and Eve was the first girl to enter the world, and probably it was she who became Cain's wife. The Bible does not say that Cain found his wife in the land of Nod, and that she gave birth to Enoch there. The inference is that when Cain went out from "the presence of Jehovah," which can signify from the vicinity and view of the cherubim and of the altar that stood before the gate of Paradise, that his wife went with him, willing to share his banishment. In ancient times it was not thought repugnant nor unlawful for brother and sister to enter the union of marriage. In Egypt, where there was no lack of women, it was the custom of the Pharaohs, and still later of the Ptolemies, for the king to marry his own sister. Even Abraham married Sarah, his half-sister (Gen. 20:12).

The reason Cain chose Enoch as a name for his son is not given. Its Hebrew meaning is "trained," "skilled," or "dedicated." During the seventeenth century the Puritans popularized it as a male name. At the time of the boy's birth, Cain was building a city or fort, and called it by his son's name. The word "city" is, in the Spanish, "ciudad," which signified a fortified place, as still seen in the term "ciudadela," meaning, "a fortress." There were no people around Cain making it necessary for him to build a city to accommodate them. Dread took possession of his guilty soul after killing his brother, and he found himself branded and banished. While there were no others around him except his own family, he could not regard himself as being secure, and so set about building a stockade for his defense. As the curse affected the animal creation, such a stockade would also preserve him from the perpetual menace of wild beasts.

4. The Child Lamech

This son of Methusael and his wife was the great grandson of the grandson of Cain (Gen. 4:18), and grew up to become renowned for three things. It was Lamech who introduced polygamy into the world when he took two wives. Paul makes it clear that the purpose of God in creating only one woman for only one man explains the teaching of our Lord (Matt. 19:4-6; I Cor. 7:2). Then Lamech became the first poet in the world as the short poem dedicated to his wives proves (4:23, 24) and his was the first poem to celebrate a murder. Two children of these two wives were to become originators of the arts. Jubal became the father of all handling the harp and pipe, and Tubal-cain, the forger of every cutting instrument of brass and iron (4:21, 22). As for Jubal, he was the first keeper of sheep on a large scale. Any other children born of these two wives, Adah and Zillah, are omitted from the record in order to fix attention on their three sons who became famous in their day. Mechanical and fine arts, and the possession of material riches, began among the Cainites.

5. The Child Seth

Eve became the mother of another son, and "called his name Seth" (Gen. 4:25, 26). Adam is also represented as the giver of the name whose sanction was necessary for in the father was vested the right of naming her son (Gen. 5:3, 4). Adam lived for another 800 years after the birth of Seth. Then Eve gave the meaning of the name she chose for her baby, "God hath appointed me another seed instead of Abel, for Cain slew him." Seth means "substitution." While there may have been other sons after Abel's death, Eve was looking to the promise of "the Seed of the woman," frustrated by Abel's tragic end, but which at last lived again in Seth – a child she received with rare delight. With the heart of a godly mother, still lamenting the loss of her pure and gentle Abel, now, after the lapse of many years, Eve accepted the birth of Seth as a special gift from God, besought, perhaps, from God with anxious desire, as Samuel was years later (I Sam. 1:27). Eve saw no hope of the promised seed from the impious race of Cain. It was from the seed of promise that our Substitute came who died in our place.

6. The Child Enos

Genesis, as we have seen, is a "Book of Beginnings," and the son born to saintly Seth was called Enos by his father, for with his coming "*began* men to call upon the name of the Lord" (4:26). The narrative has it, "Then began men to call themselves by the name of the Lord." What there was about the coming of Enos that occasioned such a circumstance we are not told. Evidently the announcement does not mean that men first began to pray or "call upon the Lord," at the time of the birth of Enos, or Enosh, as the RSV puts it. As prayer is at least as old as sacrifice, we can imagine righteous Abel often "calling upon the Lord." Then the words cannot be qualified to mean, "proclaiming the name of the Lord in public assemblies," because they would be unknown at that early stage of history. The most satisfactory sense is the alternative rendering given in the margin, "Then began men to call themselves — or to be called by the name of Jehovah."

At the time of the birth of Enos there were already two distinct classes of people, namely, the Cainites and the Sethites. With the coming of Enos, the race of pious Seth began to call themselves, or were called, by a characteristic name or a distinctive badge — the venerable name of Jehovah — which the impious Cainites had cast aside. Daniel prayed that God would have mercy upon those he described as, "Thy people are called by thy name" (Dan. 9:19). The Old Testament frequently uses such a designation. In the New Testament the disciples were "called by His name" — Christ-ians (Acts 11:26). As Christians, there ought to be more of Christ about our actions and ways.

It is most interesting, however, to observe the significance of the name Enos, the son born to Seth. The Hebrew word used implies "a feeble man," "mortal," "weakly" — a name which may have had a personal association if Enos was born with a weak constitution. Some scholars suggest that the name was a description of the character of the race with sickness and feebleness becoming the portion of men because of their impiety. Enos himself, who was one of those "poor in spirit of whom is the kingdom of God," was in the line of promise, or the descent of the covenant as Luke proves in his genealogy of Christ (3:38).

7. The Child Enoch II

In the genealogical table of the descendants of Adam, in the line of promise — the line of Christ — the promised Seed of the woman, Enoch, the son of Jared, finds honorable mention (Gen. 5:18, 21-24; Luke 3:37). Little did Jared know that when his son was born he would be a unique child in that although he had a cradle, he would not have a grave. Though he would be born into the world, he would not die and be buried in it. In all the history of the world with the millions upon millions of babies born into it, only two never died, namely, Enoch and Elijah (II Kings 2:1-15; Heb. 11:5, 6). When Jesus returns in the air for His redeemed on earth, they, too, will escape death by translation. Saints, living in the world when He comes, are to be changed instantaneously into His likeness (I Cor. 15: 51-53; Phil. 3:20, 21; I Thess. 4:13-18).

> O joy, O delight
> Should we go without dying.

The father of Enoch was not aware at the time of his son's birth, that he would become known as the most conspicuous saint in the Bible. Spoken of as "the seventh from Adam," Enoch's biography is brief yet weighted with significance (Gen. 5:21-24; Heb. 11: 5, 6; Jude 14, 15). Although Enoch lived in times of impiety, of sensuality, and of violence, he was distinct from his environment. The rottenness of his age impelled him to seek closer communion with his God. That Enoch was able to describe the godlessness of his time, and the divine judgment that would overtake the ungodly, is evident from the record he left behind to which Jude refers. From a reading of the context it would seem as if the birth of Methuselah resulted in a spiritual crisis in the experience of Enoch for, "he walked with God *after* he begat Methuselah three hundred years, and begat sons and daughters." For scores of other parents, the coming of a child into the home registered their commitment to God, not only on their own behalf, but also that theirs might be the spiritual ability to train their child to walk before God.

A further fact that should not escape our notice is the record that during his 300 year walk with God, Enoch "begat sons and daughters." The raising of a large family in no way impeded such a holy walk. Does this achievement not reprove the error of the Roman Catholic hierarchy that the state of marriage is less holy than that of celibacy? This great saint, then, not only maintained unbroken communion with God amid the atrocious sensuality and impious atheism of his age, but also amid the trials and vicissitudes of his home life with its many mouths to feed. As a reward for his faith and faithfulness, Enoch was "translated that he should not see death." One day God said to him, "Enoch, you have come so far with Me today, now come home with Me." God translated him. Adam was not born, but died. Enoch was born, but did not die. The sum total of his life was 365 years.

8. The Child Methuselah

When, at the age of sixty-five, Enoch became the father of Methuselah, we wonder whether he had any intuition that his baby boy would grow up and become famous in history as the man who lived the longest? "All the days of Methuselah were nine hundred sixty and nine years: and he died" (Gen. 5:27). He was only thirty-one years short of reaching a millennium. Although he lived the longest of any man, not a single deed of his is recorded, except that he begat sons and daughters. If, as common chronology states, Methuselah died in the year of the Flood, then he was drowned in the waters, implying that he was probably one of those "forgotten of God," whose sins brought on the world the waters of divine judgment (Gen. 6:18; 7:1). Evidently it was true of him as it was of Abraham, "He died in a good old age, an old man and full of years" (Gen. 25:8).

Although Methuselah lived 604 years longer than his father Enoch, there is no record that he emulated his saintly father's unbroken fellowship with God. It is not the length of life that counts but the quality of it. Jesus lived on this earth for a little more than thirty-three years, yet His life and death changed the world. It was Philip James Bailey (1816-1902) who, in *Festus* reminded us that –

> We live in deeds, not years, in
> thoughts, not breaths;

In feelings, not in figures on a dial.
We should count time by heart-
throbs. He most lives
Who thinks most — feels the noblest
— acts the best.

Whether our years be few or many, God grant that the rest of our time may be used ascertaining and accomplishing His blessed will for them (I Pet. 4:2, 3).

This may be an appropriate place to briefly consider the longevity of those who lived on earth until the time of the disastrous Flood.

Adam lived for 930 years,
Seth lived for 912 years,
Enoch lived for 845 years,
Jared lived for 962 years,
Methuselah lived for 969 years,
Noah lived for 950 years, dying two years before Abraham was born. Because these ancients paid little regard to chronology, and we moderns lay great stress upon it, it is a difficult matter to assess the correct temporal sequence of events to which the ancients paid so little attention. Yet accepting the enormous span of life the Bible gives those antediluvian patriarchs, as well as the traditions of nations of antiquity as to the great age to which human life attained in times long past, we examine the reason why these men, and we expect also the women, lived for so long. Scientists today affirm that by increasing sufficient human vitality you can obtain any age you please.

When God created the physical constitution of Adam and Eve it was adapted to a life without end. He made them provisionally immortal, and a great part of their extraordinary vitality remained to them and to their posterity after their fall. Adam and Eve died because they had sinned. "By sin came death." But what would have happened if they and their seed had remained sinless? Enoch and Elijah supply the answer. It has been pointed out that to those before the Flood, "Enoch's translation afforded the clearest evidence of immortality, as that of Elijah did to those of his day, and the resurrection of Christ does to us." If men had continued walking in the garden with God, unsinning, in spite of the serpent, they would never have died, but been raptured to heaven when ready for it, as Enoch and Elijah were.

But the tragic fact is that the longevity of those far-off days was one of the most prolific causes of the corruption of those times. So terrible were the moral consequences of this extraordinary vitality and consequent longevity of the race of sinners before the Flood, that God in mercy cut short the term of human life from then until now. After the Flood, the diminution of human life was rapid. Abraham is spoken of as dying "full of years," but his span of life was 175 years — short in comparison with even Enoch (Gen. 25:7). Moses was 120 years of age when he died and wrote, "The days of our years are threescore years and ten; and if by reason of strength they be fourscore years, yet is their strength labour and sorrow; for it is soon cut off, and we fly away" (Ps. 90:10). Although Job lived for 140 years, it was he who wrote that "Man that is born of a woman is of few days, and full of trouble" (14:1, 2; 42:16).

Scripture lays great stress upon the brevity of life and the certainty of eternity, and warns us against negligence of preparation for the continuation of life beyond the grave. If the sky, and not the grave is to be our goal, then it is imperative to get ready for heaven by being fully given to Him who died and rose again that we might live with Him forever more. Emily Brontë gave us the expressive thought in her *Last Lines* —

O God within my breast,
Almighty! ever present Deity!
Life — that in me has rest,
As I — undying Life — have power in Thee.

9. The Child Giants

Babies weighing ten to twelve pounds at birth are considered to be healthy, bouncing and perfect, precious bundles of humanity. What whoppers those babies must have been that were born to the giants of old and who grew up to become mighty men, men of renown (Gen. 6:4)! The spies, sent out by Moses, came back with a report of gigantic men, the sons of Anak, in whose sight the spies of ordinary stature seemed as grasshoppers. Babies born to these giants must also have been of an unusual weight and size. What strength and vigor they must have been born with!

Admittedly, there are difficulties in stating an explicit interpretation of the exact nature of the parents and their offspring, whose presence and pernicious influence accentuated the terrible judgment of the Flood (Gen. 6:1-7). At the outset, it must be noted that the giants were not apparently the product of the mixed marriages between "the sons of God," and "the daughters of men." The two phrases "and also" and "after that" imply a marked distinction between the "giants," and "the mighty men." The statement, "There were giants in those days," stands by itself. Then follows another statement, "And also after that (when the sons of God took wives of all which they chose [6:2]), when the sons of God came in unto the daughters of men, and they bare children to them, the same (not the giants but the offspring of this union) became mighty men which were of old, men of renown" (6:4).

This problematic passage may be clarified somewhat if we can discover who are meant by — (1) The sons of God, (2) The daughters of men, (3) The giants, or the mighty men of renown.

What is clearly evident is the fact that with the rapid increase of the population during almost two millenniums from Adam to Noah, marital unions were consummated which the Lord could not sanction, and which, within 125 years, He would destroy (6:1-3). The phrase, "The sons of God" or "of Elohim," is used in different ways. For instance, it describes "angels" but not exclusively so. In passages like Job 1:6; Ps. 29:1; Dan. 3:25, the angels, or mighty ones, are in the minds of the writers. From an old Jewish tradition the view has persisted that "the sons of God" who entered into union with the "daughters of men" were the fallen angels who by the association with women of human stock, produced the giants of whom the Greeks and Romans have some fantastic and impure stories. The historical references to the sins of the angels, mentioned by Peter and Jude (II Pet. 2:4-9; Jude 6, 7), are thought to have a connection with the unnatural connection of apostate angels and women.

But it is contended that if angels are to be understood as being responsible for such an unholy, unnatural brood of giant-like children, they would have been included in the record and in the judgment of the Flood, if they had been involved in the corruption and violence necessitating the Flood. Further, angels, even fallen ones, are imperishable, and therefore beyond destruction by water. Then, it must be remembered that Jesus said that angels do not marry nor are given in marriage (Matt. 22:30), which would seem to prohibit entrance into the marital realm and production of a race of wicked giants.

"The Sons of God" is also a designation of the chosen people of God, the Israelites (Deut. 14:1; Hos. 1:10; 11:1). From the days of Enos, men were called by the name of Jehovah. "Israel is my son" (Exod. 4:22). Adam is spoken of as, "the son of God" (Luke 3:38). Those born anew by the Spirit of God are called "the sons of God." "Beloved, now are we the sons of God" (I John 3:2. See Gal. 4: 6).

The generally accepted view is that the term: "the sons of God who saw the daughters of men," represents the godly line of Seth which was separated from all others who were not prepared to be called by God's name. These "sons of the Elohim," or "mighty ones," are so named not for any moral goodness or piety they possessed, but because they were conspicuous for their muscular vigor and warlike prowess. The chosen people and possessors of the birthright, these Sethites, fell into evil ways and married out of the line for mere lust of beauty, and their depravation of women of another race resulted in their utter corruption and in their terrible end in the Flood.

How the intermarriage of the pious, male Sethites with the inferior female Cainites could produce "mighty men . . . men of renown," or strong warriors, is hard to explain. But what is clearly evident is the fact that we here have two classes notably described as "sons of God" and "daughters of men," the union of which, co-operating with "their long and vigorous life, and the corresponding strong animal passions of the people of those days, cast down to the ground the last vestige that remained among men of piety and the fear of God."

a. *The Daughters of Men.* These women who became the wives of "the sons of God" were of the godless line of Cain, and with the blending of these two streams, the end of human apostasy was reached and the Flood came and took them all away. The matrimonial alliances the writer mentions completely blotted out the God-designed distinction between the just and the unjust – "the children of God" and "the children of men," and resulted in the complete ruin of a divine testimony in the world and in the complete triumph of that "old Serpent, who is called the devil and Satan." Universal and unbridled lewdness coupled with violent discord and strife forced God to declare that His Spirit would not always stive with men in their dissoluteness and destruction, but that judgment would overtake such carnal sinners guilty of their shameless excesses. Although God gave them a respite of 125 years, there was no repentance on their part, and the Flood destroyed them. (See Isa. 63:10; Acts 7:51).

Commenting upon the descendants of Cain, Ellicott remarks that Cain is described as "the founder of civil institutions and social life: the name he gives to his son testifies to his determination that his race shall be trained men. They advance rapidly in the arts, becoming rich, refined, luxurious, but also martial and arrogant. The picture terminates in a boastful hero parading himself before his admiring wives, displaying to them his weapons, and vaunting himself in a poem of no mean merit as ten times superior to the forefather Cain. His namesake in the race of Seth also indites a poem; but it is a groan over their hard toil, and the difficulty with which, by incessant labour, they earned their daily bread."

Then Ellicott goes on to describe the effect such show of might had upon the simple daughters born to men. "Enriched by the possession of implements of metal, playing sweet music on harp and pipe, and rendered invincible by the deadly weapons they had forged, must have seemed indeed as the very 'sons of the Elohim.' The Sethites could not have taken the Cainite women according to their fancy in the way described, protected as they were by armed men; but the whole phrase, 'whomsoever they would,' reeks of that arrogancy and wantonness of which the polygamist Lamech had set so notable an example. And so, not by the women corrupting nobler natures, but by these strong men acting according to their lust, the race with the birthright sank to the Cainite level, and God had no longer a people on earth worthy of His choice."

Up to the time of the Flood there was the absence of any godliness in the Cainite race. Devoted to earthly things, the Cainites lived their lives apart from God. Certainly, they had natural ingenuity, art, and civilization, which, in themselves, are not necessary evil, but with such there was no religion. As W. H. Griffith Thomas points out, "Is it not suggestive that the first time art, trade, and manufactures are mentioned they are associated with godlessness? Is it, or is it not, an accident that art has often flourished most when religion has been at its lowest? Is it not a fact that there is that in music, art, and civilization which easily panders to the very lowest in man?" Parents, whose children show an aptitude for the arts, should strive to point out that these are no substitutes for God, but can be devoted to the highest interests of life and the glory of God, thereby escaping the tragic end of those of Noah's time who left God out.

b. *The Giants.* In *Measure for Measure* Shakespeare exclaims –

> O! it is excellent
> To have a giant's strength; but it is tyrannous
> To use it like a giant.

The giants mentioned in the Bible are more or less conspicuous for using their giant strength as tyrants. Much of the violence before the Flood came from the giant-like men which the sacred historian describes as being on the earth at that time (Gen. 6:4). All children who like their parents to read to them never tire about stories of giants. The record of the massive Goliath and of the little David, who slew him never ceases to hold young minds. The giants of our text (Gen. 6:4) were apparently of the Cainite stock, and are distinguished from the offspring of the mixed marriages who became "mighty men, men of renown." These children became a race of brave fighting men, who by their martial deeds won for themselves a wide reputation. These men of name were not of giant stature but were heroes, warriors, as Nimrod was (Num. 10:8, 9).

The giants the spies saw were the sons of Anak, and Anakim, the Hebrew plural of Anak, literally means "long-necked ones" and comes from a root meaning "neck." It is a term referring to the great size or the enormous strength of the Anakim (Num. 13:32, 33). Caleb drove out the three sons of Anak from Hebron (Josh. 14:15; 15: 14). The town the Anakim occupied was called Kirjath-sepher, meaning "booktown" and can be taken to indicate that the giants housed some kind of literature there. A strip of territory on both sides of the Jordan north of Jerusalem is referred to as "the valley of giants" and Caleb is credited with driving them out (Judg. 1:20. See Deut. 2:10, 11).

The tableland of Basham, the kingdom of Og, was called, "the land of giants," and King Og himself was of an enormous size whose iron bedstead was thirteen and a half feet long and six feet wide (Deut. 3:11; II Sam. 5:18; 17:4). Goliath was more than eight feet in height (I Sam. 17:4-7). The Bible, of course, does not speak of Goliath as a giant. He was a giant-like man, yet young David killed him with a pebble taken from a brook. Other giants were slain by David, including a kind of demigod of great stature, who had six fingers on each hand, six toes on each foot. Spoken of as "the son of a giant," he must have been a child of unusual size when born (II Sam. 21:22; I Chron. 20:4-8). One wonders whether the daughters born to giants became giantesses in size. Samson was a "strong man" rather than "a giant."

Hebrew words used for "giants" like *Nephilim,* imply men of great physical strength and stature, and "nothing is more probable than that, at a time when people lived for centuries, human vigor should also show itself in producing not mere individuals, but a race of more than ordinary height. Legends of giants extol their remarkable power and performances." The average height of the human species is from five and a half to six feet, and the majority of individuals do not depart far from the average. Folklore of primitive peoples abound with stories of men who were twice as tall as the average person. An unusually tall man, say up to seven feet, is the product, not of ordinary gigantism, or giantism, but of "acromegaly," or the abnormal but permanent enlargement of certain parts of the body.

There are those scholars who feel that Nephilim, or "giants," describes men of prodigious pride and wickedness, rather than of prodigious stature, strength and rapacity. The striking fact is that the Hebrew word, *Nephilim* signifies "fallers" and may refer to the violent way giants would fall upon the defenseless. Others translate it "fallen," and understand it to refer to fallen angels or to unusually strong, apostate men, fallen away from God. What is evident is the fact that the men of gigantic stature, and also the mighty renowned men, all perished in the Flood. After David's time there is no mention of a single giant. John Bunyan gave us the dread figure of Giant Despair, who lived in Doubting Castle, and had a wife whose name was Diffidence.

10. The Child Noah

Lamech, the son of Methuselah, was 182 years old when his wife gave birth to a boy, Noah, which, in the Hebrew means, "long-lived." Lamech lived for 777 years and his son, Noah, 950 years and so lived up to his name. Wilkinson says that Noah means "rest" and hence, "comfort" and that his father named him this for, "This same shall comfort us concerning our work and toil of our hands, because of the ground which the Lord hath cursed" (Gen. 5:29). The name was an expression of hope concerning the future character and conduct of Noah to which the history of the patriarch's life gives the appearance of an oracle.

But this longing of Lamech for peace and comfort, in strong contrast with the arrogance of his namesake of the race of Cain (Gen. 4:18), was never realized. Noah brought no rest but ruin; no comfort but catastrophe, for in his days came the Flood to destroy all on earth, except Noah and his family. With the birth of Noah we have the first recorded instance, since the days of Eve, of a baby being named at his birth, and in both cases the name ended in disappointment. Are we not curious to know more about the childhood and youth of outstanding characters like Enoch and Noah both of whom are described as having walked with God? But, as in the case of Noah, we go from the announcement of his birth to his entrance into his mature life as a saint and as a family man. Would you not like to know about the boyhood and youth of Noah, the name of the mother who gave him birth, and the name of his own wife who shared with him the tragedy of the Flood, and likewise their deliverance from it? But, as Dr. Joseph Parker reminds us –

> The best part of human history is never written at all. Family life, patient service, quiet endurance, the training of the children, the resistance of temptation; these things are never mentioned by the historian.

While a veil is drawn over the early life of Noah, let us dwell upon the facts and features of his character and career revealed in Scripture.

a. *He Was a Recipient of Grace.* After the announcement of Noah's birth, there is no further mention of him until he reaches manhood and fatherhood (Gen. 5:28, 29; 6:8-13); and his divine mission (6:14-22). Little did Lamech and his wife know that the child God gave them would become the fountainhead of a new race on earth. What a distinct portrait we have of this one who witnessed the greatest catastrophe to overtake the earth. How impressive is the "but" in the context –

"The Lord said, . . . it repenteth me that I have made them.
But Noah found grace in the eyes of the Lord."

What a contrast is suggested here between disappointment and delight. When it says, "Noah found grace in the eyes of the Lord," this also included his wife and three sons with their wives, for if they had not shared Noah's separation from the corruption of that time, they, too, would have perished in the Flood. Had they been contaminated by the spirit of the age, spurning a walk with God, to have spared them for Noah's sake would not have been just. But when God said to Noah, "Come thou and all thy house into the ark," it was because all were worthy to enter, even though the father of the home was the one conspicuous for his righteousness in the sight of God (Gen. 6:18).

For such a godly man who had endeavored to warn his contemporaries of the coming doom, it must have been a heartbreak to Noah that many of his own relatives had perished in the Flood. Although three of his sons are mentioned, Shem, Ham, and Japheth, all of whom were born after Noah had passed the age of 500, it is likely that there were other children who had already died, or who were united in character and destiny with the godless around them, and so died with them when judgment came. Anyhow, there were those of the family of Noah, and of his wife's family, and with the families of the three wives of Noah's sons, who did not enter the Ark and who must have been caught up in the swirling waters of death. What an eternal separation in families sin and death bring about!

What a gulf there is between Noah whom Peter called "a preacher of righteousness" (I Pet. 3:20; II Pet. 2:5), and the wicked around him who were incorrigible when the long patience of God waited "while the ark was a-preparing." In fact, it is Peter who tells us how many *few* are –

"few, that is, eight souls." By the eight persons, Peter means Noah and seven others, the thought being that the punishment must have been almost total if only eight persons out of the inhabited world escaped judgment. After being informed of Noah's birth the next glimpse we have of him is that as a man he "found grace in the eyes of the Lord." This is the first time in the Bible where the word "grace" is mentioned, and throughout the Word implies unmerited favor. From creation to the present, the wickedness of man accelerated so rapidly that divine justice demanded his extermination. But the preservation of Noah reveals how mercy is tempered with judgment, for God's purpose was not complete obliteration, but a new beginning. Thus, with Noah a higher and better order was to begin.

Further, the patriarch found grace with God in that He looked down upon Noah, who was not ashamed to confess Him in the midst of a crooked and perverse generation. Noah was faithful to God even though he was surrounded by universal corruption. "All flesh had corrupted its way," but Noah remained "righteous before God," and so found grace in His sight. As "a righteous man," he was qualified to function as "a preacher of righteousness."

Then, the record goes on to say, that he was "perfect in his generations." This does not mean that he was of pure and unmixed blood – the word perfect is never used in that sense in the Bible – but that he shone as a diamond on the dung heap of his day. He was "just" in contrast to his evil contemporaries, one whose actions were sufficiently upright to exempt him from the punishment inflicted upon the rest of mankind. Noah's wife and sons and their wives, must also have found grace in the sight of God to have been delivered from a watery death. As for the term "perfect" it means "sound," "healthy," and does not convey the idea of sinlessness.

Noah is also spoken of as having "walked with God" a joy he shared with his great-grandfather, Enoch, whose life was spent in the immediate presence of and in constant communion with God, and must have been an inspiration to Noah. All flesh had corrupted its way upon the earth, but Noah kept to the way of holiness, walking daily in the company of the Holy One. The extreme wickedness of those of his time impelled him to yet greater intimacy with God.

b. *He Was a Shipbuilder.* "God said unto Noah . . . Make thee an ark of gopher wood," and he made it according to divine specification so perfectly that he merited the praise, "Thus did Noah; according to all that God commanded him, so did he" (Gen. 6:22). This oblong box-shaped vessel was not made to sail, but merely to float, and had small cabins arranged in three tiers, with the interlacing of the timbers holding the whole structure together.

As Noah had to build the ark before maritime cities were founded and there were no ship-carpenters, the difficulties of his unheard-of enterprise must have been many, and the task tediously slow. Probably Noah was wealthy and invested not only his time, but his worldly estate in such a venture, and his faith stands out in bold relief in that he obeyed without delay the divine commission. "A heart less valiant and full of faith than that of Noah, would have been appalled at an enterprise so superior to all his resources, and so foreign to his business, whatever that may have been." Peter speaks of the patriarch as "a preacher of righteousness," but such a designation refers doubtless to Noah's character, rather than any office he held. As to the somewhat small space accommodating so many animals, it must be remembered that the Ark contained 33,750 square feet of surface in each of its three stories, or say, 101,250 square feet in all.

As to the miracle of the Flood, doubtless God could have saved Noah, his family, and the denizens of the Ark by one display of His supernatural power, thereby obliterating the long time spent on fashioning the Ark, and another long period in it as the waters raged. But the Ark was the means God designed for this purpose, and thus illustrated that omnipotence is linked to human instrumentality. While special providence watched over and guided the Ark, in our lives such providence is exercised through and in accordance with the ordinary laws by which God governs the world.

c. *He Was an Honored Progenitor.* We are not told why Noah had no children until he had reached the age of 500 years. He might have had earlier children than Shem, Ham and Japheth, though they were unworthy of sharing their father's deliverance. Although neither of his three sons had any offspring until after the Flood, it was from them that the three great lines into which the human family is divided came.

Shem, meaning, "fame" or "glory," was the owner of the birthright and the progenitor of our Lord. From Shem came His chosen people.

Ham, signifying, "dark-colored," is the ancestor of the Egyptians, Cushites and other black races of Arabia and Africa.

Japheth implies, "the widener" or "the fair one," though the youngest son was the ancestor of most of the races of Europe, as well as some of the chief nations of Asia.

Have you ever paused to think that no children were spared to enter the Ark. Shem, Noah's first named child was about 100 years old when he entered the Ark, and his two married brothers correspondingly younger. From our Lord's prophetic use of "the days of Noah," we learn that people married and were given in marriage, and as his days covered some 500 years, there must have been a large number of babies, and young boys and girls, the offspring of those who had married, but not one baby was carried into the Ark and no baby was born in it. Innocent children, then, not yet contaminated by the corruption and violence of their parents were among those who had "the breath of life" in them, and being on the earth died. None of them were delivered to help build a new race. (See Rev. 2: 22, 23).

Because of the extreme wickedness of men, God resolved to destroy them completely, even their children, lest they should grow up and manifest inherited corruption. In His mercy, He removed them to heaven in their innocency, and began the race anew with the family of Noah. Two previous experiments had failed. Adam the first progenitor, sinned, and became the father of the first murderer and of a fallen race. Then the second experiment of the formal separation between the wicked Cainites and the pious Sethites, who from the days of Enos called themselves by the name of the Lord, ended in their mixed marriages. These failures revealed the native wickedness and depravity inherent in man, and were meant to exhibit the utter ruin of man when left to himself.

Another experiment or trial began with Noah to see whether divine judgment would constrain man to amend his perverse way before God. The covenant based on the primeval promise as to the Seed of the woman was the same promise and covenant God confirmed with Noah who, after the Flood, remained as the only earthly representative of the people of God in the world and through whom the race was not to perish. At the end of a year, Noah and his family left the Ark, and found themselves on a thoroughly dry earth, facing a new beginning of life. Noah's first act was to consecrate the new, cleansed earth to God, and build an altar for the offering up of burnt offerings – the first altar to be mentioned in the Bible (Gen. 8:20).

"The Lord smelled a sweet savour," we read, or as the original expresses it, "a smell of satisfaction." Divine justice resulting in the Flood was satisfied, and there was now peace between heaven and earth. The blessing God pronounced on Noah, the second father of the human race, is exactly parallel to the one our first Adam received (Gen. 1:28, 29; 2:16, 17; 9:1-7), with the added covenant of the rainbow. Out went the three sons to replenish the earth. "Of these was the whole earth overspread." But such is the faithfulness of the Bible as the biography of humanity, that the shameful fall of Noah is admitted. He had walked with God for so long, but he drank the juice of the vine to excess and became earth's first example of the shameful effects of intemperance. "Let him that thinketh he standeth, take heed lest he fall." Thus, the hoary head found for so long in the way of righteousness, became dishonored and disgraced by drunkenness.

Ham, the second son of Noah, saw his father's nakedness and told his two brothers, and ridiculed his father for his breach of modesty. But Shem and Japheth, with filial piety and delicacy covered the naked body of their drunken father with a robe, walking backward to lay it upon him. When Noah awoke from his stupor, and saw what had happened and pronounced a curse, not upon Ham, but on his son Canaan (Gen. 9:24, 25). Ellicott comments that in the curse "Ham is passed over in silence, as though his unfilial conduct, recorded in verse 22, made him unworthy of a blessing while it was not so wicked as to bring on him a curse. The whole weight of Noah's displeasure falls on Canaan, whose degraded position among the nations is thrice insisted upon" (9:25-27; 11). At 950 years of age, the honored life came to an end, and as an "heir of righteousness which is by faith," Noah entered the presence of the One he had walked with for so long.

11. The Child Ishmael

When Terah became the father of Abram, he had no idea as he looked into the chubby face of his baby that one day he would become "the friend of God," and the father of God's chosen people, the Jews. Abram, who became Abraham, is the first one to be called a Hebrew (Gen. 14:13). The way he went out from his own country and father's house into an unknown country in response to the divine call makes fascinating reading. His travels and trials and triumphs have been retold a million times. Although God had promised Abraham, "In thee shall all families of the earth be blessed," his wife Sara, who became Sarah, was barren, "she had no child" (Gen. 11:30; 12:1-3). The years passed and there seemed to be no sign of the fulfillment of God's promise of Sarah becoming the happy mother of the son of promise.

Impatient, Sarah adopted the expedient that was common at that time, that of giving her husband her Egyptian slave, Hagar, for a second wife. As God had promised Abraham a son, not necessarily by Sarah, the son of Hagar would certainly be his own son and eligible for the promise. But to the bitterness of her own soul Sarah found this expedient unworkable. With petulance she blamed her husband for the animosity between Hagar and herself, and Abraham allowed his wife, Sarah, to do what she liked with the maid who had become the mother of her husband's child. So we come to one of the most touching child stories in the Bible – the casting out of Hagar and her unborn child into the desert.

Ill-treated and humiliated as Hagar had been by Sarah, her mistress, she was proud of the distinction of giving a son to her master as she took the road to her own country. Being heavy with child, she rested by a fountain of water, and something wonderful happened. The angel of Jehovah who, if a divine person, was another member of the Godhead, sent by the Father, drew near and asked Hagar what she was doing in the wilderness. With hesitation she replied, "I am fleeing from the face of my mistress." Then came a most surprising request to return to her mistress and submit herself to the authority of Sarah. With the request was the promise that her seed would be greatly multiplied.

What followed must have overwhelmed Hagar for the divine speaker told her that her unborn child would be a boy, and that she was to call his name *Ishmael,* meaning "God will hear," in commemoration of the fact that God had heard her cries in affliction. The prediction was also made that her son would be somewhat conspicuous, "And he will be a wild man; his hand will be against every man, and every man's hand against him; and he shall dwell in the presence of all his brethren" (Gen. 16:12). Then came the Egyptian slave's recognition of the angel as the omniscient Lord for she said to Him "Thou God seest me: for she said, Have I also here looked after him that seeth me?" Hagar commemorated the occasion of a divine intervention by naming the heavenly Visitor, just as He had named her unborn child. It is quite probable that she, too, named the well at which the Angel and she met as "The well of the living-One who-seeth-me," the Hebrew of Beer-lahai-roi, a name long preserved in the family of Abraham (Gen. 24:62; 25:11).

Before passing on to the unfolding of Hagar's story, there are several features about the pronounced name and prophetic nature of the child she was to bear Abraham.

a. *His Name.* While there are several instances of unborn infants being named by divine command, the son of Abraham and Hagar was the first one in the Bible to be thus named, and among the first to have a name with "God" in it, for "Ishmael" means "God heareth," or "God shall hear." Hagar was commanded then, before the birth of her child, to name him thus, as the assurance and pledge of the mercy of God toward herself. It was a name attesting the compassion of God for the afflicted and destitute, and His readiness to act in their behalf.

The origin of the name, Ishmael, therefore, was not a record of an answer to prayer, but was certainly intended as an encouragement to prayer. When Hagar returned to the home of Abraham she doubtless told him of the divine vision and command, and when the child was born Abraham "called his son's name which Hagar bare, Ishmael." Some thirteen or fourteen years later, Abraham made the divinely-given name the foundation of his plea in interceding for blessings upon Ishmael when he presented the petition, "O that Ishmael might live before Thee!" God's significant and gracious reply must have reminded Abraham of the meaning of his son's name, "As for Ishmael, I have heard thee."

Later on, in the experience of Ishmael himself we have an illustration of the truth taught by his name, with the added benefit arising from a practical application of its significance. When he and his mother were banished from his father's home for good, wandering in the desert, he became exhausted for want of food and drink, and Hagar placed him under a large shrub, and then retired to another spot that she might not see her dear son die. But, as we read, "God heard the voice of the lad; and the angel of God called to Hagar out of heaven, and said to her, What aileth thee, Hagar? fear not; for God hath heard the voice of the lad where he is" (Gen. 21:17). Whether the lad's voice was the voice of prayer, or only the voice of distress and despair, the language of the narrative forcibly declares that God, for a second time in the experience of Hagar, justified the character which He had given Himself in her son's name, a God who hears and answers prayer. In later times others are mentioned as possessing this expressive name. One of Ishmael's descendants was named Elishama, a word of nearly the same meaning, "God hath heard" (Jer. 41:1).

b. *His Nature.* When the angel named the child whom Hagar was to bear, He also gave a prophetic portrait of Ishmael's nature and circumstances. "He will be a wild man; his hand will be against every man, and every man's hand against him; and he shall dwell in the presence of all his brethren. I will multiply thy seed exceedingly, that it shall not be numbered for multitude" (Gen. 16:12, 10).

As a wild man, Ishmael would be untamed, turbulent and ungovernable. The Hebrew expresses it, "a wild-ass man." That there is a nobility about the wild asses of the Arabian deserts is seen in their selection by Job as especially exemplifying the greatness of God (39:5-8). This animal is notable for its great speed, love of solitude, and an untamable fondness for liberty. The wild ass is therefore a fitting type of Ishmael's descendants, the Bedouin Arabs, who delight to rove at will over the desert, despising the ease and luxury of a settled life. They love to be free and indomitable.

Then mutual conflict and animosity are suggested by "his hand will be against every man, and every man's hand against him" — which is a vivid picture of Ishmael's offspring down to this day. Because they were uncontrollable, Arabs could not be bound by treaties or submit to any law. Plunder taken was treated as legitimate gain. Although dwelling 'in the presence of all his brethren," Ishmael and those of his race would maintain their independence, and exist as a free people in the presence of the other Abrahamic nations. Besides Ishmael and Isaac, there were other sons born to Abraham, all of whom had their descendants claiming the Abrahamic heritage (Gen. 25:2). But in the presence of all of this Ishmael would maintain himself free and independent, unconquered and unconquerable as the wild ass.

As for the unique multiplication of seed, this was indeed a great prophecy. Scattered throughout the world today are some thirteen million Jews, but the descendants of Ishmael and of those allied with him and joined to him on the faith of the false prophet of Arabia, Mohammed – an Ishmaelite of the Ishmaelites – constitute a vast host of some 150 millions. In fact, they "cannot be counted for multitude" as the angel predicted. (See Gen. 17:20). What about the mother of the prominent Arab world? The name Hagar is from an Arabic root meaning "to flee," and when she fled from Abraham's home because of Sarah's unkind treatment, as an Egyptian, she not only manifested the untamable love of freedom Ishmael was to inherit from her, but apparently illustrated her own name, which virtually means, "run away."

Following the divine command, Hagar returned to her mistress, and bore Abraham his son, whom he named Ishmael. The sacred historian informs us that Abraham was eighty-six years old when Hagar gave birth to his child who doubtless became very dear to the childless old man as we gather from his plea to God, "O that Ishmael might live before thee!" But from the birth of Ishmael to his circumcision by his father when he was a lad thirteen years old (Gen. 18:25), we have no glimpse whatever of the life he and his mother lived under Abraham's roof. Our curiosity prompts us to ask what happened to pregnant Hagar when she returned. How did her mistress receive and treat her now that she was the mother of her husband's child? Did Hagar know of the secret of the family as to God's promise of the promised "seed," and did she, on the promise of the angel, entertain the hope that she would be the mother of the "seed," and consequently assume an air of superiority over her mistress, Sarah, now that she was not only Abraham's wife, but the mother of his child? Further, do we not try to imagine what Sarah's reaction was to Ishmael as he grew up in the household? Did she shower any affection upon him, as his father must have done, or was the presence of the lad the means of feeding her envy of Hagar, especially now that she did not occupy the old position as a slave of the household?

What we do know is that a dramatic situation was reached when at last Sarah herself became a mother. When Ishmael was born, Abraham was eighty-six years old, and when Isaac was born, the patriarch had reached his one hundredth year (Gen. 16:16; 21:5). Thus, for fourteen years Ishmael had been the heir, but at the banquet given at the weaning ceremony of Isaac, the son of Hagar gave way to spiteful feelings. He derided and ridiculed the child Isaac to such an extent as to compel Abraham to cast out Hagar and her son. Hagar, who probably had never regarded Sarah with much affection, doubtless allowed her bitterness to become more intense, now that her son, Ishmael, had been disinherited. This home conflict reveals the inevitable results of polygamy in which, so often, the father's life is made wretched by the intrigues of his wives for their children.

We are all familiar with the tragic climax to the story of Hagar and her child. Their expulsion was demanded by Sarah who would not recognize Ishmael as being a joint heir with her son, Isaac. As for Abraham, we read that "the thing was very grievous in Abraham's sight because of his son." Because of his natural affection for Ishmael it would be painful for Abraham to part with him, and he possibly thought the proposal of Sarah most unjust. But the Lord, intervening, assured Abraham that all would be well, both with Ishmael and Isaac (Gen. 21:8-13). So, early one morning the parting came, and Abraham took bread and a bottle of water which he gave to Hagar. While Hagar never received full acknowledgment as Abraham's wife, she was the mother of his child, and received a noble promise from God for the father's sake.

By this time Ishmael was a young man of some sixteen or seventeen years, and before long was able to maintain himself and his mother with his bow, and later take an Egyptian as his wife. It was not long before the bottle of water was dry, and as the lad Ishmael was not accustomed to the fatigue of wilderness wandering, he became exhausted and fainted by the way. Cast down by her anguish, Hagar abandoned herself to her grief, knowing that without food and water they both must die. Resting the tired body of her son under the shadow of a shrub, she sat down within a bowshot for she did not want the agony of seeing him die of starvation. Then the touching story goes on to say that it was not her crying that God heard, but the mute prayer of the young life under the shrub – Hagar lifted "up her voice, and wept. And *God heard the voice of the lad*" (Gen. 21:16, 17).

Then the angel of God, the same august person whom Hagar met on her first expulsion from Abraham's house, came with a most assuring message – "What aileth thee, Hagar? fear not; for God hath heard the voice of the lad where he is." Then something wonderful happened. "God opened her eyes, and she saw a well of water." Abraham gave her only a bottle of water, but God gave her a well of water. How inadequate is man's provision! How inexhaustible is God's! The bottle of the world soon runs dry, but God's wells of salvation never fail. So Hagar filled her bottle with God's provided water and refreshed the boy and herself. The command was to lift up the boy and hold his hand, implying that she was to be his faithful protector until he was able to care for himself, as he did when he became an archer. When he took a wife out of Egypt, the heathen element in Ishmael and his descendants was strengthened. Yet he seems to have remained on friendly terms with Isaac, his half-brother (Gen. 25:9; 28:8, 9).

Paul, as we know, uses the experience of Hagar's casting out from the home of the son of promise, as an illustration of the conflict between law and grace. The apostle calls what happened between the two women, an "allegory" (Gal. 4:22-31). The terrible animosity between the Jews and the Arabs in the Middle East resulting in war and bloodshed is but the climax of the strife and jealousy gendered so long ago between Sarah and Hagar. Not until Christ, who came from the Abrahamic line returns to earth as its rightful King, will there be harmony between Jew and Arab. Then Israel will be His glory, and Egypt will be His people signally blessed of Him. Peace at last will be the portion of Isaac and Ishmael. They will be one in the service of Him who came as the matchless Son of Abraham (Matt. 1:1).

12. The Child Isaac

Usually, the birth of a child, begotten in a lawful way, and earnestly desired by two hearts beating as one, is greeted with joy, contentment and satisfaction. To illustrate a point Jesus said, " . . . as soon as she [the woman] is delivered of the child, she remembereth no more the anguish, for joy that a man is born into the world" (John 16:21). Coleridge would have us know that –

God's own Image fresh from
Paradise
Hallows the helpless form of
Infancy.

But parents, looking into the innocent face of their baby, see more the reflection, as well as life, of themselves. Grateful to God for His gift, supreme happiness is theirs in the knowledge that they communicated body and life to another. With the birth of Isaac we have a most unique story, for the world has never known of another baby, promised and born, amid peals of laughter, and whose very name means "laughter." His half-brother, Ishmael, who was a heathen, had a name full of God, for as we have seen, it means, "God shall hear," but Isaac's name is full of glee. If, as the dictionary explains, Laughter is a merry, chuckling or explosive sound from the throat, there were plenty of mirthful chuckles around when Abraham, who was ninety-nine years old at the time, and Sarah his wife who was ninety years old, knew they were to have a baby of their own.

Longfellow could write of one "with eyes overrunning with laughter." Think of those with similar eyes over the coming of the miracle baby, Isaac. Can it be that it was the laughter of the heart they expressed? Discussing the significance of the names of the two sons of Abraham, Wilkinson, in his most important work on *Personal Names in the Bible* says –

> It is remarkable that "he who was of the bond-woman," and "born of the flesh," received from God a name of deep spiritual import, conveying a fact and a promise of utmost value, intelligible to all who heard it; while "he who was of the free-woman by promise" and "born after the Spirit" was, by the same authority, called by a name which was the record of a circumstance of apparently a trivial character, and which of itself taught nothing and promised nothing. The name *Isaac,* means, "he laughs," or "shall laugh," or, impersonally, *there is or shall be laughing."*

What was it, then, that gave rise to the somewhat flippant name? It arose out of the incident which occurred when God announced to Abraham the near fulfillment of the promise He gave him long before the birth of his first son, Ishmael, regarding the son from whom a people and the Messiah would come (Gen. 17).

a. *The First Laugh.* At the advanced age of ninety-nine, when, as the Bible says, Abraham was "as good as dead," the patriarch received an unforgettable revelation of God as *El Shaddai,* the Almighty One, in which He made an everlasting covenant with His servant as to his posterity. His name was changed from *Abram,* meaning "high or exalted father," to Abraham, signifying "the father of a thronging crowd of nations." The name of his wife was also changed from Sarai, meaning, "My princess," most likely a pet name her husband had given this woman of extraordinary beauty, to Sarah, a princess in a larger sense, and for a numerous posterity. "She shall be a mother of nations; kings of people shall be of her." Such a change of name shows that she was admitted to the covenant, and that Abraham's spiritual heir would not be Ishmael, but the son she was to bear. The changed name, then, represented a change in her hopes and in her state. While still her husband's princess, she was to become a royal mother of nations.

When Abraham heard God say that his long barren, and now ninety-year-old wife, was to become a mother, he fell down and laughed. The ludicrous aspect of such an event completely overcame the old man, leading him to say to himself, half laughing over God saying something that was contrary to nature, "Shall a child be born unto him that is an hundred years old? and shall Sarah, that is ninety years old, bear?" (Gen. 17: 1-22). Abraham was staggered at the strangeness of such a promise.

There are expositors who affirm that Abraham's exclamation of surprise does not express unbelief on his part, but that his laughter was a mixture of wonder and rejoicing; that his eminently natural emotion was like to the experience of the disciples when, seeing their risen Lord, "they yet believed not for joy, and wondered" (Luke 24:41-43). But for thirteen years Abraham believed that the promise of a son had been fulfilled in Ishmael whom he loved and so met the divine announcement about another son with the plea, "O that Ishmael might live before thee." This "son of the house" (Gen. 15:3), had been regarded probably as the true heir, and the transference of such an honor brought a mingling of laughter and loss.

b. *The Second Laugh.* Not knowing of the good laugh her husband had had over the declaration of God about her coming motherhood Sarah, eavesdropping, heard a conversation that set her chuckling, "Sarah laughed within herself" (Gen. 18:12). The background to this hearty laugh, as if it were a joke she had heard, is well-known to all Bible lovers. About three months after he had had his laugh, Abraham was seated at the door of his tent, and lifting up his eyes he saw three respectable persons standing nearby. With sincere and unaffected gentility, Abraham courteously offered them the hospitality of his home, not knowing the three were angels, and that their Lord was also present. Abraham and Sarah quickly prepared a meal for their visitors. No wonder the patriarch earned the distinction of being called, "the friend of God" (Isa. 41:8; II Chron. 20:7; Jas. 2:23). Everything about Abraham was great and gracious.

Listeners, they say, never hear any good of themselves, but as Sarah listened to the conversation of the men as she sat behind a curtain which effectively concealed her person, she heard something good about herself but could not believe it. The messenger who spoke for Jehovah, (or could it have been Jehovah Himself?) said that He would return in a year's time, and that by then Sarah would have a son. As Sarah heard this she laughed, for it had long ceased to be with her after the manner of women, meaning, that she was well beyond the age and ability of childbearing. This is what Paul meant when he spoke about "the deadness of Sarah's womb" (Rom. 4:19). She herself said, "I am waxed old," or, "worn out as an old garment," which, doubtless she looked at ninety years of age!

The laughter of both Abraham and Sarah brought into prominence the inconceivable character of the fact seeing they were both old and incapable of parenthood. Yet when Sarah died, and Abraham married Keturah, he had six more children (Gen. 25: 1, 2). Although Sarah laughed within herself at the idea of becoming a mother, Jehovah heard the chuckle and said to Abraham, "Wherefore did Sarah laugh, saying, Shall I of a surety bear a child, which am old?" (18:13). Although Sarah was long past the natural age of conception, she was to learn that the God of Abraham was a God of miracles, therefore, the divine reply to her question, "Is anything too hard for Jehovah?" Having fashioned the complex nature of woman, He was able to turn back the clock and produce the necessary ability for childbearing. So the declaration was repeated that when He returned in about a year's time, Sarah's son would be born.

Afraid of the august presence of the speaker, Sarah denied she had laughed at what she had heard – her laugh turned to a lie, for which she was rebuked by the divine promiser. "Nay: but thou didst laugh." Sarah's unbelieving and irreverent laughter exhibited disbelief both in the omnipotence and in the omniscience of God. Struck with terror that she had ridiculed the promise of the divine speaker, she offered no excuse, but took refuge in a falsehood. Peter speaks of Sarah as an example of the holy women of old time "who trusted in God" (I Pet. 3:5, 6), so she was not ungodly nor profane, but guilty of levity and then lying. The gentle rebuke she received humbled her and when according to promise her son was born, in allusion to his name said, "God hath made me to laugh – appointed laughter for me – so that all that hear will laugh with me." The first occasion of her laughter was reproved by God, now He encourages her to laugh the laugh of the assurance of divine favor.

c. *The Third Laugh.* The Bible tells us that God laughs – "He that sitteth in the heavens shall laugh" (Ps. 2:4) – and mirth must have been His when He chose the name Isaac for the son of the laughing pair! "God said . . . thou shalt call his name Isaac" (Gen. 17:19). "The Oxford Dictionary of English Christian Names," says, "the Hebrew of Isaac means, 'God may laugh' that is, regard the hearer in a friendly light." Such a name, which became an honored one, is a perpetual memorial that Isaac's birth was naturally such an impossibility as to excite ridicule. Ellicott comments that "the name *Isaac* not only recorded the fact of the laughter of his father and mother, but was a standing memorial that Isaac's birth was contrary to nature, and one of which the promise was provocative of ridicule in the sight even of his parents."

Well, laughing Sarah had her precious son, which event seemed to her most marvelous and astonishing, causing her to say, "All that hear will laugh with me." And can we not imagine how many were merry at the thought of an old woman of ninety having a baby boy? Isaac, then, was the divine name for the heir of the covenant, and not as dignified or as spiritual as that of his brother Ishmael ("God shall hear"). Yet, as "interpreted by its history, possessed a significance which rendered it the symbol and earnest of blessings, and a token of the believer's satisfaction and complacency in the anticipation and realization of the promises of his God." Further, the history of Isaac's name reveals how fascinating and enlightening the study of names is.

13. The Children of Incestuous Origin

Behind the repeated phrase, "That we may preserve seed of our father," lies a sordid story of a night in a cave after God had destroyed the cities of Sodom and Gomorrah (Gen. 19:29-38). The father in question was Lot who turned out to be a bad lot. He remains today as one of those beacons in the Bible warning us of the peril of starting out well with every possible advantage, and then ending our career in shame and disaster. Perhaps there is scarcely a life recorded in the Bible which is more full of serious and solemn instruction to all who rise up to follow the Lord.

Along with his uncle, Abraham, he left Mesopotamia, not knowing where he was going, and remained with his uncle in Canaan until their multiplied possessions necessitated separation. Choosing, as he thought, the best part of the land, Lot pitched his tent toward Sodom, and before long was in it with a house taking the place of a tent. Caught up in the plunder of the city by the kings of the East, Abraham came to his rescue, but after his release from captivity he returned to Sodom to live. Sodom fascinated him. If it were not for Peter's commendation of him as "just Lot" we would have hardly classified him as a godly man (II Pet. 2:7). While his soul was daily disturbed by the wickedness of Sodom, somehow he had no influence to stem the tide of evil. When he tried to warn his kinsfolk of the coming doom, his plea had no power. He had lived too long as one of the Sodomites, and seemed to those he warned "as one that mocked."

When at last the stroke of judgment fell upon Sodom, the angels forcibly removed Lot, his wife, and his daughters from the burning lava about to engulf the city. Looking back, Lot's wife, walking behind her husband, was stifled by the sulphurous vapors and became a pillar of salt, and as such "a monument of an unbelieving soul." Lot and his two daughters escaped the catastrophe caused by the brimstone and fire, and found shelter in a mountain cave, which brings us to a scene of unutterable shame. The degeneracy and depravity of Sodom, by which Lot was tainted, had left a deep mark upon his godless daughters and resulted in a plan that ended their father's career in ignominy and disgrace.

What happened, then, in that cave, although horrible, is not surprising when we remember that the two girls were born among and brought up with those who were exceedingly wicked. "The utter degradation of Lot and his family is the most painful part of his story, which thus ends in his intense shame." Thinking, perhaps, that the whole world had perished and that they and their father were alone spared, and that there were no men left on the earth from which they could choose husbands, they devised the foul plot to make their father drunk, and through their revolting conduct, have children by him, thereby preserving his seed. While, in ancient times, every effort was made in a lawful way to continue the family line, the shameless and nameless daughters of Lot were flagrantly guilty of the sin of incest which the law condemns (See I Cor. 5:1).

What sorrowful stories of lust and dishonor are associated with the coming of many children into the world, and who remain forever branded through no fault of their own. It was so with the two sons of Lot which his daughters bore their own father. Never the patterns of modesty and propriety, the two Sodomite girls made their father so drunk that he did not know what he was doing during those two nights in the cave. Had it not been for his drunkenness, his daughters would never have accomplished their incestuous ends and forced their father to become the father of their children. With this act they sounded the lowest depth of degradation and caused him to die with such a stain upon his character. The names given the two infants suggest their incestuous origin. *Moab,* the son of the elder daughter means "son of my people," that is, one born of intercourse in her own kin and family. *Ben-ammi* was the name the younger daughter gave to her child, and it means, "son of my kinsman," and implies in a less repulsive way, his unchaste origin.

Have you ever thought of the mix-up as the result of this prohibited union? Those two children, conceived in that cave, had a father who was their grandfather; and who, although they were brothers were yet cousins. While both Moab and Ben-ammi were of Hebrew stock because of their father, the Moabites and Ammonites were finally merged in the Arabs, the most implacable foes of Abraham's descendants. Such, however, is the overruling mercy of God that it was out of Moab that Ruth the Moabitess came, who, in turn, was honored as an ancestress of our Lord and Saviour, Jesus Christ. In Matthew's royal genealogy of the Messiah, Ruth's name is forever inscribed. "Boaz begat Obed of Ruth" (1:5) – a striking illustration, is it not, of how God can overrule and bring good out of evil?

14. The Child Twins

There is no more appealing, romantic love story in the whole of literature than that of Isaac and Rebekah, whose charming betrothal is told with the utmost exactness of detail. Isaac was thirty-seven years of age when his mother Sarah died, and forty at his marriage (Gen. 23:1; 25:30). Being old and well-stricken in age, Abraham was anxious to see his bachelor son settled, so he placed his trusted servant under a vow to secure a wife for Isaac in his own country and from among his own relatives. How the godly servant went forth, seeking divine guidance, how he met Rebekah at the well of water, returned with her to her father's house, only to discover that she was the granddaughter of Milcah, the daughter of Haran, Abraham's brother and was therefore Isaac's cousin, is a heart-moving narrative, as is Rebekah's departure from home.

As for Isaac, as he awaited the return of the household servant in his search for a bride, he went about his work in the fields and at eventide went out into their solitude to pray. One night, as darkness began to fall, he was out as usual for his period of prayerful meditation. Looking up, he saw the camels coming, and soon learned from his father's servant the story of his successful search. As soon as Isaac saw Rebekah, he loved her. It was a case of love at first sight for them both. Quickly Rebekah filled the vacancy in Isaac's heart for he was now comforted after his mother's death (Gen. 24). Abraham, left alone by Isaac's mariage, took Keturah to wife and had six sons by her, thereby contradicting a previous objection of his about being too old to have children (17:17).

As for Isaac and Rebekah only one thing marred their ideal companionship, although they had been married for twenty years, no children had been born to them to create a family. Isaac was forty when he married, and sixty at the birth of his sons (Gen. 25:20, 26). Interceding with the Lord about the barrenness of his wife, his prayer came before the Lord as fragrant incense, and soon Rebekah conceived. Evidently she was unaware that twins were struggling within her, but with a conscious pain of strange struggles within her, she inquired of the Lord as to the meaning of her inner suffering. Immediately she received the answer, which cast in poetic form, reads –

> Two nations are in thy womb:
> And two peoples from thy bowels
> shall be separated;

And people shall be mightier than people;
And the great shall serve the small.

The sacred record goes on to say that when Rebekah's days were fulfilled, behold, "there were twins in her womb" (Gen. 25:21-26). This is the first time the word "twins" is used in Scripture. The next occasion in which twins are mentioned is in connection with Tamar who, through deception, had twin sons by her own father-in-law whose names commemorated the unfulfilled pledge of Judah to Tamar. The record as told in Genesis 38 is not a pleasant one to read, illustrating, as it does, the utter contamination of the patriarchs through their association with the Canaanites.

As for the twins Rebekah bore, they were to become the progenitors of two hostile nations. "Two dissimilar nations sprang from Abraham, but from mothers totally unlike, namely, Sarah and Hagar, so, too, from the peaceful Isaac two distinct races of men were to take their origin, but from the same mother, and the contest began while they were yet unborn." Esau, the first to appear, was red looking and was covered with hair, which betokened a strong and vigorous, but sensual nature (Gen. 27:16). Esau means, "hairy." When his brother Jacob came out of the womb he was clutching Esau's heel, proving that there was no interval between their birth. Jacob means, "one who follows at another's heels" – one who waits to take advantage of another, or a supplanter, which is the bad sense of Jacob's name which Esau attached to it as being symbolic of his character (Gen. 27:36). To be at a person's heel is to be his determined pursuer, and one who on overtaking him throws him down. Jacob's own unworthy conduct in robbing Esau of his birthright revealed him to be true to his name.

The second line of the poem God gave to Rebekah – "two peoples from thy bowels shall be separated" – indicates that in their earliest days Esau and Jacob would be unlike in character and unfriendly in disposition, and as we know from their history they developed into hostile nations. The two nations descending from Rebekah were, throughout all their history, the most uncompromising and bitterest of foes, and would have seemed to have begun their contentions before their birth (Ezek. 35:5). The poem also was prophetic in that it stated that although Esau started with the advantages of the birthright as the first to appear, and had a stronger physical nature than Jacob, yet he would finally hold an inferior position (Gen. 32:6). Radical differences between the two boys were seen in their appearance and in the circumstances of their birth. Often, twins are much alike, but here it was just the reverse.

While it is not within the province of our meditation to discuss the genetic characteristic in twins it can be said that two classes are to be distinguished, namely, "identical twins" and "fraternal twins." The former are genetically alike, and arise from a single fertilized egg, and consequently are called, "monozygotic twins." Any differences between them are due to environmental differences to which they may have been subjected before and after birth, or at both times. The latter arise from two fertilized eggs and are referred to as "dizygotic twins," and are no more similar genetically than are ordinary brothers and sisters born at different times. In many cases twins are associated with heredity.

Generally, identical twins are more often alike than fraternal twins. The former are often almost exactly alike in looks, features, height, so much so that it is difficult to distinguish them apart. They act and feel alike, love to dress alike, and do so many things together. Recently the press carried a report of two young women, twins, one of whom was married. As the time drew near for her to have a baby, her unmarried sister strangely enough seemed to suffer the same labor pains as her married sister, such was the bond of sympathy between them.

As for fraternal twins, there is little of this identity and mutual feeling. The study of Rebekah's twins, with their opposite physical appearance, characters, desires and tastes, places them in the category of fraternal twins. Esau, the first of the pair to appear, both as to his complexion and the color of hair was red, a possible indication of his violent, frank and passionate character. Jacob, on the contrary, had a smooth velvety skin, and a character no less smooth and deceitful (Gen. 27:11). As the twins grew up they developed opposite tendencies. Esau became a man of the field, a skillful hunter, and ready to fight fierce beasts or men. But Jacob was a quiet, or plain man, lacking his brother's skill, dexterity and other manly accomplishments. Although he was "a quiet man who dwelt in tents," Esau also "dwelt in tents," but with this difference: Jacob dwelt in tents by day, and Esau by night. "To dwell" means "to sit down." Esau was about all day in his bold and valiant pursuits, and did his sitting at night, but Jacob, with his timid disposition and lack of outdoor pursuits, and more pious than his brother, was content to pass his life among the tents. Yet after his Bethel experience he revealed great skill and dexterity as one who raised cattle.

Already we have remarked on the folly of favoritism in a family, and of how in the home life of Isaac and Rebekah its love, peace and harmony was ruptured because of the undisguished partiality of the parents each for the favorite son. Perhaps it is not easy to avoid preferences in a family and love children with varying degrees of affection unless all of them are cast in the same mold, and have all the same character and disposition. Often the tragedy comes in manifesting preference, or in varying treatment according to partiality. Isaac admired and loved his valiant hunter-son, Esau, because "he did eat of his venison"; but "Rebekah loved Jacob," because he was always with her at home and had her quiet disposition. But such undisguised favoritism brought about deceit and consequent separation of the twins for almost twenty years. Parents who have twins can learn a great deal about the avoidance of heartache which partiality brings about from this ancient record of Bible twins who did not have a twin spirit (Gen. 25 - 27).

One feels that he cannot let John Milton's symbolic use of twins pass by without mention. In his *Areopagitica*, he has the sentence –

> It was from out the rind of one apple tasted that the knowledge of good and evil as two twins cleaving together leaped forth into the world.

15. The Children of Leah and Rachel

As the design of this section of our study is to set forth incidents in connection with the birth of children, and not to give an exposition of their life and character as they matured, we pass over the dramatic experiences Jacob encountered after he was forced to flee from home and ultimately found himself in the home of Laban, the son of Nahor who was Abraham's brother.

At the outset of his sojourn in his adopted home, he knew what it was to reap what he had sown. Having deceived his father, which deception resulted in his flight to Haran, he found himself deceived by Laban over the matter of his daughter Rachel, beautiful and well-favored, and whom Jacob loved as soon as he set his eyes on her. Thinking that Laban had given him Rachel as his wife, Jacob discovered Leah her elder sister had been substituted.

Jacob had to serve another seven years before Rachel became his wife, but the years "seemed but a few days, for the love he had to her." Although Leah was to bear him more children than Rachel, yet Jacob "loved Rachel more than Leah" (Gen. 29:20, 30). While we are to dwell more fully upon the two children Rachel bore him, it may be profitable to briefly indicate the significant names of the children Jacob had by Leah. As we know, twelve of the patriarch's children became the representatives of the twelve tribes of Israel. The record says that "the Lord saw that Leah was hated." Doubtless the horrible imposture Laban had practiced on Jacob turned him against Leah, and doubtless changed Rachel's affection for her sister into disgust. Whether Leah entered the dishonest switch contrary to her will, or with her full consent and contrivance we do not know.

What seems evident is that the names Leah gave successively to her children by Jacob clearly reveals the thought which continually occupied her heart, namely how she could win the love of her husband. Yet her choice of names was prophetic as Jacob makes clear in his dying blessing in which he treated his sons as being predictive of the characteristics of the twelve tribes of Israel (Gen. 49).

It is not our aim to expound all the circumstances and experiences of Jacob's sojourn in Laban's home. What can be emphasized are the dire consequences of polygamy countenanced by that ancient family. "The domestic discords, the envies and jealousies between Jacob's several wives, forcibly illustrate and demonstrate the wisdom and goodness of God's law that each man should have his own wife, as well as each woman her own husband." A plurality of wives always results in discord, strife, jealousy and hatred. The protection, purity and peace of a home depend upon the recognition of God-given precepts as to the regulation of the marriage relationship.

The most prominent aspect of Jacob's life at Padan-aram is the account given of the birth and meaning of the names of his children by different wives. The genealogical record is full and explicit with the name of each child born, and in case the meaning of the given name, as well as what occasioned the selection of it. Does not this fact indicate that God would have us learn important lessons from these carefully preserved names, all of which were so closely associated with the early and latter history of Israel? Further, the order in which the twelve sons were born and the circumstances giving rise to the several names chosen correspond exactly with the order of the history of the children of Israel. The Hebrew nation became known as Israel, Jacob's new name, which fact alone compels us to look somewhat closely at the record of his sons from whom the nation sprang.

The prophetic and typical significance of Jacob's twelve sons is a most fascinating study in which chapters 29, 30 and 49 of Genesis must be viewed together. When the patriarch came to die he summoned each of his twelve sons to his bedside, and in naming them, uttered one of the most striking predictions to be found in the Old Testament. As with most prophecies, the dying utterance of Jacob had a double fulfillment. Not only did he describe, most strikingly, the past history of his descendants, but he also contemplated the fortunes of the twelve tribes represented in his twelve sons in the last days (Gen. 49:1. See Isa. 2:2; Jer. 23:19, 29). In the naming of the children at the time of their birth, circumstances giving rise to the selection of their respective names are stated, for in each case a *reason* is given why the name of the child was proclaimed by his mother. At the outset both Leah and Rachel were barren, but the Lord saw that the former was hated by the latter, and "opened her womb." Rachel's continuing barrenness led to the poignant cry, "Give me children, or else I die" (Gen. 29:31; 30:1).

H. B. Pratt in his *Studies on the Book of Genesis* reminds us that, "All the six sons of Leah and one daughter were born before Joseph (Rachel's first son), whose birth did not occur till after Jacob had completed his fourteen-year contract, and just before he began a new arrangement with Laban (Gen. 30:25-34). The seven children of Leah, therefore, were born in the space of seven years. Jacob married at the end of the first seven years he had spent with Laban; Joseph was born at the end of his fourteen years of service, in which he gained his property; and Joseph was the youngest of the eleven children born in Padan-aram, so that the Bible shows that children were born to Leah with extraordinary rapidity – one each year, for seven consecutive years." It was this fast-growing family that caused Rachel to envy her sister, and become desperate for children of her own.

a. *Reuben.* Being the first son of Leah, Reuben by birth had a pre-eminence in dignity and power. His name means, "Behold a Son!" As his mother named him she said, "Surely the Lord hath *looked* upon my *affliction*" (Gen. 29:32) – her affliction being her barrenness. This first child of Jacob proved to be as unstable as water (Gen. 49:3, 4). His unbridled passions brought about his downfall, and he fell into merited contempt. "Boiling over as water" figuratively describes Reuben's overflowing sensual passions resulting in his great sin against his father, the sin of incest and adultery. In his prophecy of Reuben, Jacob stressed three things about his first-born. How touching is the parting benediction of Jacob as with crossed hands he blessed all his sons!

He was his might, or excellency. As the first child, Reuben had excellence of dignity because the natural birthright was his.

He was to forfeit his dignity. "Thou defilest my bed." His position of excellency was lost because of his vileness. Although a man of good and humane instincts, as seen in his plea for his brother Joseph's life (Gen. 37:22, 29), he was yet a man of weak character.

His tribe was never to attain any distinction in Israel. Deborah in her song of victory mocked and upbraided the warriors of Reuben for their lack of courage. "Unstable as water" is a symbol taken from the passing away of water which had dried up like a summer stream.

Reuben did not excel. His birthright was given to Joseph. Judah, not Reuben, was the royal tribe from which God's Son sprang (I Chron. 5:1, 2). The tribe of Reuben never enjoyed numerical superiority. "Let his men be few" (Num. 1:21; 26:7; II Kings 10:32, 33).

b. *Simeon*. This second son Leah bore Jacob was named Simeon which means "heard" and the reason of such a choice is given, "Because the Lord hath heard that I was hated" (Gen. 29:33). The Hebrew *Shimeon* means "listening." Leah wanted children, and asked God for them so that she might become fully established in her husband's affections. Arthur W. Pink draws attention to the striking resemblance between the significance of the names given to Leah's first two children — "Surely the Lord hath looked upon my affliction." "Because the Lord hath heard that I was hated" — and what is recorded in Exodus in connection with the sufferings of Israel in Egypt.

> First, we read that "God looked upon the children of Israel" (Exod. 2:25). Then He said to Moses — "I have surely seen the affliction of my people which are in Egypt" (Exod. 3:7). Then, corresponding with the words of Leah when Simeon was born, God adds, "And I have heard their cry" (Exod. 3:7). It is surely something more than a mere coincidence that at the birth of Israel's first two sons their mother should have spoken of affliction, which she said the Lord hath looked upon and heard, and that these identical words should be found in the passage which describes the first stage in the national history of the children of Israel who were then hated and afflicted by the cruel Egyptians. When the Lord told Moses He had seen the affliction of His people Israel and had heard their cry, did He not have in mind the very words which Leah had uttered years before?

c. *Levi*. This third son was named Levi at his birth by his mother. Levi means "pledged" or "attached," or "union" or "united with." Giving the name Leah said, "This time will my husband be joined unto me" (Gen. 29:34). With the succeeding names Leah makes clear the thirst of her heart for some part of the tenderness which Jacob lavished upon the beloved, but still barren, Rachel. It is interesting to compare Jacob and his two wives, Leah and Rachel, with Elkanah and his two wives, Peninnah and Hannah (I Sam. 1:1, 2). In those days when a large family was regarded as a special favor and gift of God, both Leah and Peninnah could not understand why their respective husbands did not love them, at least for the children they bore them.

Levi became the father of the priestly tribe and so again the words of Leah were prophetic of the beginning of Israel's history. On the eve of leaving Egypt, through the slain lamb and its blood sprinkled, God was joined to Israel and became her husband. Then it was that He was joined to His people. Thereafter He promised to be as a "husband unto them" (Jer. 31: 31, 32). Because of the ardent zeal of the tribe of Levi, and its defense of the cause of God and of Moses at the critical worship of the golden calf, the curse pronounced upon Levi in association with Simeon was turned into a blessing (Exod. 32:25; Deut. 33: 8-11). The tribe was selected as being better able to perform the office of priests and more qualified to have a distant territory which was properly their own (Num. 35:7, 8; Josh. 21: 1-42). The book of Leviticus unfolds the function of this priestly tribe.

In Jacob's dying, prophetic utterance Simeon and Levi are linked together and termed "instruments of cruelty" (Gen. 49:5-7). Although Moses was himself a descendant of the tribe of Levi, he did not omit unworthy traits of their characters from the sacred record. Doubtless Jacob was referring to the terrible slaughter of all the males over the defilement of Dinah, the sister of Simeon and Levi (Gen. 34:25). Simeon's name is mentioned first probably because he was the "leader" in that shocking affair. Other references to the association of Simeon and Levi are Genesis 42:24; 49:7; Exodus 32:27; Joshua 14:4; 21; Judges 1:3.

d. *Judah.* Leah called her fourth child Judah, meaning "praise," and exclaimed, "Now will I praise the Lord" (Gen. 29:35). One is curious to know why Jacob's wife whom he did not choose, and had not loved, selected such a spiritual and honored name for her fourth son? Could it have been that Jacob himself, grateful to God for His goodness in giving him so many sons, was becoming more affectionate toward the one who bore them, thus prompting her to sound this note of grateful adoration? A still more distinguished mother praised the Lord for a greater son (Luke 1:46, 47).

In his last words, which were of a Messianic character, Jacob dwelt at length on Judah's praise, conquests, pre-eminence and his kingship. "Thou art he whom thy brethren shall praise" (Gen. 49:8). The germ of this prophecy is enshrined in the name Leah gave her fourth son. When Judah became a tribe, the other tribes sounded the achievements of Judah from which Jesus came (Heb. 7:14). The place of greatest honor in the family of Jacob was accorded to Judah by divine decree. The tribe's supremacy was ordained of God. "He chose the tribe of Judah" says the psalmist. Jacob predicted that Judah would remain a kingdom until the coming of the Messiah. The scepter was not to depart from Judah, and through the greater portion of its history the tribe enjoyed regal dignities, and amply justified Jacob's prophecy. The tribe of Judah was always of recognized predominance (Judg. 1:2; 21:18). Whatever may have been Judah's own moral and religious defects, his father and his brothers praised his ascendancy (Gen. 37:27; 43:3-9). May we be found singing the praises of Him who is fearful in praises (Exod. 15:11; Ps. 106:11, 12).

e. *Dan.* This fifth son of Jacob was born of another woman, or wife. Because Leah's family was increasing, Rachel became not only envious of her sister but also desperate, and cried to Jacob: "Give me children, or else I die!" But the patriarch, weary over Rachel's constant frustration, angrily answered her, "Am I in God's stead, who hath withheld from thee the fruit of the womb?" (Gen. 30:1-6). To remedy the situation, Rachel resorted to Sarah's expedient and gave Jacob "Bilhah her handmaid to wife . . . and she bare Jacob a son." The phrase "obtain children by her" implies "be builded by her" or "build herself up" by the children Bilhah her maid would bear Jacob.

The understanding was that as Bilhah was Rachel's slave so her child would be hers also (Gen. 16:2, 3). The same phrase "build herself up" or "build her house" was used by Sarah in giving Hagar to Abraham. There are Biblical passages that cannot be properly understood without the use of this key. (See Ruth 4:11; Prov. 14:1). When Bilhah bore a child on Rachel's behalf she called his name Dan, saying, "God hath *judged* me, and hath also heard my voice." *Dan* means "judge" or "judged" – to do justice to one, being the most common sense of the phrase "to judge" in the Hebrew (Ps. 43:1; Luke 18:3).

In his dying message Jacob availed himself of the implication of his son's name to convey a promise to the tribe springing from him, "Dan shall judge his people as one of the tribes of Israel." Being the first of the children of the two handmaids who became Jacob's two other wives, the meaning of his prophecy may have been that the tribe of Dan should not be in subjection to the rest of the tribes, or be held and treated as inferior to them. Dan was to have his share in the general government the tribe were to exercise, or maintain his own government as on equal terms with the rest. Dan was so named by Rachel, who looked upon him as a judgment God had given in her favor, and as He had judged Rachel so the descendants of her son by Bilhah were to provide judges for Israel, one of whom was the mighty Samson, who was of the tribe of Dan.

f. *Naphtali.* This second son Bilhah bore Jacob, and whom Rachel claimed as her child, was Naphtali which means, "My wrestlings," the origin of such a name being found in Rachel's outburst, "With great wrestlings *(Hebrew,* "wrestlings with God") have I wrestled with my sister, and I have prevailed" (Gen. 30:7, 8). Such a statement reveals the variance and strife of the two sisters, Leah and Rachel, so disastrous in the large family being founded. Rachel's saying bears testimony to the vehemence of the envy that consumed her over Leah's success as a mother. Later on, Jacob was to have his own wrestling encounter (Gen. 32:24). Naphtali and Zebulun, the sixth son of Leah, are often associated in Scripture. Deborah sang in her triumphal song: "Zebulun and Naphtali were a people that jeoparded their lives unto the death in the high places of the field" (Judg. 5:18).

Although the two boys were of different mothers, both the sons and their descendants were much alike in disposition and character – daring and defiant, valiant and vicarious (I Chron. 12:33, 34). It is somewhat striking that the word used by Rachel at the birth of Naphtali should occur twice in Israel's history and would thus seem to be prophetically anticipated by her. The same word "prevailed" describes what took place between Israel and Amalek as they wrestled together. "Israel prevailed . . . Amalek prevailed" (Exod. 17:11). Paul also had something to say about the spiritual foes the believer wrestles with (Eph. 6:12).

In his farewell blessing upon his sons, Jacob said of Naphtali that he was "a hind let loose: he giveth goodly words" (Gen. 49:21). He was as erratic as a wild gazelle and yet a gifted orator. He represented those who scamper through life aimlessly and without a purpose, having a wild extravagance spoiling his otherwise brilliant talent and magnificent capacity. There is only One who can tame the hind let loose, namely, Jesus who was able to calm the rude tempest with a word (Mark 4:39).

g. *Gad.* The birth of this seventh child is a witness to the fourth wife of Jacob. A pause in Leah's childbearing prompted her to give her servant, Zilpah, to Jacob to wife, and she bore him a son whom Leah named Gad. She was determined not to be overtaken in the rivalry of "building the house of Israel" (Gen. 30:9-11). Naming Zilpah's son, Leah said, "A troop cometh," which probably was the expression of her desire of numerous and valiant posterity. Gad means, "good fortune" or "fortunate." The name also has the implication of "a marauding troop," or guerrilla band, as Jacob suggests in his last reference to Gad (Gen. 49:19). As a tribe, Gad was situated on the east side of the river Jordan, and being exposed to the attacks of invading enemies had to learn how to defend themselves (I Chron. 5:10-22). The verb rendered "overcome" is of the same root with the term *gedud* used for troop, and so the brief blessing of the tribe by Jacob indicates the fortunes of the tribe. In the great battle in which the Gadites defeated the Hagarites we are told that they overcame because of their appeal to God.

The phrase, "Gad shall overcome at last" (Gen. 49:19), reminds us of the final overcomers John writes about (Rev. 2; 3). What a victorious air there is about the song many sing in their protest marches, "We shall overcome"! Gad was overcome, but overcame, and such is comfort for all who are temporarily conquered. The last enemy to be destroyed is death, and the full enjoyment of a glorious victory over this dread foe by Him who will overcome at last.

h. *Asher.* Zilpah, Leah's maid, bore Jacob a second son — his eighth — and Leah called the baby, Asher, which means "happy," and exclaimed, "Happy am I! for the daughters will call me blessed" or fortunate (Gen. 30:12, 13). In his dying message to the tribes, Jacob prophesied that Asher would have much cause for happiness over the royal dainties awaiting the tribe. The inheritance of Asher was considered one of the best in Israel (Josh. 19:24, 31). This portion of the tribe was better known by its Grecian name of Phoenicia, which means, "Land of the Palms," so called because of its abundant luxuriant palms. Jacob's prediction of a land preeminently rich and beautiful came true for Asher. Tyre was within the territory of Asher and supplied many "royal dainties" for King David (II Sam. 5:11; I Kings 5).

In the time of famine, Asher supplied the hungry prophet Elijah with bread, for Zarephath, where the widow sustained the prophet, was in Asher's territory (Josh. 19:28; I Kings 17:9; See also Luke 4:26). The New Testament gives us two references to "dainties" coming from the richly endowed tribe of Asher. The godly prophetess, Anna, was of the tribe of Asher, and offered a most blessed "dainty" to Israel's newborn King. As she gazed into the face of the holy Child Jesus she "gave thanks likewise unto the Lord, and spake of him to all them that looked for redemption in Jerusalem" (Luke 2:36-38). Yet once again do we read of bread coming out of Asher for when Paul was being taken to Rome, the ship reached Sidon — Asher's territory — and "Julius courteously entreated Paul, and gave him liberty to go unto his friends to refresh himself" (Acts 27:3).

Asher means "happy" and the possessions of his tribe produced the absence of any fear of want. But even "royal dainties" can fail, as the Asherite purveyors to the king experienced, for during the reign of King David the numbers of the tribe of Asher had declined to such an extent that the court had no representative amongst the chief rulers. Adversity comes hard to those who have had prosperity for so long (I Chron. 26:16-22).

i. *Issachar.* A somewhat unsavory background surrounds the birth of Leah's fifth son, Issachar, meaning "hire," or "recompense." Leah, the wife Jacob did not choose and did not love, conceived again as the result of a bargain struck with her sister. Reuben, Leah's first-born had gathered "mandrakes," or "love apples," which were coveted by women because of their supposed virtue in promoting the conception of children. Above everything else Rachel longed for children, and offered to exchange Jacob's company for Reuben's mandrakes. Meeting Jacob as he returned from the fields, Leah said to him, "I have hired thee with my son's mandrakes." Leah now envied her sister as she watched Rachel's control over the mind and person of Jacob, and entered into the agreement resulting in the resumption of her child-bearing. (See Gen. 29:31.)

The narrative said, "God hearkened unto Leah, and she conceived, and bare Jacob the fifth son" – his fifth child by Leah (Gen. 30:14-18). Leah looked upon her new son as God's recompense for having given Jacob her maidservant for a wife. Wilkinson thinks that the name should have another s and be spelled *Issaschar,* signifying, "he bringeth hire," or "he payeth me my hire." The idea of children as wages or reward of Jehovah is expressed by the psalmist, "Lo, children are an heritage of the Lord: and the fruit of the womb in his reward" (Ps. 127:3). Here the word "reward" is *sacar,* usually and more literally represented by "hire" or "wages."

The last words of Jacob concerning the tribe of Issachar are not easy to interpret. Evidently the men of Issachar were not lacking in valor, yet somehow preferred to pay tribute rather than face the toils and dangers of military service. (See Judg. 5:15; I Chron. 12:32.) Although the people "jeoparded their lives unto the death" (Judg. 18), they loved rest and their pleasant hills and dales, and came to leave the defense of the interests of the commonwealth to others. The figure used of Issachar as a strong-boned ass represents his great strength. In the East the ass is renowned for its capacity for bearing heavy burdens. The might of Issachar was revealed in time of war, but such strength was not used in the interests of their country. So they "couched down" to luxuriate in the delightful restfulness of a rural life. How careful we should be lest our power and prosperity induces indolence and, like the rich fool we, too, take our ease (Luke 12:19)! God gives a warning to those who are at ease in Zion (Amos 6:1).

j. *Zebulun.* Once again Leah gives birth to a son, her sixth, and sighing always for the good she had not yet obtained, she exclaimed, "*Now* will my husband dwell with me, because I have born him six sons" (Gen. 30:19, 20). Leah looked upon her large family as a good dowry which God had endowed her with, and so she called her infant, Zebulun, which means, "a dwelling." In connection with the prophetic intimations of Jacob's dying utterances, the order of the sayings of the mothers of the patriarch's sons corresponds to the order of Israel's history, and as Zebulun's coming is spoken of as a good dowry, the same can tell of Israel's occupation of the goodly inheritance God endowed the people with.

As previously indicated, Zebulun and Naphtali are linked together in the Bible, being contiguous the one to the other. As to the boundaries of the tribe of Zebulun, a commercial and seafaring tribe, Josephus, the Jewish historian says that it extended from "the Lake of Gennesaret as far as Carmel and the Mediterranean" (Josh. 19:19). An interesting fact to observe in the blessings of his children is the way Jacob passes from the fourth to his tenth son (Gen. 49:13). Believing as we do that the very arrangement of the words of Scripture is the handiwork of the Holy Spirit, why was there this leap? Arthur Pink supplies an answer in this way –

> When blessing his fourth son we found that the words of our dying patriarch manifestly looked forward to Christ Himself, who, according to the flesh, sprang from the tribe of Judah. Hence, because of the close connection

of our Lord with the land of Zebulun during the days of His earthly sojourn, these two tribes are here placed in juxtaposition. Having spoken of the tribe of which our Lord was born, we have next mentioned the tribe in whose territory He lived for thirty years. This is, we believe, the main reason why the tenth son of Jacob is placed immediately after the fourth.

k. *Dinah.* Again Leah bore Jacob a child, but this time it was a baby girl whom she called *Dinah* – the feminine form of Dan – which means "judged" or "vindicated." The choice of such a name reveals how Leah was thinking always on the justice which God manifested, but which man had failed to exhibit. Dinah was not the only daughter Jacob had for later on we read that "all his daughters rose up to comfort him" when he heard about Joseph (Gen. 30:21; 37:35; 46: 7). It is more than likely that Jacob had several daughters by Leah and the two handmaidens.

Of all his daughters, Dinah alone is mentioned by name, because two of her brothers, Simeon and Levi, forfeited the birthright by the cruelty with which they avenged her wrong when Prince Shechem seduced her. Shechem had wrought folly in Israel in lying with Jacob's daughter, "which thing ought not to be done" (Gen. 34: 7). Feeling that they were upholders of their sister's honor, Dinah's brothers, especially two of them, laid a snare to punish the seducer. But the punishment that resulted got out of hand for Simeon and Levi slew not only Shechem, taking Dinah out of her house, but "slew all the males" and plundered the city taking all the wives and children captive (Gen. 34: 25-31). This is not a pleasant record to read but proves what Dr. Joseph Parker said –

> How bold a Book is the Bible! It hides nothing of shame; the Bible is not afraid of words which make the cheek burn; the Bible conceals nothing of moral crippleness, infirmity, or weakness or evil.

l. *Joseph.* What a sweet phrase the historian uses – "God remembered Rachel," and the sequel is seen in the birth of her first son, Joseph (Gen. 30: 22, 23). As soon as Jacob saw Rachel, he loved her, and she had a love which none of the other three women in the patriarch's life shared. Without doubt the union of Jacob with Rachel was of God, and it was divine providence that ordered things so that they should meet at that well (Gen. 29). The first sight of his cousin's beautiful face convinced him that Rachel was the partner for him. Etiquette of the East allowed him to kiss her, seeing they were cousins. F.B. Meyer says that, "Jacob's encounter with Rachel at the first well he came to, reminds us that, though there is nothing more important than the union of heart with heart, there is nothing into which people drift more heedlessly."

We all know how the love story developed. Under the same spell as Jacob was, Rachel ran home to tell the news, and her alacrity revealed her heart. Jacob met her father, Laban, and agreed to serve his uncle for seven years, on the understanding that at the end of such a specified period, Rachel would become his wife. In this way he manifested the love he had for her. To have her to hold and to cherish, Jacob was willing to give time, strength and service, and those seven years seemed but a few days because of the love he had for Rachel.

> Selfishness seeks a gift,
> Love loves to give;
> Giving itself away,
> Love loves to live.

Love's grand munificence
Counts not the cost;
Knowing, though all is gone,
Nothing is lost.

The deception Jacob suffered when Laban exchanged Leah for Rachel has already been touched on. It was a cruel blow for Jacob but he served another seven years for Rachel, for true love knows how to wait. Yet when at last Rachel was his, the sorrow of them both was the absence of children to cheer their hearts. When Leah bore her fourth child to Jacob, Rachel was envious of her sister, and her envy gave rise to the desperate request, "Give me children, or I die!" Rachel's mistake was that she sought Jacob to meet her need, when she should have looked to God.

As for Jacob he should have sympathized with the bitterness of Rachel's disappointment, and quietly pointed out her mistake in coming to him seeing the withholding of children was not his fault. Instead he lost his temper with the one he loved. If only his spirit had not been so disturbed and he had calmly pointed out that the issue of life was not in his keeping, how greatly he would have helped Rachel to bear the cross of barrenness. But Rachel's day came, for God had not forgotten her, and with divine remembrance there came divine help. Although she had failed God when she gave her maid, Bilhah, to Jacob, yet in His mercy He gave her a son – and what a son! Among all the sons of Jacob, Joseph excelled them all (Gen. 30:22-24). After seven years of reproach and of impatient waiting, her first exclamation bears witness to her immense satisfaction on seeing "her reproach among men taken away." Most Eastern wives desired to be mothers, partly to be numbered with the ancestors of the promised Messiah.

The three verses describing Rachel's maternity are full of God. It has been said that, "The Deed which secured the emancipation of the Negroes was so written that the face of Abraham Lincoln could be clearly seen upon it." Rachel, in the mercy granted to her, clearly saw not the face only, but also the loving heart of God who had heard her passionate prayer and who gave her a child. At last the pent-up desire for years was satisfied, and when her baby came Rachel called him Joseph, meaning, "addition" or "will add," for with the prediction of a seer she said, "The Lord shall add to me another son." Such language not only manifested her yearning for another child, but the grateful, happy mother was a prophetess, for her prophecy was fulfilled by the birth of Benjamin, whose birth, as we shall see, resulted in his mother's death. That prophesied son cost Rachel her life (Gen 35:18, 19). The saints of God often prove that the brightest anticipations of life are clouded by the gloom of the grave.

Dealing with the significance of the name, Joseph, W. F. Wilkinson remarks that "when Rachel bore her first child, after a long period of hope delayed, she first said, 'God hath taken away *(asaph)* my reproach'; and then we are informed that she called her son's name, Joseph, and said, 'Jehovah shall add *(yoseph)* to me another son.' The similarity of sound seems to associate two different ideas, one being pre-dominant. The first idea is that of ablation, or substraction, in the removal of barrenness; the second that of addition, in the increase of fruitfulness. The first suggested the second, whether by sense or sound; and hence the second, rather than the first, became the expressed and permanent name."

The long cherished desire of Jacob

to have a child by his beloved Rachel was also realized. Not only so, but he must have wondered at his wife's prophecy of having another son by her. Doubtless Jacob's decision to return to Canaan was bound up in the future career of his precious Joseph whom he wanted brought up amidst the hallowed associations of the land of promise that he might know something of the memories that had nourished and inspired his own boyhood. Parents cannot be too concerned about having their children surrounded by gracious influences.

The prophetic benediction Jacob gave to Joseph was the longest given to any of his sons (Gen. 49:22-26), and is divided into two parts, Retrospective and Prospective.

(1) *Retrospective* (Gen. 49:22-24). Here the verbs are in the past tense, and as Arthur Pink reminds us, in reviewing the past Jacob mentions three things in connection with his favorite child.

First, he sees Joseph as a boy in his father's house, as an object of beauty, of tender care, and as well pleasing to his father's heart — all pictures under the beautiful figure of a "fruitful bough by a well."

Second, Jacob refers to the bitter enmity and fierce hatred which were directed against him — the archers sorely grieved him. They shot at him their cruel arrows, they vented upon him their unreasonable spite. But through it all Joseph was divinely sustained. "His hands were made strong by the hands of the mighty God of Jacob."

(2) *Prospective* (Gen. 49:25, 26). The prominent feature about Joseph's future is fruitfulness. In Egypt, where he came to great prominence, Joseph, the Hebrew, took a Gentile wife, and by her had two sons whose names are most significant. The first was Manasseh, meaning, "forgetting" for, said Joseph as he named his child, "God hath made me forget all my toil, and all my father's house." When the second child came, Joseph named him Ephraim, meaning, "God hath caused me to be fruitful in the land of my affliction" (Gen. 41:45-52). Not only did Joseph receive a double portion in the land, namely, the first-born's birthright transferred to him from Reuben (I Chron. 5:1, 2), but much fruitfulness also was his out of the double tribe springing from him, for Ephraim and Manasseh were two branches out of the parent stem. "Joseph shall have two portions" (Ezek. 47:13). Joshua was from one of the tribes springing from Joseph (Num. 13:8).

Of Joseph's two sons, Ephraim means "fruitfulness" and of Manasseh Joseph predicted, "Let them grow into a *multitude* in the midst of the earth." Jacob's prophecy concerning Joseph, his favorite son, will receive its complete fulfillment in the Millennium when the twelve tribes of Israel inherit their land (Ezek. 47:13). The message for our own hearts is that affliction need not limit addition, for like Rachel's first child, we, too, can be fruitful in our land of affliction. Because of his prophetic insight, sterling character, and special attention of his father, Joseph was hated by the rest of Jacob's children who sought to kill him. In so many ways Joseph typifies Jesus. It was because Joseph had "the genius to be loved" that he roused the scorn of those who despised goodness. (See Gen. 39:9.)

m. *Benjamin.* A tragic and heartbreaking experience overtook Jacob as the whole family journeyed from Padan-aram. Desirous of dwelling once more in the tents of the ancestral home which Jacob had been forced to leave years before, he wanted his children, especially little Joseph, to become acquainted with "the play-place of his early years." Events on the way back to Canaan such as the reunion between Esau and Jacob; the inhuman and sacrilegious vengeance taken by the sons of Jacob on those who had outraged their sister, Dinah; the awesome meeting between God and Jacob at Bethel, when the patriarch's name was changed to Israel, because behaving himself in a princely fashion he earned such a name meaning, "He acts as a prince with God" — all merit exposition which our particular study does not call for.

Leaving Bethel, which Jacob called "the place where God spake to him," the company set out for Ephrath still some distance away. Rachel, being pregnant, must have found the traveling hard, and one wonders whether Jacob lacked foresight in not waiting a little longer at Bethel for Rachel to have her child. Perhaps she might have been spared such a distressing death in giving birth to her second son. So excruciating were her birthpangs, that in giving birth to Jacob's twelfth son, she gave up her life. This is the first notice in the Bible of the extreme form of the curse which fell on the woman in the day she ate the forbidden fruit (Gen. 3:16). Since then multitudes of mothers have died in giving children life, or have been buried with them in their own grave.

As she died in great pain, she named her newborn child whom she would never fondle, Ben-oni, meaning "Son of my sorrow" — a name not acceptable to her husband, who, exercising his parental authority, substituted another name for the one which would have been the painful memorial of his dear one's greatest sorrow. Jacob chose a name expressive of supreme affection, as well as an augury of prosperity and honor. He called this now motherless baby, Benjamin, signifying, "Son of my right hand" — a name, displacing the melancholy and ill-omened Ben-oni once for all. Jacob, whose heart was lacerated with grief could not bear that his child should have a name of sadness which might shadow his character and destiny. How sad, that the birth of Benjamin was the burial of the hopes and joy of Jacob's life, for he dearly loved Rachel.

Before proceeding to face more calamities still, Jacob raised a monument over the spot where he had laid to rest the mortal remains of the beloved, beautiful woman who had been so precious to him. Her sorrowful death left Jacob with an empty heart, and with an air of sadness so characteristic of the rest of his life, at the end of which he confessed, "Few and evil have the days of the years of my life been" (Gen. 47:9; 48:7). Mohammedans still revere the burial place of Rachel. In passing, it is fitting to observe that Rachel's prediction about having another son received a partial fulfillment in Benjamin for the words, "another son" seem to anticipate that birth in a manger when "The Word was made flesh." The Son of Mary, like the son of Rachel was both "the son of sorrow" — Ben-oni (see Isa. 53: 3, 4); and "the son of the right hand" — Benjamin (see Heb. 1:2, 3).

In his appraisal of Benjamin, Jacob spoke of him "ravin as a wolf: in the morning he shall devour the prey, and at night he shall divide the spoil" (Gen. 49:27). David calls this last son of Jacob, "little Benjamin" (Ps. 68:27). While not numerically the smallest of the twelve tribes of Israel, Benjamin received the smallest allotment of land given to any of the Tribes (I Sam. 9:21). Yet it was from "little Benjamin" that great men and great achievements came. The first of the judges of Israel was a Benjamite, Ehud. The first of the kings of Israel was another Benjamite, Saul. Prominent among the apostles of our Lord was Saul of Tarsus, who became Paul, who was always proud of his ancestry as a son of Benjamin. As Saul, he went to Damascus "breathing out slaughter against the saints of life" and justified the dying words of Jacob, "Benjamin shall ravin as a wolf" – Benjamin was dear to Joseph who spoke of his brother as "my mother's son."

Before saying farewell to the sons of Jacob, preachers and Sunday school teachers might find it profitable to dwell upon the typical significance of the names, and in the order in which the patriarch's twelve children are mentioned. First of all, the Gospel and the history of sinners saved by grace can be traced in such names –

Reuben, the first-born, means "See, a Son!" which is what God says to us through the Gospel as it calls us to behold the Son of God who became the Son of Man that He might make the sons of men, the sons of God.

Simeon, whose name means "hearing," can suggest the reception of the Gospel by faith. "How shall they hear without a preacher?" Faith comes by hearing the Word, and by reading it. The promise is, "Hear and your soul shall live."

Levi, having the implication of being "joined," can stand for the blessed and eternal union by which the Holy Spirit makes us one with Christ through His Word. Atonement means being at-one with the Lord. Once rebels we are now priests and kings.

Judah, meaning "praise," can stand for the divine life lived out in the believer's life in joyous gratitude for all he possesses in Christ his "never-failing treasury filled with boundless stores of grace."

Dan implies "judgment," and reminds us of our responsibility to judge our character and conduct in the light of God's Word. Paul could say, "I judge myself," and, "if we would progress in holiness there must be the uncompromising sentence passed on self and sin."

Naphtali, with its meaning of wrestling," is a name heavy with the idea of mighty prevailing intercession, and also of our conflict with infernal and internal foes. For every true saint there is his Jabbok.

Gad, suggesting "a troop or company," brings us to the truth of Scripture that the Lord's people are His army; also that they are a fellowship, or communion of saints. How blessed is the tie binding them together.

Asher is another expressive name, and means "happy," and "Happy are the people whose God is the Lord." Such happiness or joy, however, depends upon or is the outcome of obedience to God's will and Word. "Happy are ye if ye know these things, and *do* them."

Issachar means "hire," and speaks of service for the Master. We are saved to serve. Some who are not saved try to serve Him. Others are saved but fail to serve Him as He commands. Are we servants or slackers?

Zebulun, as we have seen, means "dwelling." To abide in Christ is akin to dwelling or being at home in Him. He is ever the dwelling place of His people. Paul desired to be absent from the body and present, or at home, with the Lord for ever.

Joseph, representing "addition," can be applied in the sense of reward for diligent and faithful service. Pentecost witnessed a mighty addition both to the Lord and His church. Are we adding to our faith, virtue?

Benjamin, this name of Jacob's last

son means "son of my right hand," and can imply our privileged relationship as the sons of God. As "the right hand" denotes position and authority, both belong to those to whom God has given power as His children.

Dealing further with the prophetic and typical import of the twelve sons of Jacob, we can see in the dying prediction of his children the fulfillment of what is admirable in them, in the Lord Jesus Christ which the patriarch seemed to have a distant vision of. Arthur Pink, in his indispensable *Gleanings in Genesis,* indicates a twelvefold application concerning Christ.

(1) The prophecy concerning Reuben reminds us of the excellency and dignity of Christ's person: He is the "First-born" in whom is "the dignity and the excellency of power" (Gen. 49:3).

(2) The prophecy concerning Simeon and Levi may well speak to us of Christ on the cross. Then it was that "the instruments of cruelty" were used against Him. Jacob says, "O my soul, come not thou into their secret" – he would have nothing to do with them: so on the cross Christ was forsaken by God and man. A curse is here pronounced by Jacob upon them, as Christ, on the cross was "made a curse for us" (Gen. 49:5-7).

(3) The prophecy concerning Simeon and Levi also anticipated our Lord's priesthood, for Levi became the priestly tribe of Israel. The Book of Leviticus is the handbook on priestly functions.

(4) The prophecy concerning Judah pictures our Lord's kingship, who came of the tribe of Judah (Gen. 49: 8-11).

(5) The prophecy concerning Zebulun looks at Christ as the great refuge and haven of rest for His people (Gen. 49:13).

(6) The prophecy concerning Issachar prefigures the lowly servitude of Jesus who invited His own to share His yoke (Gen. 49:14, 15).

(7) The prophecy concerning Dan views Him as the judge into whose hands God has committed all judgment (Gen. 49:16-18).

(8) The prophecy concerning Gad announces His triumphant resurrection when He led captivity captive (Gen. 49:18).

(9) The prophecy concerning Asher looks at Jesus as the Bread of Life, the One who satisfies and gladdens the hearts of His own (Gen. 49:20).

(10) The prophecy concerning Naphtali regards Jesus as God's perfect prophet, giving forth "goodly words." Never man spake like this Man (Gen. 49:21).

(11) The prophecy concerning Joseph foreshadows Christ's millennial reign when with all things under His control He will exert His sovereignty over the earth (Gen. 49:22-26).

(12) The prophecy concerning Benjamin depicts the Saviour as the terrible Warrior as He comes forth with dyed garments, looking glorious in His apparel (Gen. 49:27. See Isa. 63:1-3).

16. The Child Moses

The story of the babyhood of Moses is one of the sweetest and most appealing ever written – and so true to life, even though it was penned thousands of years ago. When parents look into the innocent face of a babe God has given them they are not able to discern the great potential wrapped up in that tiny, fragile form. If the baby is a boy will he become a Homer or a Hitler, a Martin Luther or a Voltaire? If the baby is a girl will she grow up into a sensuous Cleopatra, or a sacrificial Florence Nightingale? When Amram and Jochebed, both of the line of Levi (Exod. 2:1; 6:20; Num. 26:59), looked into the cherub face of their baby born at a time when Pharaoh had decreed that all baby boys should be thrown into the crocodile-infested Nile, what did they see? Did they see only a lovely child or one who would become a man whose fame would fill the world as the man of men next to the Messiah, the conqueror of Pharaoh, the leader of Israel, and the giver of the law to all mankind?

We are distinctly told what the parents of Moses did see in him as he came from the womb. They saw that he was "a goodly child" (Exod. 2:2; Heb. 11:23). Stephen said that when Moses was born he was "exceeding fair" or "beautiful to God," as the margin puts it (Acts 7:20). The beauty of the baby in that crude cradle was a heavenly beauty for he had a "human face divine." Later on the people would not have been able to continually behold that face because of the divine glory glowing from his countenance (II Cor. 3:7, 13). So, the beauty of that baby was not of the body only. There was a nameless something about him that was prophetic of great things, and somehow roused his parents to save him from a watery grave. Amram and Jochebed had an intuition that their newly-born child had a body borrowing its beauty from the soul within.

What exactly is meant by the term, "goodly child" twice used in Scripture? The Greek word *asteios*, used for "goodly" has no relation to character, but expresses that which is beautiful because it is elegant. "They saw that he was a beautiful child" (Heb. 11:23) *Good News for Modern Men.* An ancient historian spoke of the child Moses as being "recommended by the beauty of his personal appearance," and it was possibly his childlike goodliness that intensified the desire of his mother to save his life, although this was not the main cause of her anxiety for his safety. Each mother thinks her baby is the most beautiful one in the world because the natural love of a parent's heart makes a child look lovely, but somehow the parents of Moses saw more than nature could. It would seem that they had a spiritual intuition that their child was destined for great things, and have a name living for ever. Their eye of faith could see in their little one, not only physical loveliness, but also a divine purpose.

A Jew would probably call a very poor boy "a child of poverty"; a boy who had outlived many dangers "a child of providence"; and a very pious boy "a child of grace." The boy Moses was all three. How different was the palace in which he was brought up from the humble home in which he was born! Actually, Moses was a foundling, or a child left by its parents and found by some passer-by. Thus, his name means "water-saved," so named from the water out of which he was drawn. But in spite of his lowly origin, Moses was to stand before kings and prove himself kinglier than they. Do we not admire Pharaoh's daughter for the way she was stirred to pity by the cry of a baby born to slaves in her father's kingdom?

But Moses was also a child of providence and was thus delivered from the king's wrath, and from a terrible death in the river. Was ever a baby in a sadder plight, left as a prey to the flood and famine, to crocodiles and vultures? Pharaoh had commanded that all the baby boys of God's people should be destroyed, knowing that in this foul way the nation would soon die out. But when the parents of Moses hid him for three months from the spies seeking out all the male children, and then placed him in a little box which was to float like a toy boat down the Nile, the faith of Amram and Jochebed feared no danger. As Levites, they believed their lovely child was one of the children of the covenant, so they hid him. Is it not the duty of all Christian parents to hide their children? And where is the safest refuge? Is it not in "the shadow of the Almighty"?

In a remarkable way God's providence brings about the greatest things by means of the smallest. It was His purpose to overthrow the haughty Pharaoh, to free Israel from bondage that He might prepare for the coming of the Messiah, and so bless the world. And how did He begin? He made a baby cry! If babies do not cry, there is usually something abnormal about them. Their cries draw attention to hunger, discomfort or pain. But why does the Bible, which often gives but a line to a nation's history, take such notice of a baby's tears? Because it was God who prompted Jochebed's precious baby to cry in the nick of time. Had he cried a few minutes sooner he might have drawn to his little ark the crocodiles or the spies on the lookout for male babies.

Had that baby not cried at the very moment the proud princess came to the waters to bathe, she would have washed herself and returned to the palace. But her presence at the water's edge and the child's scream were perfectly coordinated by the great hand of providence, and so the child was saved to make world history. By his tears he made his way into the heart of an Egyptian princess, proving that he was indeed a child of providence. Does this incident not clearly show that God's hand is in small things no less than in great?

Our life flows from a thousand springs,
 And dies if one be gone,
Strange that a harp of thousand strings
 Should keep in tune so long.

When the small ark or box containing the crying baby was brought to the curious princess we read that "she opened it, and saw the child: and, behold, the babe wept. And she had compassion on him." How different in nature she was from her cruel and callous father who had ordered the destruction of all boy babies! Here was a wicked man who had a daughter who was kind, loving and tenderhearted. What the birth name of the child who became the great Jewish lawgiver was we are not told. We know him only by the name he received three months after his birth, from Pharaoh's daughter, for it was she who "called his name *Moses,* saying, Because I drew – caused to draw – him out of the water." Speaking in the Egyptian language the name the princess gave the child must have been Egyptian, and "Moses," meaning "one who draws out," was expressive of the act of deliverance by which he was preserved (See II Sam. 22:17; Ps. 18:16).

From the moment Moses' father and mother had put their child in the water, Miriam, Moses' sister, never took her eyes off the ark. And at the moment Pharaoh's daughter came down with her maids to bathe in the river, the loving eyes of that little Jewish girl watched every movement. Seeing one of the servants returning the floating cradle for her inquiring mistress, Miriam slipped up close in order to hear and see all that would be said and done about her baby brother. We all know what followed. Looking into the cradle and seeing such a beautiful baby, the princess observed that he was one of the Hebrews' children whom her father had condemned to death. She had compassion on him, and the girl Miriam offered the suggestion, "Shall I go and call to thee a nurse of the Hebrew women, that she may nurse the child for thee?" The princess, looking down into the eager face of the small child, answered "Go!"

We can imagine Miriam running as fast as her little legs could take her to her mother and reaching home saying, "Come quickly, a princess has found our baby, and wants a nurse for him!" Without hesitation Jochebed hurried to the spot and was engaged as nurse for her own baby. She was paid for nursing her own child.

While we read that Pharaoh's daughter took the child into her own home, and "he became her son," one wonders whether she learned the identity of the nurse she hired to nurse him as being his own mother? Further, was she allowed to take her own child home occasionally, and did Moses become acquainted with his brother and sister as he grew up? Perhaps Jochebed was allowed to keep her child until he was weaned, and then surrender him to the princess at the agreed time to be brought up as her son and given a son's education and privileges as an Egyptian. But the fact remains that all the years of Moses' sojourn at Pharaoh's court could not obliterate the godly faith of his parents he was the inheritor of. As a babe, his tears saved him, and he became the saviour of his people. Reaching maturity, Moses refused to be called any longer the son of Pharaoh's daughter, but chose rather to suffer affliction with the people of God (Heb. 11:23-27). The treasures of Egypt had no lure for him. "By faith he forsook Egypt."

Another interesting feature that comes out in the study of Moses' childhood is that nothing is said about the childhood of his brother and sister, Aaron and Miriam, all three of whom became conspicuous as leaders in Israel's deliverance from Egypt, and the wilderness experiences of the nation. Children in a family are great company for each other as they grow up together, especially in a godly home such as these three children represented. But while Miriam and Aaron were never separated and shared many confidences, even to old age, Moses was taken from home when only three months old and so missed childhood years with his own flesh and blood. Moses was the youngest of the three children of Amram and Jochebed, and Miriam the eldest with Aaron in between. The first glimpse of Miriam is when she is referred to as a maid (Exod. 2:8), which term implies "a young woman" – "a virgin." We meet Miriam only once as a girl and that is when she was a helper of her baby brother at the right moment. In later life it was her task to stand beside her two great brothers. Yet there came a day when she was not willing to be known only as the sister of Moses and Aaron. Alas, she tried to turn Aaron against his brother, and was smitten with leprosy because of her jealousy. As for Aaron, the first mention of this member of the family is made when Moses shrank from the challenge of confronting Pharaoh because he was not eloquent (Exod. 4:10). God chose Aaron to be the speaker, saying, "Is not Aaron the Levite thy brother? I know that he can speak well" (Exod. 4:14). Because of his faculty of speech, Aaron joined Moses as his mouthpiece. Moses was about eighty years old at this time so Aaron and Miriam must have been a few years older. But what contact there had been between brothers and sister during the first eighty years we are not told.

After forty years in Egypt, Moses, because of his slaughter of an Egyptian whom he caught smiting a Hebrew, fled to Midian, and made his home there for the next forty years. His dress, appearance and speech marked him out as an Egyptian, but the seven daughters of Reuel, priest of Midian, soon discovered Moses' exact identity. In the course of his sojourn in the home of Reuel, Moses married Zipporah, one of Reuel's daughters by whom he had two children, Gershom and Eliezer (Exod. 2: 21; 18:1-7). These boys received wonderful names from their father, the reason for which is explained in his record of their births, for Moses wrote the first five books of the Bible.

Gershom. This name of the first child means "a stranger there," probably a different word from Gershom, the name of a son of Levi which means "to expel," or "expulsion." Moses explains that the name he chose implied, "I have been an alien in a strange land." It was a name expressing his desolate feeling and condition as an outcast and an exile. It was a memorial of the reverse of position which had befallen him, and of the contrast of his present hardships as compared with his former dignity as the son of Pharaoh's daughter.

Eliezer. The name of the second son is one of those divine names so rich in significance for it means, "God is my help." Moses tells us why he coined such a name, "The God of my father was mine help, and delivered me from the sword of Pharaoh," which speaks of adversary and danger, and also of devout gratitude and praise to God for His mercy in His gracious protection. The despondency of his earlier days in Midian were wiped out, and he came to experience that God's providence was far wiser than his own plans.

17. The Child of Jephthah

The full pathos of the story of Jephthah, a son born of a nameless harlot, but whose father was Gilead, can be found in the phrase, "His daughter . . . was his only child; beside her he had neither son nor daughter" (Judg. 11:34), or, as the margin puts it, "he had not of his own either son or daughter," apart from the daughter he was about to sacrifice. The sons of Gilead's legal wife did not want an illegitimate around the house, and so cast Jephthah out. No love was lost on him but he loved this only child of his, and he was crushed when he found that this precious girl was to be the burnt offering he had vowed, for victory over Ammon (Judg. 11). We can read between the lines that Jephthah and his daughter loved each other with a more than common love for that remote day.

Where there is an only child in a household, he or she is usually the object of great care and concern, and draws out the whole of their parents' affection. Too often the solitary child is idolized and is spoiled because of all the attention received. Furthermore, such a child misses a great deal in the formation of character, and the enjoyments of child life through the absence of brothers and sisters. When sickness or affliction overtakes the only child in the home, the anxiety of the parents is most acute. Cried the father of the demon-possessed boy, "Master, I beseech thee, look upon my son: for he is *mine only child*" (Luke 9:38). The widow at Nain had the anguish of seeing her "only son" carried to burial, but then raised again from the dead (Luke 7:12). Jairus had "one only daughter," who likewise died but was resurrected (Luke 8:42). God's only-begotten Son died for a lost world (John 3:16).

Jephthah's anguish over the fulfillment of his impetuous vow was accentuated by the fact that his daughter, whose young life was opening as a flower, was his only child. How he had guarded his only jewel, safeguarding her on every side so that her only outlook upon life was through her father! Her environment was that of the daughter of Jephthah, with her father as the representative of God in his capacity as Israel's deliverer – "He for God only, she for God in him." For a full treatment of Jephthah's vow and what actually happened to his daughter the reader is referred to the author's volume, *The Women of the Bible,* published by the Zondervan Publishing House, Grand Rapids. All that we are attempting in this sketch of Jephthah's

"... One fair daughter and no more,
The which he loved passing well,"

is to present her as an example of obedience for all children to emulate.

We certainly admire the faithfulness of Jephthah in not going back upon his vow, but his daughter's unquestioning acceptance of all that vow involved gives us a glimpse of obedience as perfect as any the world has known. She acted out to the limit the apostolic injunction of children obeying their parents. As the stroke of the vow fell upon her there was not the least whisper of revolt. In our age, too many children fail to understand the meaning of practical obedience. True, no false idea of the demand of God is laid upon girls today, yet they need to learn the gospel of obedience, and thus be in the noble line of sacrificial women of whom Jephthah's daughter was a pioneer. Obedience, such as hers, always means death to something for there can be no stepping into any kind of higher life except over a dead self.

Doubtless this daughter of old, with a nature fine and rare, felt that in obeying her father she was obeying the God he represented as a judge, and was magnificent in her calm self-control in the hour of surrender. What a heritage of pure womanhood Jephthah's daughter left for others to appropriate! Among the last words we have of Emily Bronte and which have been preserved by her sister Charlotte, we see her to be by her brave spirit a true sister of Jephthah's daughter –

No coward soul is mine,
No trembler in the world's storm-troubled sphere:
I see Heaven's glories shine,
And faith shines equal, arming me from fear.

There is not room for Death,
Nor atom that his might could render void,
Thou – Thou art Being and Breath,
And what Thou art may never be destroyed.

18. The Child Obed

We are seeing how sometimes fathers, and at other times, mothers, gave names to their children. But this is probably the only instance in which women neighbors named a baby on behalf of his parents. "The women, her [Naomi's] neighbours gave it a name . . . they called his name Obed (Ruth 4:17). Ruth, the Moabitess widow, had no children by her previous husband, Mahlon, the son of Naomi. In the land of Moab, Naomi was left alone, for she suddenly lost her children and husband. One is tempted to linger over every aspect of the "idyllic glimpse of home life in ancient Israel" which the Book of Ruth presents, but we abstain seeing that our main objective in these profiles is to concentrate on those Bible characters whose childhood is mentioned. What can be said is that the Book as a whole presents these aims –

(1) To show how a daughter of the hostile Moab obtained an honorable position among God's people by faithful love and devotion to Israel's God, in spite of the prohibition against the admission of a Moabite into the congregation of the Lord (Deut. 23:3).

(2) To enlarge upon the record of David's ancestry which is but meagerly sketched in I Samuel 16.

(3) To inculcate the duty of marriage on the part of the next of kin with a widow left childless.

(4) To show how a religious spirit may be carried unostentatiously into the conduct of daily life. (See *The Women of the Bible.)*

Coming to the marriage of Boaz and Ruth what impressed "the mighty man of wealth" was the kindness shown by Ruth in taking an old man for her second husband, and giving him a greater devotion than she had given to Mahlon and his mother (Ruth 3:10). Ruth forgot her own people and her father's house in Moab, and became grafted into the true Israel, and a partaker of the fatness of the olive tree. She became, as Jerome put it, "An Israelite not in race, but in mind; not in blood, but in faith; not by tribe, but by virtue and goodness." Although a stranger in the land of promise, Ruth came to wear the crown of faith and love, and as such was accepted and blessed of God and acknowledged in Israel as an ancestress of our blessed Lord. The women of Israel could speak of Ruth to Naomi as one better to her mother-in-law than "seven sons." What a testimony to have! A Gentile stranger by faith better than seven children of Abraham!

When Boaz redeemed the land that was Elimelech's, he took Ruth as his wife to raise up the name of the dead son of Elimelech and Naomi on his inheritance, and the offspring of this marriage was Obed. Whether there were more children we are not told. Let us enumerate the remarkable things that are recorded of Ruth's baby for whom Naomi his grandmother became nurse. Such was the good reputation Naomi herself had in Bethlehem that her neighbors said, "There is a son born to Naomi."

a. *His Name.* Why the women neighbors called Ruth's baby Obed we are not told. All that is said is that Naomi's "neighbours gave it a name, . . . and they called his name Obed." As such a fact is so carefully recorded there must have been a reason for the name, which means "a serving one," or "one who serves." Perhaps the name expressed the desire and hope of the friends of Naomi who had lost her husband and two sons, that the child would minister to her as the solace and support of her old age. As Wilkinson points out, the name "Obed" occurs in several compounds.

Obed-edom is the name of the Levite in whose house the Ark of God abode three months, and means, "Edom is serving," that is, "in a state of servitude," indicating that he was perhaps born at a time when some victory was gained over the Edomites.

Obadiah, meaning "servant of Jehovah," was the well-known name of the pious comptroller of Ahab's household, and of the prophet who proclaimed God's vengeance on Edom.

Ebed, which is nearly the same word as Obed, and has the same meaning is formed of Abdeel or Abdiel, meaning, "servant of God." This was the name chosen by John Milton for the single angel who, among the hosts of Satan, refused to join in his rebellion –

> "Among the faithless,
> faithful only he."

Allusion is made to the etymology of the name in the line supposed to be addressed to him from the heavenly throne,

> "Servant of God, well done;
> well hast thou fought."

Abdullah, "servant of Allah (God)," is a common name among the Arabs, and is borne by some celebrated personages in Mohammedan history, among whom was the father of Mohammed himself. It is akin to Abdiel.

When Ruth gave birth to her son by Boaz, the women said to Naomi, his grandmother, "Blessed be the Lord, which hath not left thee this day without a redeemer – kinsman – that his name may be famous in history." The last verse of Ruth shows how famous his name became, "Obed begat Jesse, and Jesse begat David." And the New Testament opens with the sentence, "The book of the generation of Jesus Christ, the son of David, the son of Abraham" (Matt. 1:1).

b. *His Mission.* Commendable things are recorded of the child of Boaz and Ruth. First of all, the coming of Obed meant that the line of Elimelech and Naomi would not, after all, become extinct, for in Obed they were not left without a kinsman. Then the birth of Ruth's child gave his grandmother a new lease on life, for Obed was as the restorer of Naomi's life and a nourisher of her old age. The margin has it, "to nourish thy gray hairs." Somehow, in her grandson, life began again for Naomi. Then she was not only dearly loved by her daughter-in-law, but Obed and his mother were better to Naomi than seven sons of her own. The bonds of love often prove stronger than those of nature. As prayer to God attended the marriage of Boaz and Ruth, so praise to Him attended the birth of their son (Ruth 4:11, 14).

Of the significance of the name Obed meaning, "a servant" or "a servant who worships," Matthew Henry suggests that the good and happy neighbors chose it "either in remembrance of the meanness and poverty of the mother, or in prospect of his being hereafter a servant, and very serviceable, to his grandmother." To the end Ruth was faithful to that sudden inspiration which told her to follow her widowed mother-in-law whom she loved into an unknown land, and she was rewarded when she became the mother of the child of Boaz, Obed, in whom she also became the ancestress of King David and of the Jesus, the Saviour of the world.

19. The Child Samson

What child is not fascinated with the life and exploits of Samson with his giant-like strength? So compelling is the story that Hollywood made a film of it. The prodigious power of this man who became the last Judge of Israel before Samuel was the "Hercules" among the Israelites being greatly feared and hated by the Philistines who had oppressed Israel for some forty years (Judg. 13). Actuated by personal vengeance, Samson seems to have been a strange champion for Jehovah and worthy of mention among the heroes of faith (Heb. 11:32). Then this mighty man who fought with his wits as well as his fists received a birthname corresponding to his muscular prowess. Samson means "son of the sun," or "sun-man," just as his home at Beth-shemesh means, "house of the sun." The Sun being the reservoir of strength in the solar system, Samson's name symbolizes his strength, just as the name Delilah, the woman who betrayed Samson, implies "treachery."

Unique as the life of Samson is among O.T. biographies, all that concerns us in this discussion of him are the recorded events of his birth — which are full of spiritual import for all parents anticipating the coming of children into their home. Not all parents know that the Bible offers them full directions as to the training of their children. With each child, and each of its separate needs, there is always need of a wisdom which parents of themselves do not possess, but which comes to them from above in response to believing prayer (Jas. 1:5). Such intercession is the secret of the effective training of the children we are responsible for. Each child is a gift of God as truly as the one He gave to Manoah and his wife, and, as with their child, must be reared for the service of God.

a. *Prediction of Samson's Birth.* Manoah and his wife were childless, and a supernatural being appeared to them predicting the birth of an unusual child, who would be a Nazarite to God from his birth and a deliverer of God's people. The days in which the barren couple lived were those of trouble as the result of the sin of the nation. Because of its evil in the sight of the Lord, the people were in bondage to the Philistines for forty years. The name of the man of the family of the Danites, Manoah, means, "rest," and expressed the yearning of the Israelites for rest from strife and servitude. As for Manoah's wife, although the Bible does not give us her name, *The Talmud* says that it was Zelelponi of the tribe of Judah, and that it means, "The shadow falls on me."

The redundancy in language with the announcement that Manoah's "wife was barren, and bare not" (Judg. 13:2), is common to the Bible and other forms of ancient literature (See Gen. 11:30). "I am indeed a widow woman, and mine husband is dead" (II Sam. 14:1). Within such phrases we have both a positive and negative statement, as further seen in the declaration, "Thou shalt live, and not die." A supernatural being appeared to Zelelponi with the prediction that she was to become a mother. "Thou shalt conceive, and bear a son." Telling her husband the glad, good news, she revealed that she was so struck by the majesty of the angel in human form, that she omitted to ask him where he came from. "A man of God came unto me, and his countenance was like the countenance of an angel of God, very terrible" (See Matt. 28:3, 4).

Receiving the heartwarming prediction from his wife, Manoah prayed that the same angelic messenger might return to them both, not to confirm his prophecy, but to teach them how to educate "the child that shall be born." In answer to his prayer the angel returned. Zelelponi had said of the angel of God, "neither told he me his name." When Manoah faced the august visitor he did not know that he was an angel of the Lord, and curious-like asked, "What is thy name?" The reply he got was surely a revelation of the Lord Himself. "Why askest thou thus after my name, seeing it is secret?" (Judg. 13:18). While "secret" is an adjective, and not the actual name of the angel, the fact is that this is the same word given as "Wonderful" in connection with Christ in Isaiah 9:5. "The angel did wondrously" when he ascended in a flame from the altar upon which Manoah had offered a burnt offering to the Lord.

Such was the impact of this wonderful sight upon the godly couple that they said, "We shall surely die, because we have seen God" (Judg. 13: 22).

b. *Preparation for Samson's Birth.* Along with the intimation of the birth of a child there were specific instructions as to how the parents should prepare themselves for the coming of the predicted child, impressing thereby on them as well as on the nation the separated character of the promised son (Judg. 16:17). He was to be a Nazarite from his mother's womb. The Nazarite vow involved abstention from all intoxicating liquor and unclean food and for a man uncut hair (Num. 6). These requirements indicated separation to special purity and holiness and were enforced upon Zelelponi, for the coming Nazarite child must have a Nazarite mother. The spiritual training of her child would come not so much by lip as by life. The life of self-denial, consecration, and prayer form the most effective preparation for parenthood.

When the angel appeared to Zelelponi the second time, and she ran to fetch Manoah to meet him, seeing the Angel asked, "Now let thy words (as to the birth of the child) come to pass. How shall we order the child, and how shall we do unto him?" Literally, when he prayed to be taught what to do for the child about to be born, he was asking for wisdom and guidance to train the child in Nazarite ways. The angel gave no definite rules as to how Manoah should educate the child, but simply reiterated the command about Zelelponi practicing the outward signs of dedication to God.

God's answer to Manoah's plea, "How shall we order the child?" was, in effect to say, "As you live, you train. Live a Nazarite, holy to the Lord, and your child will be a Nazarite unto God, a deliverer of My people Israel." In a way we cannot explain in the holy time of mystery, when mother and child are still one before the latter's birth, influences from the mother's spirit pass into the child. Solemn, therefore, was the warning of the angel, "Of all that I said unto the woman let her beware" (Judg. 13:13). God loves to answer the cry of godly parents for guidance as to how to prepare their children aright for His service.

The name of the parents' God is still Wonderful. He opens their eyes to see how wonderful He is, and what wondrous things He can accomplish in the lives of their children. Wonderful is His love – His ways – His work, and also wonderful in what He can do for parents and through them for their children. Praying Manoah and Zelelponi give us a picture of the way in which husband and wife lovingly help each other to all that concerns their children. Blessed is the fellowship of love and faith, of prayer and worship between husband and wife, to which the coming and the training of a child can lead!

c. *The Performance of Samson's Birth.* How explicit is the phrase, "And the woman bare a son" (Judg. 13:24), but behind it was the overwhelming joy of a barren wife who, by godly living, had prepared the way for his coming. A few things are said about the baby born to Zelelponi –

"The woman . . . called his name Samson."

Added to what we have already said about this name in the rendering of Jerome who gave its meaning as "strength of the sun" or "sunny." The combination of "the sun" and "strength" are natural. (See Judg. 5: 31; Ps. 19:5, 6.) The rabbis say that Samson was "named after the name of God, who is called Sun and Shield of Israel" (Ps. 84:11). The renowned scholar, Ewald, connects the name Samson to an Egyptian root, and makes it mean, "Servant of God," in reference to his being a Nazarite.

"The child grew, and the Lord blessed him."

Because as a young man Samson had enormous strength, he must have been born a strong, healthy baby, and as the years went by strength and courage were multiplied to him. In his moving confession to Delilah, Samson seems to suggest that his strength was in his uncut hair, but that if it were cut, his strength would leave him (Judg. 16:17). When his hair grew again, his massive strength returned (Judg. 16:22-30). "But the hair of Samson was no magical amulet," comments Ellicott. "It was only a sign of dedication to God. While he kept his vow the strength remained; it only departed when the vow was shamefully broken." The long, strong hair of Samson testified to the divine ownership of his life, and of a consecration to God by a wholly special calling.

"The Spirit of the Lord began to move him at times."

When the angel appeared to Zelelponi, Manoah's wife, and announced her coming motherhood, he said of the child, that after his birth "He shall *begin* to deliver Israel out of the hand of the Philistines" (Judg. 13:5), which we can combine with "began to move him." As soon as he was grown, Samson experienced the vehement and overwhelming impulses to courageous deeds on behalf of Israel which occasionally possessed him (Judg. 14:6; 15:14; 16:20). Alas! Samson's sexual weakness robbed him of the privilege of achieving a complete deliverance for Israel.

Between Samson and his parents there seems to have been close fellowship, although they were much displeased when their God-promised and given child took one of the daughters of the Philistines for a wife (Judg. 14: 3, 5, 16). Probably his father and mother were dead by the time Samson was blinded by the Philistines, and he was avenged of his two eyes when, with the return of his former strength, he destroyed the temple of Dagon and slew more Philistines at his death than during his life. They buried his mangled body in the burial ground of his father, Manoah. He was born with great potential, but during the twenty years he judged Israel with indomitable energy and power Samson was guilty of sinning against his Nazarite vow. However, the wonderful, pardoning God who gave him to his parents, restored to him the years the locusts had eaten, and at his end, as John Milton expressed it –

"Samson hath quit himself like Samson, and heroically has finished a life heroic."

20. The Child Samuel

Another Bible figure whose childhood never fails to arrest the attention of children is Samuel. Perhaps his story is the most favorite one that boys and girls like to hear and read about, for he is conspicuous among Bible children who were called by God. Because there is nothing under the sun that is more beautiful than piety in a child, "the child Samuel" never loses his charm for young and old alike. Martin Luther in his gentler moments would dwell with great tenderness on the boyhood of Samuel because he found in him what he longed for in his own small sons, and in all boys. The secret of how Samuel became the boy and then the man he became is revealed in his ready, unfailing reply to the voice of God. The early piety of Samuel demonstrates the truth that the highest honor of God belongs to those who begin as young as Samuel began to serve Him, and continue serving him through a long life. It was this characteristic feature of God-awareness in Hannah's precious child that inspired one of the finest hymns for all the children of God to sing –

O give me Samuel's ear,
The open ear, O Lord,
Alive and quick to hear
Each whisper of Thy Word;
Like him to answer at Thy call,
And to obey Thee first of all.

O give me Samuel's heart,
A lowly heart that waits,
Where in Thy house Thou art,
Or watches at Thy gates;
By day and night, a heart that still
Moves at the breathing of Thy will.

O give me Samuel's mind,
A sweet unmurmuring faith,
Obedient and resigned
To Thee in life and death;
That I may read, with child-like eyes,
Truths that are hidden from the wise.

There are various aspects of the childhood of Samuel that parents and teachers can emphasize and illustrate as they seek to lead the young around them to know the Lord. In many ways, this child of the sanctuary is a model for all boys – and girls – to copy.

a. *He Was Earnestly Desired and Prayed for* (I Sam. 1:5-8, 17) Elkanah, the father of Samuel, was a godly man who had two wives, and as a polygamist was responsible for the envy and grief marring his home life. One wife, Peninnah, had many sons and daughters (I Sam. 1:2, 4), but Hannah the other wife, had no children. "The Lord had shut her womb," meaning that there was a divine purpose for her barrenness. The record says that "Elkanah loved Hannah," but nothing is said about his love for his other wife, Peninnah. To Hannah, her husband gave "a worthy portion" or, as the margin puts it, "a double portion." This one portion for two persons was an expression of Elkanah's deep love for his childless wife, as if to suggest, "Thou art as dear to me as if thou hadst borne a child." Was he not better to her "than ten sons"? (I Sam. 1:8).

But while Hannah's husband was dear to her, she longed for a child of her own to clasp to her heart. Every time she looked at the other wife's healthy brood of children, her yearning for children she could care for was intensified. Then her grief was accentuated over the way Peninnah taunted her because of her childless condition. As Hannah's "adversary," Peninnah angered her, and caused her to fret. This jealousy and malice would never have arisen if Elkanah had only observed the divine law of one man for one woman. But what might have been a quiet, affectionate and God-fearing household was poisoned by the sin of polygamy. To add salt to the wound, on the yearly visit to the sanctuary in Shiloh, Peninnah took the occasion of taunting Hannah because of her barrenness.

The cruel treatment of the fertile wife for the sterile one caused the latter to weep and lose her desire to eat. But bitter of soul, she found her way to the mercy seat – "She prayed unto the Lord," and saturated her supplication with tears. We can image how all her pent-up feelings gushed out in the heartfelt prayer she offered. Out of the depths she cried to the Lord in continuous prayer, for the phrase "she continued praying" (I Sam. 1:12), implies that she "multiplied to pray." Her fervent prayer, however, was not audible for "she spake in her heart." Her lips moved but no words were uttered, and Eli wrongly judged the weeping, worshiping woman as one who was drunk. Although Eli the high priest, had falsely accused Hannah, she answered him with all due reverence and humility. The old man, sorry for insulting a blameless woman, promised Hannah that what she wished so ardently should be hers, and Hannah asked the aged priest to pray for her at his temple ministrations.

What a delightful touch the historian then gives us. "She went her way, and *did eat,* and her countenance was no more sad." Hannah experienced the composing influence of prayer. Having cast her heavy burden upon the Lord, her own grieved spirit was relieved of its load, and returning to the family feast she ate her meal with a cheerful heart, confident that God had heard her prayer and that He would answer accordingly. Having asked, she believed she would receive. "The Lord remembered her," and the prayed-for son was nestling in her loving arms about a year later.

b. *He Was Given to the Lord Before He Was Born* (I Sam. 1:9-11). Not only did Hannah pray that she might be blessed with a son, "Give unto thine handmaid a man child," but she vowed a vow that if God gave her a son, she would give him back to Him for service in His cause "all the days of his life." Actually, Hannah made two promises. The first one was that the son she longed for would be surrendered to God, but she never knew what a famous prophet and great reformer he would become. The second promise she gave regarding her yet unborn son was that he should be a Nazarite all his life. From previous Scriptures like Numbers 6:5 and Judges 13:5, we learn that the Nazarite vow including three things is symbolic of separation from sin and separation unto God –

Abstinence from all intoxicating drinks.
Allowing the hair to grow,
Avoidance of all ceremonial defilement by corpses even of the nearest kin.

The first requirement typified the absence of all sensual indulgence which cloud the mind and render one unfit for prayer and service.

The second injunction regarding uncut hair declared to all that the owner of the untouched hair was a consecrated man determined to be separate from the world, and to devote the whole strength and fullness of life to God's work.

The third stricture indicated that the person under the vow renounced all moral defilement, being willing to despise anything that would stain and soil the life yielded to God's service.

Samuel, after his birth, observed the vow, and became as *The Talmud* describes, "a perpetual Nazarite." As we know, the prophet throughout his long life never wavered in the dedication his mother had vowed for him.

Having received her child from the Lord, although he was only "young" (I Sam. 1:24), Hannah brought him to Eli, and said, "For this child I prayed; and the Lord hath given me my petition which I asked of him." How the aged priest must have been delighted to see Hannah again and to take her child in his arms! Eli must have been overwhelmed when he heard the godly, glad mother say, "I have lent him to the Lord; as long as he liveth he shall be lent to the Lord." Then comes a remarkable touch, "And he" – that is, the young child Samuel – "worshipped the Lord there." Ellicott comments that by this act "he puts his own child-seal to his mother's gift of himself to God."

Every Christian mother as she looks into the face of her first-born, so eagerly and prayerfully anticipated, feels that the love and joy of her heart can find no better way of expressing itself than in the surrender of her child to the Lord, to be His as long as he or she lives. It should be true of each one of us, "As long as he liveth he shall be given to the Lord." There is a sense in which the child is already His, for as the Creator, God fashioned the babe and gave it life. But by the surrender by the parents, the child becomes doubly His. Not only so, but the child so dedicated becomes doubly our own, and this double act becomes the link of a most blessed friendship and intercourse between God and the parents. God needs children for His temple, and He has a place for each child in it. Are you praying that as a consecrated parent you may have a consecrated child or children who will hear the same voice the boy Samuel heard, and who will respond in child-like simplicity as he did, "Speak, Lord, for thy servant heareth"?

We often say that God is no man's debtor! Well, He amply rewarded Hannah for the lifelong loan of her son, as her Magnificat reveals. "The barren hath born seven; and she that hath many children is waxed feeble" (I Sam. 2:5). As Eli accepted the child Samuel for service in the Temple, he blessed Elkanah and Hannah his parents saying, "The Lord give thee seed of this woman for the loan which is lent to the Lord" (I Sam. 2: 20). And He paid her back with large interest for three more sons and also two daughters came to bless her home (I Sam. 2:20, 21). In the Song of Hannah inspired by her own experiences, the phrase, "The barren hath born seven children" is used as an evidence of the full number of the divine blessing in the gift of children. (See Ruth 4:15; Jer. 15:9.) The Jews have a curious legend to the effect that for each boy child born to Hannah, two of Peninnah's died as a judgment for her cruel treatment of Hannah through her years of barrenness.

c. *He Was Named by His Mother* (I Sam. 1:20). The history of names may be an intriguing subject, but the naming of a baby often means the expenditure of more time than the gathering of the baby's layette. Parents rarely decide on their children's name capriciously. Anyone can name a baby, but too often it is not done well. To give a child an absurd or insignificant name is like tying a stone around its neck. What must be remembered is the fact that the name chosen will be a part of the child's identity for life, and affects its personality and popularity – especially when school begins.

Hannah called her son, Samuel, to commemorate a deep, spiritual experience. She earnestly prayed for a child, and God gave her one, and the name she gave him means "asked of God." Hannah herself explained its significance, "Because I asked him of the Lord." What must be borne in mind is that the name Samuel was in existence long before Hannah adopted it for her much-prayed-for son. In the Hebrew it is the same as Shemuel, one of the commissioners appointed by Moses to divide the land of Canaan (Num. 34:20). Shemuel, meaning "heard of God," is identical with Ishmael, meaning, "God will hear" and with Simeon, meaning, "a hearing" or "accepting," that is, on the part of God.

Hannah, then, chose this name for her child with the express and avowed object of recording the fact that he was born in answer to prayer. (See under *Asked of God* in our previous chapter.) Its implication "heard of God" perfectly represents the sentiment contained in Hannah's statement, "Because I have asked him of Jehovah." The name Shealtiel, used after her day as the name of the son of King Jeconiah, means something similar, "I have asked of God." Further, the transition from "asking" to that of "lending" is conveyed in the words uttered at his birth.

"The God of Israel grant thee thy petition *(shēlā-thek)* that thou hast asked *(shā-alte)* of him."

When Hannah brought Samuel to Eli to present him to the Lord, she said, "For this child I prayed and the Lord hath given me my petition *(she-ē-lathi)* which I asked *(sha-alti)* of him; therefore also I have *lent (hishilti)* him to the Lord; as long as he liveth he shall be *lent (shā-al)* unto the Lord."

As can be seen, the terms used are conjugational forms of the verb *shā-al*, meaning "to ask." The combination of asking and lending is to be found in the name Saul, or "Sha-ul," meaning "asked for," or "borrowed," and hence "lent." Saul of Tarsus was "from his mother's womb separated" by God for His service, and called "by his grace" (Gal. 1:15); and designated as one "separated unto the gospel of God." It is one thing to have a good name, and often a different matter altogether to have a character corresponding to that name. A soldier who had committed a crime bore the same name as his commander, Alexander the Great. Brought before the great leader, he was asked his name: "Alexander, sir." Then said the famous Alexander,"Go, change your name or your character."

d. *He Ministered Before the Lord.* That the child Samuel had a godward tendency is seen in the way his piety is described. "He worshipped the Lord there" (I Sam. 1:28). "The child did minister unto the Lord before Eli the priest" (I Sam. 2:11; 3:1). "Samuel ministered before the Lord, being a child, girded with a linen ephod" (I Sam. 2:18). Being set apart for lifelong service before the Lord, young though he was, Samuel wore priestly dress – the ephod being the official garment of a priest: "The child Samuel grew on, and was in favour both with the Lord, and also with men" (I Sam. 2:26; 3:19). None of the divine words from the lips of this youthful priest and prophet fell to the ground. Although he grew up in dark days of sin and shame, the young Samuel stood firm; his early life being a perpetual protest against surrounding covetousness and iniquity.

We must be careful not to misinterpret the phrase, "Now Samuel did not yet know the Lord, neither was the word of the Lord yet revealed unto him" (I Sam. 3:7). The latter phrase qualifies the first. God called the boy three times but he was ignorant only of the fact that it was God who had called him and not Eli. Further, there are two kinds of knowledge expressed by two different words. One word is used for knowing about a person, the other word for knowing the person himself. As a Britisher, I know all about Queen Elizabeth II, but I do not know her in person. Mine has never been the honor of meeting and coming to know her. A child knows about his mother – better still, he knows her. His is not the cold and distant knowledge, but a close and warm knowledge because the child can clasp her close, and say, "You are my mother!" From his godly mother, Samuel had learned about God, but in the Temple he came to know Him personally, and soon came to an understanding of God's will and word for "the Lord revealed himself to Samuel in Shiloh by the word of the Lord" (I Sam. 3:21).

How the heart of Hannah must have been filled with gratitude as she saw her first-born become a consecrated son, and be made the recipient of the divine word so rare in those days (I Sam. 3:1)! Coleridge, the Christian poet affirmed, "My faith in Christianity is bound up with my mother's child, and with the earliest remembered tones of her blessed voice." Samuel's intimacy with God began in the Temple when he heard God's voice. At first the boy did not recognize the speaker. Had he known it was God speaking to him, he might have been afraid, but graciously God imitated the tone and accent of Eli's voice, and Samuel took it for the voice of the gentle Eli who was too gentle to speak harshly to his own erring sons.

"The Lord called Samuel . . . and he ran to Eli" (I Sam. 3:3-6). The child-prophet was awakened by a voice calling his name, and naturally he thought it was his half-blind master who had summoned him. Three times this happened, and then Eli knew that Samuel had had no dream. "Eli perceived that the Lord had called the child." Eli told his devoted pupil to go to his chamber, and if the voice should call him by name that it would not be his voice but that of the invisible King calling him, and that he should answer,

> "Speak, Lord; for thy servant heareth."

This time the name was repeated, "Samuel, Samuel" (I Sam. 3:10), such repetition implying divine emphasis and urgency. That God loves holiness in children is manifested in the way His voice spoke directly to Samuel, and young though he was, he immediately obeyed that voice.

Samuel's obedience to the call of the Eternal was prompt, hearty and lifelong. Although as a prophet he lived long, and in power and intellect became a spiritual giant, Samuel was always in heart a child, saying night and day, "Speak, Lord; for thy servant heareth." To benefit from the radio one must "listen in," and listening became a precious part of Samuel's close fellowship with God. "Speak, Lord; for thy servant is listening." Later on in his life, when Samuel became the famous prophet, priest, and judge of Israel, and the people clamored for a king as a substitute we read that "the Lord had told Samuel in his ear a day before Saul came" (I Sam. 9:15). Literally, this phrase means, "The Lord uncovered the ear of Samuel" to whisper the word about the deliverance of His people. The image suggests the pushing aside of the ringlets of Nazarite hair, as well as the headdress, in order more conveniently and confidentially to whisper the message. "This is one of the few more direct intimations in the sacred records of one of the ways in which the Spirit of God communicated divine thoughts to the human spirit."

The child Samuel will always remain as the model of early piety, enabling him to be an example of true service for God, and of perseverance in such service. He was about eight or ten years old when his mother took him to the Temple and left him there, and as he was probably about ninety years of age when he died, Samuel continued serving God until the end of his life (I Sam. 25:1). Boys and girls who begin to serve God when they are young, and learn to persevere in spite of all difficulties, become conspicuous in His cause. It was the grace of God which made Samuel pious when he was a child, and which enabled him to continue serving God through the years of his long life. And it is because the same divine grace can do the same for any boy or girl, that those of us who have any contact with children, whether in home, church, or school should strive in every possible way to win them for the Saviour while they are young and tender and undamaged by sin and the world.

A sad ending to our coverage of Samuel's childhood years will not be deemed out of order when it is remembered that godly though he was, he came to have two sons of his own who were most ungodly, even though Samuel had made them judges over Israel. Trained by him to share his high duties, since the infirmities of old age began to make his hard life more burdensome, Samuel had to have the anguish of seeing the honors and dignities he had earned, pass from his house for ever. Samuel called his first-born son Joel – a divine name meaning, "Jehovah is God." His second son he named Abiah, which means, "Jehovah is my Father"; but both of Samuel's sons belied the honored names they bore. Let the record of these unworthy sons of a most worthy father speak for itself – "Samuel's sons walked not in his ways, but turned aside after lucre, and took bribes, and perverted judgment" (I Sam. 8:3).

It was the corruption of these sons that disgusted the people of Israel, and brought the elders to Samuel with the demand that the theocracy should cease, and that as a people they become a monarchy. "Make us a king." Samuel, the long-respected prophet-judge, was sorely displeased, but he carried the matter to his God-Friend who comforted the old man by telling him that his rejection by the people was directed not so much against him, as against the King of heaven Himself.

21. The Child Ichabod (I Sam. 4:19-22).

Both Eli and Samuel shared a common heartbreak. Godly though this priest and prophet were, they both had children who did not know the Lord; and who, by their scandalous conduct, contradicted all their honored fathers had stood for through the long years of their service for God. While parental sanctity can greatly influence children in the home grace does not run in the blood. Although parents seek to fear God and to walk in His ways, their relationship with Him is no guarantee that their children are safe in the fold. Each individual has a personal responsibility, and is saved or lost according to his own attitude toward God and His requirements.

Often children reared in a religious home throw off all restraint when youth is reached, and walk no longer in the ways of their God-fearing parents. But the sad tragedy of the sons of Eli and also of Samuel was that they continued to hold high religious offices in the Temple – offices their godly fathers represented – and at the same time were unbelievers whose unbelief resulted in moral worthlessness. Eli's two sons, Hophni and Phinehas, are described as "sons of Belial." While it would seem from Paul's reference, that "Belial" was an idol, or the personification of evil (II Cor. 6:15), the word as used in connection with Eli's sons was not the name of some pagan deity, but simply means "worthlessness," being employed in this way several times in the Books of Samuel. Hophni and Phinehas were "sons of worthlessness," good-for-nothing men, just as the sons of Samuel were (I Sam. 8:1-3).

It was to the boy Samuel, as a Temple assistant to aged Eli, that God revealed the solemn truth that He would judge Eli because he condoned the sacrilegious conduct of his two sons. "I will judge his house [Eli's] for ever for the iniquity which he knoweth; because his sons made themselves vile, and he restrained them not," or "he frowned not upon them" (I Sam. 3:13). An indulgent father, Eli did not have the courage to remove his sons from the high office they were prostituting by their profligacy. When Eli demanded from the lad Samuel what God had revealed to him, he told Eli all God had said, hiding nothing from him (I Sam. 3: 11-18). Learning of the terrible verdict, Eli, thoroughly devoted to God Himself, accepted without a murmur the divine judgment upon himself for his foolish partiality for his sons, and upon their unholy conduct. As an old man – Eli was 98 when he died (I Sam. 4:15) – he seemed to be as a puppet in the hands of his godless sons. So, having sown to the wind, in his last days he reaped the whirlwind.

Judgment soon overtook Hophni and Phinehas, for in the battle between Israel and the Philistines Israel suffered a heavy defeat, losing some 4,000 of her men (I Sam. 4:2). Thinking that the presence of the Ark of the covenant would save them from further slaughter, the two sons of Eli – who were its guardians – brought it to the camp, but Israel had no longer the unseen help of Him for whom the Ark stood. Another battle ensued, and this time "there fell of Israel 30,000 footmen. And the ark of God was taken" (I Sam. 4:10, 11a). Predicted judgment upon the sons of Eli was fulfilled for "Hophni and Phinehas, were slain" (verse 11). Poor, blind Eli, hearing the tragic news that his sons had died in the great slaughter, and that the Ark had been taken by idolaters, the old man's heart broke, and falling off his seat by a gate, he broke his neck and died after having judged Israel for 40 years (I Sam. 4: 14-18).

Such a record is necessary for an understanding of the name of Ichabod – the child whom his father and grandfather never saw – the child whom his mother died in bringing to birth. The wife of Phinehas was about to have a baby when her husband was killed, and hearing the news of Israel's defeat, the Ark taken, and the death of her husband and father-in-law, doubtless added to her birth pains and contributed to her death as her son was born. Women attending her tried to console her by saying, "Fear not; for thou hast borne a son" (I Sam. 4:20), but somehow her heart was not in what they said, "Neither did she regard it." Her husband's bloody end on the field of battle, or news of the swift, fatal end of her father-in law, did not affect her as much as the news of the Ark being taken by Israel's enemies did. Hers was a deep love for God and the Tabernacle with its sacred contents, and as it has been remarked, "The wife of this deeply corrupt man shows how penetrated the whole people then was with the sense of the value of its covenant with God."

As the nameless widow died she named her son *I-chabod*, meaning, "Where is the glory?" or "There is no glory." She herself gave the significance of such a name, "The glory is departed from Israel: for the ark of God is taken" (verse 22). The first syllable "I" is followed by "chabod," and the "I" can suggest the query,

"Where?" – "chabod" means "not glory" that is, "there is no glory." The "I" can also stand for an exclamation of bitter sorrow, "Alas!" The name then could be translated, "Alas! the glory." "Where is the glory?"; the answer is, "It is nowhere." Such a sorrowful name then was a memorial of disaster, being given, like so many others by mothers who died in childbirth, and who had no need of the congratulations of surrounding friends in such an hour of anguish. We cannot do better than conclude this brief notice with the observation of Wilkinson written well over 100 years ago in his great work on *Personal Names in the Bible* –

> We cannot fail to perceive in this affecting record the signs of the deep and spiritual piety of the wife of Phinehas. Great as was her personal and domestic affliction, it was not the trouble that weighed most heavily upon her soul. She was the wife of a bad man and faithful husband, just cut off in the midst of his sins. She was suffering bodily anguish, and was at the point of death. But, evidently, her thoughts were not so much occupied with her own particular distresses as with the great calamity which had befallen her country, the bereavement sustained by the Church, the dishonor done to the name, and cause, and service of her God. The symbol of God's covenant with His people, the pledge and token of His presence, the depository of His law, was, in her estimation, the true glory of Israel; and that glory was dearer to her than a mother's joys, dearer than life.
>
> She mourned not for herself, but for the anticipated spiritual desolation of her fellow-believers, her fellow-worshipers, and her children. *I-chabod* – Where is the glory? The name thus bequeathed by the dying mother, heard day by day in the lullaby of the orphan child, would be a perpetual wail in the great princely and priestly household, to be taken up and re-echoed throughout the dismayed and sorrowing tribes of Israel. And still, at this day, when sin, or error, or whatever other spiritual evil there may be, has invaded the sanctuary of God, or corrupted a Christian community, or vitiated a sacred cause, this is the all-expressive word in which the faithful utter their lamentation over the fallen – *Ichabod!*

22. The Child Solomon

King David, father of Israel's most colorful king, is one of the notable characters of the Bible of whose childhood we have no record. Our first glimpse of him is as a youth when he was anointed by Samuel as successor to King Saul. The youngest of Jesse's eight sons, David was not present when the prophet, guided by God, made his selection of the young shepherd. As a baby, David must have been a lovely child for when Samuel saw him, "he was ruddy . . . of a beautiful countenance, and goodly to look to" (I Sam. 16:12). Yet God did not choose young David because of his attractive countenance but because of what He saw in the godly lad's heart (I Sam. 16:7). The divine voice warned Samuel that the external advantages of mere beauty of face and form were no evidence of true greatness. From the hour of his choice, the Spirit of the Lord was upon Jesse's youngest son.

When David began as the sweet psalmist of Israel he could write: "O Lord God: thou art my trust from my youth" (Ps. 71:5). As the future king of Israel, he derived his early lessons of wisdom from the venerable Samuel whose last years were spent training his pupil in poetry and music and in the things of God. The events of David's life are familiar to young and old alike. As the result of his triumph over the giant, Goliath, David married King Saul's daughter, Michal, who had "no child unto the day of her death." In our previous chapter under the section, *Born to Die,* we dealt with David's child born as the result of his seduction of another man's wife. By his many wives David had many children. His much-loved rebellious Absalom was his third son by Maacah, daughter of Talmai, King of Geshur. The tragic death of this favorite son of great charm and beauty was a source of deep grief to the fond and aged father. When David heard the sad news he forgot he was the king and became the tenderhearted, grief-stricken father expressing in tender language a lament that was to become a classic in literature, as well as a model for the expression of the feelings of parents for wayward children down the ages (II Sam. 18:33).

The children born to David in Hebron by different wives are given in II Samuel 3:2-5, and the sons and daughters by wives and concubines from Jerusalem are stated in II Samuel 5:13-15. Of all his children, only those he had by Bathsheba have we facts of their childhood. The first, deeply-loved by David, died shortly after birth, and gave rise to a remarkable witness to a life of consciousness beyond the grave, and of the future recognition of those loved on earth. Some time after the death of this nameless baby David and Bathsheba were comforted as another son was given them, a son whom the Lord loved (II Sam. 12:24), and whom the Lord Himself named "Solomon." "The word of the Lord came to David, saying . . . Behold, a son shall be born to thee, who shall be a man of rest; and I will give him rest from all his enemies round about: for his name shall be Solomon, and I will give peace and quietness unto Israel in his days" (I Chron. 22:9).

Nathan named Solomon "Jedidiah" meaning, "Beloved of the Lord," but such a name never came into use as a personal title. It was intended to do no more than express the divine acceptance of Solomon. "He called his name Jedidiah, because of the Lord" (II Sam. 12:25), that is, because the Lord loved him. These two birth names deserve, we think, a closer consideration.

a. *Solomon.* Solomon is one of the sacramental names of Scripture, which names have a high degree of significance being "names imposed either immediately by God Himself or under His inspiration, in association with some promise, or covenant, or declaration of His will, as to the character, destiny, or mission of those to whom they were given." After Moses, no name of a strictly sacramental nature occurs until we come to the birth and naming of Solomon.

Solomon was not only the heir of the royalty of David, but when, by divine command, he was so named, it was to denote his character and that of his reign. Thus, Solomon means "a little man of peace," or "peaceable." God said, "His name shall be Solomon *(Shelomo),* and I will give peace *(Shalom)* and quietness unto Israel in his days" (I Chron. 22:9). Such a promise, given and sealed, was symbolized in the name God appointed for David's successor. It was a promise amply fulfilled, for during Solomon's reign, "he had peace on all sides around him" (I Kings 4:24). The name was likewise a prophetic pledge of a far more blessed and more enduring peace than that which Israel experienced under Solomon. The psalmist, while alluding to Solomon in connection with the blessing of peace, takes a leap forward and depicts One who will come, far greater than Solomon, and who will exercise universal dominion as the true Prince of peace (Ps. 72).

b. *Jedidiah.* This comparatively private name which Nathan gave to the child of David and Bathsheba is mentioned only once in Scripture, yet all it implied was never forgotten. Jedidiah means, "beloved of Jehovah," and Nehemiah in later days could say that, "among many nations was there no king like him, who was beloved of his God" (Neh. 13:26). Jedidiah, a name preferable for dignity and sanctity, is singularly expressive of divine favor. Solomon was the name given in obedience to a divine command issued before the royal infant's birth, and took precedence over Jedidiah through priority of announcement as the child's ordinary and historical name. It is also said that "Solomon loved the Lord."

Jedidiah, however, being a name of a more personal nature, was not used or proclaimed publicly, but cherished in domestic use and likely regarded as possessing a peculiarly hallowed and mystic character. It is, in fact, a name akin to David his father, which means "beloved" or "darling." Jadid – the Hebrew term for David – only expressed the affection of an earthly parent, and was so chosen by Jesse for his youngest son. But Mah, meaning, "Jehovah" added to Jadid indicated that David's child was the object of parental love to God Himself. Did He not say concerning David's heir, "I will be his father, and he shall be my son"?

Although Solomon came to great eminence as a king, there is no evidence that as a child he was a prodigy. When he came to the throne God offered him any gift of his choice, and all he asked for was an understanding heart which was granted in abundant measure, hence, his famous judgments and prodigious accomplishments (I Kings 3:2-28; 9:1-10). Through Solomon the line passed to the Messiah, and so, in the Davidic covenant of kingship as given by Matthew. Solomon finds honorable mention as the son born in an honorable way of "her that had been the wife of Uriah" (Matt. 1:1-7), who, in spite of her past shame was not excluded from being included in the Messiah's line of ancestry.

23. The Child of a Harlot (I Kings 3:16-28)

At the conclusion of this remarkable specimen of Solomon's wisdom involving the settling of a dispute between companion harlots as to the parenthood of a baby boy accidentally smothered to death at night we read that, "All Israel heard of the judgment which the king had judged; and they feared the king: for they saw that the wisdom of God was in him, to do judgment" (I Kings 3:28). The baby in question lived for only three days, and can be added to the list, *Born to Die*, in our previous chapter. Solomon had just prayed for wisdom telling God that he was "but a little child" (I Kings 3:7).

The king was not a child in respect to age for he had reached manhood (I Kings 2:9), but in understanding to rule as sovereign of the people. About twenty years old at this time, he was raw and inexperienced in matters of government, but God answered his prayer and gave Solomon wisdom not only to qualify him for the administration of justice, and the government of a kingdom, but also to attain general knowledge of nature. In the sordid story before us he reveals the intuitive sagacity God made him the recipient of. A seemingly hopeless situation faced the king, but appealing to the principles of human nature a solution to the problem of conflicting testimony was reached. It is said that, "the modern history of the East abounds with anecdotes of judicial cases, in which the decision given was the result of an experiment similar to this of Solomon upon the natural feelings of the contending parties."

The parties in question were two harlots who had become mothers about the same time. These two fallen women lived in a house together, where each of them gave birth to a son within three days of one another. One of the unmarried women "overlaid her child," or suffocated it, and in the darkness of the night exchanged the dead child with the living child of her companion who was soon aware of the switch and appealed to the king for justice. If the case had been brought before a lower court and the judges were unable to determine who was the mother of the living child, then it came before Solomon who listened patiently to the mothers both of whom were vehement in their claim and deeply concerned about it. Neither would own the dead baby.

Having heard what both women had to say, Solomon sums up the evidence and then orders the living child to be cut in half by a sword, and the two halves divided between the contenders. This verdict proved an effectual discovery of the truth. To find out the true mother, Solomon could not see which one the child loved best, for since he was only a babe of three days there was no recognition. So he had to find out which mother truly loved the child. Both women showed motherly affection, but sincerity could be proved only by putting the baby's life in danger – which Solomon resolved to do. One wonders whether he had discerned beforehand by the faces of the women, their way of speaking and grief which of the two was the mother of the living child?

The woman who knew in her own heart that the dead child, and not the living one was hers, yet contended for the crying infant, and standing upon a point of honor was content with the decision of the judge to have the child cut in two.

The other woman who, with maternal instinct, knew the child was hers, rather than see him cut in two, gave him up to her adversary. Feelingly she cried out, "O, my Lord, give her the living child," which cry meant, "Let me see it hers, rather than not see it at all." Such an act of surrender proved her love. Solomon knew that she was not the careless mother responsible for the death of her baby, but the true mother who, having compassion on the son of her womb could not bear to see him die in such a terrible way. That settled it for Solomon who said of the child's own mother, "Give her the living child, and in no wise slay it: she is the mother thereof" (verse 27). Men might call Solomon's handling of this case, "a touch of genius" – the Bible calls it "the wisdom of God" (I Kings 3:28).

24. The Child Hadad (I Kings 11:14-22)

Because of the way Solomon came to traffic in wives and concubines who were of heathen origin, his heart became divided between the true God and the idols for whom he built shrines. For this the breaking up of his kingdom was predicted, and toward the end of his reign the Lord stirred up adversaries to trouble him. Among these was Hadad the Edomite, of whom it is said that he was only "a little child" when he was carried away and thus preserved from the terrible slaughter when Joab cut off every male child and man in Edom. Hadad was the last descendant of the royal house of Edom, and escaped from the slaughter of his male relatives. Does not this child refugee remind us of the frightful pictures of children being carried by distraught parents fleeing from cruel oppressors? Jesus knew all about this refugee problem, for He had to flee with His own mother and foster father from Herod's slaughter of innocent babes. As Jesus fled to Egypt, so did Hadad where Pharaoh sheltered this remaining branch of a royal family. When he grew up he married the queen's sister and by her had a child which the queen herself was very kind to. With David and Joab both dead, Hadad had returned to his own country bent on settling the score of the slaughter of his kindred.

Since Solomon had sinned away his wisdom, as Samson did his strength, he forfeited divine protection and was thus weak against his adversaries. What vexation Hadad, the one-time refugee child gave Solomon we are not told. Along with the other foes of Israel, Hadad must have been a formidable enemy of Solomon in his declining years. The record says that Hadad "abhorred Israel" and created a lot of "mischief" for king and people (I Kings 11:25). Along with his fellow-adversary, Rezon, a Syrian, possession of Damascus was regained, and they reigned there and over the country round about, thereby creating a good deal of trouble for Israel. After his apostasy, Solomon was too weak to ward off his adversaries, and after his death his illustrious kingdom was rent in two as God said it would be because of his departure from Him.

25. The Child Abijah
(I Kings 14:1-20)

Parental concern over sick children is a marked feature of Bible records of families. We have David, broken-hearted over the fatal illness of his first child by Bathsheba; the widow of Zarephath distraught over her son; the nobleman, whose boy was at the point of death and earnestly sought the aid of Jesus; Jairus, melted with grief, pleading for his little girl, his only child; the woman of Canaan at her wits' end over her demon-possessed girl! And here is Jeroboam, the flagrant idolater, deeply concerned about his sick son, Abijah. What happened to these distressed parents is an experience almost every home passes through at one time or another. It would seem as if sickness is never absent from some homes, and often comes as a blessing in disguise.

We have written much about the training of children by parents, but in the training of parents through children God sometimes uses sickness as one of His special means of grace. The testimony of many a home is that the sick room has often been the place when a parent first fully found his way to the child's heart, to guide it to Jesus and to the distinct confession of faith in Him. Sick children, too, have ministered as God's messengers to their anxious parents, for in their fear lest the sick child should die they were drawn nearer to God. When Christ was here on earth, the sickness of a child was one of the cords with which God drew men to His Son. The lives of children were spared for His service and His glory, as well as to gladden and sanctify the parents' heart by His grace.

In a previous chapter under the caption, *Born to Die,* reference will be found to the early death of Abijah which came as divine judgment upon his father, Jeroboam, who made Israel to sin. Persisting in his contempt of God, Jeroboam prostituted and profaned the priesthood (I Kings 13:33), but as soon as his child sickened he sent his wife to inquire of Ahijah the prophet what should become of his child. The gods Jeroboam served could give him no advice or relief, but the blind prophet of God still blessed with visions of the Almighty could. God gave His faithful servant notice that Jeroboam's wife, disguised, was coming to inquire as to the recovery of their sick boy. How surprised she was when, reaching the door of the prophet's home, Ahijah called her by her name and told her what her visit was about! "Come in, thou wife of Jeroboam; why feignest thou thyself to be another?" (verse 6).

The prophet, anticipating the distressed mother's inquiry concerning her child, foretold his death and the ruin of the house of Jeroboam because of his wickedness. Matthew Henry, commenting on God's act of mercy in taking the child to be with Himself, says, "Had Abijah lived, he might have become infected with his father's sin, and involved in the ruin of his father's house." Observe the character given of the sick child – "In him there is found some good thing toward the Lord God of Israel, in the house of Jeroboam" (verse 13).

The divine image in miniature has a peculiar beauty and luster in it. Abijah only, of all Jeroboam's family, shall die in honor, shall be buried, and shall be lamented as one that lived desired. This hopeful child dies first of all for the family, for God often takes those soonest whom He loves best. "Heaven is the fittest place for them; this earth is not worthy of them."

The death of the child Abijah was a sign of divine wrath upon the family which would be ruined when he was taken by whom it might have been reformed. The child's mother went home with a heavy heart to Tirgah, the meaning of which seemed to be a mockery – "a sweet delightful place"! As soon as she crossed the threshold of her home, the child died, and all Israel sorrowed for the loss of so hopeful a prince. Abijah's godless father died soon after, but all Israel did not mourn for him. After reigning for twenty-two years Jeroboam left his crown to a son who lost it, and his life, too, and all the lives of his family, within two years after. What grief and disaster innocent children are spared when they die young!

26. The Child of a Widow (I Kings 17)

Reference can be found to the heart-moving record of hunger and death in a widow's home in the previous chapter of our study under the section, *Born to Die.* We return to Elijah's experience at Zarephath to add a few touches. As a recompense for her kindness to the prophet, the widow's dead boy was restored to life. God had arranged for her to care for and sustain Elijah, and she herself was sustained by a miracle, and doubtless thought that God would continue to bless her and her child. But most unexpectedly the child died and the mother's heart was crushed. She accused Elijah as if he had been responsible for her great loss. The prophet did not answer the widow – often silence is best in the house of sorrow. Elijah went to God and reasoned with Him about the child's death and interceded for his resurrection which took place. Here we have a striking illustration of the power of prayer and of the almightiness of Him who hears and answers prayer. He who kills is able to make alive.

The widow could hardly believe her own eyes as Elijah brought her once dead child, but now alive, down to her room. Excitedly she cries out, "Now by this I know that thou art a man of God" (verse 24). She knew it before as she watched the increase of her meal, but now she is doubly assured of the power and holiness of Elijah. Jesus said of the death of Lazarus that it was for the glory of God which was manifested in the resurrection of this man whom Jesus loved; and it was thus with the death of the widow's child. By it, God was glorified and His prophet was honored. With the passing of the apostolic age, the miracle of the resurrection has never been repeated. Now, concerned parents can earnestly pray that their sick child may be healed. But if God takes the child to be with Himself, a multitude of prayers cannot bring the lamb back to the earthly fold.

27. The Child of the Shunammite
(II Kings 4:8-37)

This record of child resurrection has also been touched upon in our previous chapter (which see). The great woman of Shunem and her husband had given up hope of having any children, but when by God's grace a baby boy came to fill their hearts and home with joy, life began anew. As we have already dealt with all that happened in that ancient family, all we desire to add is that the method used to restore the dead child is typical of the sympathy which all who are in health should have for those, whether old or young, who are dead in their sin. In barbarous heathen times the life of sick or deformed children was not thought worth preserving. Sickly children were thrown out as not worth saving. One of the prominent changes Christianity brought about was that sick children should not be left to perish. Hospitals came into being in which they could be cared for. Godly souls adopted sick and unwanted children and brought them up as their own. They gave life and happiness to these unfortunate boys and girls, a taste of their own life and happiness: their words were words to them, their eyes were eyes to them, their hands were hands to them. They stretched themselves out, as it were, upon these needy children and they lived as they had never done before.

Complete indentification with those who are not as well and blessed as we are brings its reward. It will be well for them and it will be well for us. It was the day of days in the history of the Shunammite when she folded her living son in her bosom. Is not the chief crown and joy of any home or flock, the fresh, warm life of believing children, who have life before them, and who wait to be led to lay themselves on God's altar? How we need to intercede that in homes and churches children may be touched, moved and saved, and made mighty channels of blessing both in the church and the world! What a scene of unspeakable tenderness it must have been when Elisha called to the mother, and, pointing to the living child, said, "Take up thy son"! Once alone with God we can imagine how she would yield her resurrected child to Him. At Elisha's touch life streamed out of the living into the dead. Children all around us need the life-giving touch of the Saviour, and through godly parents and teachers they can be warmed into life in Him as heart touches heart.

28. The Child Josiah
(II Kings 22; 23; II Chron. 34)

Child psychologists and theologians differ on the age children begin to manifest personal understanding and responsibility, and are able to discern the distinction between right and wrong. Works on child psychology generally agree that between five to seven years, a typical child has discovered that objects have a permanent identity; that he is able to take fairly good care of himself; that his memory increasingly provides practical service and retentiveness rapidly improves; that he is able to defend himself and his small possessions; that his conscience is developing and finds it difficult to conceal or to bear any sense of guilt; that as yet he has no broad ethical principles, except the maxims of his parents or teachers.

Some children are born with unusual gifts and at a very early age are prodigies in music, languages, or mathematics. Others, with a long heritage of godliness, seem to have a keen religious outlook even in their earliest years, as in the case of the child Samuel. Before us is Josiah, a royal miracle of grace, who in spite of his evil ancestry and surroundings, at the age of eight sought to do that which was right in the sight of the Lord. Surely, he must have been a remarkable child to many of his elders, seeing he began to reign in Israel when he was only eight years old. One wonders what his mother, Jedidah, thought of her godly, gifted child? Without question the boy's evil environment throws into bold relief his sterling qualities. Too often a royal boyhood is a poisoned boyhood. But with Josiah it was different.

The people of Israel surrounding the little boy were worse than heathen. His grandfather, Manasseh, had filled Jerusalem with innocent blood, although his character changed before his death. Josiah's father, Ammon was a bad man, and was murdered by his people with his murderers being murdered in their turn. The sins and sorrows of that time are described in the Book of Lamentations by Jeremiah whose heart the people had broken. Yet it was in such a sordid atmosphere that Josiah, as a child, sought to do that which was right in God's sight. Brought up in a palace stained with blood, and foul with the vilest sins, where virtue was a crime and evil good, the will of this royal boy, empowered by God, was determined to rise above the wickedness of court and country. Though, as a babe, he had "lien among the pots," he arose above them like a white dove and spent his life in the clear, unsullied light of God.

At sixteen he sought the God of his ancestor David with great earnestness. In the twelfth year of his reign, Josiah, then about twenty and reaching his full legal age, became his own master, and set out purging Judah and Jerusalem. This godly youth hated idols just as much as he loved God. The hatred he manifested toward idolatry sprang from love, and was stayed in love. We are told that his servants destroyed the altars of Baalim "in his presence." He had to be present and feast his eyes on the idols being ground to powder. Josiah was not like Alexander the Great of Russia who used to say, "I reform my country, and am not able to reform myself." Josiah grew up hating sin, not only in others, but also in himself. He did not hate in others the sins he practiced himself. Josiah hated sin in any shape or form, especially in himself. What need we have of many noble-minded young Josiahs who love the Lord, and hate evil!

With conscience as his king, he went forward boldly, even though his mission of reformation put his life in peril. His was the spirit of Chrysostom, who replied to the threats of the Empress Eudoxia, "I fear nothing but sin." As boys have glowing eyes as they follow the adventures of their favorite heroes, all who labor to win boys for Christ are amply repaid as they dwell upon the boy Josiah who was every inch a hero. Yes, it was the Word of God that infused his holy heroism. When the ancient and perfect copy of the Law was found, Josiah, in a most fearless manner, applied its commands to the life of the nation. Edward VI, another youthful king, who has been called "the English Josiah," revealed the same reverence for Scripture. One of his servants placed the Bible on a chair to stand upon it. King Edward at once rebuked him saying, "Respect the Bible."

Josiah reigned for some thirty years, and then was slain in the thickest of the battle, in the valley of Megiddo, bravely defending his country. The whole land mourned for him as if for an only son. The mourning for him was the greatest ever known among the Jews and passed into a proverb for bitterest grief. No wonder the rabbis said "that the memory of him was like costly incense, and sweet as honey in the mouths of all." Josiah was not among the number the poet predicts who —

> . . . Doubly dying, shall go down
> To the vile dust, from whence he sprung,
> Unwept, unhonored and unsung.

The name Josiah signifies, "Jehovah hath founded, laid the foundation, or established." God certainly laid the foundation of His rule in the heart of the child Josiah who built upon it a life that glorified God and which also left its impact upon a nation.

29. The Child Joash or Jehoash (II Kings 11:2-21; 12:1, 2)

Another royal child who came to the throne at an early age was Joash or Jehoash, who was only seven years old when he began to reign, and reigned for forty years. This ninth king of Judah spent the formative years of his life under the spiritual and moral influence of Jehoiada, the priest of lofty character and devout spirit. Alas, however, the historical record of the long reign of Jehoash is that "he did that which was evil in the sight of the Lord" (II Kings 13:10, 11).

30. The Children of Isaiah (Isa. 7:3; 8:1-4)

This great evangelical prophet of the Old Testament had two sons with significant and symbolical names, which, along with other symbolical names in the Book of Isaiah were characteristic of the spirit of prophecy in his age. As with Isaiah, so with Hosea, as children were born to them they gave them names which were hopefully significant. Each child was, as it were, a sign and portent (Isa. 8:18). The wife of Isaiah and mother of his sons was herself a prophetess, and, sharing her husband's hopes and fears, was one with him in the choice of prophetic names for their sons.

The birth of the first son, Shear-jashub, is not recorded. By the time he accompanied his father to meet king Ahab, he would be a youth of sixteen or eighteen. His name means, "The remnant shall return." Isaiah received the revelation of the remnant of the people returning to their land after his awesome vision of the Lord, high and lifted up on a throne (Isa. 6:11-13). Thus when his son was born, Isaiah gave him the name, Shear-jashub, which embodied such a prophecy of a literal and spiritual return. Later on, in a prophecy on the remnant's return, the words composing the name of this son were so used as to make it plain that this name had been given by God for the purpose of attesting and sealing the promise conveyed by its meaning, "The remnant shall return."

"It shall come to pass in that day, that the remnant of Israel . . . The remnant shall return (shear-jashub) . . . a remnant of them shall return" (Isa. 10:20-22).

This first son, then, "bore a name which was a recognized symbol of a great, divine promise, implying the fulfillment of a great threat: and was on this occasion after the manner of prophetic action in those days, presented to the notice of king Ahaz as a visible pledge of the divine intention."

When the prophet received the divine call to go to Ahaz, he was also commanded to take a great roll, or large tablet, and to incribe upon it the words Maher-shalal-hash-baz, meaning, "haste to the spoil, quick to the prey," which brings us to Isaiah's second son who was born within a year after the reception of the prophecy.

With the record of this son's birth is also the notice that it was God who instructed Isaiah to call his child's name Maher-shalal-hash-baz (Isa. 8:3), to which was added the announcement – "Before the child shall have knowledge to cry, My father, and my mother, the riches of Damascus and the spoil of Samaria shall be taken away before the king of Assyria."

Thus this child, with the longest name in the Bible, was of course to be both before and after the event which his four-syllabled name symbolized, a living witness by that name of the truth of God in His threats against the idolatrous and apostate kingdom of Israel. In the prophecy Isaiah delivered after the birth of his second son, he said – "Behold, I and the children whom the Lord hath given me, are for signs and wonders in Israel from the Lord of hosts, which dwelleth in Mount Zion" (Isa. 8:18) – a clear witness to the sacramental character of both of Isaiah's sons.

Is there not a tender touch in the prediction of the Assyrian invasion? As soon as a child is able to mumble what are the first two words they try to pronounce? Are they not, mummy and daddy? And how thrilled parents are to hear these terms! Here is Isaiah saying that before the first cries of the child, with his mysterious name – "My father, my mother" – were heard, that within a year of his birth the spoils of the two capitals of the kings of the confederate armies should be carried to the King of Assyria. Compare with another sign of doom (Isa. 7:14-16).

31. The Children of Hosea

As human relations have not changed much since the ancient Scriptures were written, how up-to-date they seem to be in their records of family life long ago. The prophet Isaiah and his prophetess-wife were drawn together by united thoughts and counsels. Their hearts beat as one for in the things of God they acted in harmony. There are countless homes today in which such unison is repeated, and husband and wife, father and mother, are one in spiritual matters. Without doubt, they are heirs together of the grace of life (I Pet. 3:7). Theirs is a mutual pact to make Christ Lord of the home.

We have mention of another home in which a priest and his wife were bound together as one. They loved each other and placed God first in heart and home. A sudden bereavement, however, was to rend them apart and leave the home desolate. Such was the experience of Ezekiel, the priest-prophet, whose life's partner was so swiftly taken from him by death. What a crushing blow it is when such a tragedy occurs, and the remaining one faces the lonely future with half of their heart in heaven!

We are not told whether there were any children to grace the home of Ezekiel and his wife. Perhaps there were not, and the prophet was able therefore to abandon himself completely to the service of God when with a stroke the desire of his eyes was taken from him (Ezek. 24:15-27).

The God who is the dispenser of life has the prerogative to give and take it. In His goodness He prepared Ezekiel for the blow about to befall him. Notice was given in advance that he must suddenly lose the beloved wife who was the desire of his eyes. God said, "I take away from thee the desire of thy eyes." When the desire of our eyes is removed with one swift stroke, we must see and recognize the hand of God in it all (Job 1:21). But the command was that Ezekiel, although so tragically bereaved, was not allowed to sorrow over the death of his much-loved wife. No mourning nor tears were to be his. It must have been hard for him not to lament the death of one he loved so dearly, but Ezekiel obeyed the divine voice. His wife died at night, and the next morning he appeared in public without any sign of sorrow. God was his inner source of consolation. Able to function as a husband to the widow, God can likewise be as a wife to the widower.

By his extraordinary self-denial, Ezekiel was to be a sign to the people who knew that the death of his wife was a great affliction and yet he appeared so unconcerned. The calamities about to overtake Jerusalem were to be too great to be lamented, so great that they should sink down under them into a silent despair. The public pride of the people, the Temple, would be plundered and burned; their family-pleasure would be destroyed by the sword of the Chaldeans. "Your sons and daughters shall fall by the sword." Such was to be the punishment for sin; and as Ezekiel wept not for his affliction, so neither were those perishing by famine, pestilence and the sword to weep over their anguish. Calamities were to come upon them thick and fast that they would find themselves stupefied or hardened in their sorrows. (Job 6:10), and then remember that Ezekiel was a sign to them.

Because his prophecy is saturated with tears of compassion, Jeremiah is known as the "Weeping Prophet," and, as such, is a type of the weeping Saviour who foretold the destruction of Jerusalem by the Romans just as Jeremiah predicted the plunder of the same city by the Chaldeans. Of all the prophets of the Old Testament, Jeremiah stands out as the supreme prophet of God to the human heart. Throughout his long and loyal career he laid siege to the hearts of his hearers. As Alexander Whyte expresses it, "The care of all your families, he cried, and all your plagues and all your defeats and all your captivities – the cause and the care of them all is in your own heart: in the heart of each inhabitant of Jerusalem and each captive in Babylon."

Although Jeremiah was a prophet of unwelcome truths he was never afraid. No coward could have undertaken his task of declaring fearlessly the commands of God to kings, princes, priests and prophets. He was equally hated and feared by all as he delivered unpalatable truths in the royal chamber, temple and street. One of the most striking features of this great figure in ancient history is the way he stands out as a solitary fortress, one grand, immovable, lonely saint, amid the apostasy of his age. As by divine decree, Ezekiel's dear wife was suddenly taken from him, so by the same decree Jeremiah was not permitted to have a wife or children. In contrast to other prophets, his was to be a celibate life. He learned that it was God's will for him that he should not marry and have a companion to lighten the burden he was forced to bear. Cardinal Newman was impressed in early manhood with the conviction that God's will for him was that he should never marry.

The Roman Catholic Church forces celibacy upon her priests, but many are now rebelling and marrying. Jeremiah's celibacy was ordered of the Lord that he might be a sign to the people (Jer. 16:1, 2), yet, as Professor A. S. Peake expresses in his commentary on the prophet –

> Jeremiah, whose heart was so exquisitely fitted for love, and to whom a home would have been a welcome refuge from the scorn and cruelty of his fellows, was doomed to a life of loneliness uncheered by wife or children. And yet with deep sympathetic insight into a joy his vocation forbade him to share, the prophet sees in a glad wedding the type of human happiness (Jer. 3:14; 16:9). He was not of a naturally morose temper, nor had his isolation soured him; he looked at the felicity of others with no jaundiced eye but only with the sad conviction that it would soon utterly cease. He felt this to be one of the penalties of his vocation, that he must have no share in the innocent pleasures of his fellows.

By life Jeremiah had to conduct himself as one who expected his country to be brought to ruin, and was thus forbidden marriage or mirth; and, like Ezekiel, no mourning for the dead. Wives and children were to die grievous deaths (Jer. 16:3, 4), but Jeremiah in his loneliness was to illustrate that it was better to have no wife and children than to possess them only for the murderer to destroy. The prophet's sorrow for the destruction of his nation generally must swallow up his sorrow for particular deaths of his relatives and neighbors. It is interesting to compare the renunciation Jeremiah was called to make with our Lord's pronouncements (Matt. 24:19; Luke 23:29), and also with Paul's motives for a like abstinence on account of "the present distress" (I Cor. 7:26).

After such an introduction we come to Hosea for whom marriage was to be a tragedy through which he was to learn how to comprehend the love of God. The miseries of his union are in sad contrast to the bliss of that between Ezekiel and his wife (Hos. 1:2). We hold that these opening chapters are not merely an allegorical representation, "designed to exhibit in vivid colors the terrible moral condition of Israel," but "an historic occurrence, the only too real tragedy of the author's personal experience, employed for the purpose of illustration." (See Isa. 8:1-4.) That such an unwholesome marital experience was to be a divine sign can be gathered from the command – "Go, take unto thee a wife of whoredoms and children of whoredoms: for the land hath committed great whoredom, departing from the Lord" (Hosea 1:2).

The name of the wife Hosea took to himself was Gomer, meaning "perfect" or "complete." Whether external beauty, or wickedness of character is implied by such a name is not easy to determine. The question has arisen whether Gomer was guilty of adultery before or after her marriage to Hosea. We can hardly conceive of God asking His holy prophet to marry a whore. Thus, it would seem that after their marriage the wickedness of Gomer became manifest to Hosea, and that the sorrow of his agonized heart was transfigured to the inspired prophet as he saw in his grief an emblem of his own nation's wrong to God. Hosea must have suffered acutely, but his agony was part of the divine plan to illustrate the way Israel had outraged the love of God.

As a Book, Hosea pulsates with a divine love and compassion for a people living in spiritual whoredom. As Dr. G. Campbell Morgan in his study of the Book reminds us, "The greatest revelation of the Book of Hosea is that of love. In the midst of his own overwhelming sorrow God called Hosea, and commanded him to seek again the sinning Gomer, and to bring her back into the wilderness of seclusion for a while, but ultimately into the place of love and privilege at his own side." The moving message of the Book, then, is that the sin of Israel as it was understood by God, was symbolized in the tragic marriage experienced by Hosea.

After Hosea's heart was broken by the tragic experience overtaking his own domestic life, he entered into fellowship with God as He sorrowed over the infidelity and unfaithfulness to love he saw in his people. The prophet passed into fellowship with the broken heart of God through his own suffering, and out of this fellowship of suffering Hosea had a most poignant and appealing message for his nation. This is why his Book "thrills with emotion, and flames with light, from beginning to end." Hosea was made a sign to the people in that his longsuffering love for a wife who proved faithless to him, and whom he brought back from a life of shame, was a picture of God's love for a rebellious people who had broken their covenant with Him and had given themselves up to the worship of idols – which idolatry is often described as spiritual adultery.

Three children were born to Hosea and Gomer, two boys and a girl, and with each God decreed how they should be named.

a. *Jezreel.* It is profitable to observe not only the resemblance in sound between Jezreel and Israel, but the historic associations of the former. Jezreel was the name of a fertile plain in the tribe of Issachar, and was the scene of terrible struggles (Judg. 4:13; 6:33; 7:1; I Sam. 29:1). It was also the name of a town associated with the guilt of Ahab and Jezebel in the murder of Naboth (I Kings 21); and with the final extinction of Ahab's house by Jehu (II Kings 9:21; 10:11).

Between the two names, Jezreel and Israel there is a similarity of sound – "izrahel." John Calvin, writing on the name as typically given to Hosea's first-born, represents God as saying, "Ye are not Israel, but izrahel, a people whom God will scatter and cast away." Later on, the name is used in connection with the promise of the restoration of the people –

"They shall hear Jezreel. And I will sow her unto me in the earth" (Hos. 2:22, 23a). Israel, once called izrahel, as "the dispersed of God," shall now be called izrahel, as "the sown of God." See also "the branch of my planting" (Isa. 60:21).

As a name Jezreel means, "God shall sow," and is susceptible of two senses – "God scattereth" or "God planteth." Having discovered the faithlessness of his wife, and that his marred married life was symbolic of his nation's history, Hosea could understand why God named his son, Jezreel – "I will avenge the blood of Jezreel upon the house of Jehu . . . I will break the bow of Israel in the valley of Jezreel" (Hos. 1:4, 5). An adulterous people were to reap what they had sown. Yet the promise was that scattered in judgment they would be regathered in mercy (Hos. 1:11).

b. *Lo-ruhamah.* Gomer conceived again, and this time had a daughter whom God said should be called Lo-ruhamah, meaning "not having obtained mercy," or "unloved," or "unpitied." Her father's own growing despondency about the future of Israel is revealed in her name after receiving its divine significance. "I will no more have mercy upon the house of Judah," or, as the margin puts it, "I will not add any more to the house of Judah" (Hos. 1:6). The latter part of the verse can be rendered, "For I will no longer have pity on the house of Israel, that I should indeed forgive them."

c. *Lo-ammi.* Gomer's third child was to be a type of utter and final repudiation of a faithless people by God, for Lo-ammi means, "Not my people," and God explains in the bestowal of the name, "Ye are not my people, and I will not be your God" (Hos. 1:9). But that judgment is mixed with mercy is evident from the fact that the language of rejection is followed by that of reconciliation and promise — "It shall come to pass that in that place where it was said unto them, ye are not my people, there it shall be said unto them, Ye are the sons of the living God." Then follows the words of the divine oracle, "Say ye unto your brethren, Ammi" (Hos. 2:1), Ammi, "my people" being the expression of God's recognition of Israel's restored filial relationship to Himself.

After the tragic unfolding of the first chapter of the Book of Hosea, the prophet's domestic misery and his symbolically named children pass out of sight. God is then represented as taking up the language of Hosea and uttering His terrible and yearning cry over Israel who had been unfaithful to Him, and who, by her idolatries, had forfeited all claim to His covenanted love and mercy. For characteristic features of the Book as a whole, the reader is directed to the author's work, *All the Books and Chapters of the Bible.*

Doubtless there are other characters whose childhood if not specifically stated, is implied, that we might have lingered over. Some there are who are described as children but were in fact youths. For instance, Daniel and his three companions are mentioned as being "children in whom was no blemish" — "children which are of your sort" (Dan. 1:4, 10). But "these four children" (Dan. 1:17) were actually youths "who had knowledge and skill in all learning and wisdom." Daniel had "understanding in all visions and dreams" (Dan. 1:17). Then in several places the term children is used symbolically as we shall discover in our next chapter. It is to be hoped that the coverage of Old Testament children which we have given is sufficient to prove how true to life the Bible is even in filial relationships.

New Testament Children

Between the Old and New Testament there is a silent period of some 400 years. As we turn the page from Malachi 4 to Matthew 1 we must not forget that we cross a bridge of four unrecorded centuries, and that the New Testament did not come directly out of the Old, but from it through the Intertestamental Period. Much of the language of the New Testament is from the literature produced during these four hundred years, as well as from Old Testament Scriptures. Conspicuous amongst the literature of this intermediate era is the Septuagint translation of the Old Testament. This Greek translation of the Hebrew Scriptures was largely used by New Testament writers, and also the Apocrypha, which is the collection of fifteen books.

As for the Apocrypha, it has been included in whole or in part in the Bible through the ages. The Roman Catholic Church includes it in its version, and all the earlier English translators of the Protestant churches retained it. But during the Puritan Era the question arose as to whether the Apocrypha was worthy of inclusion in the Bible. The Westminster Confession placed it under a ban, and although it was still included in some editions of the Bible, the British Bible Society finally excluded it in 1827 on the grounds that its books were inferior to those of the Old Testament, having come out of a period when divine revelation seemed to be in abeyance. That there is much of a moral and spiritual value in the fifteen books of the Apocrypha none can deny.

Dealing as we are with children, the reader who cares to wade through the Apocrypha will find gems of wisdom as to parental responsibility and also exhortations for children to heed. All that we have space for are a few illustrations of how fathers, mothers, and children should live and act in their home –

> Mothers, embrace thy children, and bring them up with gladness, make their feet fast as a pillar: for I have chosen thee, saith the Lord (II Esdras 2:15).
>
> Honour thy father with thy whole heart, and forget not the sorrows of thy mother.
>
> Remember that thou wast begotten of them; and how canst thou recompense them the things that they have done for thee (Eccles. 7:27, 28).
>
> The children of sinners are abominable children . . . The inheritance of sinners' children shall perish . . . The children will complain of an ungodly father, because they shall be reproached for his sake (Eccles. 41: 5-7).

In the History of Susanna there is the account of beautiful Susanna who feared the Lord, whose husband was Joacim, a rich man of Babylon. The parents of Susanna were righteous and taught their daughter according to the Law of Moses.

During the terrible slaughter of The Maccabees, "they hanged the infants about their necks" (I Macc. 1:61). "Thus there was killing of young and old . . . children . . . infants (II Macc. 5:13). This grim record is akin to the massacre of infants by Herod after he heard of the birth of Jesus.

As we take up the New Testament children we cannot but be impressed with the way it opens with the birth and childhood of John the Baptist, and also of his illustrious cousin, the Lord Jesus Christ; and how their entrance into the world and consequent teaching brought to men a higher concept of the value of childhood. Through His experience as a child and His constant references to children, Jesus taught both disciples and parents the vast potential wrapped up in a precious child; and of how parental love, care and wisdom can transform a house into a home. With the advent of Christianity, parenthood and childhood were clothed with a higher dignity. Although every day new lives begin, the motherhood of Elisabeth and Mary, which introduces the New Testament, teaches us that the miracle nonetheless remains fresh and unique for every mother and that the godliness of parents is a vital factor in the life of a child.

As we shall presently understand anew, no one thought of a child as Jesus did. It is due to His elevation of childhood that all over the civilized world today children are thought of with such tenderness, that an appeal to help starving children always finds a response in the hearts of Christians and non-Christians alike. Jesus was born in a poor, humble home, grew up in it and remained in it for thirty years, and thus experienced how fundamental the family unit is to the development of one's own character. Karl Marx, founder of communism, was outspoken in his denial of the concept of the family as a unit bound together by mutual love and care. In his *Communist Manifesto* he asks the question and gives the answer –

> On what foundation is the present family, the bourgeois family, based? On capital, on private gain . . . The bourgeois family will vanish as a matter of course with the vanishing capital . . . The bourgeois claptrap about the family and education.

Marx advocated the shift of the cultural center of gravity from the home to public institutions, and said that the breakup of the family is not incidental but central to the working of Communist ideology. Today Communist leaders know only too well that as long as the family unit remains strong, and retains its cultural and spiritual independence, the state cannot claim complete supremacy. Engels, Marx's partner, and whose money helped to keep Marx alive, declared that if revolution failed to abolish the long-established institution of the family, the gradual stronghold of communism would destroy it. "The family will not be abolished, it will be allowed to wither away." Alas! in so-called Christian lands where the tenets of communism are abhorred, the subtle inroads of materialism, affluence, worldliness and indifference to moral values are withering up a wholesome and happy home life.

How different was the idea of home in the estimation of Thomas Jefferson, the third child in a family of ten, who became the third president of the United States! It was this noble man who wrote, "The happiest moments of my life have been the few which I have passed at home, in the bosom of my family . . . Abstracted from home, I know no happiness in the world." He believed that good homes are the cornerstone of a free and peaceful society. If our civilization is crumbling it is because good homes are not as plentiful as they should be. Will Durant, the eminent American educator and writer, after having studied the great philosophies of life tried to answer for his own satisfaction the question, *What is happiness?* and here is what he wrote –

> Many years ago I lost happiness. I sought it in knowledge, and found disillusionment. I sought it in writing, and found a weariness of the flesh. I sought it in travel, and my feet tired on the way, I sought it in wealth, and I found discord and worriment. And then one day, at a little station out on a wooden cliff near the sea, I saw a woman waiting in a tiny car, with a child asleep in her arms. A man alighted from the train, walked to her quickly, embraced her, and kissed the child gently, careful lest he should awaken him. They drove off together to some modest home among the fields; and it seemed to me that happiness was with them.

The whole drift of New Testament teaching is in the creation of holy, happy homes in which children can grow up in the nurture and admonition of the Lord, and in turn become commendable citizens of society, as well as laborers in His vineyard. Examples of such homes are before us in the New Testament.

1. The Child John

What fascinating stories of child life there must be behind the mechanical, cold list of begats with which the New Testament opens. Although this section of the Bible begins with the birth of Jesus (Matt. 1:18-25), chronologically the birth of John the Baptist, His forerunner, comes first (Luke 1:1-25, 57-80). Because his was a birth many were to rejoice over, it is essential to understand the many features of this babe who was to become "great in the sight of the Lord." Luke, the beloved physician, gives us a full account of the conception and of the coming of John.

a. *His Coming Was Divinely Proclaimed.* While Zacharias the priest was in the Temple at Jerusalem offering incense before the altar, the angel Gabriel came to him as the spokesman of God to announce that Elisabeth and he would have a son. But parenthood seemed impossible for this godly couple. "They had no child, because that Elisabeth was barren" (Luke 1:7). Yet, as we have seen, other barren women were made to become the joyful mothers of children. It is the next phrase that affirms the hopelessness of Zacharias and his wife becoming parents. "They both were now well stricken in years," or "far advanced in their days," meaning that they were beyond the age of procreation. Thus, the promise of a son implied a miracle which Zacharias did not believe possible, for in response to Gabriel's announcement, he said, "Whereby shall I know this? for I am an old man, and my wife well stricken in years" (Luke 1:7, 18). John, then, was to be one of the miracle babies of the Bible for God reversed the natural process in the body of Elisabeth and gave her the childbearing she had longed for.

As a penalty for not believing the words of Gabriel concerning the divinely-promised son, Zacharias was stricken dumb and did not speak again until John was born. Zacharias asked for a sign that parenthood would be his, and the request was granted in the muteness he experienced. The vision and message of such an august angelic messenger as Gabriel should have assured Zacharias that a divine promise is certain of performance. But his was a lack of faith for which he suffered some nine months of speechlessness. Emerging from the Temple after this awesome experience, Zacharias was not able to speak to the people. He was mute and remained so (Luke 1:22). A Sunday school teacher was trying to impress her nine-year-old scholars with the wonder of the arrival of a baby to bless Elisabeth and Zacharias who were so old. One little fellow, somewhat puzzled, asked the teacher, "What's so strange about that? My mother's just had a baby, and she's *thirty-two!*"

b. *His Name Was Divinely Published.* When Gabriel said to Zacharias, "Fear not Zacharias: for thy prayer is heard; and thy wife Elisabeth shall bear thee a son" (Luke 1:13), we are not to assume that he had been praying for a son. Such a hope had died out long ago. His prayer was in harmony with the whole multitude of people praying at the time of incense, and the burden of the intercession of priest and people alike was for the coming of the Kingdom of God, or the redemption in Jerusalem which godly souls had waited so long for (Luke 2:25, 36, 38). Praying thus, Zacharias received more than he asked for. The long but abandoned yearning of his heart for a son who might have a share in manifestation of the Messiah was to be realized, and the name of this one who should prepare the way of the Lord was divinely given, "Thou shalt call his name John" (Luke 1:13).

Wilkinson observes that, "In the gospel age we find some eminent, though not numerous, examples of the employment of proper names for the purpose of recording some great truth, or representing some divine blessing conferred, for the sake of the Church, upon certain individuals. In the very introduction of the gospel a name was selected by God Himself for the great prophet in whom the series of Old Testament ministrations and disclosures were to end, and the first manifestation of the glories of the new covenant were to be revealed . . . his name – *John.*" For the one who was to become the greatest of the prophets, God chose one of the most common Jewish names.

Under its Hebrew form, "Johanan," or "Jochanan," John was a well-known and ordinary name which several Old Testament persons were known by (I Chron. 3:15; Ezra 8:12, etc). Meaning "Jehovah is gracious," or "Jehovah has favored," or "Jehovah has granted grace," John was indeed a most appropriate name to denote the nature of the mission of the Baptist which was to mark the epoch of grace for the world. Evidently the neighbors were not satisfied with the name Elisabeth and Zacharias, under divine direction were giving their infant. They explained that it was not a family name, "There is none of thy kindred that is called by this name." Making signs to the dumb father what name his son was to have, he wrote on a slate, "His name is John," "Jehovah is gracious" – and He was indeed gracious, for as soon as Zacharias wrote the name of the babe, "his tongue was loosed, and he spake, and praised God" (Luke 1:59-65). The name was not a question to be discussed. It had been given already by God.

Had the choice of a name for their son been left to his aged parents, they could not have selected a more meaningful one to express their gratitude to the God of all grace as granting their heart's desire for a child. But as the name was God-given and was accompanied with illustrative words of promise, we cannot fail to discern in the name an exhibition of the grace and favor of God to Israel and to the world. The song of praise uttered by the child's father on the occasion of the name of the child has for its keynote the sentiment of such a sacramental name (Luke 1:68, 69). John was also to be the name of Christ's much-loved apostle.

c. *His Work Was Divinely Prescribed.* As the child of Elisabeth and Zacharias grew up, and "waxed strong in spirit, and was in the deserts till the day of his shewing unto Israel" (Luke 1:80), his prophesied mission became evident. We cannot do better than itemize what Gabriel predicted of the mission of the one he named –

"Many shall rejoice at his birth.
He shall be great in the sight of the Lord, and shall drink neither wine nor strong drink.
He shall be filled with the Holy Spirit, even from his mother's womb.
Many of the children of Israel shall he turn to the Lord their God.
He shall go before Him in the spirit and power of Elijah, to turn the

hearts of the fathers to the children, and the disobedient to the wisdom of the just;

To make ready a people prepared for the Lord" (Luke 1:14-17).

What a precise and prodigious task this unique child was to undertake; and as he came to fulfill his mission he little knew that, like the Saviour whose way John prepared, his witness would cost him his life! C. H. Spurgeon once said that, "John was the first Baptist minister to lose his head through dancing." (See Matt. 14:8-22.)

Again and again in Scripture we see how God in securing and preparing those He desires to use, loves to begin at the beginning, and from the birth, from the first conception of life, to take charge and to sanctify the vessel He wants to employ. Paul speaks about being separated from the womb for the exercise of his great ministry. To all contemplating parenthood there is a deep truth of unspeakable preciousness. John was to be filled from – or, in – his mother's womb, with the Holy Spirit. As Andrew Murray puts it, "The mother's womb was the work-place of the Holy Spirit." As for the mother herself, hers must be a heart in harmony with the selfsame Spirit. "It is of holy parents that God would take a holy child."

The promised child was to grow up as a Nazarite, which meant a life utterly consecrated to God and the absence of all lower forms of stimulation in order to experience the Spirit's infilling. (See Eph. 5:18.) The godliness of the parents provided the foundation of their child's separation unto God. "They were both righteous before God, walking in all the commandments and ordinances of the Lord blameless." To quote Andrew Murray again, "It is the God of nature, who in this world of cause and effect has ordered that like begets like, who is also the God of grace. With omnipotence at His command, ready to work any miracle He pleases, He yet most carefully observes His own laws, and when He wants a holy child, seeks for holy parents. . . . A righteous and blameless life prepares for, and may also count upon the power of the Holy Spirit in the unborn child."

The marks of a child born under the covering of the Spirit are distinctly seen in Gabriel's delineation of the character and mission of John. "Many shall rejoice at his birth" (Luke 1:14). Well, Elisabeth and Zacharias rejoiced, for we read they had "joy and gladness." Many came to bless God for the birth of John, for when he became the wilderness preacher his converts were many. Several of those who repented under his preaching became our Lord's first disciples. Some parents wish their children had never been born because of the pernicious influence of their lives. Did not Jesus indicate a thought like this in His condemnation of Judas Iscariot? If parents desire their children to be blessed and made a blessing so that many will rejoice at their birth, then they must prepare the way for their seed to serve the Lord.

d. *His Fame Was Divinely Prophesied.* The crown on the whole of the promise of John's birth is in the declaration – "He shall be great in the sight of the Lord" (verse 15). The Baptist became the model of greatness, but how are we to view his greatness? Well, there is the negative view, or in what it did not consist. John's greatness did not consist in a long and honored life for he was only thirty-two or thirty-three years of age when he was beheaded by the wicked Herod. It does not require a long life to do what is right in the sight of the Lord, and to bring souls to Him. John was great in God's sight for he excelled in these areas.

Further, true greatness does not require great riches. That the child whom God said would be great was in fact a poor man is proven by the clothes he wore and the food he ate – the kind of clothing and food of the poorest of the land (Matt. 3:4). He owned no land and had no house of his own to live in, yet in spite of his voluntary poverty he was "great in the sight of the Lord." Some men are rich without being great; others are great without being rich.

Then, John did not become great because of "the honor that cometh from man." Cardinal Wolsey sought this kind of honor, and received it from King Henry VIII, but what good did it do him? In a single day he lost everything – position, prestige, and riches – and died a poor, miserable, heartbroken man. Just before he ended his career, Wolsey is said to have written to a friend – "O Cromwell, Cromwell! had I but served my God with half the zeal with which I've served my king, He would not now have forsaken me."

Character is what we are – reputation is what men think of us. John, ever careful about what he was in the sight of God, cared nothing whatever about man's estimation of his ways. What his eye was upon in his ministry was honor from God, and in His sight the Baptist was great! As there are some ways in which his greatness did not consist, let us find out in what it did consist.

One of the virtues contributing to John's prominence was his humility. Solomon affirms that, "Before honour is humility" (Prov. 15:33). It was John's humility that led to his honor. When the Jews sent messengers from Jerusalem inquiring about the identity of this fiery preacher, his answer to their question was, "I am the voice of one crying in the wilderness" (John 1:23). He did not say, "I am a prophet," or "I am the forerunner of the Messiah," but "I am a *voice*" – a little breath put in motion – that's all. John's humility also appears in what he said about Christ. After me is coming a man mightier than I; One who was preferred before me; whose shoelace I am not worthy to untie. The same humble spirit is seen when he declined to baptize Jesus saying, "I have need to be baptized of thee" (Matt. 3:14). Yet again in the declaration, "He must increase, but I must decrease" (John 3:30).

> The saint that wears Heaven's brightest crown,
> In deepest adoration bends;
> The weight of glory bows him down
> The most, when most his soul ascends;
> Nearest the throne itself must be
> The footstool of Humility.

Then, is it not evident that self-abnegation added to John's greatness? Think of the years spent in the desert before he appeared as the revivalist! Although all men came to him, he never displayed the air of importance. Some of his disciples, jealous of their master, requested him to do something to manifest his greatness. But John's response was, "A man can receive nothing, except it be given him from heaven" (John 3:27). The Lamb he exalted had to have all the glory for he knew that he could not make much of the Saviour and of self at the same time.

One of old could confess, "Thy gentleness made me great" (II Sam. 22:36; Ps. 18:35), but with John, God-given courage made him great. Fearing God, he had no other fear, not even the fear of man. The preaching of repentance and of the kingdom of God by John attracted all strata of society to hear him. Herod, king of Judea, had pleasure in listening to John preach and became his friend. Herod, however, lived in sin, and John had the courage to tell him that by living with another man's wife he was breaking God's law. For his brave witness, John was thrown into prison and shortly thereafter died as a martyr for daring to tell the truth.

A child, prayerfully prepared for, is a joy to his parents who endeavor to dedicate him to the Lord's service. How rewarded they are if he grows up to be a blessing to men, and great in the sight of the Lord! He may not make a name for himself among men, nor be conspicuous in gifts and talents, yet by divine grace he can be great in the sight of Him who sees not as man sees. Like John, he can be a voice and vessel, a true way prepared for the Master into the hearts of men. As a parent, are you constant in prayer that your child, or children, are under the overshadowing of God's heavenly grace, and are among those who will be great in His sight?

2. The Child Jesus

Among all born into the world from Cain the first child, down to the multitudes of babies born at the very moment these lines are being read, the birth of Jesus stands out as the most momentous one humanity has known. His was an incomparable birth in so many ways. The uniqueness of His birth is implied in the repeated phrase "*thy Holy Child Jesus*" (Acts 4:27, 30). Approaching a meditation of Him who was "made of woman" we have the same feeling of awesomeness Moses experienced when, standing before the burning bush, he heard God's voice calling to him out of the bush, saying – "Draw not nigh hither: put off thy shoes from off thy feet, for the place whereon thou standeth is holy ground" (Exod. 3:5).

On the walls of an old Swiss church there hangs a somewhat curious yet wonderful picture. The artist tried to paint a subject which it was impossible for him to represent. He endeavored to depict God the Father, and in the painting He is shown in the act of throwing down a tiny Baby to the people of the waiting earth. Is this not what the Incarnation is actually all about? At the town of Bethlehem was the biggest "giving" that has ever been, or ever could be. God gave His only Son. Surely that was the greatest moment of time, when God the Son appeared on earth as a human Baby, holding out a pair of tiny hands!

We have two historical accounts of the birth of Jesus. Matthew begins his record with the phrase, "Now the birth of Jesus was on this wise," and then proceeds to tell us of the way the angel prepared Joseph for the revelation of the Child whom Mary was to bear; and also of the visit of the wise men from the East to see her Child (Matt. 1:18-25; 2:1-12). Luke concentrates upon the annunciations preceding the birth of Jesus; the journey to Bethlehem and the presence of angels and shepherds in the field (Luke 1:26-28; 2:1-20). Both writers dwell upon the cardinal truth of Christianity, namely, that "the holy Child Jesus" had a human mother but not a human father. The finest statement of the Christian reason for belief in such a virgin birth was expressed by Professor H. R. Macintosh in his work on *The Person of Christ* – "The present writer can only say that to him supernatural conception appears a really befitting and credible preface to a life which was crowned by resurrection from the dead."

That the birth of Jesus is the most notable of births is borne out by the fact that every day we date the letters we write from the birth of Christ – The year of our Lord, 1970. Further, the entire history of the world is divided into two general sections B.C. – "Before Christ," A.D. – "Anno Domini," or "The Year of our Lord," just as "Anno Mundi" means "In the year of the world" – a phrase used in computing dates from the period of Creation. Jesus, then, could not have been an ordinary child. Had He been, His birth would never have changed the calendar of the world. What, exactly, constituted His birth as a unique and remarkable event?

a. *His Was a Predicted Birth.* Centuries before Jesus was born His coming was prophesied by holy men who, in advance, saw His day and rejoiced. Prophecies as to His lineage are well-known to all Bible lovers. The Bible practically opens with the first prophecy of the birth – and death – of Jesus. As soon as Satan caused our first parents to sin, he received the prophecy that One would be born of a woman to destroy his works. Thus, He came as "the seed of the woman" (Gen. 3:15; Luke 2:7). It was further predicted that He would come of the line of Shem (Gen. 9:26; Luke 3:36); of the tribe of Judah (Gen. 49:10; Luke 3:33); of the seed of Abraham (Gen. 12:3; Matt. 1:1). Then there are explicit prophecies as to His coming as God (Isa. 7:14; Matt. 1:22, 23), as Man (Ps. 8:4-6; Heb. 2:5-9); that His mother would be a virgin (Isa. 7:14; Matt. 1:18). We also have predictions as to His name (Isa. 7:14; Matt. 1:21-23), the place of His birth (Mic. 5:2; Luke 2:4-7), His forerunner (Isa. 40:3; Matt. 3:1-3).

b. *His Was a Virgin Birth.* Because this aspect of Christ's birth is both deep and delicate, infinite and incomprehensible, one needs to have a mind overshadowed by the Holy Spirit if it is to be expressed in "acceptable words" (Eccl. 12:10). To grasp, in some measure, the tremendous miracle of our Lord's birth, there must be a corresponding spiritual experience, namely, a regeneration of soul made possible by the same Spirit who made Christ's physical birth a reality (John 3:6).

At the outset let it be said that the Virgin Birth will always remain a mystery. "In Scripture a mystery may be a fact which, when revealed, we cannot understand it in detail, though we can know it, and act upon it," says Dr. Handley Moule. "It is a thing only to be known when revealed." It is thus with the holy miracle before us of which "there can be no fitting attitude of the human intellect save that of acceptance of the truth, without any attempt to explain the absolute mystery." It was of this mystery of "God manifest in flesh" that Paul wrote "without controversy great is the mystery of godliness" (I Tim. 3:16). Theologians indulge in heated controversy over the Virgin Birth, but the Early Church believed it and sang about it. Human reason may reject it because it is against the law of natural generation, yet even an unbeliever like Huxley had to confess that as a scientific man he could not reject Christianity on the ground of the Virgin Birth, as there were millions of such births in the lower forms of life. The attitude of a true believer is –

"I will seek
to believe rather than to reason;
to adore rather than to explain;

to give thanks rather than to penetrate;
to love rather than know;
to humble myself rather than to speak."

As we come to examine what is meant by the Virgin Birth it must be made clear that the actual birth of Christ was in no way miraculous. The process of His birth was natural. He came from the womb of His mother, as do all children. Supernaturalness is associated with the manner of the initial conception, or the begetting of His body which was "made of a woman," not of a man *and* a woman. By a divine creative act, apart from human generation, the formation of the body was set in motion when it was conceived by the Holy Spirit (Luke 1:31, 35). Dealing with the unusual births of John and Jesus, Scofield says that, "both births were supernatural: that to Elisabeth because it was too late: that to Mary because it was too soon."

Christ's birth is called "virgin" because Mary at the time of the birth was *virgo intacto,* which simply means, there had never been any intercourse with man. "A virgin shall conceive" (Isa. 7:14). "A virgin shall be with child" (Matt. 1:22, 23). Cruden's Concordance explains a virgin as "a young unmarried woman who had preserved the purity of her body." After Mary's first-born who did not have a human father, she had other children by Joseph (Matt. 13:55, 56).

If Christ had been born according to the laws of procreation He would have been defiled and numbered among those conceived in sin, or born with evil tendencies because of the sin of our first parents (Ps. 51:5). But Jesus came forth from Mary absolutely sinless, "holy, harmless, undefiled, separate from sinners." His substance was pure and immaculate because there was no mixture of human seed in His conception. Within Mary, the Holy Spirit as the Alchemist laid hold of that part of her flesh out of which His body was to be formed and purified it, as dross is removed from metal, thereby making possible "that Holy Thing" born of her.

Approach, Thou gentle Little One,
Of stainless Mother born to earth,
Free from all wedded union
The Mediator's two-fold birth.

What joys to the vast universe
In that chaste maiden's womb are borne:
Ages set free from sorrow's curse
Spring forth an everlasting morn.

This act of the Spirit must not be confused with what the Roman Catholic Church wrongly calls "The Immaculate Conception," which implies that "the blessed Virgin Mary was from the first instant of her own conception by a singular grace and privilege of Almighty God, in view of the merits of Christ Jesus, the Saviour of man, preserved from all stain of original sin." But Mary was born in sin like every other woman and in her Magnificat over the birth of Jesus was the first to recognize her need of His saving grace, "My spirit hath rejoiced in God *my* Saviour" (Luke 1:47).

Further, the word "incarnation" means to "embody in flesh," and this is what really happened in Mary's first Child who, as the Word, became flesh and dwelt among men.

Veiled in flesh the God-head see,
Hail the incarnate Deity!

Within Mary the Spirit laid hold of deity and humanity and fused them together, thereby becoming the love-knot between our Lord's two natures. Thus, when He came forth from the womb, it was not as God exclusively, or as man exclusively, but as the God-man – God manifest in flesh! No wonder an old divine confessed, "I can scarce get past His cradle in my wondering to wonder at His cross. The infant Jesus is in some views a greater marvel than Jesus with the purple robe and the crown of thorns." This, then, is the mystery our finite minds cannot fully comprehend –

> The Ancient of Days became a Babe at Bethlehem.
> He who thunders in the heaven cried in a cradle.
> He who gives to all their meat in due season, sucked the breast.
> He who made all flesh was made flesh.
> He was older than the mother who bore Him.
> He who clothed the heavens was wrapped in swaddling clothes.
> The mighty God became a helpless infant.
> The everlasting Father became a child.
> God and man became one Person.

Jesus came as "the Offspring of a virgin's womb" for with God nothing is impossible. He was born clean, although born of a woman (Job 25:4), because of the overshadowing of the Holy Spirit who wrought a miracle in the production of this new humanity, securing from its earliest germinal beginnings freedom from the slightest taint of sin. Yes, and in taking Mary's flesh our Lord rolled away the reproach from woman which became hers by the seduction of the serpent, the devil. In taking her flesh, He honored her sex and untied the knot of her disobedience. "As at the first the woman had made man a sinner, so now, to make him amends, she brings him a Saviour."

c. *His Was a Lowly Birth.* At His birth He became familiar with the "housing problem," for there was no room for Him in the wayside inn. Born the Prince of life, Jesus did not see the light of day in a palace but a stable surrounded by cattle. As for the home into which He was born, it was so poor that all Joseph and Mary could offer as a sacrifice was the offering of the poor – two small pigeons! How little children love to sing hymns about "the Child Jesus."

> Once in royal David's city
> Stood a lowly cattle shed,
> Where a mother laid her Baby
> In a manger for His bed.
> Mary was that mother mild,
> Jesus Christ her little Child.

It was Richard Crashaw (1612 - 1649) who gave the church his most expressive *Hymn of the Nativity* –

> Gloomy night embark'd the place
> Where the noble Infant lay.
> The Babe look'd up and shew'd His face;
> In spite of darkness, it was day.
> It was Thy day, sweet! and did rise
> Not from the East, but from Thine eyes.
>
> Poor world, said I, what wilt thou do
> To entertain this starry stranger?
> Is the best thou canst bestow,
> A cold and not too cleanly manger?
> Contend, ye powers of heav'n and earth,
> To fit a bed for this huge birth.
>
> Welcome, all wonders in one sight!
> Eternity shut in a span.

d. *His Was a Welcome Birth.* The birth of a baby, prayed for and eagerly, carefully and rightly planned for, always brings joy to the hearts of expectant parents. Knowing of all His birth meant to His own mother, Jesus could say, "As soon as she [woman] is delivered of the child, she remembereth no more the anguish, for joy that a man is born into the world" (John 16:21). Then He also declared that Abraham "rejoiced to see my day: and he saw it, and was glad" (John 8:56). Christ's birth was the historical fulfillment of the joy of all Old Testament saints who saw from afar such a Messianic event. When the wise men came to where "the young Child was . . . they rejoiced with exceeding great joy" (Matt. 2:10). Mary herself rejoiced in the privilege of being the mother of her Saviour. The angel brought to the shepherds and to all people, "good tidings of *great joy* . . . unto you is born this day . . . a Saviour." A multitude of the heavenly host praised God, as did the shepherds also, for the birth of Christ (Luke 2: 10, 13-20). Godly Simeon had been assured that he would not die until he had seen the Lord's Christ, and when, at last, the Babe came, the aged saint took the Child "up in his arms, and blessed God" (Luke 2:28). The prophetess Anna also shared the same joy over the birth of Jesus and "gave thanks likewise unto the Lord, and spake of him to all them that looked for redemption in Israel" (Luke 2: 38).

Countless multitudes through the ages have rejoiced over the Saviour's coming, and have magnified God for the gift of the Son whom Mary bore. What a dreary, songless world this would have been if Jesus had not taken, "frail flesh, and died." But a joy came to the world from His manger that will never end.

> Hark the glad sound — the Saviour comes!
> The Saviour promised long:
> Let every heart exalt with joy,
> And every voice be song.

The only one who did not rejoice over the birth of the Saviour was Herod who trembled for his throne when he heard that One had been born a king at Bethlehem (Matt. 2:3-18). From the wise men, Herod requested full knowledge of the place of Christ's birth under the pretense of a journey to worship Him, but there was murder, not music, in his heart, for he sought "the young Child to destroy him." When Herod found he had been outwitted, there came his cruel and callous commandment concerning the brutal slaughter of all babies up to two years of age. But "the holy Child Jesus" escaped those bloody massacres of innocent children who became the first martyrs for His sake.

e. *His Was a Royal Birth.* The wise men who studied the Scriptures and the stars were among the noble hearts in the East who looked for a great king to appear from among the Jews. Such a Messianic expectation was begotten by the prophecies of Moses, Isaiah, and Daniel. (See Num. 24:17; Isa. 9; 11; Dan. 7). This hope fermented in the minds of Gentiles as well as Jews, and led many to welcome the birth of the King as the One fulfilling all expectations. But His was an unbefitting entrance as a King for He was born in a stable, and not a palace, surrounded by poverty and not wealth. Jesus came precisely as men did *not* expect Him, shattering their earthly hopes to pieces. There was no royal beauty about Him, that they should desire Him, hence His rejection. "He came . . . they received him not" (John 1:11).

Further, is there not a deeper significance in the statement that this Child was born a King? It is rare indeed for one in a royal family to be born a king. Born a prince, yes, but not a king. The prince becomes the king only on the death or abdication of his kingly father. But Jesus was born a King. How? The simple answer is that Jesus lived before He was born, and when He assumed the body of a baby He was the King in disguise. Does not Paul remind us that He is "the King *eternal,* immortal," and now, to our human eyes, "invisible" (I Tim. 1:17)? Pilate asked Jesus, "Art thou a king then?" Jesus answered, "Thou sayest that I am a king. *To this end was I born*" (John 19:37). As the King, He established a kingdom which is not of this world, or according to worldly standards of royalty and dominion. Out of Bethlehem, "least among the princes of Juda" came Jesus, "a Governor, that should rule my people Israel" (Matt. 2:6).

f. *His Was a Beneficial Birth.* Multitudes of babies are born into the world, grow up and live in it, and then die, without ever benefiting it. The one life they had to live was lived in vain. But no child has meant as much to the world for almost two millenniums as "the Child Jesus." For a full treatment of what God's Son and Mary's Child has meant to mankind the reader is referred to my two volumes on *The Man Who Changed the World.* Christ's impact upon humanity arises from the fact that He was born, not only a King, *but also a Saviour.* The angelic army of the great King magnified Him for coming as a Saviour to bring glory to God, peace on earth, and good will among men.

Before He was born, His name was divinely decreed – "Thou shalt call his name Jesus: for he shall *save* his people from their sins" (Matt. 1:21, 25; Luke 1:31; 2:21). Jesus was a name full of meaning, and in its Old Testament form is Joshua (Num. 14: 6; Neh. 8:17), which means "Jehovah is Salvation," and given to Mary's Child became a specially sacred name. As He was manifested to take away our sins, the salvation He provided was one not only from the guilt and penalty of sin, but also from sin itself. Thus Jesus came not as a teacher, social reformer, model of obedience, or a martyr willing to die for what He believed. No, He was born to die as the Redeemer of the souls of men. He was "made of a woman," to "redeem," and to make sinners the sons of God (Gal. 4:4-7). Because of the way the name Jesus has been greatly enhanced by His life, death and resurrection, it is "the name which is above every name" and the name to which every knee will yet bow (Phil. 2:9, 10). At Bethlehem, that cold night in a manger, a Brother was born for our adversity (Prov. 17:17).

> Jesus, Jesus, let us ever say it
> Softly to ourselves as some sweet spell;
> Jesus, Jesus, troubled spirit lay it
> On thy heart and it will make thee well.
>
> Jesus! Jesus! in the home of glory,
> Still that lovely name shall tune our lays
> Jesus! Jesus! all the wondrous story
> Of His love shall fill eternal days.

Having considered the birth of Jesus, there are several features of His childhood we can profitably meditate on, especially if we are associated with children. Perhaps we can begin by pointing out that Jesus had two homes. His real home was not Bethlehem, where His human life first dawned. It was heaven, known to Him as His Father's house or home (John 14:2, 3). It was to Mary and His foster father, Joseph, that He said, "Did you not know that I must be in my Father's house" (Luke 2:49 RSV). Then there was His declaration, "The Son of man [shall] ascend up where He was before" (John 6:62). Heaven, then, was His native place, His true atmosphere. Before He became Mary's Son, "he was with God," "he was in the bosom of the Father" – words spelling a blessed, uninterrupted intimacy. Listen to Him as He says, "Thou lovedst me before the foundation of the world" (John 17:24).

As Christ's earthly life was closing, He could look through the murky darkness of His agony and think of "the glory I had with thee [God] before the world was" (John 17:5). When He had nowhere to lay His head, He was consoled by the remembrance of the home He had left where "love is its lord and king." But in His humiliation as the Lord of heaven "He became domiciled on one of His own distant estates to reclaim the tenants by lodging with them," and that through His poverty they might become rich. It is His express wish that we might share His heavenly home, beholding His glory (John 17:24). John Oxenham reminds us that –

> The good intent of God became the Christ
> And lived on earth – the Living Love of God,
> That men might draw to closer touch with Heaven,
> Since Christ in all the ways of man hath trod.

One day His first disciple came to Him asking, "Master, where dwellest thou?" The humble home of Joseph and Mary was His earthly dwelling for almost thirty years. It takes a father and mother both to make a home for the normal child, but it is striking to observe that in His first home Jesus had a Father but no mother, while in His second, or earthly, home He had a mother but no father after the flesh. Through His Incarnation He had the experience of a loving home in which He was provided with a mother's care just as in heaven He had a Father's love. All who have children of their own, and boys and girls who love the Child Jesus, are interested in the life He lived as He grew up with brothers and sisters (Matt. 13:56).

As Joseph toiled and Mary spun, the Boy Jesus watched, and when He left to teach and preach the truth of God, He drew many illustrations from His home life in Nazareth. Often He looked out of the cottage door and saw the clucking hens calling their chicks under their wings, and noticed how some willfully stayed outside. This was what the people of Jerusalem did, though He called them again and again under His wings (Matt. 23:37). Wrong-doing and wrong-speaking on the part of parents often leave a searing mark on the character of a young life, just as a home in which habits are regulated by Christian principles produces God-loving children. We have no evidence that, although the family at Nazareth was a large one, there was any element making for disunity; that although it was humble, it was not holy. The constant presence of Jesus must have sanctified it.

A pastor records that one of the saddest things he ever heard spoken came from the lips of a lady who said, "It means nothing to me that God is a Father, for every memory of my father is shadowed and shamed." Although Jesus had a human mother but no human father, yet He was subject to Joseph, His foster father, who, was a just man and obedient to the voice of God (Matt. 1:19, 24). They must have had many a wonderful talk together as they worked side by side in the carpenter's shop. The memory of Joseph was one Jesus would not forget, just as His last thought was about His mother's future welfare. Jesus was never forgetful of the blood relationship. One of the first things He said after His resurrection was, "Go and tell My *brothers* I have risen from the dead, and let them meet Me in Galilee" (Matt. 28:10). Yes, He had blood ties and so do we, for it is the bond of Calvary's blood which makes us brother and sister in Him.

Having considered the birth of Jesus, we now come to several features of His childhood which tradition has loaded with many legends – some of which are ludicrous. Scripture does have some pertinent things to say of His very early years, but nothing of His youth. The only glimpse we have of Him between His first years and the age of thirty when He left His Nazareth for His brief ministry of three years or so, is when he was twelve years old and visited the Temple with His parents. What is written of Him as a child is full of instruction for growing children today, and for those with responsibility of training boys and girls for their life ahead. The renowned hymnist, C. F. Alexander in his ever popular hymn, *Once in Royal David's City,* wrote –

> For He is our childhood's pattern,
> Day by day like us He grew;
> He was little, weak, and helpless,
> Tears and smiles like us He knew;
> And He feeleth for our sadness,
> And He shareth in our gladness.

It is not enough to teach our little children that there is a Friend for them above the bright blue sky, we must impress upon their soft hearts that "the Holy Child Jesus" who developed normally as a child and who was crucified when He reached young manhood, is with them here on earth; that He knows all about their childish tears and smiles and can help them mature as He did.

g. *He Was Circumcised* (Luke 2:21). The first thing we read about Jesus after the description of Him as a babe wrapped in His baby clothes, lying in a manger, is that when He was only eight days old, like John the Baptist, He was circumcised (Luke 1:59; 2:21). Behind the physical aspect of this rite was a separation from the taint of imperfection and sin attached to every child entering the world. But as Jesus was born holy and undefiled and separate from sinners, circumcision was not necessary in our Lord's case. At this stage, however, the whole mystery of His birth had not been revealed to Mary who therefore acted as any loyal Jewess would with a male child, namely, in devout obedience to the law under which she lived (Lev. 12:1-6).

In Christ, even as a child there was not the remotest taint of original and universal corruption, nothing unclean for the circumcising knife to cut away. Yet the wonder of wonders is that when He was only eight days old He was numbered with transgressors. Although He knew no sin, in the act of circumcision He was made sin for us. As Alexander Whyte expresses it, "Mary's firstborn Son was a lamb without blemish and without spot, but before He was a week old, He began to hear the sins of many." Already He was made a sacrifice for sin and for uncleanness not His own. It was the physical pain, as well as the spiritual significance of circumcision that John Milton cast in poetic form –

> He Who with all Heaven's heraldry whilst He
> Entered this world, now bleeds to give us ease.
> Alas! how soon our sin
> Sure doth begin
> His infancy to seize!
> But, oh, ere long
> Huge pangs and strong
> Will pierce more near His heart.

Related to Old Testament circumcision is New Testament baptism with this distinction, the former was associated with blood shedding, and represented, more completely, the intensity of our sin and of our universal and urgent need of the removal of all our sin and imperfection. Such a sacrament of blood signifies our ingrafting into Christ, and our surrender to be the Lord's. The latter ordinance, however, was associated with water, and symbolized the washing away of sin from the heart of the repentant sinner. But Christ had no sin to repent of for He came as the spotless Lamb of God. John, at first, refused to baptize Him, as he had been baptizing repentant sinners, but Jesus submitted to the rite as an indication that He was identified with the sinners He came to save. As He came into the world, He became sin for us. It was in His circumcision as a Babe a week old that He began to save us from our sins.

> Jesus! Name of mercy mild,
> Given to the Holy Child
> When the cup of human woe
> First He tasted here below.

With His circumcision, there came the reaffirmation of His God-given name, Jesus, and His presentation to the Lord by Joseph and Mary who "brought him to Jerusalem, to present him to the Lord" (Luke 2:22-24). The surrender of the child had to be accompanied by a sacrifice commensurate with the means of the offerers. For the poorest who were not able to bring a lamb, a pair of young pigeons could be offered which was all Joseph and Mary could afford. Rich, for our sakes He became poor (Lev. 12:8). Parents, believing their children are gifts from God, should bring their precious offspring into His sanctuary soon after they are born and present them to Him for His benediction and service.

h. *He Grew* (Luke 2:40). Going home after the Dedicatory Service in the Temple, and settling down to the life ahead we have the simple phrase describing a natural process, "And the child grew." Much attention is given to the childhood of the Messiah in prophecy (Isa. 7:14; 9:6), which prepares us for the New Testament infancy narratives, revealing how He came as a helpless Babe and grew up through a normal childhood. Luke, who wrote one of these narratives, doubtless had the satisfaction of a doctor, as he watched the fine physical frame of a sturdy lad developing naturally. We sing of Him as "Gentle Jesus, meek and mild," but although meek, He was not weak. As His body grew big, His muscles kept pace with it.

He grew! Not only did He grow in stature, but also in character. In no way was He stunted in growth. "When the early years of any child's life are neglected, wasted, and mismanaged, all the afteryears of that child's life are bound in shallows and miseries." But Jesus escaped all the stagnation in His early days because "the very first foundation stone of life, character, and service was laid in that body which the Holy Spirit prepared for our Lord as the *instrumentum Deitatis* – the organ and the instrument of His Godhead." As He grew up, His figure would be conspicuous in stateliness and strength, so different from Paul who confessed that his bodily presence was weak. An ancient proverb reads *Mens sana in corpore sano* – "a sound mind in a sound body." Jesus had a stately mind and character in a corresponding bodily stature. With Him, the body was "the inseparable companion and the fit coworker with the mind."

Working, as Jesus did, in a carpenter's shop for some fifteen years enabled Him to develop a powerful physique standing Him in good stead through three years of most arduous service. He could labor hard through the day, and yet forfeit sleep to spend the whole night in prayer. But strong though He was there were occasions when He was weary and needed sleep. Young men are not long in discovering the value and honor of becoming strong in body – to have an active frame, firm limb, fleet foot, sturdy arm, and a hardiness enabling them to toil without too much fatigue, and to conquer in the game. Natural health and vigor is God's gift, and parents must guard their children against spoiling it. It is one thing, however, to have a strong body, and different thing to have a strong, hardy conscience. Many sportsmen or athletes have massive, physical frames but lack stout hearts to resist temptation. What natural vigor is to the body, strength of character is to the mind, so we come to the next feature.

i. *He Waxed Strong in Spirit.* Added to His youthful and childlike powers was strength of character. There was a daily advance within as well as without. In the delightfully well-chosen phrase, "waxed strong in spirit" we are reminded that as "Jesus grew in the number of His years, and the stateliness of His bodily presence, so He waxed strong in spirit; in the endowments of His mind, and in the affections of His heart." Alexander Whyte further wrote in *The Walk, Conversation and Character of Jesus Christ Our Lord* –

> There was not one atom of what we censure as precocity and prematurity about the Holy Child. Not one atom. At eight days old, He was just what an eight days' old child should be. And at twelve years old, He was just what a twelve, or, say, sixteen years' old lad should be. Take Him at any year of His life you like, and He was neither a year younger, nor a year older, than that. When he was a child, He spake as a child, He understood as a child, He thought as a child. And it was only when He became a man that He put away childish things. There was first the blade, and then the ear, and then the full corn in the ear. And it was not till the fruit was brought forth, that the sickle was put in, because the harvest was come.

Alan Whicker, an outstanding British TV personality, well-known for his remarkable interviews, recently visited the U.S.A., and staged a TV program called *America '69*. In a magazine layout of his documentary film, he referred to "The Cult of Childhood, whose followers are those remarkably self-assured pre-teens, the first media generation which Marshall McLuhan describes as 'far more interesting and exciting a bunch that ever appeared on the face of the earth.' Americans would rather have their children well-adjusted than well-behaved, so it is common knowledge they're unspeakable loudmouths who bully their parents. Foreigners have known this for two centuries. It is not necessary to meet American children to be aware how awful they are."

Americans, with the same empty authority, see English children unresponsive, unchildlike, repressed. Depending on your side of the Atlantic, "American children are admirably at ease in an adult world, or spoiled brats who chant beer commercials but don't know their national anthem." How far Whicker is right in his appraisal of American childhood, others must decide! This we do know, that if youth today would only follow the youthful Christ as He developed physically, mentally, and spiritually, they would not be in the mess they are. How strong and noble they would be if only they remembered Him in the days of their youth!

j. *He Was Filled With Wisdom* (Luke 2:40). He who came as the personification and perfection of wisdom, and was made unto us wisdom, yet had a human mind that expanded with His growing body. As His mind opened, wisdom was poured into it from different sources. He drank in whatever wisdom there was in knowledge of those about Him. The good and great King Alfred used to regret in later years nothing so much as that, owing to his long wanderings and troubles when he was young, he had not had the opportunity of regular instruction at school. The childhood of Jesus was more sheltered and regular, and He learned wisdom from the Scriptures, from rabbinical teaching at the Jewish school, and from asking and answering questions, as He did in the Temple. Nothing is more charming than to hear a child asking questions in order to learn.

Because, as Solomon says, "Wisdom is the principle thing; therefore get wisdom" (Prov. 4:7), it is said that Jesus was filled with wisdom, not knowledge or great talents. Knowledge is necessary but so often puffs up; wisdom always edifies. All Jesus heard, read, and saw was turned into wisdom to Him, like the water He turned into wine. "Everything He learned in His head, straightway descended into His heart, and then out of His heart were the issues of His wise, and holy, and heavenly life." Combining the physical and the mental, Luke says that "Jesus increased in wisdom and stature" (Luke 2:52). Is it any wonder then that when He came to teach in the synagogue those hearing Him were astonished and said, "From whence hath this man these things? and what wisdom is this which is given unto Him?" (Mark 6:2). Christ grew every day in divine wisdom until He was filled with this wisdom every day. Doubtless His first instructors in wisdom from above were His parents, which is what God meant all parents to be.

Was not our Lord a little Child,
  Taught by degrees to pray;
By father dear and mother mild
  Instructed day by day?

And loved He not of Heaven to talk,
  With children in His sight;
To meet them in His daily walk,
  And to His arms invite?

k. *He Increased in Favor With God and Man* (Luke 2:52). What more beautiful words than these could be found to describe anyone's character? There was never any youthful folly in the pure life of Jesus to grieve His heavenly Father's heart, or to break the hearts of His earthly parents. Phillips gives us the translation, "He grew also in the love of God and of those who knew him." The word "favour" has the idea of "good graces," and Jesus was always in the good graces of God and of those who knew and loved Him. Life upward then outward are implied in the words, "With God and man." Pleasing to God, He was pleasing to others. "This man hath done nothing amiss."

So as the child grew into boyhood, and the boy grew into youth, and the young man into manhood, the purity and lowliness and unselfish sympathy which Jesus manifested earned Him His Father's benediction and drew the hearts of all men to Him. Alas! however, there were those like the scribes and Pharisees who admired His God-like character until His holiness became aggressive against their hypocrisy and roused in them an antagonism bitter in proportion to any previous admiration they may have had for Jesus. Too often our desire to remain in God's good graces brings us into conflict with men who are adverse to honoring Him in all His ways. Further, seeking to court the favor of man causes us to lose the favor of God. Young though He was, Jesus increased in favor with God — God first — and with man. He never sinned against God or man.

l. *He had the Grace of God Upon Him* (Luke 2:40). By "grace" as used here it implies the gracefulness of a person, and not the ordinary evangelical acceptation of the word as in the phrase, "By grace are ye saved." This grace implies more than favor which may be deserved or gained. Saving grace is a free gift which repentant sinners accept by faith. The grace of God that came upon Jesus was not the grace bringing salvation, for as the sinless One He had no need of such. We might render the phrase, "The good pleasure of God was upon Him." At His baptism the divine voice said, "This is My beloved Son, in whom I am well pleased" (Matt. 3:17).

Surely no child, no boy, no young man in all Galilee was in such divine and universal favor. The graciousness of God became more manifest in Jesus as He grew up. In Him it increased more and more, and evoked gratitude from man. His disposition was always fragrant and sweet and kind, and as we linger in His gracious presence our lives become "like a watered garden, full of fragrance rare." James Learmount in stories for children in *The Year Round*, tells a delightful one about a little flaxen-haired child who went into a chemist's shop with the request:

"I want two pennyworth of glory divine."

The people in the shop laughed at the child's order, but the man behind the counter looked rather serious.

"Are you sure it is glory divine you want?"

"Yes, sir," was the wee girl's prompt reply.

"For what does mother want it?" asked the kind salesman.

"To throw around the room and in the backyard," said the little one innocently.

"Isn't it chloride of lime she wants?" asked the chemist.

The small girl nodded her assent, and was soon supplied. But was she not right as far as we are concerned? We all want more of the glory divine to carry around with us.

"Chloride of lime," sounding very much like "glory divine," is a wholesome thing, killing evil germs wherever it goes, and when one carries glory divine in the heart, he carries about with him an atmosphere, a sweetness, a fragrance that kills all evil things that are around us — bad temper, selfishness, unkindness, evil talk and deeds. It is not so hard to be good when a friend is near who has glory divine in the heart.

When it is said that graciousness covered Jesus as a robe, it simply means the fragrance, or glory divine, He scattered made other lives sweet and beautiful. And the more we live in His perfumed presence, the more will the glory divine shine through us.

m. *He Was Subject Unto His Parents* (Luke 2:51). The word "subject" is a military term implying the obedience of a soldier to his superior officer. Used here by Luke, it expresses a great deal respecting Christ's early life. Joseph and Mary were poor, humble, working people, and if Jesus was subject or obedient to them, it means He did what they told Him, and thereby endeared Himself to them. Subject means that He must have done the work of poor people, have eaten the bread of carefulness, have shared the life of a humble household, and have been content to do the lowly tasks assigned Him. Children should obey their parents because of their wider experience and mature wisdom, and because they are the natural guardians appointed by God for the welfare of their children.

Through all His wondrous childhood
He would honour and obey,
Love and watch the lowly Maiden,
In whose gentle arms He lay.
Christian children all must be
Mild, obedient, good as He.

When Henry Grady the great southern Christian statesman made his first trip to Washington, he had a strange experience. He had looked forward to seeing the nation's capitol building. Standing in a position where the building stood out in bold relief, he said in deep emotion, "So this is the home of the nation." Upon his return to Georgia he had occasion to spend a night in a humble planter's home. Before retiring, the father called about him the family, and in flickering candlelight he read the Bible and they knelt in prayer. It was an old-fashioned family altar. Stirred again, Henry Grady said, "I was mistaken about the home of the nation being at Washington. That pile of marble, as magnificent as it is, is not the home of the nation. The home of the nation is found in the dugout, cottage, cabin, and every home where they teach the children to honor the Word of God and serve the Christ it reveals."

The famous preacher, Spurgeon, has given this description of the home: "The word home always sounds like poetry to me. It rings like a peal of bells at a wedding, only more soft and sweet, and it chimes deeper into the ears of my heart. It does not matter whether it means thatched cottage or manor house; home is home, be it ever so homely, and there's no place on earth like it."

When Jonathan Edwards, of revival fame, was a lad living in his father's manse, he made several resolutions. Here are two of them we can all take to heart –

No. 46. Resolved: never to allow the least measure of any fretting or uneasiness at my father or mother. Resolved: to suffer no effects of it, so much as in the least alteration of speech, or motion of the eye; and to be specially careful of it with respect to any of our family.

No. 47. Resolved: to cultivate assiduously a temper good and universally sweet and benevolent, quiet, peaceable, contented and easy, compassionate and generous, and ever patient, moderate, forgiving and sincere; and to do at all times, what such a temper would lead me to do; and to examine strictly at the end of every day and every week whether I had so done. Sabbath morning, May 5, 1723.

It was from Christ that Jonathan Edwards learned about those home graces he resolved to exhibit. In His deference and obedience, subjection and submission to His parents in the small house in which He lived with His younger brothers and sisters, Jesus has left an example for all boys and girls to copy. In all things He is the model of perfection (Heb. 5:9). He is like a jewel with many surfaces. Each is different from the rest, but all are perfect in their kind. He was perfect in home relationships, just as He was perfect in His life godward; and it was because of the perfection of His character, as a child, youth, and man, that, by His death and resurrection He became the perfect Saviour.

In Him all virtues are consummated, and His adequacy as the ideal for all ages has never changed. The children can sing – "Gentle Jesus, meek and mild." Youth can sing – "The Son of God goes forth to war." The mature can sing – "How firm a foundation, ye saints of the Lord"! The aged sing –

> While life's dark maze I tread,
> And griefs around me spread,
> Be Thou my Guide!

Having been a child, no one before spoke so tenderly of children as Jesus, and living at home as long as He did, He likewise understands the heart of a parent. It is because no one thought of a child as "the Holy Child Jesus" did, that it is due to Him that children all over the Christian world are treated with tenderness. Further, to the spiritually trained child the Lord Jesus, as He is presented, not only in His childhood, but in His life and death, is in reality the chief among ten thousand and the altogether lovely. The exhortation of Alexander Whyte to Christian parents is well worthy of repetition.

> Pray importunately that your child may be made of God, both to Him, and to you, a twin brother of the Holy Child Jesus. Pray without ceasing that your child may be sanctified with the self-same sanctification as Mary's Child. And if that may not be perfected all at once, as His sanctification was, pray that at least it may be begun as long as you are here to see it and to have a hand in it. Take your child apart, as long as he is docile and will go with you, and ask on your knees, and in his hearing, something like this –
>
> > O God, the God and Father of the Holy Child Jesus, make this, my dear child, a child of God with Him. And after I am gone make him and keep him a man of God.
>
> Take no rest yourself, and give God no rest, till you see a seed of God not only sown in your child's heart, but till you see him, as Mary saw her first-born Son, subject to her in everything in her house at home, and growing up every day in wisdom, and in stature, and in favour with God and man.

As we leave the soul-absorbing theme of our Lord's begetting within Mary, and of the Holy Spirit's part in preparing a body for God's beloved Son, there are several applications one could make. The two main ones are –

(1.) *The Virgin Birth Is a Figure of Regeneration.*

It must be evident to every spiritually-minded believer that the mystery of the Virgin Birth of our Lord is related to the new birth of the sinner. Take for instance passages like,

"Which were born . . . of God" (John 1:13).
"That which is born of the Spirit is spirit" (John 3:6).
"Through the Spirit . . . being born again" (I Pet. 1:22, 23).

And what do we find within such? Why, just as our Lord was born of the Holy Ghost and thereby received another nature, namely, a human one, so the sinner is born again by the same Spirit and receives as a consequence a new nature, namely, a divine one.

It is because Christ took our flesh and was born of a virgin that He can be spiritually born in our hearts. And what will it profit us that Christ was born into the world unless He be born in our hearts? Yes, and once we experience the Holy Spirit's work of regeneration there is no difficulty regarding the Virgin Birth! Why, it is the fact of the Virgin Birth that gives power to the appeal for man's regeneration.

"If we realize," says Prebendary Sadler, "that He who died to save us is God Incarnate, we never can be tormented with doubts about the ability and willingness to save, or whether we have an interest in Him. We are raised into an atmosphere above all this.

"Able to save you? – Why, He is your God.

"Willing to save you? – Why, He took your flesh for this one purpose."

The Virgin Birth is both the figure and the pledge of regeneration; thus with true hearts we sing the carol –

Mild He lays His glory by,
Born that man no more may die;
Born to raise the sons of earth,
Born to give them second birth.

Yet the tragedy of it all is that although Christ's Virgin Birth gives such efficacy to the blood He shed, an efficacy which can be experienced only by those who trust it, so many fail to believe such a stupendous fact. Indeed, one can detect the shadow of Calvary gathered around Bethlehem that night our Lord was born. "The little village of the least of the tribes said truly it had no room for the Immense and the Incomprehensible. There was an unconscious truth even in its inhospitality." "And," as F. W. Faber goes on to say, "as He was born outside the walls of Bethlehem, so must He die outside the walls of Jerusalem. Alas! the spirit of Bethlehem is but the spirit of a world which has forgotten God! . . . Bethlehem is what the Creator does to His creatures, Calvary what His creatures do to Him!"

(2.) *The Virgin Birth Is a Foreshadowing of Sanctification.*

Keeping in mind the outstanding features of our Lord's Virgin Birth, we can understand more fully the doctrine of sanctification as we have it in Paul's mystic phrase of Gal. 4:19 – "I travail in birth again until Christ be formed in you." Many things are beyond the range of our understanding in connection with the Virgin Birth, but these factors are open to us, namely, Mary's faith and self-surrender, and on the other hand the operation of the Holy Spirit. Paul's desire for the believers at Galatia, which is but an echo of the inner message of the Virgin Birth, is that the reincarnation of Christ is possible only when we have Mary's self-surrender and faith, and when, like her, we allow the Holy Spirit to produce Christ in and through us.

O Jesus Christ, grow Thou in me
　And all things else recede:
My heart be daily nearer Thee,
　From sin be daily freed.

In Mary's submission of her body, yes, and of her reputation also for the time being, we see the only pathway to a life that is radiant with the image of our Lord. Let us look in closing at her word of full acquiescence regarding the divine will. Here are her beautiful words, breathing it would seem the very air of Gethsemane and Calvary – "Behold the handmaid of the Lord; be it unto me according to thy word" (Luke 1:38). The word "handmaid" we are told is *doulee* signifying "the female slave." There are two Messianic Psalms where the phrase "The son of thine handmaid" occurs (Ps. 86:16; 116:16), and in both instances the word "handmaid" means the same thing, namely, "the female slave."

Such a word not only reveals the depths of humiliation that our Lord descended to when He became the Son of God's female slave; it also speaks to us of Mary's entire surrender to the Lord. She called herself the slave of the Lord! And as a slave her body was not her own but her Master's, and thus to Him it was surrendered in full and glad obedience.

Before reader and writer part company, shall we not put this question to our separate hearts – Am I willing to become the slave of the Lord in order that Christ may be formed in me? Are we prepared to follow Mary in her blissful submission and say – "Behold the female (or male) slave of the Lord; be it unto me according to thy word"? Can we each say, as we bow silently before "Our glorious Victor, Prince divine," that we are "glad vassals of a Saviour's throne"? If we can, then we have caught the inner meaning of the Virgin Birth, and the Holy Ghost will assuredly overshadow us, even as He did the virgin, and extract the dross from the silver until in all our ways, thoughts and words, Christ is formed.

And so at the end of our meditation upon such a sacred theme we return to our opening thought; that is – the holy, virgin life of the believer is necessary if the Virgin Birth of our Lord is to be rightly comprehended. Professor A. B. Bruce once wrote, "With the denial of the Virgin Birth is apt to go denial of the Virgin Life." Not only so, but it is the constant presence of Christ within us that keeps our lives like His own. Or as Watson in his *Body of Divinity* would have us remember – "As Christ was conceived in the womb of a virgin, so, if He be born in thee, thy heart is a virgin-heart in respect of sincerity and sanctity. Art thou purified from the love of sin? If Christ be born in thy heart, it is a *Sanctum Sanctorum,* a holy of holies. If thy heart be polluted with the predominant love of sin, never think Christ is born there. Christ will never lie any more in a stable. If He be born in thy heart, it is consecrated by the Holy Ghost." With such a spiritual application John the apostle agrees when he declares that "Whatsoever is born of God overcometh the world," and "Whosoever is born of God sinneth not" (I John 5:4, 18).

Such is God's ideal for your life and mine, and it can be blessedly realized as the result of the Virgin Birth of our Lord. How shall we respond?

3. The Child Born Blind (John 9:1, 20)

Previous mention has been made of this tragic accident at birth. "Blind from his birth"! Can we not picture behind this bald statement the anguish of his parents when they realized the child they eagerly anticipated came into the world with sightless eyes, and that as he grew up he would be only a beggar pleading for alms from passers-by? Those who are born with sight but lose it forfeit the enjoyment of light, but those who are born blind have no idea of it. We can imagine that a person born blind would be thrilled to have his curiosity satisfied with but one day's sight of lights and colors, shapes and figures, though he were never to see them again. How we should bless God if we have eyes that can see! Personally, I never meet a blind person without thanking the Creator for my sight.

Christ cured many blinded by disease or accident, but here He revealed His power to help in the most desperate cases by curing one who was born blind. Ellicott observes that "of the six miracles connected with blindness which are recorded in the gospels, this is the only case described as blindness from birth. In this lies its special significance, for 'since the world began, was it not heard that any man opened the eyes of one that was born blind'" (John 9:32). Such a miracle had a threefold result. First of all, curing this blind man was a kindness to the public whose sympathy kept the man in food. By His noble act Jesus served the public by relieving the passers-by of having to care for the beggar who, now that he could see, would be able to work for a living and be a charge upon his friends and neighbors no more.

The second result was that once the man came to know who the Benefactor was who gave him the priceless gift of sight, he became one of His grateful followers. As He revealed Himself as the Son of God with power, there came the response of the once-blind man, "Lord, I believe. And he worshipped him" (John 9:38).

Then in the third place this miracle gave Jesus the opportunity of using physical blindness as an illustration of spiritual blindness and of the difference between spiritual light and satanic darkness (John 9:35-41). We have a saying that, "None are so blind as those who won't see." Spiritually, the Pharisees lived in a denser darkness than the blind man had experienced. This miracle was a specimen of the work of His grace upon the souls of sinners which gives sight to those who were by nature blind.

"Once I was blind, but now I can see,
The light of the world is Jesus."

The question arises why this man was born blind. The disciples felt that sin must have been the cause of the affliction either in the man or his parents. The Pharisees went further and told the beggar who now saw that he was altogether born in sin and therefore born blind (John 9:34). As the man had come into the world as a baby with sightless eyes, it was most cruel and unjust to condemn an innocent babe with having sinned – Jesus gave the reason for the blind baby's entrance into the world, namely, "that the works of God should be made manifest in him" (John 9:3). The disciples sought to trace the blindness back to sin; Jesus traced it back to the region of divine council, where purpose and result are one. Often, to our finite minds, the ways of Providence are unaccountable, yet every time –

"Behind a frowning providence
He hides a smiling face."

What God permitted in the case of the blind beggar, He yet overruled in order that light might dawn upon spiritual as well as upon physical blindness. We would never have had the revelation of Jesus as "The Light of the World" had it not been for this man born blind.

Can we not say that one by-product of the miracle Jesus performed as He passed by one of the gates of the Temple is the effort through the centuries to train and educate blind children to become independent of charity? Had those parents had a school for blind children their baby would never have become a beggar. But babies born then never had a chance to know how to learn to write and read and work with their hands. Now, thanks to Christianity, the education of blind children cannot begin too soon. Deprived of sight, they are taught early to develop other senses through experience.

While from early times gifted persons, blind from birth, have achieved fame, organized efforts to care for those born blind, or who have become handicapped through being blinded after having sight, sprang from the example of the compassion of Christ who gave sight to the blind. Back in the fourth century St. Basil founded an inn for blind persons in Cappodocia. Then in the fifth century the hermit, St. Lymnaeus, established a refuge for the blind in Syr in Syria, erecting special cottages for their use. Reaching the seventh century we find St. Bertrand of Le Mans opening an institute for the blind at Pontlieu. In the eleventh century we have the classic case of William the Conqueror who, in expiation of his sins, founded several inns in Normandy for blind and infirm persons.

But it was not until the close of the eighteenth century that more widespread and definite efforts were made to educate those without sight to become useful members of society. Pity for such an affliction was not enough. Valentin Haūy (1745 - 1822), who earned the title, "Father and Apostle of the Blind," was led to set out on his determination to help the blind by listening to Marie Theresa Von Paradis, the noted blind Austrian pianist. In 1784 Haūy opened in Paris his School for the Blind with twelve blind boys and girls as his first pupils. He invented a kind of raised print – forerunner of Braille – which they could read. Such was his success in teaching the blind to read and study that Haūy was asked to organize similar schools in other countries.

The first in Britain was opened in Liverpool in 1799. In 1833 three Schools for the Blind were opened in America. By 1837 the first entirely state-supported U.S. School for the Blind was opened in Ohio. Several efforts had been made to teach the blind to read, but it was Louis Braille, a French blind teacher who, in 1829, invented a system of reading which with a few modifications was universally adopted throughout the English-speaking world. Now blind children can go to school, then to a university, and out into the world to live useful lives. Organizations like The National Institution for the Blind teach the blind to become efficient as craftsmen.

Thinking again of the man who was born blind it is to be questioned whether we realize what a vast and complex problem universal blindness is. First of all, why are some babies born blind today? Apart from the divine explanation of the reason for the beggar's blindness at birth, what are the causes behind the birth of blind babies in our generation? Such a pertinent question is forced upon us as we remember that in India alone there is a blind population of around 2,000,000. Other related countries face the same tragedy of blindness. In fact, it is calculated that seventy-five to eighty percent of the world's sightless people live in the countries of Asia. While governments, schools, and voluntary agencies are making great efforts, the problem is still acute, especially in the aspect of child blindness.

The man born blind had what is now called congenital blindness, that is the blindness of prenatal origin resulting in a baby being born blind or with very serious eye defects. In the early part of this century, babies' sore eyes, or ophthalmia neonatorum, as the affliction is called, acquired from gonorrhea organism in the birth canal of the mother was the major cause of blindness in children. But it was found that the use of silver nitrate drops in the eyes of infants immediately after birth practically eliminated this serious affliction.

Basic research into prenatal factors producing blindness has proved that an accident during pregnancy or an attack of German measles, or a maldevelopment due to the presence of syphilis, or leprosy, or a tumor result in babies being born blind. Medical science is intensifying its efforts to prevent babies, perfect in every other way, from entering a "land of darkness and blind eyes." Those who are unfortunate enough to be born without sight are not as helpless as the blind beggar was. They can be taught now to live normally and to achieve the highest position in almost every sphere. Colley Cibber (1671 - 1757) wrote a poem called *The Blind Boy,* a verse of which goes –

O say! What is that thing called Light,
Which I can ne'er enjoy? . . .
Whilst thus I sing, I am a King,
Altho' a poor blind boy.

There are many who cannot see, but they can sing because like the blind man Jesus cured they have come to see with the inner eye of faith that in Him is no darkness at all. Physically blind they still are, but they walk in the light as He is in the light. Theirs is no longer "a blind life within the brain," of which Tennyson wrote in *The Idylls of the King.*

4. The Child of the Nobleman (John 4:46-54)

What a heart-moving plea this ruler presented to Jesus, "Sir, come down ere my child die"! (verse 49). The death of a child often leaves a deep scar, with all hope buried in a tiny grave. But in the case of courtier or high-ranking military officer, human sorrow became the birth-pang of faith. In his utter helplessness the distressed father cast himself upon the mighty God for the life of his child, and although his faith was weak, it was there. A strong faith in a wrong object can never bring relief, but a weak faith in a right object always produces results. The nobleman did not realize that Jesus could speak the word, and the child, although some distance away, could be healed. The distraught father felt that the presence of Jesus in his home was necessary for his son's life and so pled with Him, "Come down, ere my child die."

Parents who never have children's sickrooms, and the experience of the certain nobleman we are thinking about, are rare indeed. Dread sickness and disease often attack the children of the godliest parents, and agonized by the sight of little ones suffering, or in fear of losing them, these parents ask themselves the question, Why does God permit small innocent children to suffer? One answer is for the purification and the strengthening of faith, as in the case of the nobleman who came to know what it was to meet the extreme sickness of his child by faith in Jesus. A general faith begotten by what he had heard of Christ's compassion and power brought him into contact with the Healer which resulted in an experiential faith. "The man believed the word that Jesus had spoken unto him" (verse 50). Such a faith became a shared faith for "himself believed, and his whole house."

The divine purpose, then, in sickness, whether in child or parent, is to foster that simple, childlike faith in divine ability, which, while it cannot give account of its assurance to reason, yet through the Spirit has the assurance that having asked, the need will be met. In the school of sickness, parents learn how to offer the prayer of faith, and if healing is granted or denied, rest in the fact that God's will is the best for them and theirs. Further, sick children are sometimes God's messengers to parents convicting them of parental shortcomings. Heart and life and home are searched as to whether the children have been wholly devoted to the Lord, or if unworthy parental conduct has prevented the young from seeking Him. Does He not still take parents into the sick room of their little ones, that there they may learn to seek and find Him, and to receive a fuller revelation of His power and love?

5. THE CHILD LUNATIC (Matt. 17:14-21; Mark 9:14-29; Luke 9:37-43)

Emphasis is upon the fact that this demon-possessed son was a child whose lack of balance caused him to fall frequently "into the fire and into the waters." In his record of this demoniac child, Luke the beloved physician reveals his tender sympathy for, as also in the case of the widow of Nain, he is the only writer who calls attention to the boy being an *only child* – which added poignancy to the father's plea for help. An only child is cared for as a treasure, and draws all the love and attention of parents upon himself. But a child who is a member of a large family is trained and restrained by those among whom he lives, and becomes a sharer in what his parents can give. A solitary flower in a garden is always conspicuous, but loses its sole attractiveness when other lovely flowers grow up beside it.

It is interesting to observe that in this record cited by the first three writers of the New Testament Jesus used a stronger word than He did when He said to His disciples, "*Suffer* the little children to come unto me, and forbid them not" (Mark 10:14). When the father of the lunatic child told Jesus that His disciples were unable to cast out the evil spirit, He rebuked their unbelief when He said, "*Bring* the child to me." Little ones were always willing to come to this loving Friend to be blessed, but this poor child had to be brought, no matter how he may have rebelled. Every parent has the liberty and the power to bring his child, no matter how desperate resistance may be, to Jesus. In every extremity of sin or need, the voice of Jesus calls, "Bring the child to me."

As the father brought his child, over whom Satan had such a hold, to Jesus, telling Him the touching story how from childhood his boy had been the victim of such terrible possession, he pleaded "*If thou canst do* anything, have compassion on us, and help us" (Mark 9:22). But Jesus tossed the ball back again, and throwing the whole responsibility of the case upon the father said, "*If thou canst believe*, all things are possible to him that believeth" (verse 23). It was not a question whether Jesus could or would relieve the demon-possessed child, but whether the father had faith enough to believe Jesus could do it. If he had such faith, the healing was sure: if he lacked it, then the miracle would not be performed. "All things are possible to him that believeth." Faith is the exercise of a will that yields itself to God's holy will to take possession of it and work out its pleasure.

Thus, in speaking to the father of the poor child as He did, Jesus gave us for all time the secret of fruitful parental training and prayer. Every Christian parent needs to exercise strong faith as he brings his child to Jesus for the deliverance He alone can give. Some parents may think the attitude of Jesus in His dealing with the father who was almost at his wits' end, somewhat hard. Surely the pitiable condition of the child should have been a sufficient reason for a cure – without strings attached. Others may argue that although they bring their children to God, it is His sovereign will whether they should be saved, and that all the responsibility should be thrown on them. The comment of Andrew Murray is –

> Scripture reveals to us most clearly God's sovereignty; His grace is electing grace; the final decision of each man is in His hands. Scripture reveals as clearly man's responsibility, and the all-prevailing power of faith. True humility accepts both statements without reconciling them; it bows under the solemn truth Jesus utters here, that if the parent can believe the child can be saved.

Made to feel that his unbelief could rob his dear, demented child of relief, the father, bursting into tears, cried, "Lord, I believe; help thou mine unbelief" (Mark 9:24), and amid his crying and confession the faith was exercised which resulted in his child being made whole. When a father pleads for his child's liberation from Satan's power, his tears and confession of unbelief have power. "The first step in the path of an overcoming faith is the confession of sinfulness, and the sins of which it is the index and symptom." Parental sins hinder the answer to parental supplications for a child's salvation. A lesson so hard for parents to learn is that if only they allow their children to first bring them to Jesus in confession, prayer, and truth, then their faith can bring the children out of the power of the evil one.

6. The Child of Jairus (Matt. 9:18-26; Mark 5:22-43; Luke 8:41-56)

Jesus called the only daughter of Jairus a "maid." Her father spoke of her as, "My little daughter." Luke says that she was an only child, "about twelve years of age." The word Jesus used, *Talitha,* means, "My lamb." Harrington C. Lees in *The Divine Master in Home Life,* says that "Jesus stands by the dead girl and says some of the tenderest words in all the gospel story, words which perhaps He Himself had been awakened many a morning by His mother in the little bed chamber at Nazareth – *Talitha Cumi.* 'My lamb, it is getting up time.' This is the same as used for rising from sleep in Deut. 6:7; II Kings 6:15. 'And the maid arose.' Was any sweeter sentence ever said over the still form of a child?"

Actually the resurrection of this little Jewish girl was a miracle within a miracle, for when Jesus was on His way to the home of death a woman approached Him and insisted on being cured of her disease. It was while Jesus was dealing with her that messengers came to Jairus and said, "Thy daughter is dead: why troublest thou the Master any further" (Mark 5:35), indicating that it was all over – too late to do anything for the girl. They were not aware that no time is too late for Him whose power has no limit. "There are no dates in God's leisure." We are not told what strange feelings the girl must have had when her soul came back into the body it had recently forsaken. Was she startled or frightened? Perhaps she could say about her return to life what Malan of Geneva said of his new life in Christ, "I was awakened as a mother awakens her child with a kiss."

Would you not like to know something of the later history of the resurrected daughter of Jairus? One thing is certain, she must have loved the One who gave her back to her father and mother, and that she became His by every tie of gratitude. What impresses us is the way the Lord of the living and of the dead speaks about dying. Once in the house of mourning, He would not have the word "dying" used. "The damsel is not dead, but sleepeth" – a figure used only of the body, not of the soul! The body falls asleep, but whether it sleeps for a few moments, as did this girl's, or a thousand years, at the Resurrection it awakes never to fall asleep again.

When a child sickens and dies, Jesus is still near saying to grief-stricken parents and to all mourners, "Fear not, only believe." "Fear not the seemingly dark and dreary void into which thy loved one has passed. Fear not that God will desert thee in thine hour of need. Fear not but that thou wilt once more see the child, or other loved one thou hast lost. Only believe in the lovingkindness of God our Saviour. Only believe that He who makes the flowers to spring and the buds to come forth again, will raise that little flower, will help that bursting blossom of the human soul."

In telling this story of the daughter of Jairus to children, parents and teachers can stress that there is a spiritual sleep that can overcome little lambs who are always precious to the Good Shepherd; and that they must bestir themselves and get up from idle, selfish, or wrong habits, and live again in Jesus; that they can be lambs of His fold. All lovers of children must teach them the significance of one of their hymns –

It is a thing most wonderful,
Almost too wonderful to be,
That God's own Son should come from heaven,
And die to save a child like me!

Dealing with the name Jairus, W. F. Wilkinson reminds us that this ruler, whose daughter Jesus restored to life, has the name "Jair," first mentioned as that of a successful chieftain of the tribe of Manasseh, and next as that of a judge of Israel, a Gileadite belonging to the same tribe. The meaning of such a name is, "He shall enlighten," and may be either a prayer that God shall from the birth of a child, or by His means, give light, that is, "prosperity," to the family, or the expression of a hope that the child shall prove a light or blessing to others.

The prayer and the hope were both fulfilled in the experience of Jairus, for the light of divine truth and of spiritual life shone upon him and his when his daughter was redeemed from death by the almighty power of Jesus. Although He forbade the grateful father to proclaim the glory and goodness of his great Benefactor at the time of the miracle, we can image how afterward he freely testified of Him who had in so marvelous a fashion revealed Himself under the roof of his home as "The Resurrection and the Life," giving proof, thereby, of His readiness to receive the prayer of faith, to increase the faith of all who come to Him, and to manifest Himself to His own as He does not do to the world.

7. The Child of the Syrophenician (Matt. 15:21-28; Mark 7:24-30)

A somewhat striking and surprising feature of the gospels is the fact that many of the most precious and encouraging words of Christ in regard to faith were spoken to parents in reference to their children, and to, and about, children themselves.

"Fear not, only believe."
"All things are possible to him that believeth."
"Great is thy faith; be it unto thee even as thou wilt."

These "faith" utterances have frequently been the strength and comfort of sinners seeking divine pardon, or have encouraged believers pleading for some blessing from above. But it must not be forgotten that in the first place these utterances of Jesus are the property of parents, assuring them that there is no case in which a child, under Satan's power, is beyond the reach of the Master's power and love and a parent's faith. The well-known story of the Syrophenician mother proclaims that there is hope for a child who may grow up in sin, and pass out from beyond the reach of a parent's influence.

a. *Her Description.* Matthew describes the distressed mother as "a woman of Canaan." As a Canaanite, she was of Phoenicia whose inhabitants were so called (Exod. 3:8, 17; Ezra 9:1). She was thus a "Syrophenician by nation." The Emperor Hadrian divided the province of Syria into three parts – Syria proper, Syro-Phoenicia, and Syria-Palestina. Mark, who had a liking for Latin forms, also spoke of her as a "Greek," a term meaning "Gentile" – the sense in which Paul used it (Rom. 1:16; 2:9, 10). The way in which this Canaanitish woman addressed Jesus, "thou son of David" proves how the fame of the Prophet of Nazareth had traveled beyond the limits of Galilee. Learning of this remarkable healer with a Messianic name she cherished the hope that somehow He must come within her reach and heal her demoniac daughter.

What a thrill it must have been when, beyond all expectation, Jesus did cross the boundary of Israel, and she was able to see Him in her own country. In His incomparable story of "The Good Samaritan," Jesus spoke of him as coming to where the robbed, half-dead traveler was – an illustration of His own eagerness to find His way where need is. Nationality, position, religion, and age made no difference to Him with whom there was never any respect of persons. He was always drawn to the physical, material and spiritual needs of men as filings to a magnet. In the incident before us Mark informs us that to avoid undue publicity Jesus, as He crossed the borders of Tyre and Sidon, entered a house to be in seclusion for a while, "but he could not be hid." You cannot hide the beautiful fragrance of a rose, and so a Gentile found Him.

b. *Her Despair.* What anguish dominates the cry of this mother, "Have mercy on me, O Lord, thou son of David; my daughter is grievously vexed with a devil." This poor girl was young – how young we are not told. At an early age Satan entered into her. What misery this girl had in the plague of her own soul! In the ancient world the human soul was often represented on canvas or in marble as a young girl with wings, but torn and bound by evil spirits. In the daughter of the woman of Canaan we see what Satan does in the soul he enslaves – he "grievously vexes." What terrible fear, misery, torment, so unnatural in a girl, this satanically-controlled one must have endured! This was not some form of physical sickness but the possession of the soul by an evil spirit.

The question may be asked as to whether young boys and girls of our time can be subject to demon-possession. What other explanation is there for the crime, violence, hooliganism and the cruel treatment of parents by many young people than that they are demon-possessed? Many a loving mother cries out in prayer to the children's Redeemer, "My child is grievously vexed with the devil." In our permissive society too many children are under the power of Satan and are enemies of God as well as a menace to a well-ordered society. How we should concentrate intercession on the misguided, evil-inspired young people around us that they might be delivered from the devil and translated into the kingdom of God's dear Son!

We all know that the miracles Jesus performed for the sick, diseased and demon-vexed were parables of what He is able to do for diseases of the soul. Where sin is, there is Satan, the cruel despot, for he is "the spirit that worketh in the children of disobedience." He it is who tempts young people to lie, steal, swear, destroy and to dishonor and disobey parents. The casting off of all moral restraint makes them Satan's slaves. How terrible is his power over a sinning soul: it is just like his power over the girl's body in the record we are considering! That Satan is the worst of tyrants and tormentors is seen in that in the end he vexes the soul as grievously as he tormented this writhing girl, the Syrophenician's daughter. And just as all the gods and physicians in Tyre and Sidon could not set her free, so no human power can free one from the shackles of Satan. A pastor once spoke of the hymn:

> "How wretched was our former state,
> When slaves to Satan's sway."

But he made a deep impression on the congregation when he announced that perhaps some present should read it —

> "How wretched is our *present* state,
> As slaves to Satan's sway."

Is it not true that the sun shines on no sadder sight than a young life, so full of promise, becoming a willing slave of Satan? How the tears of the church should mingle with the tears of good parents over such, as the mother from Canaan, a stranger from the commonwealth of Israel though she was, wept over her daughter whom Satan was claiming as his slave! (See Acts 16:16-19.)

c. *Her Disappointment.* One would have thought that such a heart-cry for help as left the mother's lips would have received an immediate answer from Him who came proclaiming liberty for the captive. What was the response of Jesus to the urgent plea of the mother for her wretched child? "But he answered her not a word." The disciples also wanted to get rid of this desperate pleader — "His disciples came and besought him [Jesus], saying, Send her away; for she crieth after us." Here was a mother, probably a widow seeing there is no mention of the girl's father, who made all her young daughter's grief her own, for her prayer was, "Have mercy on *me,* O Lord, help *me.*" Her terrible sorrow bettered what was best in her, and lifted her nearer to God.

All the rabbis scorned Gentile women, but here was one who had a gleam of that "Light who was to lighten the Gentiles" (Luke 2:32). How she was drawn to the Jewish Teacher with such faith and hope we are not told. What is evident is that she knew that He alone could ease her of her burden. There are graceless women today among so-called atheists and humanists who seek to descry and oppose Jesus, but it is interesting to notice that no woman ever opposed Him in the days of His flesh. It is recorded that even children always drew back for the eagle-like, serpent-like eyes of Voltaire, the brilliant French sceptic. He had no love for them, and somehow they all sensed it, and shrank back from him as a young bird flees from a hawk seen for the first time.

But in some instinctive way children and parents felt that while in the presence of Jesus they were in the presence of One who knew their need and loved them, just as a blind man knows a flower by its perfume. It was thus that the Syrophenician was drawn to Jesus, lover of children, exalter of woman, and friend of all mankind; and revealed by her desperate plea that there is no stronger love on earth than that of a mother's for her suffering child. Her soul was like a harp, which does not give out its sweetest music till its strings are strained. *But Jesus was deaf to her passionate entreaty.* Why? When He did speak, His answer was worse than His silence; it cut off all hope: He was not sent to heathen Gentiles. Then as the disappointed mother drew nearer and fell at His feet and worshiped Him, saying, "Lord, help me!" still no direct reply. The answer Jesus did give seemed to heap contempt on her misfortune. He spoke about it not being meet to cast children's bread to dogs. As a Gentile, the mother was not only a heathen but a *dog* – a term used by professionally religious rabbis to describe godless Gentiles.

What Jesus meant by this seemingly harsh reply was that "Charity begins at home," that because He was sent, not to the lost sheep of Gentiles, but to the lost sheep of the house of Israel, there was no reason why He should respond to the desperate plea of a woman of Canaan. Why, then, did Jesus seem to act in such a harsh manner? Was it His purpose to comply all along with her request but act as He did only to test and manifest her faith? Certainly Jesus did not dismiss her with a word: His constant tenderness toward sufferers forbade such an action. On the other hand did He feel that the normal limitation of His mission to Israel made difficult any help for an outcast Canaanite – a member of the most scorned and hated of all heathen races (Gen. 9:25), who, as yet had given no evidence of conversion to the faith of Israel although she confessed to the Messiahship of Jesus?

Is not the fruitless appeal of this mother a true picture of what passes in the heart of many a pleading parent? Christ's love and power are believed in, and prayer is offered with great urgency for a dear child in deep physical or spiritual need, but heaven's door seems to be closed and no change is seen in the loved one interceded for. If the salvation of a wayward child is sought, but a miracle of grace does not take place, too often the praying parent settles down in a quiet despondency or a vague hope that some day a change will take place. Theirs is not the persistency in prayer enabling them to say, "I will not let thee go except thou bless me!"

What we have to learn, is what the Syrophenician learned, namely, that the Lord's delays are not denials, but always full of meaning. By His delay He taught the woman patience and trust, and prepared for greater blessings than she could have received at an earlier period. In His own wise and merciful way Jesus brought out her faith and humility, and taught all men that the feast of His love is for all men, whether Jew or Gentile. An ancient writer quaintly expresses it thus –

> Christ's love is wise. There is an art in His strange delays which make us lovesick. We cheapen what is easily got, and underrate anything that is at our elbow; but delays heighten and raise the market value of Christ's blessings. He wishes to make our faith stronger, and His trials are for the triumph of our faith. He did as we do when we hold toys dangling before our children, that we may make them desire and enjoy them more. He acts as we do with musicians at the door; for when they please us, we

do not give them their penny at once, that we have to hear their music longer.

d. *Her Determination.* Here was an anxious mother who refused to be denied, and so backed up her plea with perseverance, and by such has left all parents an example to follow. Silence, argument and contempt with one invincible weapon — more prayer, more trust. Somehow her faith grew stronger by its trial. As James Wells puts it: "It was like the water lily which lives and thrives amid storms; for though its head is tossed with wind and waves, its roots are sheltered deep in the earth." Having heard of the wondrous Man and His compassion, and now face to face with Him, the Canaanite could not believe that He would send her away empty. Even in the voice that refused her there was something inspiring her to hope against hope, and believing she triumphed.

This Canaanite woman with her grief-stricken face and burdened heart was one who had to have help. She could not go back and look into the face of that tormented child of hers, dying while she lived. Something simply had to happen, and we can sense the desperation as she pressed her case. Her words were heavy with agony, and was manifest in her gestures. She had to have help for her hopeless child; and in her approach to Jesus manifested the two virtues He valued, namely, a sense of need, and the faith that He was what He claimed to be, and could do what He knew needed to be done.

What aroused Christ to action on her behalf was that when He said that it was not meet to take the children's bread and give it to the dogs, she was willing to be a dog, willing to be anything, if she could only get some of the crumbs under the table. From a heathen country though she was, she yet had the spiritual insight to know that the table was so loaded with bread that there was more than sufficient for both children and dogs alike, and that even a crumb of Christ's grace would serve her purpose. Parents who plead for a prodigal child have what this determined mother never had — a thousand promises and the revelation of the Father's will and of the Saviour's love she never knew. How her faith, pleading and perseverance put us to shame! Yet we are not to trust to the fervency of our desires or the wrestling urgency of our petition, but only in God's promise, love, faithfulness and power.

e. *Her Delight.* The record of the Syrophenician and her daughter is of special interest for Gentile children, most of all for Gentile girls. The mother was the first Gentile to whom Christ plainly opened the gate of mercy; and her daughter was the first Gentile girl whom He healed, and the first of a mighty multitude of Gentile children of every age and nation whom Christ has freed from Satan's sway. Can we not imagine the delight of the mother when she saw her child who had been "grievously vexed with a devil" lying peaceably on her bed? Her deliverance was complete, for we read that she was "made whole." To be whole and to be holy mean the same thing for the words whole and holy came from the same root.

Further, the girl was healed by remote control, for Christ cured her though she was at a distance from Him. The daughter knew the exact time of her deliverance from the devil; it was from "that very hour." Many of us know that we have been healed by Christ but we cannot give the day and date. David Livingstone tells how he once asked a chief how old he was.

People around burst into laughter. "The idea," they said, "of a man remembering when he was born." But they knew they had been born, though they knew not when. Whether their second birth came early, or so gently that they cannot remember it any more than they can remember their first birth, as long as there are the true signs of the new birth, we need not trouble about anything else.

But what added delight must have been this mother's, whose daughter Christ did heal when she heard Him praising her faith, and felt that by the miracle He performed her faith had been increased. She received a wondrous blessing — a spiritual blessing — the Master's delighted approval of her perseverance and faith. Matthew says, "O woman, great is thy faith: be it unto thee even as thou wilt" (Matt. 15:28), and our Lord, as in the case of the centurion, found in this woman a faith greater than He had met with in Israel. Mark records that Jesus said to her, "Go thy way; the devil is gone out of thy daughter" (Mark 7:29), and we can imagine how after expressing her gratitude to Jesus, she bounded home and found her precious child calm and peaceful, and fully delivered from all restless frenzy. The lesson of the narrative for all parents concerned about deliverance of any of their children from Satan's control, is to tarry in prayer and to trust the Lord to undertake in His own way and time. Laying the wayward, rebellious child at His feet, parents must rest in His love and persist in claiming deliverance for the child vexed by the devil. Despair must never be yielded to when the answer seems to be delayed. The full assurance of hope is bound to triumph.

Monica, the mother of Augustine, prayed that her godless boy might not go to Rome, for she feared that Rome would be his ruin. God did not grant that request because He had something better in store for her. Augustine went to Rome and found God there, and later explained God's apparent refusal of his mother's prayer in this way, "O God, Thou gavest her not what she asked then, that thou mightest give her what she asked always." Is this not the reason why Christ seemed, but only seemed, to say No to the distressed Syrophenician? Christ never says No to the sincere seeker, though He often does not say Yes in the way, and at the time expected.

8. The Child Timothy (II Tim. 1:1-6; 3:14-17)

Under the previous section, *Children and Scripture,* mention will be found of how much the child Timothy owed to his godly heritage, and of the prominent place he has in the portrait gallery of Bible children. Along with Abel, Joseph, Josiah and Daniel, Timothy is one of the unblamed youths of the Bible, one of the sacred band of young immortals who wore "the white flower of a blameless life" — one of the same spiritual breed, and of the same house and lineage — one of the company showing the fair fruit of a noble nature under the power of divine grace. Would that much of the youth of today without any beneficial purpose in life could be found following in the footsteps of this godly child of a godly mother!

Timothy will always remain as a shining example of what we might call the three loyalties, or reverences, namely, his Bible, his Home, his Saviour.

a. *His Bible.* While the Old Testament was the only part of the Bible that Timothy knew, what he had he dearly loved from his childhood days, and with the passing years his reverence and loyalty for the Scriptures were intensified. Books in his day were scarce, and probably the Old Testament was the only Book in the house. His mother Eunice and his grandmother Lois who lived in the home were godly women and surrounded the young child with godly influences. These two women whom Timothy owed so much to, were Jews and believers in the Messiah, but his father was a Greek, or Gentile, and evidently an unbeliever, for nothing is said of his faith. In those times heathen fathers thought more of their young dogs and horses than of their young children.

Timothy was an apt learner, and became famed for his Bible knowledge. He proved that the Bible was the best children's treasury, and in later days revealed that he knew more of the spirit of the Scriptures than the Pharisees did. The Holy Scriptures made the boy Timothy wise unto salvation. A literary critic records how while studying the poems of the renowned agnostic, Matthew Arnold, something of the sad and hopeless spirit of the poet passed into him, and he felt most miserable. Laying down his study of the poems, he went out for a walk. It was a bleak wintry day. As he reached Brodick, in Arran, Scotland, the hills were in a winding sheet of snow, the sky was of a leaden hue, and the sea made a melancholy moan amid the jagged, dripping rocks.

The gloom all around him joined the gloom within him, and made him feel most wretched. All at once he came upon some boys shouting merrily at play. "Are you at school?" he asked. "Yes," was the reply. "And what are you learning?" "I learn," said one, "what is man's chief end." "And what is it?" the reviewer asked. The boy replied, "Man's chief end is to glorify God and to enjoy Him forever." The man at once felt that the boy was being taught a religion of grandeur and joy, while the poems of Arnold, which he was seeking to understand, contained a religion of darkness and despair.

From his childhood Timothy yielded himself up to the spirit and teachings, yea to the God of the Scriptures and found his life shaped by them. Adolph Monod, the French critic, when he came to his deathbed wrote a small homily he touchingly called, "The Regrets of a Dying Man." One of his saddest regrets was that he had not from the first taken the Bible plan of life, and the Bible means of reaching it.

But Timothy had no such regret, for from his earliest years he had taken the Bible as his guide.

b. *His Home.* We have no means of knowing how old Timothy's father was when he died. If he had his father, say, until he was a youth, Timothy might have been tempted to follow his heathen father into all excess of riotous living, characterizing Gentile society at that time (I Pet. 4:3, 4). But it speaks volumes for the boy that he preferred to follow his devout mother and grandmother. Gladly he gave himself up to the spiritual influences of his home and thereby his mother became his mother in a threefold way – she gave life to his mind, and to his soul, as she had given life to his body at birth.

With us piety means the whole of religion, but long ago it meant only faithful love to parents. Thus, in the only place in the Bible where piety is used, it is employed in this way. "Let them learn first to shew piety at home, and to requite their parents" (I Tim. 5:4). This verse written to Timothy is full of deep significance. He knew that the right feeling to good parents is so like the right feeling to God that people used one word for both. Timothy's own inner piety so made him one with his Christian mother that he had no interests of his own apart from hers. If we look around us we will find that some of the noblest characters are found among those who in youth yielded to a saintly mother's influence. West, the renowned artist once said, "A kiss from my mother made me a painter." Another, equally blessed by a good mother could write, "In my best moments I find again my mother in myself."

It is to be regretted that not all children have the godly home that Timothy enjoyed, and do not love their parents as they should. What a lamentable breakup of family life we are witnessing! Many children representing Christian homes seem to cast off all restraint as they reach years of independence, and never think of requiting or recompensing their parents for all the sacrifice, care and love of the past. Such children would be more noble in character if they shared Timothy's love for the Bible and for his mother. Why, even the agonies of the cross and the near prospect of seeing God did not separate Jesus from His mother, for as He came to die, He could say, "Woman, behold thy Son!"

c. *His Saviour.* Timothy's deepest love and loyalty were toward the Saviour he came to know more fully through personal conversation with Paul, the mighty apostle. There are children like Samuel who cannot remember a time when they did not trust God. Their love to Him was not an after love, but a first love. But there are others who, like Timothy, have a well-marked and a well-remembered conversion. I can more easily give the place, date and hour of the day when God gave me second birth, than of my first birth. The main thing is to know that we have been born anew, and that our life testifies to the fact that we are the children of God.

As previously indicated, although Timothy had a godly heritage, knew his Bible, loved his parents and was outwardly blameless, he lacked the assurance of God's salvation. His mother had brought her boy up in the fear of the Lord, but He gave the honor of bringing young Timothy to Himself to a preacher, as is often the case. So Paul speaks of him as, "My own son in the faith, . . . whom I have begotten in the Gospel." Eunice, rather than find any fault with the instrument God had used for the conversion of her son, magnified Him for His goodness in claiming him for Himself. Through the preaching of Paul, or through personal contact, Timothy yielded his life to the Saviour and became the close friend and companion of his spiritual father.

At the time of his surrender to Christ, Timothy must have been a mere boy, and but a youth when ordained to preach the Gospel. Writing to him Paul said, "Let no man despise thy youth" (I Tim. 4:12). Perhaps he was somewhat boyish-looking, with people taking him to be younger than he was. The youthful piety of Timothy proves that God is able to save the very young, and hold them to Himself with the cords of love and trust. Bishop Burnet said of the renowned John Newton, "He had the whitest soul he ever knew, and was as a very infant in purity of mind." It was so with Timothy who will always remain an inviting example of God's grace and youthful godliness.

There are many who find Christ late

in life, but who because of their long delayed conversion have to confess,

> Alas, that I so lately knew Thee,
> Thee so worthy of the best;
> Nor had sooner turned to know Thee,
> Truest good and only rest.
> The more I love, I mourn the more,
> That I did not love before.

But Timothy came to Christ in the glad morning of his life, and had a charming character formed by the union of the three loyalties of the Bible, home and the Saviour. May those of us who have young children to care for constantly pray that they may be children of Timothy's mold, and experience that God has no better gift for them but heaven itself!

> Go, while the day-star shineth, go, while the heart is light;
> Go, ere thy strength declineth, while every sense is bright;
> Sell all thou hast, and buy it: 'tis worth all earthly things –
> Rubies, and gold, and diamonds, scepters and crowns of kings.

9. Children in Heaven

Having written much of the life of children on earth, it is but fitting to conclude with a brief observation of what the Bible says about their life in heaven. In the author's small volume on *The Gospel of the Life Beyond,* a section will be found dealing with the question of children in heaven. As there are no babies and children who died under the age of responsibility in hell, all of them must be in heaven surrounding the throne of God singing, Glory! Glory! Glory! Do children remain children up there, or are growth and increase theirs until they reach a glorified maturity? We must correct the idea that children become angels in heaven. It is wrong to teach the young to say –

> I want to be an angel
> And with the angels stand;
> A crown upon my forehead,
> And harp within my hand.

In a volume which he presented to Dick Hall, of Dartmouth, after his son's death, Calvin Coolidge wrote the following inscription: "To Edward K. Hall, in recollection of his son and my son, who have the privilege by the grace of God to be boys through all Eternity!" The president pictured the loveliness of a life in which his son could be spared the hardening of body and mind that often accompanies age.

To be boys through all eternity may be a pleasing thought for those whose children died young, but are they to go on in an eternity of perpetual immaturity, of never growing into interests deep and strong? When William R. Harper, one-time president of the University of Chicago, approached death he prayed: "May there be for me a life beyond this life; and in that life may there be work to do, tasks to accomplish." As the saints are to serve the Lord, as well as see Him in heaven, eternity for them will offer the pursuit of glorious enterprises.

Like all the saints and martyrs, children are glorified human beings in the land where years are not counted. If you have a baby or child in heaven, you have the assurance that the precious one is safe in the bosom of Him who never ceases to be the Friend of little children, and that, reunited, you will be lost in wonder, love and praise as you dwell forever in the presence of Him whose shed blood avails for all ages. As the lover of children, the Lord placed them among the beloved on earth and those who passed over are among the blessed in heaven.

Zechariah describes boys and girls playing in the streets of the city, and gladness grew in him as he watched in vision the children at their games, and heard their ringing laughter (Zech. 8:5). The Jerusalem he spoke of was the city of God on earth and the picture of the city of God in heaven, which John so vividly portrays (Rev. 21; 22). War had laid the city waste in the prophet's day: the old people and children who could neither fight nor flee had been slain; and grass was growing in its deserted streets. But better days were to come, and joyous life again would pour its tide into every corner of the city when it would be "full of boys and girls playing in the streets thereof."

Jerusalem the Golden, at its best, not at its worst, is an impressive image of the New Jerusalem, the heavenly city, full as it will be, with a mighty multitude of happy children. The poet Wordsworth imagined himself on a heavenly island by an immortal land and of seeing –

. . . The children sport upon
the shore,
And hear the mighty waters
rolling evermore.

Near the Rhine stands the city of Carlsruhe, or Charles' Rest, so called after its founder It has the shape of an outspread fan, and all the streets branch out from the palace, in front of which stands the bronze statue of the prince. No other city so fills the visitor's mind with the name, image and achievements of its originator. In almost every street the child at play can see the shining image of the prince. Is this not a faint picture of how the glorious Prince of Peace fills the "city of peace" with His sacred and eternal presence? While the Bible does not give us many full statements about children in heaven, a marked feature in all Christ's parables of the judgment is that we do not find one hint about little children being at the Great White Throne. Only those who were old enough to think and act for themselves are to stand before the august Judge. Early deaths of children remind us that although they died through the fall of the first Adam of whom they knew nothing, they live forever through the act of the second Adam, of whom also they knew nothing.

Further, the picture Zechariah gives us of children playing in the streets, implies that life for them is full of happiness and that for them in heaven there are pleasures for evermore. The Saviour, whose coming brought joy to earth, is the Source of unending joy in heaven. John, the apostle of love, closes the Book of Revelation with a sad list of outcasts, with "the fearful" heading the list. Liars are mentioned three times (Rev. 21:8, 27; 22:15). But children are not included in such a list. Rowland Hill the stirring evangelist used to say, "If I were permitted to drop a tear on the golden street, as I enter the city of my God, it would be a tear of regret at bidding farewell to my beloved and lifelong companion, penitence." But those who die young before being able to discern right from wrong are not children of sin and have nothing to repent of. For them grace abounds, and in, and with, the Saviour, theirs is a never-ending life.

There's a home for little children,
Above the bright blue sky;
Where Jesus reigns in glory,
A home of peace and joy.
No home on earth is like it,
Nor can with it compare:
For every one is happy,
Nor could be happier, there.

Now that we have reached the conclusion of our coverage of the children of the Bible, it is with the feeling that we have no idea how much we owe to the Bible for its unfolding of God's purpose concerning family life. The various religions of the world each have their sacred books, but the Bible is the only divine Book that takes a deep interest in boys and girls. Who of all religious figures in the world, but Christ, took up children, laid hands upon them and blessed them? Christianity changed the thoughts and feelings of men about children. Christ's tenderness toward them taught men to be human-hearted, and to show mercy to children and treat them as if they were "little majesties."

Before communism took over China, and missionaries were allowed to settle and evangelize in the country, Dr. Carstairs Douglas told of explaining the sixth commandment — "Thou shalt not kill" — to a group of Chinese. He said that the commandment meant that even children were not to be killed. A Chinaman stepped forward, and asked, "What, do you mean to say that we cannot kill our own children? I have killed five of mine, and I had a perfect right to do so." Those around the speaker agreed with him. Another missionary of that time wrote of a city in which he labored in which there was a place called "The Child's Ditch," into which parents threw the children they did not wish to bring up. Where the Bible was, and is, unknown, there is little loving concern for children.

History records that when a child was born in a Greek or Roman home, it was laid at the father's feet. If he stooped down and took it in his arms it became a member of the family: if he left it unnoticed it was often cast out to die, or to be devoured by beasts. Some of those fathers were so well-educated that their writings are read by men today. Yet in almost every home of these intellectuals, for the first seven or eight years the children rarely saw their father's face, who, until they came of age, had the power of putting them to death.

Now, in our much vaunted civilization we murder babies by abortion before they are born. In many back streets criminal abortionists flourish. In Britain, since the Abortion Act of 1968 came into being, well over 35,000 abortions have been carried out. In a period of three months over 1,000 women had legal abortions in England and Wales among whom were almost 300 girls under sixteen years of age. Last year in London alone there were 12,000 operations.

Out of the above figure of 35,000, forty-seven percent were single women; about seventeen percent were under twenty years of age. What else can we expect for this wanton, wholesale slaughter of babies before they are born but divine judgment upon those who make such laws to get rid of unwanted children! The tragedy is that the present Archbishop of Canterbury went into the lobby of the House of Lords to vote for the Abortion Bill of which the grave disadvantages are now showing.

All the kindness and happiness now showered upon children they owe to Jesus, who went about as a Lover of the young. God was indeed the Creator of the universe with all its marvels. He was the nursing Father of the created world as Dr. A. J. Gordon expressed it well —

> When the universe was in its cradle, it was His hand that rocked that cradle and rocked the universe into life. He remembers the birthday of every star in the sky and every angel in heaven as if it were yesterday for He gave them birth.

The glory of grace is that God is also the loving Father of all who are His through His own beloved Son the Saviour.

It is also hoped that our study has shown that we cannot underrate the importance of childhood. Christ's word was "Take heed that ye despise not one of these little ones" (Matt. 18: 10). Most suggestively the Greek has it, "Do not think down upon" – an interpretation reminding us of what Francis Thompson said in his essay on Shelley, the English poet –

> We play at being children, and the result is that we are not more child-like, but our children are less child-like. It is so tiring to stoop to the child, so much easier to lift up the child to you. To be a child is to have a spirit yet streaming from the waters of baptism. It is to believe in love, to believe in loveliness, to believe in belief.

We have further learned that parents who profess and call themselves Christians must lay it to heart that they are to glorify God not only with their lips, but also in their lives, lest they cause any of His little ones to stumble. John Bunyan in his *Pilgrim's Progress* makes Christian to say,

> I am very wary of giving my children occasion, by any unseemly action, to make themselves averse to going on pilgrimage.

Parents, who are God's children, believe that parental prayer tends to make Christian children of the finest type, and that when matters of child care and training reach a certain stage, "prayer for the child is as instinctive and as inevitable as the kiss," as Harrington Lees reminds us. "In the very earliest days let the children be prayed for, even audibly prayed for, over the cot where the infant lies half awake or sleeping. And increasingly will the parent pray *with* the child, until it be mature enough to pray for itself."

In his inspiring volume, *The Path of Prayer*, Dr. Samuel Chadwick, the renowned Methodist preacher, tells of the daughter of a minister with whom he was staying who stole into the visitor's bedroom before breakfast. The little one talked blithely of the wonders of her little world. Dr. Chadwick asked her if her father was up. She looked radiantly into his eyes and said, "Oh, my Daddy always talks with God in the drawing room before breakfast." Chadwick's comment is, "Happy daddy! Happy daughter! Happy God!" One of the most touching poems concerning prayer for our children is that by Edith Nesbit –

> To no vast Presence too immense to love,
> To no enthroned King too great to care,
> To no strange Spirit human needs above,
> We bring our little intimate, heart-warm prayer.
> But to a God who is a Father too,
> Who loved and gave to us His only Son;
> We pray across the cradle, I and you
> For ours, our little one.

EMBLEMS

Children of Israel

Children of God

Children of Humility

Children of Obedience

Children of the King

Children of Light

Children Who Are Faithful

Children of Zion

Children of Promise

Children as Heirs

Children of the Bridechamber

Children of Spiritual Birth

Children Who Never Mature

Children of Darkness

Children of Disobedience

Children as Backsliders

Children of Belial

Children of Murderers

Children as Fools

Children of the Devil

Children of Hell

Children of Wrath

Children of This World

Children Who Are Strange

4
EMBLEMS

A striking evidence of the divine estimation of family life is the way many of its relationships are used to symbolize divine, and also devilish, relationships. Prominent among the emblems of Scripture are those associated with fatherhood, motherhood and childhood. We have endeavored to bring together some of the examples of such symbolism with the hope that our comment on each will prove profitable to Bible lovers.

Children of Israel
(Gen. 50:25; etc.)

The term "children" is applied to any descendant or descendants of a particular person, tribe, or area. Children of Israel are descended from Jacob, who received the new name of Israel (Ps. 103:7; Hos. 11:1), their common ancestor (Gen. 32:24-32). It was the custom to designate the members of various tribes as the children of the one from whom the tribe originated, and it was thus natural that the people who boasted of Israel as their ancestor should be so designated. Sometimes they are called "children of Jacob" (Num. 1:20-43; II Kings 17:34). When Jews are referred to as "the children of Abraham" moral likeness or spiritual kinship are implied (John 8:39; Gal. 3:7).

"The children of Eden," who were destroyed by the Assyrians, were so named because they were a tribe which inhabited a region of which Telassar was the center (II Kings 19:12; Isa. 37:12). In like manner, "the children of the East" describes in a general way the inhabitants of the country east of Palestine. Jews thought of their own country as occupying the central place, and of the other parts of the world in relation to this (Gen. 29:1; I Kings 4:30; Job 1:1; Jer. 49:28). Inhabitants of the east country regarded themselves as descendants of Abraham.

Children of God

This oft-repeated designation in Christian usage means "the sons and daughters of God." In the Old Testament the term is used of angels (Gen. 6:1-4; Job 1:6; 2:1; 38:7, etc.); of Israel (Isa. 1:2, 4; 30:1, 9; Hos. 11:1). This common expression describes all who belong to God, and is based on the relation between parents and children, and in general indicates God's affection for His own, and their dependence upon Him, and moral likeness to Him (I John 3:1-4, 7, 10). Believers are styled "children of God" from mere dependence, from special privilege, from moral likeness, and from a full and willing response to the divine fatherhood in filial love, trust, and obedience. In the Old Testament this fatherhood toward Israel is manifested in protecting and redeeming love; and involved the divine faithfulness, to which His children made their appeal (Jer. 31:9, 18-20; Isa. 43:6; 63:18; 64:8-12).

Coming to the New Testament we see how the above term takes on added significance. Contrary to what is said *all* men are *not* the children of God. Certainly they are all His creatures (Acts 17:28), but not His children. A child implies a birth and parentage, and in the family of God or His church, inclusion is as the result of the new birth, as Christ clearly taught (John 3:3-16; Eph. 5:1; Jas. 1:18; I

John 3:9, 10). Both phrases, "the children of God" and "the sons of God" are used by John and Paul as expressive of a relationship through faith in Christ, and imply a status and privilege conferred upon all who have accepted Christ as Saviour. Such an honored relationship is attested to by the indwelling Holy Spirit and His fruits (Rom. 8:14, 18; Gal. 3:26; Phil. 2:15). All, male or female, young or aged, are truly the children of God if they have come to the Father through His Son, Jesus Christ (John 14:6). Such a relationship is based on His mediatorial work.

Children of Humility

When Jesus and John spoke of "little children" they were not referring to actual small children, but were addressing themselves to grown men and women who were disciples (John 13:33; I John 2:1, 18, 28, etc). Little children are simple, innocent and trustful – features which Christian adults must manifest. When Solomon confessed, "I am but a little child: I know not how to go out or come in" (I Kings 3:7), he was a robust man beginning his reign as king of Israel. But he prayed for humility, docility, and a child-like dependence upon God for the wisdom he required to reign.

Jeremiah offered a similar plea, "Ah, Lord God! behold, I cannot speak: for I am a child" (Jer. 1:6). Although desiring childlike innocency in His servant, God did not want Him to act childishly and so rebuked him, "Say not, I am a child . . . Be not afraid of their faces!" (Jer. 1:7, 8). Setting a little child in the midst of His disciples Jesus gave them a lesson on humility, as well as on kindness to children. "Whosoever therefore shall humble himself as this little child, the same is greatest in the kingdom of heaven" (Matt. 18:4).

Discussing the confusion caused by people speaking in different tongues, Paul urged the believers in Corinth not to be children in understanding, "howbeit in malice be ye children (or babes) but in understanding be men" (I Cor. 14:20). Paul was rebuking their immaturity of judgment. Matthew Henry's comment is suggestive –

> Children are apt to be struck with novelty and strange appearances. Do not you act like them, and prefer noise and show to worth and substance: be like children in nothing but as innocent and inoffensive disposition. Christians should have wisdom and knowledge that are ripe and mature.

Peter's admonition is "Be clothed with [put on the apron of] humility" (I Pet. 5:5).

Children of Obedience

It is Peter who instructs us to live and labor in the light of our Lord's return as "obedient children, not fashioning yourselves according to the former lusts in your ignorance . . . Be ye holy, for I am holy" (I Pet. 1: 14-16). The first lesson a child has to learn is that of obedience, and as they obey they become commendable and loved. As the children of God we prove ourselves as such by our obedience to God. Once we become His children we differ exceedingly from what we were formerly. We had our times of lust and ignorance, but now as new creatures in Christ Jesus it is our obligation, not only to obey God, but also to reflect His holiness. Scripture has much to say about obedience to God, to parents, and to those who have the rule over us. There are many phases of this virtue. In his, *A Song of the English,* Rudyard Kipling has the verse –

Keep ye the Law – be swift in all obedience –
Clear the land of evil, drive the road and bridge the ford.
Make ye sure to each his own
That he reap where he hath sown;
By the peace among our peoples let men know ye serve the Lord!

Children of the King

Inquiring as to the kind of men his followers slew at Tabor, Gideon received the answer, "As thou art, so were they; each one resembled the children of a king" (Judg. 8:18). Evidently they had the air of royalty and nobility about them. Theirs was a conspicuous regal bearing. The phrase used here was "an Orientalism for great beauty, majesty of appearance, uncommon strength, and grandeur of form." But there is "another king, one Jesus" (Acts 17:7). As His children do we resemble Him? Children in a family, royal or otherwise, usually resemble their parents in features and actions. Our Lord referred to children who, although they belonged to the kingdom, were so unlike the King that they were cast into outer darkness (Matt. 8:12).

A rousing hymn would have me know that –

Tho' exiled from home, yet still I may sing:
All glory to God, I'm a child of the King!
I'm a child of the King,
A child of the King:
With Jesus, my Saviour,
I'm a child of the King!

We read of the King's Son that He was "the express image of his person" (Heb. 1:3), or as Phillips translates it, "the flawless expression of the nature of God." Jesus was so like His Father that He could say, "He that hath seen me, hath seen the Father" (John 14:9). He was the perfect facsimile of God. Ours is the hope of complete resemblance to the King when we see Him in all His beauty. How satisfied we shall be when we awake with His likeness! (Ps. 17:15).

But what about the present? As we journey on toward the palace of the King, are we manifesting "the likeness of his resurrection" (Rom. 6:5)? Man was originally created in the likeness of God, but sin defaced the image. Grace restores the resemblance. The question is, As children of the King do we resemble Him in every aspect of life? How pleased you are as a father, when a friend says of your son, "My, how like your father you are!" Have we a Christlikeness of character pleasing to Him who was a true image of His Father?

Children of Light

All who are illumined by Him who came as the Light of the world are designated "children of light." Our Lord spoke about "the children of this world" being "wiser than the children of light" (Luke 16:8). Urging those around Him to walk in the light while they had it, He said, "Believe in the light, that ye may be children of light" (John 12:36). Contrasting our life out of Christ, then in Him, Paul reminds us: "Ye were sometimes darkness, but now are ye light in the Lord: walk as children of light" (Eph. 5:8). A similar exhortation is found in his letter to the Thessalonians: "Ye are all the children of light, and the children of the day: we are not of the night, nor of darkness" (I Thess. 5:5).

The term "walk" which Paul uses is not the one we employ in the ordinary sense of taking a walk down a road. It is an old English word meaning a man's manner or habit of life. As those whose hearts and minds have been enlightened, our lives are to be worthy of the One who is the Light. Children of the light are those who have the very nature of light, and no darkness at all. Of natural light three things characterize it – light dispels darkness – light brings joy, hope and opportunity for work – light always shines for others. Is it not in these three things we show ourselves as true children of light? All living things love light.

1. Light Dispels Darkness

Darkness and light cannot exist together. Shut out light and you have darkness. Good and evil, unselfishness and selfishness, right and wrong, truth and falsehood, God and Satan – these opposites can never agree. If the light of God's love and mercy has streamed into our lives, then it is incumbent upon us to talk in that light.

2. Light Is Necessary to Labor

The value of light is seen in that it brings opportunity for labor. As the sun rises, city streets become alive with those who, after a night's sleep, are ready for a day's work in the light. The hymn has it, "Let me labor for the Master, from the dawn to setting sun," and children of light rejoice in spiritual activity, while it is day, knowing that the night is coming when no man can work.

3. Light Shines for the Benefit of Others

When it is a mere candle, or the majestic sun, both never shine for their own sake. The sun is created by God to give light to the earth. The moon and stars reflect this light. Children of light are reflectors of Him in whom there is no darkness at all, and as they shine, others, living in the darkness of sin, are brought to experience that the Light of the world is Jesus. For the sake of others, we reflect the light of God's righteousness, mercy and love. May we so walk that the people around us walking in darkness can see a great light! God forbid that anything in our lives should hide the light from others!

Children Who Are Faithful

Writing to Titus, Paul urged the elders to be exemplary in every way, particularly in having "faithful children not accused of riot or unruly" (Tit. 1:6). The island of Crete, now known as Candia, once had a hundred churches, brought into being through the ministry of Paul and Titus. A great harvest was reaped in this island, and the spread of truth came about, in some large measure, through the faithful children of believing households. They were the seed – corn all over the island famed for its lying and gluttony. Not all children of elders' homes are faithful and unaccused of riot or unruly, but these Cretian children were. What a blessed thing it is for any community to have whole families of saved and separated children!

The word "faithful" used here can mean two things, both of which should be true of all children of God whether young or otherwise.

1. Full of Faith

"Faith-full," or full of faith was the evidence that those described had accepted the faithful saying that Christ Jesus had come into the world to save them. Unless there is faith within, we cannot be full of it.

2. Truthful, or full of fidelity.

Titus urges Christian parents to train their children by example and the Scriptures to speak the truth, and to be true in their actions. They were to be like the little maid who was servant to Naaman's wife – so truthful that her mistress could trust every word she spoke.

Can we say that we are faithful to God in all things, constantly recognizing that faithfulness, and not fame, is to be the basis of reward in eternity (Rev. 2:10)?

Children of Zion

In one of his magnificent Hallelujah Psalms the writer urges, "the children of Zion be joyful in their King" (Ps. 149:2). Joel expresses a similar exhortation, "Be glad then, ye children of Zion, and rejoice in the Lord your God" (Joel 2:23). God is often pictured as having His dwelling place in Zion (Joel 3:17). Zion, or Jerusalem, was known as "the city of David" (II Sam. 5:9). The name Zion itself means "sunny mount," thus we can understand why joy is associated with it. The inhabitants of His holy hill of Zion are justly expected to do more in praising God than others. If believers, we have come to Zion (Heb. 12:22), and as the children of Zion should be joyful in the Lord.

Reasons why Israel could acknowledge God's name before the world and publicly praise Him was because He had pleasure in them as His people. Had He not communicated His favors to them, and beautified them with His salvation? Says Matthew Henry, we must have "much of the power of godliness in the heart which consists in making God our chief joy and in our solacing ourselves in Him. We must sing a *new* song, sing with new affections, which make the song new, although the words have been used before. The Gospel Canon for Psalmody is to sing with the spirit and with the understanding."

The hill of Zion yields
A thousand sacred sweets:
Before we reach the heav'nly fields,
Or walk the golden streets.

Children of Promise

To Jews of old, "the children of promise" were the seed of Abraham, not in the line of mere fleshly descent from Abraham did election run; else Ishmael, Hagar's child, and Abraham's first son, and even the sons by Keturah, would be included, which they were not – "In Isaac shall thy seed be called" (Rom. 9:7). Paul emphasizes the same truth in his Galatian epistle where he explains that the children of promise were given to Abraham (Gal. 4:28-31). Ishmael mocked Isaac probably because of his piety and faith in God's promise which God gave to his father. It was according to promise that God raised unto Israel a Saviour (Acts 13:23-25).

The children of the promise, then, were the only ones counted for the seed. "Those that have the happiness of being counted for the seed have it not for the sake of any merit of their own, but purely by virtue of the promise, Isaac was a child of promise; he was also conceived and born by virtue of the promise, and so a proper type of those who are now counted for the seed, even true believers, who are born, not of the will of the flesh, nor of the will of man, but of God." As those in Christ, who came according to promise, we are children with great and precious promises to rest in, and constantly claim,

Standing on the promises that cannot fail,
When the howling storms of doubt and fear assail,
By the living word of God I shall prevail,
Standing on the promises of God.

Children as Heirs

The Bible has much to say about "inheritance" and "heirs." In Israel the first-born son, as the new head of the family, responsible for providing for the rest, inherited the land and had also his claim to a double portion of other kinds of wealth (Deut. 21:17). Every Jew regarded himself as an inheritor of the land of Canaan, and in like manner every Christian is an inheritor of all God has treasured up for him in Christ. As heirs of God, we are also joint-heirs with Christ (Rom. 8:17). We are heirs of God through Christ (Gal. 4:6, 7). In his *Commentary on Galatians,* Bishop Lightfoot remarks, "Our Father never dies; the inheritance never passes away from Him; yet nevertheless we succeed to the full possession of it." Already the saints are in the position of assured privilege conferred upon them with absolute validity.

But let us not forget the condition linked on to co-heirship with Christ. We are possessors in prospect of our Father's heaven, in union of interest and life with our First-born, in whom lies our right, "if indeed we share His sufferings." These "sufferings" are "those deep but hallowed pains which will surely come to us as we live in and for Him in a fallen world, that we may also share His glory, for which that path of sorrow is, not indeed the meriting, but the capacitating, preparation." Under Jewish law, "if children, then heirs" did not hold with earthly inheritances, only the first-born were heirs. But heaven is a glorious inheritance that all saints are heirs to, and such will not be theirs through any virtue of their own, but purely by the grace and mercy of God. As heirs of salvation we have the present enjoyment of the treasures in Christ.

Children of the Bridechamber

One of the marvels of the Incarnation of our Lord is the way He alludes to the affairs of earth as naturally as He talks of the things of heaven. During His three years of ministry, He made full use of the constructive value of the atmosphere of Nazareth where He spent thirty years in the trivial, common round of things. Nothing escaped His attention during those somewhat cramped years, the accent of which we can detect in His teachings. In the days of His flesh our Lord was no mystic as He moved among men. As He walked and talked with them, He spoke of familiar things and experiences, making them sacred for ever.

Among all the events and affairs He was fully aware of before He left home were weddings. Doubtless He had attended many during His Nazareth days, and had often seen the wine running short at a wedding breakfast. The first miracle He accomplished was at the marriage in Cana where He added to the joyfulness of the occasion both by His presence and the manifestation of His power as the Lord of glory. Thereafter, His references to weddings are full of spiritual import.

When Jesus was chided by the Pharisees about His association with publicans and sinners, and about His absence of fasting which His critics scrupulously observed, He asked —

> Can the children of the bridechamber mourn, as long as the bridegroom is with them? but the days will come, when the bridegroom shall be taken from them, and then shall they fast" (Matt. 9:15).

Usually the children, or sons, of the bridechamber were those friends or companions of the bridegroom who were usually numerous. Any wedding guest, or anyone taking part in the bridal procession and remaining for the wedding feast might be included in the children of the bridechamber. When Christ used this illustration He had His own disciples in mind. The heavenly Bridegroom's best men go and fetch the bride; the apostles and evangelists seek to bring sinners to Jesus and to heaven (Matt. 25: 1-13).

At the marriage supper of the Lamb only those who are *called* will be the privileged guests at the feast, and these called ones, blessed of the Lord, form the Lamb's wife or His Bride — the true church (Rev. 19:7-9; 21:9) — the heavenly Jerusalem (Heb. 12:22, 23). Then the bride will not eye her garment but her Bridegroom's face, for the Lamb is all the glory in Emmanuel's land.

Children of Spiritual Birth

The Bible makes it clear that the basis of such an honored relationship as children is regeneration by the Spirit of God's Son (John 1:11, 12; 3:1-16; Gal. 4:4-7). God is our heavenly Father and we are His sons and daughters (II Cor. 6:18). The consciousness of that wonderful unity of the Spirit in which all the redeemed are as one family before God is found in the language put into the mouth of Jesus, "Behold I and the children which God hath given me" (Heb. 2: 13). As a term of special endearment, those who are the Lord's are sometimes called "little children," which He used of His own both before and after His resurrection (John 13:33; 21:5). Paul also employed the same term in writing to the believers in Galatia who were not very old in the faith (Gal. 4:19). And that John loved the expression "little children" is evident from his frequent use of it. In fact, the Greek word he employed is even more endearing than the *one* Paul used — it means, "little ones" or "babes" (I John 2:1, 12, 13, 18; 4:4; 5:21; III John 4; See I Pet. 2:2).

As John was well over ninety years of age when he wrote of the saints as "little children," we can understand why he spoke of them as affectionately as he did. Legend has it that when the aged apostle could no longer walk or speak as he used to, that some of his faithful followers would carry him into the market place. As the people, old and young, gathered around to hear the farewell message of their venerable and venerated teacher, he had only one word for all who sought his benediction. It was "Little children, love one another." The designation was perhaps a token of his great love for all the lambs of the Good Shepherd, and also a way of impressing upon those who were his spiritual children the beautiful grace of humility.

In the natural realm, little children know little of the wonderful and mighty works of God. They are likewise weak and fragile, needing the support of stronger arms. Are not the most advanced believers still "but little children weak," and in constant need of the strength of Him "who is so high and good and great"? Did not Jesus say to those He called His "little ones" that without Him they could do nothing (John 15:4, 5)?

Children Who Never Mature

While milk is used as a metaphor to describe abundance — "a land flowing with milk" (Exod. 3:8; Deut. 6: 3), and also gospel blessings (Isa. 55: 1); and is a leading element in man's diet, in the New Testament it is employed as a symbol of the simplicities of the gospel which spiritual babes are able to understand. Writing to newborn babes in Christ, Peter urged them to desire "the sincere milk of the Word" (I Pet. 2:2). Paul wanted to feed the Corinthians with "strong meat," that is, the deep, doctrinal truths of Scripture, but they were not able to bear it, or to masticate such heavy, spiritual food, so he had to feed them with milk – the ABC of the Gospel – seeing that they were still as babes in Christ (I Cor. 3:1, 2).

Spiritual immaturity is also suggested by the apostle in the Book of Hebrews, where he warns those who should have been teachers of truth but who still had need to be taught the first principles of the oracles of God. All they were able to do was to drink milk seeing they lacked experience in the word of righteousness. Still in spiritual babyhood they did not have the teeth or stomach for the strong meat belonging to those who are full age (Heb. 5:11-14). In another connection Paul reminds us that when he was a child, he thought, spoke, and ate as a child, but when he became a man he put away childish things (I Cor. 13:11). While he still drank milk, having physically matured he was able also to eat more solid food. There is nothing more beautiful in all the world than a healthy baby; but if a baby remains a baby it becomes a monstrosity.

The tragedy in church life today is the presence of too many spiritual babies who never seem to grow up and develop into a full stature in Christ. They never appear to increase in the knowledge of Him, or follow on to know Him in a fuller measure. When they hear the deeper truths of the Word expounded they seem to be over their heads altogether. Give them a sip of milk, and, like a baby, they are content, but don't serve them a plate of strong meat. There is no sight more pathetic in the family of God than that of a believer of many years with no desire to grow in grace and in the deeper knowledge of the Christ who brought about his initial salvation. "Why art thou, being *the king's son,* lean from day to day?" (II Sam. 13:4).

Children of Darkness

In the contest with Pharaoh, the ninth plague overtaking the Egyptians was that of darkness, "even darkness which may be felt" (Exod. 10:21-23). "All the children of Israel had light in their dwellings," and conversely by the same supernatural power all the children of Egypt had a thick darkness in their homes. The contrast threw into relief the judicial character of the plague (See Isa. 13:9-11.) Darkness is used as an emblem of spiritual ignorance and unbelief. "The darkness shall cover the earth, and gross darkness the people" (Isa. 60:3). Think of the millions living in heathen darkness, and millions more in the darkness of sin! Every minute of the day countless numbers of children are born into a world in which myriads live blinded by the god of this world, and consequently revel in their "works of darkness" (Eph. 5:11).

As children of light walk in the light, or live in uninterrupted fellowship with the Father and the Son, so children of darkness are actuated by Satan in whom is no light at all. In God there is no darkness at all (John 1:4, 5; I John 1:5-7). Jesus came as the Light of heaven into the darkness of the world, but "the darkness comprehended it not," or as Phillips puts it, "The light still shines in the darkness and the darkness has never put it out" (John 1:5). The apostle has the pregnant phrase, "The life was the light of men." The Life was the Light, and it ever is! It is not so much what we say, but the Christ-likeness of life that illuminates surrounding darkness.

But those who are not "enlightened with the light of the living" are those whose lives never see the light (Job 33:28, 30). "They are of those that rebel against the light" (Job 24:13). How true it is that none are so blind as those who won't see! Only the Spirit of Light Himself can enlighten their eyes, and deliver them from the power of darkness, making them, thereby, "meet to be partakers of the inheritance of the saints in light" (Col. 1:12, 13).

> Ye dwellers in darkness with sin-blinded eyes —
> The Light of the world is Jesus:
> Go wash at His bidding and light will arise —
> The Light of the world is Jesus.

Children of Disobedience

Parents who love the Lord and seek to obey Him in all their ways, and have a heartfelt obligation to bring their children up in His fear, are always grieved over their acts of disobedience to their will. Obedience is one of the first lessons a child has to learn. Coventry Patmore (1823 - 1896) in *The Toys*, has the appealing lines —

> My little Son, who look'd from thoughtful eyes
> And moved and spoke in quiet grown-up wise,
> Having my law the seventh time disobey'd,
> I struck him, and dismiss'd
> With hard words and unkiss'd,
> — His Mother, who was patient, being dead.
>
> * * *
>
> Then, fatherly, not less
> Than I whom Thou hast moulded from the clay,
> Thou'lt leave Thy wrath, and say,
> "I will be sorry for their childishness."

Scripture clearly states that divine chastisement overtakes the children of men who disobey divine commands. "Because of these things cometh the wrath of God upon the children of disobedience" (Eph. 5:6; Col. 3:6). Peter writes of the blessedness of "the children of obedience" (I Pet. 1:14). John the Baptist came "to turn the hearts of the fathers to the children, and the disobedient to the wisdom of the just" (Luke 1:17). It was through one man's disobedience that all phases of disobedience came into the world (Rom. 5:19). John Milton, in *Paradise Lost*, describes this first sin —

> Of Man's first disobedience, and the fruit
> Of that forbidden tree whose mortal taste
> Brought death into the world, and all our woe,
> With loss of Eden.

For the disobedient children of Israel, their Holy One had some solemn words of warning for they were not only rebellious children but also "lying children, children that will not hear the word of the law" (Isa. 30: 1, 9). Yet grace can prevail in the lives of such for Paul could write of those who were "sometime disobedient" but who according to divine mercy had been saved (Titus 3:3-5).

Dealing with the subject of parental self-culture, Andrew Murray has this heart-searching paragraph; "The child must control himself to be able to render obedience to his parent, that is that he may be trained to what will be his liberty and his glory, obedience to God. But here again the parent's obedience will be contagious, and it will inspire. If the parent's position be all one of privilege and liberty and command, the child may feel that the burden of obedience is all put upon him, the weaker one." In the matter of obedience, our Master is our exemplar, for we read that He learned obedience by the things He suffered. May we never be found guilty of disobeying the mouth of the Lord! (I Kings 13:21).

Children as Backsliders

A backslider is one who slides back instead of making daily progress in the Christian pilgrimage. Our experience in grace is never static. If we are not going on, then we are going back. We advance or retreat. Think of God's exposure of His backsliding children! — "Hast thou seen that which backsliding Israel hath done? . . . Backsliding Israel committed adultery . . . The backsliding Israel hath justified herself more than treacherous Judah . . . Return, thou backsliding Israel, saith the Lord" (Jer. 3:6-12).

Without doubt, Jeremiah was the prophet to backsliders in Israel whose "backslidings were many" (Jer. 14:7), and was commissioned to pronounce God's judgments upon them. Yet mercy is mingled with judgment for God promised to heal the backslidings of His children if only they would turn back to Him (Hos. 4:7; 11:7; 14:4). It is to be hoped that we are going forward and not backward (Jer. 7:24). Do you remember Macaulay's lines? —

> Was none who would be foremost
> To lead such dire attack;
> But those behind cried "Forward!"
> And those before cried "Back!"

The recurring theme of the epistle to the Hebrews is, "Let us go on unto perfection." In such spiritual progress there is always peace and satisfaction, whereas "The backslider in heart shall be filled with his own ways" (Prov. 14:14). The proverb has it, "The bad man reaps the fruits of his act." One meaning of backslider is "apostate." Paul describes those who once walked with the saints, but who became the enemies of the cross of Christ (Phil. 3:18). Judas walked with Christ for almost three years but at the end he walked away from Him into a suicide's grave.

Children of Belial

Although "Belial" became a proper name for Satan, or for Antichrist, which is the sense in which Paul uses the word when he asked, "What concord hath Christ with Belial?" (II Cor. 6:15), its frequent occurrence in the Old Testament carries the idea of worthlessness, baseness or wickedness (Deut. 13:13; Judg. 20:13; I Sam. 30:22; II Sam. 23:6). Poets have retained such an interpretation of the term. John Dryden (1631 - 1700), for instance, has the couplet —

> During his office treason
> was no crime,
> The sons of Belial had a
> glorious time.

In *Paradise Lost,* John Milton makes double mention of Belial —

> When night
> Darkens the streets, then wander forth
> the sons
> Of Belial, flown with insolence and
> wine.
>
> Thus Belial with words clothed in
> reason's garb
> Counselled ignoble ease, and peaceful sloth,
> Not peace.

The word itself, used by personification, broken up means, *Beli* — "without," and *ya'al* — "uselessness," or good for nothing. Thus "a man (of child) of Belial" was a worthless, lawless fellow (Deut. 13:13; I Chron. 17:9). Nabal, whose name means a "fool" is called "a man of Belial" (I Sam. 25:

25). But the word has come to imply that as Satan is opposed to God, Antichrist to Christ, so Belial standing in contrast to Christ must denote all antichristian pollutions personified (II Cor. 6:15). In these days of extreme worldliness, the truth of "separation" seems to be a distasteful one among some professing Christians who like to be known as good mixers. But light and darkness cannot mix, and Christ and Belial are contrary one to the other. They form an unequal yoke. No true friendship can come out of an affinity between believers and unbelievers. "There is more danger that the bad will damage the good than hope that the good will benefit the bad." Mary Slessor, the renowned missionary, was known to say that, "Complete separation from the world spelled power for God."

Children of Murderers

What a terrible stigma rests upon the children of a murderer! To go through life always with the shadow over memories that your father murdered someone and either was sentenced to life-imprisonment or was hanged or electrocuted for his crime, must be a source of continual shame. How the finger of scorn is pointed to the family by the neighbors because one of its members went to the chair for taking the life of another! The Bible has much to say about murder which was viewed as an outrage on God's likeness in man. Whoso sheddeth man's blood, by man shall his blood be shed; for in the image of God made he man" (Gen. 9:6). To cut short a person's day of grace and probation was the greatest wrong to man and an insult to his Maker.

The world's first child, Cain, who became the world's first murderer, was doomed to a life full of fears, remorse and guilt. As the law concerning murder was not in force at such an early stage of history, Cain's life was temporarily spared. Our Lord made it clear that Satan is the instigator of murder for He referred to him as a "murderer from the beginning" (John 8:44). John himself goes further and declares that not only the killer but the hater is a murderer before God (I John 3:12, 15). Love, sympathy and character can be killed, as well as the body.

As for the phrase, "the children of the murderers he slew not," the same occurs in the reign of King Amaziah who although he began well, did not persevere (II Kings 14:6; II Chron. 25:4, 7). Under the Mosaic law it was expressly stated that children should not be put to death for the crimes of their fathers. Traitors had murdered the father of Amaziah, and once he was established as king, he avenged the assassination of Joash his father – an act of justice no less than of filial piety. But the moderation of Amaziah in sparing the children of his father's murderers displayed his knowledge of the Mosaic law (Deut. 24:16), and likewise his good character. The course he pursued toward the families of the murderers was directly contrary to the prevailing customs of antiquity, according to which all connected with criminals were doomed to unsparing destruction.

Children as Fools

In his answer to the false charges of Eliphaz, Job speaks of those who "were children of fools, yea, children of base men: they were viler than the earth" (Job 30:8). The implication is that the children were as bad, if not worse than their wicked parents. They became impious, nameless as low-born rabble, just as their parents were among the most contemptible of mankind. In this chapter, Job continues his complaint of the great disgrace he had fallen into, from the height of honor and reputation.

The patriarch is affronted as he realizes that he has become like one of the vagabonds and rogues he describes. "I am their song and their byword." He found himself shunned as a loathsome spectacle, a child of a base man, and one to be abhorred and fled from (Job 30:10). Even his so-called friends misrepresented him, censured him in a most uncharitable fashion, reflected upon him as a tyrant because he had ministered justice upon them. But out of all his troubles Job was ultimately delivered. Children of fools need not become foolish children. Grace can prevent parental folly continuing in a family.

Children of the Devil

No one has ever spoken so scathingly against religious hypocrisy as the Saviour who was meek and lowly in heart. Can you not imagine the shocked appearances of those Pharisees who prided themselves on being children of Abraham when they heard Jesus say to them, "Ye are of your father the devil, and the lusts of your father ye will do"? What severe condemnation this was to affirm that the devil who was a murderer and a liar was their father (John 8:44). No wonder those religious frauds tried to kill the Man who dared to tell them they were children of the devil. How differently the children of the Father, who is in heaven, act! (Matt. 5:45).

Had God been the Father of the Pharisees who told Jesus to His face that He was a liar (John 8:13), they would have borne something of the moral image of God, as children carry their father's likeness. As their father was the devil, they manifested his impure, malignant, ungodly propensities, inclinations and desires. Dean Alford commenting on our Lord's statement, "Ye are of your father the devil," says that, "This is one of the most decisive testimonies to the *objective* (outward) *personality* of the devil. It is quite impossible to suppose an accommodation to Jewish views, or a metaphorical form of speech, in so solemn an assertion as this."

The charge Jesus made sounded harsh and insulting, but He had a deep understanding of the cruel and cunning character of His religious foes; and knowing that their actions were satanically inspired, He mercilessly exposed their hypocrisy. As children trained up with and by their father learn his words and grow like him by imitation as well as by a national image, so these Pharisees made themselves like the devil as if they had industriously set him before them for their pattern. How appalling it is to think that the majority of the godless around us today are children of the devil, exhibiting more than ever, as morals and truth decline, the lusts and lies of their satanic father. John also designates those who are like the devil in thought and action, "children of the devil," and contrasts them with "the children of God" who seek to be free from the works of the devil (I John 3:8-10).

Children of Hell

Closely allied to our Lord's piercing exposure of the Pharisees as "children of the devil" is His denunciation of them as "the children of hell" (Matt. 23:15). They were born of a person and in a place similar to their evil character. Jesus called them "children of hell" because of their rooted enmity to the kingdom of heaven, which was the principle and genius of Pharisaism. When the Pharisee gained a proselyte he made him twofold more a child of hell than himself. The scholar outdid the master. Saul of Tarsus, a Pharisee of the Pharisees, held a bitter hatred toward the Christians, while his master, Gamaliel, seems to have been more moderate.

How could these children of hell escape the damnation of hell when they were the murderous children of those who killed the prophets! When Jesus told the Pharisees to fill up the measure of their fathers who had slain the prophets He had in mind His own slaughter which He knew these selfsame children of hell would bring about. When He called them serpents and vipers He unmasked their true character, and delighted to pour contempt upon their proud yet false profession. Repentance and faith is the only way by which any one can escape the damnation of hell, but the Pharisees were wedded to their prejudice against Christ and His Gospel, and so perished in their sins. They had shut up the kingdom of heaven against men and in the end found themselves shut out of heaven because in spite of their religious profession and pretence, their hearts were evil and unrepentant.

Children of Wrath

Those who become children of disobedience through the inworking of the evil spirit controlling them are liable to a particular, terrible fate. They become both by nature and practice "the children of wrath" (Eph. 2:2, 13). These are likened to the "cursed children" which Peter describes in no uncertain terms (II Pet. 2:14). All under the curse of the law are exposed to the wrath of God. It is true that Christ died to redeem sinners from the curse of the law, but if such redemption is spurned and finally rejected, then divine wrath operates in justice.

The phrase "children of wrath" is a Hebraism, that is, they are objects of God's wrath from childhood, in their natural state, as being born in the sin which God hates, "even as others," meaning, as the rest of mankind are. They are such children by generation, they enter the world with innate corruption – an incidental proof of the doctrine of original sin. "Those who in their very nature are children of wrath." The Anglican Common Prayer Book, under *Article IX* has the forthright statement –

> Original, or birth-sin, standeth not in the following of Adam, but is the fault and corruption of the nature of every man, naturally engendered of Adam (Christ was *supernaturally* conceived by the Holy Ghost of the Virgin), whereby man is very far gone from original righteousness, and is of his own nature inclined to evil; and therefore, is every person born into this world, it deserveth God's wrath and damnation.

Paul declares that the Jews, who boasted of their birth from Abraham, were by natural birth equally children of wrath as the Gentiles, whom the Jews despised on account of their birth from idolaters (Rom. 3:9; 5:12-14). What must not be forgotten is the fact that wrath abideth on all who disobey the Gospel in faith and practice (John 3:36). How blessed to know that God who is rich in mercy waits to deliver repentant sinners from the wrath to come (Rom. 5:9; I Thess. 1:10; Rev. 6:17). As Bengel puts it, "*Mercy* takes away misery; *love* confers salvation" (Rom. 8:1).

Children of This World

In our Lord's parable on the unjust steward, He counseled His disciples to do righteously what the steward did unrighteously. Shrewdness, prudence and wisdom were qualities the steward manifested, even though he was not a child of light (Luke 16: 1-13). By the term "children of this world," twice used by our Lord (Luke 16:8; 20:34), we are to understand those who are the opposite of those named "the children of light," or "the children of God," or "the children of the resurrection" (Luke 16:8; 20:36). Children of this age are those men of the world who have "their portion in this life" (Ps. 17:14). "They are among the number who mind earthly things" (Phil. 3:19). Belonging to the world, they are only worldly in outlook and practice.

Worldly-wise, the unjust steward knew all about the adaptation of means to ends and of the energetic, determined prosecution of his principles, but none of his shrewd actions were for God and eternity. All of his wise manipulation of money was for the groveling and fleeting age of which he was part. He was a stranger to the realm of light, the atmosphere of which he never breathed. He was not a child of God. To him, grace was an undiscovered world, seeing his was an unborn existence as far as God is concerned.

Yet our Lord urged His disciples to be as wise as serpents and to learn lessons from the successful men of this world, even though as "night-birds see better in the dark than those of the day – owls than eagles," they seem to act more successfully than men of God. The steward made friends of money that he might show mercy to the poor. (See Luke 12:33; 14:13, 14; Dan. 4:27). In like manner the saints are to take advantage of the ability to make money honorably for the cause of Christ. The steward may have had prudence but he did not have faithfulness or fidelity. He may have had all the wisdom of a serpent in his stewardship but he was a total stranger to the harmlessness of the dove. What children of light learn is that fidelity depends not on the amount entrusted, but on the sense of responsibility; that as faithful stewards all they have and are able to secure must be held on trust. Money is neither to be idolized or despised; we must sit loose to it and use it for God's glory.

Children Who Are Strange

Three times over we have the phrase, "strange children" (Ps. 144:7, 11; Hos. 5:7), and as used by Hosea is equivalent to "children of whoredoms" (Hos. 1:2; 2:4). Strange, or "foreign," implies that the idolatry of these people was imported from abroad; and that being reared in idolatry they were regarded by God as strangers, and not His worshipers. The case of these strange children was desperate, as Hosea shows, when not only the existing, but also the rising generation is reared in idolatry and apostasy. The Lord is the true portion of His little children who keep themselves from idols (I John 5:21), but idols are the portions of strange children.

Are these idolatrous children not likened to "the children of transgression, a seed of falsehood," who enflame themselves with idols under every green tree, that Isaiah mentions (Isa. 57:4)? The phrase the prophet uses implies that "the children of transgression" were not merely children born of transgressors, and a seed of false parents, but were of transgression and falsehood itself, utterly unfaithful to God who was not in their thoughts. They were among the fools who said, "No God for us" (Ps. 14:1). From the Christian standpoint the term "children" implies the recognition of God as Father, and of the necessity of regeneration which is the basis of such a privileged relationship.

The Lord, the Maker, was not only the Husband of His people, but their Father and their Mother, too (Isa. 54:5; 64:8; 66:13). Jesus taught His disciples to pray to God as their Father in heaven (Matt. 6:9). A remarkable fact about God is that He combines in Himself all the virtues of a perfect character. The best among men are usually lacking in one or more graces, but God possesses them all in perfection. Because He created male and female, all manly virtues and womanly grace meet in Him. The noblest characteristic features of father and mother are resident in His loving heart. He has fused together in His own Person the strong, protective love of the man; and the patient, tender, comforting, and sacrificial love of the woman. Both are part of Him who loves us as the father, and comforts us as a mother, as John Oxenham so beautifully expresses in his poem, "The Father-Motherhood" –

> Father and Mother, Thou,
> In Thy full being are –
> Justice with mercy intertwined,
> Judgment exact with love combined,
> Neither complete apart.
>
> And so we know that when
> Our service is weak and vain,
> The Father – justice would condemn,
> The Mother – love Thy wrath will stem
> And our reprieval gain.

God speaks of Himself as the Father of Israel, because by His power He begat them by delivering them from Egypt, nourished them in the wilderness and then established them in the land of promise as His sons and daughters (Deut. 1:31; 3:26-28; 8:5). Alas! they dealt corruptly with their heavenly Father, so much so that "they are not his children" (Deut. 32:5). Sonship carried with it the obligation of filial response. "A son honoureth his father . . . if then I be a father, where is mine honour?" (Mal. 1:6).

Coming to the gospels, in the self-revelation of Jesus, as well as in His teaching, the characteristic designation of God is Father. In a unique sense He knew God as "his own Father," and Himself as "the Son of God." In the deepest experiences of triumph and trial, His faith rested in the name "Father" (Matt. 11:25; 26:39; Luke 23:46). As for His disciples, they became "the children of God" through their faith in Him, and surrender to His claims. In this age of grace we become "the sons of God" by the action of God Himself through the shed blood of His Son, and through the regenerating power of His Spirit (John 1:12, 13; 3:1-8; 14:6). The impulse of attraction to Jesus Christ is itself from the Father (John 6:44, 65). As obedient children we must endeavor to be subject to our heavenly Father in all things.

> What I have, He claims;
> What He claims, I yield;
> What I yield, He takes;
> What He takes, He fills;
> What He fills, He uses;
> What He uses, He keeps;
> What He keeps, He satisfies.

In his illuminating chapter on Jesus being subject to His earthly parents, Dr. Alexander Whyte urges that human fatherhood should be a reflection of divine fatherhood. "A child's father is much more than his mere father to him. His father is both his father and his god to every child. A little child cannot rise above his father, he cannot see beyond his father. To every child his father is the man of all men to him on earth or in heaven. There is nothing his father cannot do for him, if he pleases. There is no strength, no resource, no nobleness, no wisdom, with which every child's own father is not endowed.

"The young heart that will yet rise to the love and the adoration of its Father in heaven, for a long time knows Him only by His paternoster name. And in all this 'earthly fathers learn their craft from God.' For God, for a long time, clothes every father on earth with His own attributes and prerogatives and duties and dues. The divine throne, the divine scepter, the divine sword, are all as good as made over into every man's hand into whose house a little child is born."

As parents, then, what a solemn and heavy responsibility rests upon us to be subject to our heavenly Father in all things whose Fatherhood is manifested in protecting and redeeming love, and in divine faithfulness to which His children can appeal in times of need (Jer. 31:9, 18-20). If we are not obedient to Him, what right have we to demand obedience from our children? If we do not love the Father with all our heart, how can we be disappointed if our children do not love us as they should? By His grace we must strive to be perfect in parental example, even as our Father in heaven is perfect.

APPENDICES

Children's Stories

Children's Poems

Children's Hymns

Children's Prayers

Children's Literature

5
APPENDICES

Children's Stories

It was Sir Richard Steele (1672-1729), the eminent British essayist who wrote, "I have often thought that a good storyteller is born, as well as a poet." Parents and teachers who have the spiritual and mental culture of children at heart, realize the necessity of being good storytellers. Since a child's first teacher is his mother, although she may not be a born storyteller, she develops such an art as with his expanding mind her child says, "Mummy, tell me a story!" Young children love to hear stories, and when old enough, to read them. As their little minds cannot take in too much at once, the stories should be short. In a letter to a friend, Thoreau (1517-1562), the American philosopher said, "Not that the story need be long, but it will take a long while to make it short." The necessity of using clear, simple, and intelligible words was once emphasized by the former Bishop of Bristol, who delighted to tell of a six-year-old boy who went home after a children's service he had conducted and told his mother that the bishop had been telling them about "Jesus and His twelve *bicycles*" (disciples).

When read or recited feelingly, and with necessary inflections, stories or nursery rhymes never fail to attract and exert a formative influence over the wondering mind of a child. It is taken for granted that there are no stories comparable to those to be found in the Bible which, rightly told, are never forgotten by children. Little ones never tire of hearing —

> . . . the Old, Old Story
> Of unseen things above,
> Of Jesus and His glory,
> Of Jesus and His love.

Parents who love the Lord, and have a passionate desire to train their precious children in His way, know the constant delight they have in hearing Biblical stories again and again. They never seem to wear thin.

What we have endeavored to do in this section is to bring together from a hundred and one sources, stories, legends and traditions, some of them about children, but all of them which parents and teachers will find useful in the spiritual and moral training of the boys and girls around them. Longfellow, in his Introduction to "The Song of Hiawatha" asks —

> Should you ask me whence these stories?
> Whence these legends and traditions?

Then the poet goes on to answer his own questions —

> I should answer, I shall tell you,
> "From the forests and the prairies."

Being the fortunate possessor of a large selection of books especially designed to help preachers to make the message of the Gospel simple and plain for the young to grasp, the following stories and incidents have been taken from some of them, with the prayerful hope that their re-telling will be blessed to those in "life's sweet morning." Pastors who follow the custom of having a sermonette for children at the Sunday morning service can gather many parables and points from books of sermon helps, one of them being *The Zondervan Pastor's Annual,* published by Zondervan Publishing House, Grand Rapids, Michigan.

A Little Peddler

Robbie was a little fellow about ten or eleven years old, and he used to go about with a basket on his arm, and sell pins, tapes, pocket combs, and odds and ends. One day he came into the waiting room of a railway station, crying out –

"Pins and pocket combs!
Pins and pocket combs!"

His voice was weak, for he was tired and faint for want of food. The crowd in the waiting room took no notice of the poor little peddler. But a lady heard him, and as she had had the misfortune to tear her dress, she said, "Here, my boy, you have just what I want. Give me a paper of pins, that I may pin up this ugly tear in my dress, until I get home." Then, turning to her brother at her side, she said, "Harry, will you pay this little boy for a paper of pins?" As he was finding the money, Robbie said to the lady:

"No, no, ma'am! Don't take that sheet; it isn't a whole one. I cut off a row of pins from it this morning for my little sister to dress her doll with."

"Never mind, my little man," said the lady, "there are more than I want now, and I shall only have the less to throw away."

"Then don't pay me so much," said Robbie, and he handed two cents back to the lady's brother who had given him ten cents.

"Well, my little merchant," said the man, "you are too honest. How do you expect to make a living unless you cheat a little now and then?"

Robbie's brown eyes opened wide when he heard this question:

"But," said the boy, "I'd rather not live at all, than live by cheating."

"And who taught you this?" asked the man.

"My mother, sir, before she died and went to heaven. And I am sure she would rather have me die, and come to her at last an honest, upright boy, than live ever so well on money got by cheating."

"You are right, my boy; and you are a noble little fellow to remember your mother's teachings."

Now it so happened that this man who paid for the pins was a merchant, but in need of money, and was tempted to take some that did not belong to him in order to help him out of his trouble. But the simple honesty of that little peddler had such an effect upon him that he resisted the temptation to steal, and by God's help, got out of his trouble honestly. Some time later he sent for little Robbie, and gave him a position in his office, feeling sure that a boy who was so honest in pins and pennies, would be one to be trusted in more important matters. Robbie started as an office boy, and gradually rose until he was taken into the business as a partner. So you see it pays to be honest, or, as the Bible puts it, "have a conscience void of offence toward God and man."

Saved by a Brave Soldier

Years ago during a review of Austrian cavalry before the then emperor and empress, in the public square in Vienna, a courageous act saved a child's life. Just as one of the squadrons swept out from the main body of 30,000 horsemen, a little girl, only four years old, dashed out from her mother's side, before the crowd, and ran out onto the open field just in front of the soldiers. The squadron was at full gallop, and so close that to stop was impossible. It seemed as if the child must be crushed to death. A thrill of horror ran through the crowd, who saw the danger, but were unable to prevent it.

The empress saw it all from her carriage, and uttered a cry of terror at the thought of the little one being trampled to death. But, at the very moment that the squadron reached the child, a brave soldier swung himself down from the saddle, holding on by the horse's mane, and catching the child as he swept on, lifted it, with himself, safely into the saddle, without slackening his speed or losing his place in the ranks. The child was saved. Ten thousand voices raised a shout of joy. The empress and the child's mother wept tears of grateful thanks. The emperor summoned the noble soldier into his presence, and taking from his own breast a richly ornamented diamond cross, hung it around the brave soldier's neck, and thanked him before the crowd for his swift, courageous action. Greater glory, however, belongs to Jesus who, in His effort to save us from sin and death, died a brutal death at Calvary. Now we can live and live eternally with Him, because He bore our sin and died our death.

Regaining a Lost Inheritance

The English statesman and administrator in India, Warren Hastings (1732 - 1818), when an old man, used to tell the story of his early life. He was a poor orphan of seven when he learned that all the broad acres around him — the lands of Daylesford — had once belonged to his ancestors, and should have been his birthright. One day as he lay on the bank of the stream, he resolved that he would win back his inheritance. When a ruler in India, he constantly remembered his vow and did not rest until he was the proprietor of Daylesford.

Although only a boy of seven, he was not too young to brood over a lost inheritance, mourn its loss, and yearn and work for its recovery. All of us have lost our birthright, like Warren Hastings, by the fault of our ancestors, Adam and Eve; and, like Esau, by our own choice and fault. Unlike Hastings we cannot win it back, even though we may be successful as he was in making an empire and a fortune. Yet we can gain it back. If we put our case in Christ's hands He will secure for us a perfect right and title to the glorious inheritance on high. But if we delay in accepting such a title, we may come to shed tears as bitter and as unavailing as Esau's who sold his birthright for a bowl of pottage.

Ye who have sold for nought
Your heritage above,
Receive it back unbought,
The gift of Jesus' love.

The Wrong Climate

A distinguished traveler returning from a northern climate brought with him a rare plant for a little girl of his acquaintance. Presenting it to her, the great student of flowers told her to place the plant in a particular part of the garden where the cold wind could beat upon it. Day by day the girl looked upon the prized plant, and it seemed to her that it was withering up. She went into a nearby greenhouse and saw beautiful plants blossoming in the heat, and decided that this was what her plant needed. Up it came and, placed in a pot, was deposited in the greenhouse where the small girl believed it would blossom as gloriously as the exotic flowers thriving in the heat. The next morning when she came to see her plant, it was dead. The heat had killed it. What made other plants blossom, according to God's law of nature, had killed the plant He had created to blossom in the cold. Is there not a lesson for our hearts in this fact? The Ark which blessed the Israelites to whom God had given it, cursed the Philistines who stole it. If God places us in a position, preserved by those who love us from all cold blasts, let us be satisfied; but if He places us in His mercy and love where the storm of trial and temptation beat upon us, it is only there we will blossom.

The Language of Conscience

When Sir H. M. Stanley (1841-1904), the British explorer, started through Africa, he knew that he would find wild tribes who could not understand his language, but he also knew that they would understand the language of conscience – the same in him and in them. So he ordered his men never to steal from a savage, never to break a promise, however insignificant it was, and never to harm a human being. One day the traveler met the fiercest of tribes. Expecting they would attack him as other tribes had done, he was surprised at their kindness. When he learned to understand a little of their language, he asked why this was. They said, "Because we sent a canoe up the river, with a woman and a boy, and plenty of provisions. If you had been bad people, you would have taken the canoe. Then you would have had to fight us; but, see, we have left our spears on one of the islands."

Stanley was right in supposing that the language of conscience was universal, and had not been confounded as our tongues were at Babel. There is not a boy or girl who does not know what is right and what is wrong. The infallible guide for conscience is, of course, the Bible, so full of advice of what to do, and what not to do. If we venture too near forbidden territory, an inner voice says, "Avoid it, pass not by it, turn from it, and pass away" (Prov. 4:15). Stolen waters may seem to be sweet, but they soon turn to bitterness. May grace be ours always to follow the dictates of a God-directed conscience!

A Nest of Rabbits

The story is told of a boy strolling through the fields with his sister. They found a nest of rabbits, and the girl was charmed with it, so snug and warm and lined with down, and with the tiny occupants so content. But her brother seized them, and mimicked their squeaks and their struggles. In vain his little sister wept and intreated, as he flung the little rabbits up in the air, and shouted as each fell dead on the stones. "Confound your tears," said her heartless brother, "you should hire yourself as an undertaker." Ten years later, that sister sat weeping again at her brother's side. He was in chains, sentenced to be hung for shooting a farmer who caught him poaching.

"Sister," he said, "do you remember the nest of rabbits ten years ago, how you prayed and I ridiculed? I sincerely believe that from that day God forsook me and left me to follow my own inclinations. If I had yielded to your tears then, you and I would not be weeping these bitter tears now." Only God can deliver us from such callousness, if we will let Him, and from all the sorrow it produces. Boys who begin by tormenting cats or dogs often graduate to delight in cruelty to their fellowmen, and at last are heroes in all but their power to cause suffering.

There is an old saying to the effect, "He who snatches shall be covered with scratches." God teaches us by bad examples as well as by good ones. The good are like those tugboats which guide a ship into a harbor, the bad are like the black and shattered wrecks on a sand bar, which seem to say, "Keep far away from here." It is better for girls to be like Ruth than Salome, and boys, like Samuel than the Prodigal Son.

A Girl and Her Watering Can

A preacher tells of a cottage across the road from where he lived which belonged to a poor widow whose chief delight were a few flowers outside the door. The woman fell ill, and lay in bed a long time, and friends showed her kindness. From his window the preacher could see the doctor go in at the door, and the kind neighbors who brought her comforts both for body and mind. But there was one who showed the sick woman a real, practical piece of kindness. It was the little girl who lived next door, who did not go into the house, nor make herself conspicuous in any way. At dusk she would come with her watering pot and water the poor woman's flowers that would certainly have died in the hot summer sun. She continued this act until the sick one was better again.

The first day the widow was able, she came tottering out to see her favorite flowers, and there they were, all well and healthy. The preacher never inquired whether the poor woman knew who had kept them alive, but whenever he saw the little girl watering the sick woman's flowers, he knew that God witnessed the kind act and wrote it down in His great book of remembrance. It does not matter how young and little you may be, you can always be kind and helpful to those in need. Do you remember what happened to the mouse that once did a good deed to a lion? Jesus, we read, went about continually doing good. How happy you will be if you can make this hymn your prayer –

God make my life a little light
  Within the world to glow:
A little flame that burneth bright.
  Wherever I may go.

Something to Look Forward To

Jimmy was a little boy, only nine years old, and when his ninth birthday came around one of his uncles thought he would give Jimmy a great surprise. When the birthday morning arrived, the uncle sent him a brand new bicycle, which was just what Jimmy had been wanting for so long. The uncle did not let his nephew know the bicycle was coming because he wanted it to be a great surprise. He felt that all children like a thing better if it comes as a surprise. That night as Jimmy's mother tucked him in bed, and they had a talk about his birthday, she said, "Wasn't that a wonderful bicycle your uncle sent?"

"Yes," said Jimmy, "it was super." Then he said something else, worthy of taking special note: "But I wish he'd promised it to me, mom, months ago, instead of sending it!" What the boy meant was that he would have enjoyed the looking forward almost as much as getting it. Day after day he would have been wondering what it was going to be like; he would have been thinking of how he would take it out for the first time and what his friends would say when they saw the new bike.

All of us like looking forward to things, such as looking forward to the holiday at the seaside we are going to have, weeks before it comes. Before

Jesus went back to heaven, He gave His disciples a promise that He would return and take them to be with Himself (John 14:1-3), which is something all who love Him can look forward to. He has told us well in advance of some of the glories of heaven, and ours can be the joyful anticipation of all He has treasured up for us.

A Sack of Feathers

Have you ever heard the story of the feathers at the four crossroads, teaching us that you can never get back what goes out? A king gave a great feast for all his knights who returned from one of his wars. The day before the banquet one of the greatest of his knights fell from his horse, and was so badly injured that it was thought he could never recover, and of course he could not attend the feast. The king thought that this would cast a gloom over the happy occasion, but he was surprised to find that it made no difference at all to the gaiety of the knights, and no one seemed to miss the chief.

So the king asked them the reason of their lightheartedness in spite of their chief's absence. "Sire," they said, "we do not feel the loss of our chief very much, because when he is with us we fear the power of his lashing, sarcastic tongue, and we are always afraid of what he is going to say next."

This caused the king to think a great deal, and when, as it happened, the knight recovered and became well again, the king sent for him and ordered him to get his horse and come for a ride with the king. He was also to be particularly careful to bring with him a large sack full of feathers. The knight was greatly mystified, but naturally he obeyed the king's commands. In due time they set off on horseback, the knight carrying with him the sack of feathers. When they reached a place four miles out in the country they found crossroads there. The king thereupon ordered the knight to get down from his horse and empty the feathers on the road. They then turned their horses and rode back again. The king did not explain his rather curious proceeding and the knight dare not ask.

The next day the king sent for the knight again and told him to bring his horse and the empty sack with him. Again they rode out to the place four miles distant where the crossroads met. Then the king ordered the knight to dismount and to refill the sack with the feathers he had emptied out the day before. It is not difficult to guess what had happened – the feathers had all blown away.

Then said the king – "I did this for a purpose. The feathers were meant to represent your words. You cannot get them back, and in your case your words do a great deal of harm, and cause much sorrow." We can imagine how rebuked the knight was, and how he profited through such a unique object lesson. While the words leaving our lips cannot be drawn back, what we can do is to be careful about the words we utter. Herod was guilty of using rash words, without thinking, and they cost John the Baptist his life. Much evil is wrought by want of thought. How we need to pray before we speak – "Set a watch, O Lord, before my mouth; and keep the door of my lips" (Ps. 141:3).

The Broken Jug

Sir William Napier who gave us, *The History of the Peninsular War,* tells us how affected he was to see at the Battle of Busaco, in Portugal, a beautiful Portuguese orphan girl coming down the mountains, driving an ass loaded with all her property through the midst of the armies. She passed over the field of battle with a childish simplicity, scarcely understanding which were French and which were English soldiers, and no one on either side was so hardhearted as to touch her. Does this not illustrate how the strongest men are open to those tender kindly feelings which little children are given by our heavenly Father to promote in all of us.

Sir Napier then goes on to describe how while out for a walk one day he met a little girl of five years of age sobbing over a cheap jug she had broken, and who, in her innocence, asked Sir William to mend it. Kindly he explained he was not able to repair the jug, but that he would give her the money to buy a new one, if she would meet him there at the same hour the next day, as he had no money in his purse just then. Reaching home, however, he found that there was an invitation waiting for him which he particularly wanted to accept. But he could not then have met the little girl at the time stated, and so he declined the invitation, saying, "I could not disappoint her, she trusted in me so implicitly." When this true Christian gentleman and soldier found the small girl waiting for him the next day to receive his promised gift of money for a new jug, he was amply rewarded by her smile of gratitude.

The Right Spelling

Dr. A. P. Stanley, Dean of Westminster more than eighty years ago told the story of a small girl who lived with her grandfather who was not a very good man. The child, however, loved Jesus, and had a simple trust in His care of her. One day, when she came back from school, she found her grandfather had put over her little bed a large sheet of paper on which he had written, *God is nowhere.* You see he did not believe in God and tried to make his small granddaughter believe as he did. But all his arguments were beyond her. All she could do was to read the statement, one syllable at a time. Exercising her little mind she read the words. *God - is - now* - (nowhere was too big a word for her to grasp, so she broke it up) - *here.* That was more assuring to her than *God is nowhere.* As for the grandfather he was touched by the way the girl read the words, and was made to think of the omnipresent God. There is a sense in which *God is nowhere* is true if we take the sentence to mean that He is in no particular place, but everywhere at the same time. God is in every place; He is with you *now,* for He is always everywhere — your present Companion and your Hope for years to come.

The Figure in the Looking Glass

A young man who was leaving his quiet country home to take up work in London, was given an impressive object lesson by his father who was anxious how his son would fare in the great city. On the day the boy was to leave home, his father took him to a room where there was a large mirror in which one's figure could be reflected from head to foot. The father said to his son, "Now, my boy, stand in front of this mirror, double your fists and strike a fighting attitude." Wondering what was coming, the boy did as he was told. Of course the reflected figure in the mirror did the same. "Put your hands down," said the father. "Now hold out your right hand as if you were going to shake hands with someone." He did so, and the figure in the looking glass responded in the same way.

"Now," said the father, "you are going alone to the great city. You will meet many strangers. Remember this – it largely depends on your attitude to them what theirs will be to you. If you are pugnacious and quarrelsome, people will meet you in the same spirit, just like your reflection in the mirror; but if you are kindly disposed and exhibit a friendly spirit, people will respond in the same way. Hold out your hand and you will be met by the friendly hand, just as your counterpart in the mirror does." A verse of a hymn sometimes sung at harvest services goes –

> Sow flowers, and flowers will blossom,
> Around you wherever you go;
> Sow weeds, and of weeds reap the harvest,
> You'll reap whatsoever you sow.

The Dog That Forgave

Have you read of that brutal man who wanted to kill his dog? Having no further use for it, he took it to a deep river and threw it in. Each time the poor animal swam to the bank the man gave it a cruel blow. In aiming one of these blows the man himself slipped into the deep water, and would have drowned had not the poor dog, bruised and bleeding though it was, seized him and held him up until he could be rescued. Then the first thing the man saw when he gained consciousness was the poor animal cruelly wounded, bleeding from his blows – in fact, dying – yet lying on the ground licking the hand that had given the death blow and looking affectionately into his face.

Too often we pierce Jesus with our sins, folly and negligence, yet He always waits to be gracious. He seeks to love us and save us from every danger, and at last guide us safely through the valley of the shadow of death unto our heavenly home, but we crucify Him afresh by wrong deeds. Yet as that dog licked the hand that struck it, the Bible reminds us that the Lord is merciful and gracious and always ready to forgive.

The Toy Maker's Secret

There is an old legend about a toy maker who made more wonderful toys than anyone else. When one of the dolls he made arrived at any house, that house began to be happier, and all his toys seemed to bring joy and happiness with them wherever they were received. Do you know the secret of those toys? Well, when he made them, he took a little bit of his own heart and put it into them. He gave each toy a heart, in its tiny degree, like his own, and so the toys took his heart and his spirit with them. The old toy maker used to say –

> But each little doll I sell
> I give it a heart as well.
> I make a hole there,
> Put a soul there,
> When you walk with it
> You may talk with it.
>
> Can you keep a secret?
> I wonder if you can?
> My toys are all enchanted
> I'm a wise magician man.

Have you ever thought that God is like that toy maker? When He sent His Son to earth to die for sin and sinners, He put heart into the hopes of men. Old Simeon was quite prepared to die happy, once he had seen the lovely face of the holy Child Jesus. His coming has made humans and homes happier.

> Can you keep a secret?
> I wonder if you can?
> Our whole world is enchanted
> By God becoming Man.

Do we so live that those around can see that the great Toy Maker has put

His heart into us? He came, not only to put His heart into the world, but to break it for the world's sins. If He has given us a new heart, then many should see our changed lives and rejoice.

A Framed Text

In a Lancashire town there lived an old lady by the name of Esther Walmsley. One day a small boy was taken to meet her. Hanging on the wall of her small house was a framed text. Old Esther pointed to it and asked the boy to take it down and bring it to her. The boy climbed on the chair and took down the text. Esther then read the text aloud, and asked the boy to say it after her, which he did. The text was, "Thou God seest me."

"When you are older," Esther Walmsley said to the boy, "people will tell you that God is always watching you, to see if you do wrong, in order to punish you. I do not want you to think of it in that way, but I want you to take this framed text home with you and remember all your life that *God loves you so much that He cannot take His eyes off you.*" That is what "Thou God seest me" means.

This incident made a deep impression on the small boy's mind. Old Esther never dreamed that she was giving the text to one who, one day, would be a bishop. That poor boy became a bishop of Chelmsford, and old Esther Walmsley's text always had a place of honor on the wall of his study.

Several times a year the bishop took down the text and told its story to young men being ordained as ministers. At every ordination, the bishop told the story of Esther Walmsley and her text. These four words "Thou God seest me," were first spoken by Hagar, a woman turned out of the house of Abraham because of the jealousy of Sarah. Wandering for some time in the wilderness, at last, tired and footsore, she came to a fountain, and, as she rested there, the angel of God found her and told her to go back to the house from which she had been expelled. Surprised that God's angel had found her in such a desert place she exclaimed, "Thou God seest me," which reminds us that no matter where we are His eye is upon us.

A Quaint Name

In the far North Riding of Yorkshire, under the shadow of the Hambleton Hills, a moorland village lies on the hillside, bearing the quaint name of Osmotherley. From an old legend we learn that long ago, in Saxon times, a prince was born on those lonely hills, and it was predicted of him that he should die of drowning at the age of twelve.

He was his mother's only son, and to prevent such a disaster she carried him off to this remote part of the moorland, far from the presence of any water. But alas! though the fatal age was reached in safety, it was not passed. An unsuspected spring gushed out of the ground and Os, the boy, perished in its flood, and his death broke his mother's heart. Giving a modern meaning to this ancient legend we know that we may try to avert and avoid the eternal voices speaking to us within, but there comes a moment when we must turn and listen. So often, because we have refused to hear the still small voice, we must listen to the voice in the whirlwind. If we are persistently deaf to that voice in grace, we shall be compelled to hear it hereafter in judgment.

A Life Motto

Known throughout the Christian world is the Keswick Convention, which takes its name from the somewhat small town situated alongside the beautiful lake of Derwentwater. Through the long course of its history, myriads visiting the convention have admired the shadows of the mountains close upon the water, changing every hour from one mystic beauty to another. A favorite spot for all visitors to Keswick is a wooded crag in which is a block of stone inscibed to the memory of John Ruskin who dearly loved this place seeing it was there that he first consciously felt the beauty of the earth. On one side of the stone is a medallion of Ruskin's youthful head. On the other side is carved his life motto – *today* – which was the secret of a large part of his great life work. *Today,* says the Bible, as you hear God's voice, harden not your heart. If our ears are dull today, and we cannot distinguish the Voice among the voices, tomorrow will indeed never dawn for us. In a beautiful garden in the south of England is a sundial bearing the inscription –

Yesterday returneth not.
Perchance tomorrow cometh not.
Thine is today – misuse it not.

Where the Angels Always Sing

Several years ago the papers carried a touching account of a boy called Harry, the little eight-year old son of a God-fearing, laboring man who lived on the shores of the lovely Lake of Coniston. One day, during the hay season, the boy set off carrying his elder brother's dinner to the field where he was mowing. Approaching, he saw his brother hard at work, and boyish-like, Harry thought it would be fun to give his brother a scare, so he crept up softly behind him through the long sweet hay.

But, alas! just as he was about to spring, the brother, quite unconscious that Harry was near, suddenly reversed the movement of his scythe, which, sweeping through the grass, severed the tendons of the little fellow's legs. With a cry of horror – William – that was the brother's name – caught the poor, bleeding boy up and rushed off home with him. But before the doctor got there, and the wounds bound up, the loss of blood had been so great that Harry could not live.

"Did he speak at all?" asked a friend who had come to see the sorrow-stricken mother.

"Bless you, yes, sir, toward morning. When the birds began to chirp, and all the world to wake, he opened his dear blue eyes, and then, very low, he talked and sang."

"What did he say? What did he sing?"

"Oh! just little bits of texts and scraps of hymns, mostly what he learned at the Sunday school. He'd a wonderful store of them in his heart, and they comforted him sure, then – "

"Well?"

"He sang on, sir, and said his texts, until the sun came pouring in all ablaze. Then he stopped. We couldn't hear his little voice down here; but I like to think he's still singing and talking about Jesus up yonder, where the angels always sing."

Was not that distressed mother right? Her boy who died so soon and tragically, was not really dead. He was only fallen asleep on earth to awake in heaven. Because death overtakes us all, whether in childhood, youth, middle life or old age, how essential it is to have Jesus as a personal Saviour, so that when the call comes to leave this earth, ours will be the translation into His presence above.

Soap and Water

One day Jesus called the Pharisees "whited sepulchres" – tombs erected along the wayside which were carefully whitewashed on the outside but inside were full of the corrupting bones of dead men. Some are much concerned about having clean bodies but appear to be negligent of the necessity of a clean heart within. What's the use of washing the outside of a cup or jug, if the vessel is dirty and defiled within? Here are two stories emphasizing the importance of inner, as well as outer, cleanliness. The first concerns D. L. Moody, the renowned evangelist, who tells us that one day he promised to take his little boy William out for a drive. The child, however, played about in the dirt, and made himself quite unfit to be seen.

"Let me come with you in the buggy, daddy," the boy pleaded.

"No, Willie, you are not ready. I must take you in and wash you."

"Oh, daddy! I'm all right," the child replied.

"No, you are covered with dirt," was the answer.

"Mummy washed me; I'm clean," Willie said.

Finding that he could not convince his child that he had made himself dirty since he had been washed, Mr. Moody lifted Willie in his arms and told him to look at his face in the looking glass, and, says Moody, "The looking glass stopped his talking about being clean, but I did not wash my boy's face with the mirror." The Bible functions as a looking glass and reveals our need of cleansing, and then sends us to the only source of cleansing, namely the precious blood Jesus shed at Calvary.

The other story concerns a little boy who had been out in the garden playing in the dirt. His hands were grimy; as for his face, mud-covered, it looked like a miniature garden patch. Instead of seeking the soap and water he sat down on a chair in the best room, saying, "I'll never touch anything dirty again." As for the room itself, it was spotlessly clean, but everything the boy touched and handled showed the marks of his dirty fingers.

"Johnny, how could you touch the music with such fingers?" asked his mother. "Look at those dirty marks on the keys of the piano."

Even the chair on which Johnny was sitting bore traces of his presence. In fact, he was soon making everything he touched like himself. "Why, Mamma, I have not touched a dirty thing since I left the garden," Johnny protested. "No, perhaps not; but you are dirty yourself, and are spoiling my furniture."

This lesson is evident. We are all stained and polluted and cannot enter our heavenly Father's home in such a condition. We must be cleansed and pardoned. Suppose the boy had said, as he sat in the chair, "I'll not bother about what Mamma says. I'm clean enough." Would that have sufficed? Not at all, even if he believed himself to be as white as snow. Another detected the stains on him, and urged him to seek the cleansing soap and water could provide. Unless the boy desired to remain dirty – he must be washed. It is useless to say that all sinners require is just to be left alone, and they will come out all right. Left alone, they remain and die in their sin. If they are to be made fit for Christ's presence they must be cleansed from all filthiness of the flesh.

Not Dead Yet

R. W. Stewart writes of going to a hospital in a slum area with some beautiful flowers that had been used to decorate his church at the harvest Thanksgiving services. Near the hospital a crowd of small boys was playing, and as the minister passed by, a chrysanthemum fell out of the bunch of flowers he was carrying, Picking it up he said to one of the boys, "Would you like to have this flower?" A look of utter disgust came over his face and he turned from Mr. Stewart, saying scornfully, "I'm not dead yet!" The boy had an idea that flowers were only for people about to die or for a funeral, and not for the living and healthy to enjoy. Too often we save our flowers for people when they are dead. Is it not far better to let them have the fragrance and beauty of the flowers while they can appreciate them? An unknown writer has put it –

> It is better to bring a cheap bouquet
> To a living friend this very day,
> Than a bushel of roses,
> To lay on his casket when he's dead.

The dead in their graves cannot feast upon the beauty of the flowers above them, nor be delighted with their lovely fragrance.

Rich Although Poor

Richard Newton, author of several books for children, tells of a young minister who took charge of a small, country church in New York State. One day he was asked to call and see an aged widow who had once been an active member of the church. Calling upon her, the pastor found that she was both poor and blind. Pausing at the door he heard someone praying in a low voice. Waiting until the prayer was ended, he entered the cottage, and making himself known to the blind widow, said, "How are you today, my good friend?" With tears of gratitude streaming from her blind eyes, she replied, "I am very well, thank God."

The pastor then asked her if there was anything he could do for her. "Yes," she said, "I would be much obliged if you could bring me a loaf of bread. We have not had much solid food for a day or two."

"What, my friend," asked the astonished visitor, "how is it you keep going as you do?"

"God is very good to the poor," she replied. "The woods are full of huckleberries, and my two little grandchildren gather them. Our cow gives milk: so we have milk and huckleberries; and *we have God too.*"

Her secret of contentment was in those last four words – *we have God too.* No matter how little of this world's goods we may have, if we can only say, "We have God too," we are richer than if we had thousands of gold and silver without Him. Is this not what the good poet Cowper meant, when looking up to God, he said? –

> Give what Thou canst;
> without Thee we are poor,
> And *with Thee rich;*
> take what Thou wilt away.

Children's Poems

Poetic literature for, and about, children, whether in the form of nursery rhymes, religious and secular poems, or hymns is both vast and varied. Occupying a unique place of honor amongst the great classics of this particular literature is the incomparable book, *A Child's Garden of Verses* by Robert Louis Stevenson, through which he bequeathed to successive generations the key to the door of childhood's enchanted garden. Graciously he dedicated his book to Alison Cunningham who was his devoted nurse, as a sick child, and whom he described as –

My second Mother, my first Wife,
The angel of my infant life.

At the conclusion of this dedicatory poem to his wonderful nurse, Stevenson has the verse –

And grant it, Heaven, that all who read
May find as dear a nurse at need,
And every child who lists my rhyme,
In the bright fireside, nursery clime,
May hear it in as kind a voice
As made my childish days rejoice.

We would urge all parents to secure *A Child's Garden of Verses*, the timeless charm and poetic imagery of which have now been so beautifully illustrated by Hilda Boswell. A sample of Stevenson's genius is "My Bed Is a Boat," which goes –

My bed is like a little boat;
Nurse helps me in when I embark;
She girds me in my sailor's coat
And starts me in the dark.

At night, I go on board and say
Good-night to all my friends on shore;
I shut my eyes and sail away
And see and hear no more.

And sometimes things to bed I take,
As prudent sailors have to do;
Perhaps a slice of wedding-cake,
Perhaps a toy or two.

All night across the dark we steer;
But when the day returns at last,
Safe in my room, beside the pier,
I find my vessel fast.

Another verse of his occurring in "The Whole Duty of Children" reads –

A child should always say what's true
And speak when he is spoken to,
And behave mannerly at table;
At least as far as he is able.

From sources far too numerous to mention we have culled the following specimens which parents and teachers might like to recite or teach the children to recite. As the majority are anonymous – that most prolific writer – we give the verses as we found them in a large quantity of books and magazines. John Bunyan's picture of the Man at the gate has found expression in the lines –

I am only a little child, dear Lord,
And my feet already are stained with sin,
But they said He had sent the children word
To come to the Gate, and enter in.
And the Man at the Gate looked down and smiled,
A goodly smile and fair to see;
And spoke as He looked at the trembling child,
"I am willing with all My heart," said He.

That little children should be like the stars that "come twinkling one by one from out the azure sky" is suggested by the prayer-poem –

Make me Thy child – a child of God,
Washed in my Saviour's precious blood:
And my whole heart, from sin set free,
A little vessel full of Thee.

A star of early dawn, and bright,
Shining within Thy sacred light;
A beam of grace to all around;
A little spot of hallowed ground.

That we should never think lightly even of a little child is borne out by these expressive lines –

A child touched a spring;
The spring closed a valve;
The labouring engine burst.
A thousand lives were in that ship,
Wrecked by an infant's finger.

What a treasure this children's poem "Big Things," by Howard T. Ussher is! –

Like any child, I used to think
The big things was the best;
And I was sure that I should find
The golden eagle's nest.

Right through the bracken and the heath
I climbed, but only found
That far above me was the sky,
And underneath — the ground.

I never found an eagle's nest,
Nor yet the bird of gold;
But I have learned that little things
Mean more as I grow old.

A little smile, a little word,
A handshake, or a nod,
May be a hint to tired folk
The world is full of God.

Well over fifty years ago I came across these two poems in an English religious paper, both bearing the initials D. S.

"The Boys That Are Wanted"

The boys that are wanted are good boys,
That are noble in mind and heart,
Who would scorn to oppress the weak ones,
But would bravely take their part.
The boys that are wanted are true boys,
Who have taken CHRIST for their LORD,
Who have given their lives to HIS service,
And who strive to obey HIS WORD.

The boys that are wanted are pure boys,
Whose goings are kept by the LORD,
Who at home, at school, and in play-time
Shed their influence abroad —
An influence gentle but mighty,
That all around them can tell
They are noble and pure and CHRIST-LIKE,
And copy their MASTER well.

"The Girls That Are Wanted"

The girls that are wanted are good girls,
Good from the heart to the lips,
Pure as the Lily is white and pure
From its heart to its sweet lip tips.
The girls that are wanted are home girls,
Girls that are mother's right hand
That fathers and brothers can trust in,
And the little ones understand.

Girls that are fair on the hearthstones,
And pleasant when nobody sees,
Kind and sweet to their own folks,
Ready and anxious to please.
The girls that are wanted are wise girls
That know what to do and say
That drive with a smile and a loving word
The gloom of the household away.

Mary Howitt has a poem in which the good thought about doing everything to please God is put into the lips of a very small child she called "Willie." One day his mother saw him sitting very silent in the sunlight, with all the men and women and the beasts and birds of his Noah's Ark set out in a row. "What are you thinking about, Willie?" asked mother. Willie answering said —

You know that God loves little children,
And likes them to love Him the same;
So I've set out my Noah's Ark creatures,
The great savage beasts and the tame,
I've set them all out in the sunshine,
Where I think they are plainest to see,
Because I would give Him some pleasure
Who gives so much pleasure to me.

A little girl came one day to the noble Charles Kingsley with the request: "Dear Mr. Kingsley, give me a song." Kingsley, who had a great love for children, wrote for her:

Be good, sweet maid, and let who will be clever;
Do noble things, not dream them, all day long;

And so make life, death, and the vast
for ever,
One grand, sweet song.

While children should be taught to put their best into the most menial tasks, those who instruct them must be careful to point them to God as an impressive example of carefulness and thoroughness. "God saw every thing that he had made, and, behold, it was very good" (Gen. 1:31). The young should be taught to persevere and reach the top.

If I were a cobbler I'd make it my
pride
The best of all cobblers to be,
If I were a tinker no tinker beside
Should mend an old kettle like me.

But whether a tinker or whether a
lord,
Whatever my station may be,
Determined to play second fiddle to
none,
I'll climb to the top of the tree.

There is a simple child's poem which teaches beautifully the way God blesses children who seek to do helpful things. The first two verses go –

Only ten little fingers!
Not very strong, 'tis true,
Yet there is work for Jesus
Such little hands can do.
What though it be but humble,
Winning no word of praise,
We are but little children,
Working in little ways.

Only ten little fingers!
But little things may grow;
And little hands now helpless
Will not be always so.
And if we train them early,
Unto His work alone,
They will do greater service
When they are stronger grown.

The Jews of old felt that they could not sing the Lord's song in a strange land, yet Paul and Silas were in a strange land – in prison – yet they could sing the songs of Zion, and the other prisoners hearing them were doubtless encouraged. Among the verses of Robert Louis Stevenson already mentioned, is the only one on singing which all boys and girls should learn. The little poem has only two verses –

Of speckled eggs the birdie sings
And nests among the trees.
The sailor sings of ropes and things
In ships upon the seas.

The children sing in far Japan,
The children sing in Spain,
The organ with the organ man
Is singing in the rain.

The wonderful saying of Jesus about praise being perfected in the mouths of babes and sucklings (Matt. 21:16) suggested to Robert Browning a poem he called "The Boy and the Angel." It was about a boy the poet named Theocrite, and the poem begins –

Morning, evening, noon and night
"Praise God," sang Theocrite,
Then to his poor trade he turned
Whereby the daily meal was earned.
Hard he laboured, long and well,
O'er his work the boy's curls fell.

Then the poem goes on to tell the story of how the boy had the opportunity of going away to study books and of how he became a learned and a great man. But God, listening in heaven, missed his song and said so to the angels. One of the angels thought of a plan. He flew down to earth and changed himself into a boy and took up the boy's work and

Morning, evening, noon and night
Praising God *in place of Theocrite.*

Somehow the kind angel thought that his song would make up for what God missed and would do instead. But it didn't. Although loud and clear and beautiful, really better in a way than the boy's song, there was a difference about it which God noticed, and He said –

I miss My little human praise.

The poem ends with the angel flying away and bringing Theocrite back to sing himself as he used to.

Well over 1,000 years ago now the Duke of Normandy was very proud when he became the father of a little baby boy. One day he showed the infant to some of the knights of his court, one of whom remarked, "He's small, but he'll grow." And grow he did, to become William the Conqueror, the first Norman king of England. You may be small, but you will grow, and yours must be the determination to grow well. Paul wrote about those who grew up to become "lovers of their own selves" (II Tim. 3:2). They were the people who finished up the jam, leaving none for others. Here is a short poem about one who lived only to please himself.

I gave a little tea-party
 This afternoon at three.
'Twas very small, three guests in all,
 I, myself, and me.
Myself ate up the sandwiches,
 While *I* drank all the tea,
'Twas also *I* that ate the pie,
 And passed the cake to *me*.

The great American poet, Longfellow, who had an affectionate place in his heart and in his poetry for the children, has been rightly named, "The Children's Poet." Often he makes his bright pictures brighter by referring to the children. What child has not learned to recite "The Village Blacksmith"? An illustration of his inclusion of children in his poems is in the verse –

And the children coming home from school
 Look in at the open door;
They loved to see the flaming forge,
 And hear the bellows roar,
And catch the burning sparks that fly
 Like chaff from a threshing floor.

When Longfellow reached his seventieth birthday, the young people of Cambridge, Massachusetts, took a large bough from the chestnut tree under which the village smithy stood and made a chair out of it and brought it to the dear old man as an expression of their love. When it arrived, it made the poet so pleased and so young that he wrote another expressive poem as his reply to the children –

And thus, dear children have ye made for me
 This day a Jubilee,
And to my more than threescore years and ten
 Brought back my youth again.

It was this same poet who wrote of children as "living poems," because he found so much of his poetry in the children he loved. Here are a few lines in which he speaks of them in this happy way –

Come unto me, O ye children! for I hear you at your play,
And the questions that perplexed me have vanished quite away.
For what are all our contrivings, and the wisdom of our Books,
When compared to your caresses, and the gladness of your looks,
Ye are better than all the ballads that ever were sung or said;
For ye are *living poems*, and all the rest are dead.

A previous Bishop of London, Mandell Creighton, told in his biography something of the power that a look had upon his childhood days. Having done something wrong, he was punished, as he described in these words: "I remember once as a child being shut up in a room for some misconduct, and sitting there in a condition of helpless obstinacy trying to foster my sense of injury in spite of the reproaches of conscience. There was in the room a photograph of my father, and when this caught my eyes I seemed to see him looking at me with a stern, reproachful look that penetrated into my heart, and sweeping aside all excuses I had been constructing for myself, made me realize my fault at once."

As Jesus is an actual Person, boys and girls must understand that they have the look of His face to deter them from evil, and as a guide to conduct; and that it is most essential always to have His smile of approval. This is a poem which sums up for us the joy of having the kind, loving face of Jesus watching us all the time. The poem is called "The Face of the Lord"

In my childhood's days which have long since fled,
A picture of Christ was above my bed;
And through all these years I see it now,
The face of our Lord with the thorns on His brow.

Whenever I knelt at my bed to pray,
I felt that He heard what I had to say,
As I rose from my knees and glanced again
The face wore a smile or was shadowed with pain.

And every night as the day had been,
So the smile or the pain on that face was seen;
And, O, how I tried every day to do right,
For I dreaded the pain on that face at night.

Many now are the years that have fled,
But I still see the face at the head of my bed,
And many a check does it bring through the day,
Lest I see that pained face when I kneel to pray.

A number of boys were coasting with their sleds. One of them ran against a man who, in anger, asked, "What are you boys good for?" One little fellow looked up and answered, "We are good to make men of, sir." God who loves all the little children of the world, even the bad ones, wants them all to grow up to love Him, and to be noble and true.

God wants the happy-hearted boys,
The stirring boys, the best of boys,
The worst of boys!
He wants them soldiers of his cross,
Brave to defend his righteous cause,
And so uphold his sacred laws;
That good and true
The world may be,
Redeemed from sin
And misery.
God wants the boys!

God wants the happy-hearted girls,
The loving girls, the best of girls,
The worst of girls!
He wants to make the girls his pearls,
And to reflect his holy face,
And bring to mind his wondrous grace;
That beautiful
The world may be,
And filled with love
And purity.
God wants the girls!

Over thirty years ago, when J. R. Edwards was pastor of a London Baptist Church, he wrote several books for young people one of which he called *Everybody Happy*, and which he dedicated to a baby coming into his home –

Dear Margaret Ann,

A year ago we welcomed you into our family circle. Your words have been few, but your smiles have been many and you have made everybody happy. On your first birthday I am dedicating this little book to you – without permission. When you find out what I have done, I hope you won't mind. For you, may there be many happy returns of the day: and, for us, may there be lots of pretty sayings – and more smiles.

With love,
J. R. E.

Then following this lovely dedication is a poem by M. B. C. –

God of the heart and hand,
Teach me to understand!
I know so little of the thought that lies
Back of the shining of those childish eyes;
I guess so little of the wonder there,
Under the curling of the sunny hair.
It is so very, very long ago
Since I too knew the things that children know,
Yet hast Thou given them to me to lead:
Out of Thy wisdom grant me all I need –
Patience of purpose, faith, and tenderness,
Trusting Thy perfect love to lead and bless.
Help me to remember. Ah! for this I pray –
Make me a child of yesterday.
God of the heart and hand,
Teach me to understand!

The road of life is strewn with worthless things, yet there are treasures, too – treasures that are ours for the taking, if we but use our eyes, our hands, and our hearts aright.

Two men looked out of prison bars,
One saw mud, the other saw stars.

Young, though you are, have you eyes for the good things around you?

Two boys who went tramping one fine summer's day
Were asked as to things seen and heard on the way:
Said one of them sadly: "I'll never forget
Those pestering flies, and the dust that we met."
Cried his friend: "I'll remember, through all my life long,
That lovely white lily, that lark's perfect song."

A baby in its helplessness is a striking illustration of human need and weakness, whose life is preserved by having everything done for it – washed, clothed, fed, and nursed.

A babe is,
A sweet, new blossom of humanity,
Fresh fallen from God's own home to flower on earth.

But as a very frail flower, the babe requires so much care and attention, and fittingly symbolizes our need of the care of Providence.

The baby wept,
The mother took it from the nurse's arms,
And soothed its grief, and stilled its vain alarms,
And baby slept.
Again it weeps,
And God doth take it from its mother's arms
From present pain, and future unknown harms,
And baby sleeps.

If it is true that there is no instructor in courtesy like love, then our loving Lord will always remain "the first true Gentleman that ever breathed." He was always too big and good for petty words and meanness, and we owe it to His court to be courtly in manner and speech and behavior. "Be courteous," says Peter. All boys and girls should cultivate courtly ways, which means saying and doing the right thing at the right time and in the right way.

Christian courtesy is like the fragrance of a flower, or often like the sun shining through on a cloudy, dark day. It helps to create gladness all around, and enables us to live out the maxim – "To thine own self be true."

As the year goes by, dear, as the year goes by,
Let us keep our sky clear, little you and I,
Sweep up every cloudy scowl, every little thunder growl,
And live and laugh, laugh and live,
'Neath a cloudless sky.

Have you ever noticed that the little word *on* when read backwards says *no*? And no boy – or girl – can ever get *on* in life unless they are determined to say *no* to many temptations luring them from the true paths of life.

There are many verses urging boys and girls to be better than they have ever been; never to neglect again what they neglected yesterday. Do you know that in some parts of Italy it was a custom for a peasant girl when she was married to make a fine muslin bag, in which year after year rose petals were placed, and when she came to die the bag of gathered rose petals became a beautiful, fragrant pillow that her head laid on in her coffin? May you have a bag into which good and noble deeds can be stored daily to bring you reward when at last you lay your head on the Saviour's breast.

This school year I mean to be better!
To bind myself down with a fetter,
I'll write out a plan
As strong as I can,
Because I am such a forgetter.
Resolved – but I'm sleepy this minute;
There's so much when once you begin it!
Resolved: with my might
I'll try to do right!
That's enough! for the whole thing is in it.

Some of these days when you are able to read the stories of saintly men and women, you will come across *The Letters of Samuel Rutherford.* He was a remarkable minister who, because of his faith, was made to languish in a Scottish prison. He sent out his *Letters* from his prison cell to various friends, and always addressed them – "From Christ's Palace in Aberdeen." In one of these remarkable letters Rutherford said, "Do you know I thought of Jesus till every stone in the wall of my cell glowed like a ruby." Perhaps you have noticed how the sunlight makes even the worst and most horrible objects beautiful. It is so with the light of Him who is the Sun of Righteousness, as He makes the most ordinary, lovely and bright.

Once I knew a little girl,
Very plain;
You might try her hair to curl,
All in vain;
On her cheeks no tints of rose
Paled and blushed, or sought repose:
She was plain.

But the thoughts that through her brain
Came and went,
As a recompense for pain,
Angels sent:
So full of many a beauteous thing,
In her young soul blossoming
Gave content.

Every thought was full of grace,
Pure and true,
And in time the homely face,
Lovelier grew;
With a heavenly radiance bright,
From the soul's reflected light
Shining through.

So I tell you, little child,
Plain or poor,
If your thoughts are undefiled
You are sure
Of the loveliness of worth;
And this beauty, not of earth,
Will endure.

Children who are always ready to learn, always ready to do a kindness, and to obey their parents, earn the reward of heaven. A little boy said to his mother one day, "Wouldn't it be wonderful, mommy, if we could work miracles!" Kindness can produce some of the finest miracles. By being kind and true and by listening to nothing but what is kind and true and charitable from, and about, others, can work wonders.

It is pleasant to dream of glory,
Or earning a hero's fame;
Of writing an epic or story,
Or gaining a world-known name.

Better, far better than dreaming
Is an act of kindness done;
More noble the doing than seeming,
Though glory remains unwon.

How oft there are hearts slowly breaking
For the love we waste in dreams!
How oft for the sympathy aching
That we spend in airy schemes!

A smile, or a word kindly spoken,
Is better a thousandfold
Than the grandest dreams that, when broken,
Remain but as tales untold!

We ought always to be kind and gracious, looking for the best in people and things. If we are always looking for the ugly and nasty things in life, the unhappy result is that we become like these very things. Being the best yourself is a good way to find the best in others.

If I make a face at Billy,
He will make a face at me;
That makes two ugly faces,
And a quarrel, don't you see?
And then I double up my fist
And hit him, and he'll pay
Me back by giving me a kick,
Unless I run away.

But if I smile at Billy,
'Tis sure to make him laugh;
You'd say, if you could see him,
'Twas jollier by half
Than kicks and ugly faces.
I tell you all the while,
It's pleasanter for any boy
(Or girl) to laugh and smile.

One of the first phrases parents teach their children to repeat is, "Say, Thank you!" The Bible tells us that in everything we should give thanks. Genuine gratitude is one of the sweetest yet rarest of the Christian graces. We are apt to take too many things for granted. What a benediction of peace is ours if, in our hearts, there is a constant doxology of praise to Him from whom all blessings flow.

Three little words, nine letters wide;
And yet how much these words betide,
How much of thought or tenderness
This short "I thank you!" may express.

* * * * *

When spoken with a proud disdain,
'Twill chill the heart like frozen rain;
Or when indifference marks its tone,
Turns love's sweet impulse into stone.

Be not afraid, my little one,
As time goes on beneath the sun,
While marching in life's motley ranks,
For all our blessings to "give thanks."

To thank your God for life so fair,
For tender mercies great and rare,
For health and strength, for home and friends,
And loving care that never ends.

Then thank the ones, whoe'er they be,
That do a kindness unto thee.
'Twill cost you little, pain you less,
This sweet "I thank you!" to express.

No matter what task is ours, we should endeavor to put our best into it and never skimp our work. We read that Jesus was a carpenter, and because of all He was in Himself we know that whatever He made was of the highest quality; and as His friends our work must never be slipshod.

If Jesus built a ship,
She would travel trim;

If Jesus roofed a barn,
No leaks would be left by Him.
If Jesus planted a garden,
He would make it like a Paradise;
If Jesus did my day's work,
It would delight His Father's eyes.

David McPhail lived in a beautiful part of Scotland yet could not see the trees and flowers and birds, for Davie, as he was called, was blind. One day two great preachers, Dr. Thomas Guthrie and Dr. John Ker came for a holiday in the lovely country where David lived. Strolling along they saw in the distance a boy's kite, and behind the brow of the hill they came across Davie, crouching in the fern, holding the string.

"Why, Davie, lad," said Dr. Ker, "what's the good of *your* having a kite? You can't see it!"

But Davie, whose face radiated happiness, answered, "No, sir, but I like to pull."

The three spent some time together talking, and as the good ministers were about to leave they said to Davie, "Some people will say it's no good praying to God: you can't see Him." Davie replied, "No, I can't see Him, but when I pray I know that He is real" Although Davie could not see his kite, neither could he, or anyone else, see the wind bearing the kite up and up. We cannot see God, but we know that He is a living, bright reality.

We do not see the wind,
We only hear it sigh:
It makes the grasses bend
Whenever it goes by.

We do not see God's love,
But in our hearts we know
He watches over us
Wherever we may go.

We do not have to see
To know the wind is here;
We do not have to see
To know God's love is near.

Now let me tell you of a little blind girl and of what she saw in her mother's face and in her father's face, and how she saw God. Children who are blind learn to see with their fingers, their ears, and their sense of smell. Well, whoever *saw* love? Yet there is what the blind girl saw who had no eyes with which to see –

I know what mother's face is like,
  Although I cannot see;
It's like the music of a bell,
It's like the roses I can smell,
It's like the stories fairies tell –
  All those it's like to me.

I know what father's face is like,
  I'm sure I know it all.
It's like his step upon the stair,
It's like his whistle on the air;
It's like his arms which take such care,
  And never let me fall.

And I can tell what God is like –
  The God whom no one sees.
He's everything my mother means;
He's everything my father seems;
He's fairer than my fondest dreams,
  And greater than all these.

One of the most precious things written about Jesus is that "he went about doing good." This was the secret of His wonderful life. Jesus had to do good, because He was good. How apt are the lines John Wesley gave us!

Do all the good you can,
By all the means you can,
In all the ways you can,
In all the places you can,
At all the times you can,
To all the people you can,
As long as ever you can.

There is a saying almost as common as daisies in a field. Boys and girls often feel that *it doesn't matter much* what they do or say, because after all, they are only boys and girls, and because it doesn't make very much difference, and – because of a lot of other things. What do you think Jesus would have said if someone had asked Him, "Can a little boy or a little girl make much difference in the world?" Why, He would have replied that it is the little things in life that count. Michelangelo is credited with saying when asked why he spent so much time over minor details in his great sculpture-work, "Trifles go to make perfection — and perfection is no trifle." Does not the well-known verse emphasize the importance of little things? —

For want of a nail, the shoe was lost,
For want of a shoe, the horse was lost,
For want of a horse, the message was lost,
For want of a message, the battle was lost,
For want of a battle, the kingdom was lost!
And all for want of a horse shoe nail!

How full the world is of things that come and go! — out and in — ebb and flow. The moon waxes and wanes. The birds and the flowers come and go, as do our feelings. One day we are jubilant — the next day despondent. Do you remember the rhyme? —

There was a man of our town,
And he was wondrous wise;
He jumped into a bramble bush
And scratched out both his eyes.
And when he knew his eyes were out
He jumped with might and main,
He jumped into the bramble bush
And scratched them in again.

Praise God, there is at least one thing that doesn't come and go; and isn't in and out. Paul says, "Love never fails." Whatever else may ebb and flow, God's love is always the same for children, whatever their race; and for all men.

In the foregoing chapters of this book we have had much to say about the marvel and mystery of the little baby coming into a home. What a world of surprise the infant child brings the parents into! Where did he come from? Where is he going? A wise man tried to answer these hard questions and here is part of his answer —

Where did you come from, baby dear?
Out of everywhere into the here.

Where did you get those eyes so blue?
Out of the sky as I came through.

Where did you get this pearly ear?
God spoke, and it came out to hear.

How did they all just come to be you?
God thought about me, and so I grew.

But how did you come to us, you dear?
God thought about you, and so I came here.

How important it is to teach the children, young in life though they be, that God put them in this world for some great purpose; and that He cares for them more than He does for the beautiful flowers. God is, indeed, the great Gardener who makes all that is lovely, not only in a garden but *in a life*. How expressive is the poem —

He leaned, at sunset, on his spade.
(Oh, but the child was sweet to see,
The one who in the orchard played!)
He called, "I've planted you a tree!"

The boy looked at it for a while,
Then at the radiant woods below;
And said, with wonder in his smile —
"Why don't you put the leaves on though?"

The gardener, with a reverent air,
Lifted his eyes, took off his hat —
"The Other Man, the One up there,"
He answered, "He must see to that."

We have already written about those dear children who are born lame or who, like the boy Mephibosheth, became lame. An appealing verse reads, "Love envieth not," and while no one envied Jonathan's son because of his lameness, they might have envied his friendship with King David whose kindness greatly cheered the lame prince. It has been said that if we knew all that is in the heart of every man, we would envy no one. Here are some verses you might like to learn and recite –

Most every day a little boy comes driving past our house
With the nicest little pony – just the color of a mouse –
And a groom rides close behind him, so he won't get hurt, you see,
And I used to wish the pony and the cart belonged to me.

I used to watch him from our porch and wish that I could own
His pony and his little cart, and drive out all alone,
And once when I knelt down at night I prayed the Lord that He
Would fix it so the pony and the cart belonged to me.

But yesterday I saw him where he lives, and now I know
Why he never goes out walkin' – 'cause his legs are withered so! –
And last night when I was kneelin' with my head on mother's knee,
I was glad he had the pony and the cart instead of me.

Although we have already drawn attention to the appreciation boys and girls have for the stories of the Bible, not all of them understand that there are sixty-six books forming the one grand Book – the Bible. One who had a deep love for the whole Bible wrote these lines about it –

Sixty-six singers, singing sweet and true,
And setting all the world to singing too.

Sixty-six soldiers, vigorous and strong,
Valiantly attacking cruelty and wrong.

Sixty-six judges, learned in the law,
Uttering decisions, free from fear or flaw.

Sixty-six artists – wondrously they paint
Kings and sages, common folk, angel, devil, saint.

Sixty-six explorers, keen to search and find
All the hidden secrets of life and death and mind.

Sixty-six masons, marvelously skilled;
One majestic temple they unite to build.

Sixty-six farmers, planting holy seed,
Happily upspringing in holy thought and deed.

Sixty-six teachers, keeping perfect school,
Where faith the law is, and love the rule.

Sixty-six doctors, knowing well to cure,
Masters of a medicine healing swift and sure.

Sixty-six sailors, bearing us away
To a better country, to a brighter day.

One has read of a boy who did not appear to be very bright, and had he come to nothing no one would have blamed him. But this apparently dull lad was determined to get ahead, and one day in a most unusual way the tide turned in his favor. At school he had to write out the English translation of some Latin sentences. One of them was – *Possunt quia posse videntur*, meaning, "They can, because they think they can." The boy looked upon this axiom as his turning point, and, thereafter, things felt easier because he had more confidence in himself. Great saints like Moses and Elijah were somewhat chicken-hearted in themselves, but conscious that God was with them, they were as bold as lions. Sir Edward Pellew, in commemoration of deliverance from shipwreck chose as the motto of his family – *Deo Adjuvante* – "With the help of God." Robert Louis Stevenson reminds us that –

Happy hearts and happy faces,
Happy play in grassy places;
That was how, in ancient ages,
Children grew to kings and sages.

Some of those happy children had to face many trials and difficulties but they became "kings and sages" because they had confidence both in God and in themselves.

If you think you're beaten, you are,
  If you think you dare not, you don't,
If you'd like to win, but think you can't,
  It's almost a clinch that you won't.
If you think you'll lose, you're lost.
  For out in the World you find
That success begins with a fellow's will;
  It's all in the state of mind.

The true secret of confidence, however, is the assurance that if God is for us then nothing can be against us. This is the state of mind so necessary if we are to triumph.

Life's battles don't always go
  To the stronger or faster man,
But soon or late, the man who wins
  Is the fellow who thinks he can.

What wonderful surprises we are to have in heaven! Think of those Jesus may introduce to us! While walking on the golden street He may say, as He pauses, "Do you know who this is? This is the small boy who gave Me his two little loaves and a few little fishes one day on earth. He saw a big crowd of hungry people who had been listening to Me preaching, and shyly and awkwardly he said, 'Here, Jesus, You can have my lunch to feed them.' Is not the Saviour's heart always gladdened by the gifts of those who love Him?

What can I give Him,
  Poor as I am?
If I were a shepherd,
  I would bring a lamb;
If I were a wise man,
  I would do my part;
Yet what I can, I give Him —
  I give Him my heart.

Many years ago, the famous Methodist preacher, Mark Guy Pearse, was standing in a London railway station and noticed a young man who was evidently in trouble. Asking the boy if anything was wrong, the preacher learned that he did not have enough money to take him home for the holidays and had no friends near to help. Mr. Pearse gave him some money, and while waiting for the train told him how, years ago, a similar thing happened to him. A kind gentleman was at hand to help and as he said goodby remarked, "Some day you may have the chance to help someone else in the same way. Mind you pass on what I have done for you today."

"Now," said Mr. Pearse to the boy, "that's what I am doing for you, and be sure you pass it on to someone else."

"All right," replied the boy, as the train pulled out and he waved his hand. "I'll pass it on! I'll pass it on!" How we would like to know how he did!

Have you had a kindness shown?
  Pass it on;
'Twas not given for thee alone,
  Pass it on;
Let it travel down the years,
Let it wipe another's tears,
Till in Heaven the deed appears,
  Pass it on!

All boys and girls studying history at school know all about "The Crusaders" who, in the early centuries of Christianity, sought to rescue Jerusalem out of the hands of the Turks who persecuted the Christian pilgrims who loved to visit the Holy City where Jesus died. There were some seven crusades, one of which was known as "The Children's Crusade," the unbelievable story of which is told by Longfellow in poetic form. In the year 1212 an army of boys and girls from France and Germany conceived the idea of banding themselves together as an army, hoping to do what the soldiers had failed to accomplish. Forth they went a brave, joyous, hopeful band, with banners flying, but the way was wild and rough and many children perished. Of those who reached Palestine, nothing more was heard. That Children's Crusade was the first "Band of Hope." Longfellow puts it –

Who shall answer or divine?
Never since the world was made
Such a wonderful Crusade
Started forth for Palestine.
Never while the world shall last
Will it reproduce the past;
Never will it see again
Such an army, such a band,
Over mountain, over main,
Journeying to the Holy Land.

O the simple, child-like trust!
O the faith that could believe!
What the harnessed, iron-mailed
Knights of Christendom had failed,
By their prowess, to achieve,
They, the children could and must.

Many years ago there lived a noble man who became Sir John Kirk because of the way he had spent his long life caring for the poor and crippled children of London. Because of his constant efforts to better the lives of unfortunate boys and girls, he became known as "The Children's Friend." A still greater Friend of little children is the One who became "the holy Child Jesus," and must have been the One whom Robert Louis Stevenson had in mind when he wrote his fine poem, three verses of which we here cite –

When the children are playing alone
on the green,
In comes the playmate that never was
seen.
When children are happy and lonely
and good,
The Friend of the children comes out
of the wood.

Nobody heard him and nobody saw,
He is a picture you never could draw,
But he's sure to be present, abroad
or at home,
When the children are happy and
playing alone.

He lies in the laurels, he runs on the
grass,
He sings when you tinkle the musical
glass;
Whene'er you are happy and cannot
tell why,
The Friend of the children is sure to
be by.

In Scotland they have a saying – "Every mickle makes a muckle," which is another way of saying that little things can become big things. The Bible says that we must not despise the day of small things. One match is able to set a forest ablaze; one good true word we speak may echo around the world and down through the centuries. Don't forget that the wisest of men had to begin in the infant school. Even Shakespeare had to learn the ABC's.

Only a thought in passing – a smile
or encouraging word,
Has lifted many a burden no other
gift could have stirred.
Only! But then the onlys
Make up the mighty all.
It was only a glad "Good morning,"
As she passed along the way,
But it spread the morning's glory
Over the livelong day.

What boy has not heard the proverb, "If at first you don't succeed, try, try again"? Someone had tried and failed, and tried again, and so the words of the poem to follow. A great violinist was asked how long it would take to learn to play the violin, and replied, "Twelve hours a day for twenty years." His idea was different from that of a mother whose boy had just come into possession of a violin, and was eager to learn how to play it. "Oh, stop that noise," she said, "and put that fiddle away until you are able to do something with it." She forgot that only by perseverance would her son be able to bring rich music out of the instrument.

Now if at first you *do* succeed,
 Try again.
Life is more than just one deed,
 Try again.
Never stop with what you've done,
More remains than you have won,
Full content's vouchsafed to none —
 Try again.

If you've won a bit of fame,
 Try again.
Seek a still more honored name,
 Try again.
Sit not down with folded hands,
Cramp not hope with narrow bands,
Think what prowess life demands —
 Try again.

If at first you *do* succeed,
 Try again.
For future harvest sow the seed,
 Try again.
Rise with sacred discontent,
Realize that life is lent
On highest searches to be spent —
 Try again.

In Peter's exposure of the sin of Ananias and Sapphira is a most solemn word — *lied* (Acts 5:4). Lies are among the blackest things in God's world, and must be hated and dreaded. The dictionary gives the explanation that "a lie is a false statement, uttered to deceive." One Sunday, the lesson was on Ananias and Sapphira, and the teacher explaining their sin asked one of the boys in her class, what a lie was. Somewhat mixed up he answered that "a lie was an abomination in the sight of the Lord, and a very present help in time of trouble." The dark career of the history of a lie is told for us in the following verses —

First somebody told it,
Then the room would not hold it,
So the busy tongues rolled it,
Till they got it outside.
When the crowd came across it,
They never once lost it,
But tossed it and tossed it,
Till it grew long and wide.

This lie brought forth others,
Dark sisters and brothers,
And fathers and mothers
A terrible crew;
And as headlong they hurried,
The people they flurried,
And bothered and worried,
As lies always do.

And so evil-boded,
This monstrous lie goaded,
Till at last it exploded
In smoke and in flame,
While from mud and from mire,
The pieces flew higher,
Till they hit the sad liar,
And killed his good name.

Doubtless you have read that verse in the Bible telling us the God we love and serve is a "God of order, and not of confusion" (I Cor. 14:33, 40). An old adage is that, "Order is heaven's first law." Not all boys and girls appear to believe that there is a place for everything and that everything should be in its place. How often does mother have to say — "I am always picking up after you"? Orderliness in our habits helps to make life easier, not only for ourselves, but also for others.

He hunted through the library,
 He looked behind the door,
He searched where baby keeps his toys
 Upon the nursery floor.

He asked the cook and Mary,
He called mamma to look,
He even started sister up
To leave her Christmas book.

He couldn't find it anywhere,
And knew some horrid tramp
Had walked in through the open gate
And stolen it — the scamp!
Perhaps the dog had taken it
And hidden it away,
Or else, perhaps, he'd chewed it up
And swallowed it in play.

And then mamma came down the stairs,
Looked through the closet door,
And there it hung upon its peg,
As it had hung before.
And Tommy's cheeks turned rosy red,
Astonished was his face.
He couldn't find his cap — because
'Twas in its proper place!

What boy does not like the story Charles Dickens gave us of *David Copperfield*. Picture the parting scene between Steerforth and the hero of the story, with young Steerforth placing both his hands upon Copperfield's shoulders, saying: "Let us make this bargain! If circumstances should separate us, and you should see me no more, remember me at my best." In the most unworthy person we should look for what is good and commendable; honor that, rejoice in it, and try to imitate it.

Don't look for the flaws as you go through life;
And even when you find them
It is wise and kind to be somewhat blind,
And look for the virtue behind them.
For the cloudiest night has a hint of light
Somewhere in its shadow hiding:
It is better by far to look for a star
Than the spots on the sun abiding.

One could go on ad infinitum citing verses composed for the pleasure and profit of boys and girls. If only we could gather them all together what a poetic treasury they would form. We trust the selection we have made out of a large quantity will prove to be of service to those who have the responsibility of the spiritual and moral welfare of children around them.

Children's Hymns

Children love to sing. Soon after they discover they have voices they are not long in mimicking the singing they hear at home. Their little ears quickly catch the words, and their memories retain them, as well as the music accompanying them. How pleasurable it is to hear and see a crowd of children singing away to their heart's content! Further, the hymns they learn to sing at home or at Sunday school remain with them through the years. This fact is borne out in the recently-published biography of Marilyn Monroe bearing the title of her original name, *Norma Jean*. The friends this Hollywood celebrity was brought up with, the Bolenders, sent her to Sunday school where the first song she learned there was, "Jesus loves me this I know," and it remained her favorite. Once in a crowded cafeteria Marilyn Monroe sang the hymn impromptu.

The Bible reminds us that out of the mouths of babes God is able to perfect praise. Isaac Watts reminds us that —

People and realms of ev'ry tongue
Dwell on His love with sweetest song,
And *infant voices shall proclaim*
Their early blessings on His name.

The psalmist would have "young men, and maidens; old men, and children" to "praise the name of the Lord" (Ps. 148:12). Perhaps more praise ascends to Him from children than from old men. What a vast collection of children's hymns and choruses boys and girls of today can choose from! A few, however, stand out as favorites, and children never tire of singing them, such as –

"Jesus Wants Me for a Sunbeam"
"Tell Me the Old, Old Story"
"Jesus Bids Us Shine"
"We Are But Little Children Weak"
"When He Cometh"
"Gentle Jesus, Meek and Mild"
"Jesus Loves Me"
"There's a Friend for Little Children"

Not so long ago a letter in the daily press ridiculed the sentiments expressed in a hymn –

There's a Friend for little children,
Above the bright blue sky.

But the writer got a comeback from another reader who suggested that the critic might prefer today's version –

There's a spaceship for little astronauts
Above the dark blue stratosphere.

Early in life children should be taught A. F. Bayly's expressive hymn about the value and blessedness of a Christian home, two verses of which read –

Teach us to keep our homes so fair,
That were our Lord a child once more,
He might be glad our hearth to share,
And find a welcome at our door.

Lord, may Thy Spirit sanctify
Each household duty we fulfil,
May we our Master glorify
In glad obedience to Thy will.

Then there is the appealing hymn of Marianne Hearn which, although written for those beginning life, I always love to sing. What a message these three verses contain!

Just as I am, Thine own to be,
Friend of the young, who lovest me –
To consecrate myself to Thee,
O Jesus Christ, I come.

In the glad morning of my day
My life to give, my vows to pay,
With no reserve and no delay –
With all my heart, I come.

Just as I am young, strong and free,
To be the best that I can be
For truth and righteousness and Thee,
Lord of my life, I come.

When children come to leave home and go to school or college, they often set out with heavy hearts, and settling down in a strange place among strange faces have constant longings for home. A godly mother taught her daughter in girlhood years a brief but beautiful prayer as she faced her home-leaving experience – "O God, prepare me for all Thou art preparing for me." Recalling his own school days when the moral tone of the school was low, and he often suffered from homesickness, H. W. Shrewsbury, a notable Methodist preacher and writer of a past decade, wrote the following "Hymn for Youth" to cheer the hearts of those leaving home for school –

Beneath Thine eye, O watchful Love, we rest,
Life's morning wanes with sunny memories blessed;
Into Thine ear, O listening Love, we pour
Each anxious thought for years that lie before.

The peaceful ignorance of childhood flies,
Life's sin-stained pages pass beneath our eyes;
Give, for the innocence that knew no wrong,
The steadfast mind in cherished pureness strong.

The merry days of youth are hurrying by,

Toil, care, and conflict coming years supply;
O, for the gladsomeness of fleeting Spring,
Grant us the Autumn's rich ingathering.

Beneath Thine eye, O watchful Love, we rest,
We only lose to be more largely blessed;
Into Thine ear, O listening Love, we pour
Our anxious thoughts, and learn to doubt no more.

Feeling that parents and teachers would like to know something of the background of the hymn writers who gave to the church the well-known children's hymns sung almost around the world every Sunday, we will tabulate a few of the best known among them.

It may not be generally known that it was late in the history of the church before any provision was made for children in the worship of the Sanctuary. For example, in respect to children's hymns only one or two can be found in the seventeenth century, and even these do not seem to have been intended for public worship.

"To all intents and purposes," says Mr. Garrett-Horder, "no special provision was made for children until Dr. Watts published his 'Divine and Moral Songs,' so that he is the first founder of the choir of the children as that of their elders . . . We must give him his due as opening and first cultivating the field of children's hymnody. Moreover, as he never married, the instinct and knowledge of fatherhood were hidden from him, and his hymns for children, as a consequence, suffer."

The finest contribution from his pen is his cradle hymn, which somehow has dropped out of sight. We quote the first of the eight verses —

Hush, dear child, lie still and slumber,
Holy angels guard thy bed,
Heavenly blessings without number
Gently falling on thy head.

For a considerable time Dr. Watts' hymns for children practically held undisputed possession of the field, his two volumes of "Hymns for Children" being widely used. It was not until women, however, with their deeper insight into, and tenderer sympathy with child life, entered into the field, that anything like adequate or suitable provision was made for children's song. With the entrance of women into this sphere a new era dawned. Hence a large proportion of the writers mentioned in this section of our study belong to that sex. As this new era dawned in 1810, when Ann and Jane Taylor issued their "Hymns for Infant Minds," let us glance at their work first.

Ann and Jane Taylor

Nothing can be written about Jane Taylor without introducing her elder sister, Ann, who was her co-partner in various literary enterprises. These two sisters worked together until Ann's marriage to the Rev. Joseph Gilbert, in 1813. The father of these two gifted women was Isaac Taylor, the painter and engraver who illustrated Boydell's edition of the Bible. In 1786 he became the pastor of the Independent Church at Lavenham. After that he went to Colchester where for fourteen years he labored with great acceptance. In 1810 he settled at Ongar.

Ann Taylor was born at London 30 January 1782. She died at Nottingham in 1866. Although Ann is associated with her sister Jane because several of their hymns were published under their joint names, several favorites are known as her own composition, such as "Great God, and Wilt

Thou Condescend"; "God Is in Heaven, Can He Hear"; "Jesus Who Lived Above the Sky"; "A Captain Forth to Battle Went."

Jane Taylor saw the light of day at Red Lion Street, Holborn, on 23 September, 1783. She died in that Essex village, Ongar, in 1824, at the age of forty. Her gift in writing verse displayed itself at an early age. Entering the full light of Christ's saving power in more mature years, she strove to express in sacred song the truth she embraced.

Jane Taylor is one of the few authors who wrote consistently for children and for children only: and she wrote with unique understanding of the child-mind. What child does not know "Twinkle, Twinkle, Little Star," which is only one of the scores of memorable poems and hymns written by her, in what was probably the golden age of children's books, a century ago.

This poetess had a deep and tender love for children – to whose Christian training she devoted many of her later days in the village Sunday schools – and her endeavor, in the hymns, was to present the truths of the Gospel in words that the tiniest lisping child might find easy. Without diluting the Gospel, she translated Christian doctrine into poetic phraseology the children still love to sing.

Among her many hymns, all of which are marked by great simplicity and directness, the most popular and one of the best is "There Is a Path That Leads to God." Other child lyrics worthy of mention are "When Daily I Kneel Down to Pray"; "Love and Kindness We Must Measure"; "Good David, Whose Psalms Have So Often Been Sung."

That the Taylors had a happy knack of conveying Scripture history and teaching in simple verse, is evidenced by the following best definition of repentance it is possible to find:

> Repentance is to leave
> The sins I loved before,
> And show that I in earnest grieve
> By doing so no more.

Charles Wesley

Though Charles Wesley was fond of children and wrote many hymns for their benefit, he was not altogether successful as a writer for the young. He started with the wrong idea in attempting to lift children up to the level of adults by merely adapting his compositions to them by simplicity of diction.

Still it was he that wrote those lines, constituting the first prayer we learned in childhood at a mother's knee:

> Gentle Jesus, meek and mild,
> Look upon a little child;
> Pity my simplicity;
> Suffer me to come to Thee.

This was one of Wesley's earliest hymns, being written about the year 1740. It was written expressly for children, and in later years, when Charles had children of his own, they loved to sing it even as the children of today do.

F. A. Jones tells the story of an old man over eighty years of age, who, when he lay dying, endeavored in vain to recall a single prayer or hymn which might help to comfort him in his journey into the unknown. Since the age of twenty he had lived a godless life, forgetting the truths he learned in earlier days. Suddenly his vision cleared, and he saw himself a little lad again, kneeling at his mother's knee, repeating his evening hymn; and unconsciously from his lips issued these tender words which for nearly seventy years he had neither uttered nor heard – *"Gentle Jesus, Meek and*

Mild." It is the same with many of us. The language of Wesley's beautiful hymn comes back to us after many years.

Thomas Rawson Taylor

This author of "I'm But a Stranger Here," knew exactly what was required in a children's hymn, but unfortunately he died too early to leave more than one or two. One, the first verse of which we quote, has never been excelled.

> There was a time when children sang
> The Saviour's praise with sacred glee,
> And all the hills of Judah rang
> With their exulting Jubilee.

T. R. Taylor was born at Ossett, near Wakefield 9 May 1807. After a short but brilliant career he died in 1835, being only twenty-eight years of age.

Elizabeth Parson

Previous to her marriage to Mr. T. E. Parson, Mrs. E. Parson conducted a class for young people in the vestry of her father's church on Sunday evenings, to which was given the name "Willing Class," because those who came, came "willingly." For this class she composed several hymns known as the "Willing Class Hymns," many of which have found a place in children's hymnbooks. Two of these hymns are exceedingly popular, being full of movement and melody – "Jesus We Love to Meet," and "O Happy Land! O Happy Land!"

Dr. Julian says that for tenderness, "Saviour, Round Thy Footstool Bending" is the most moving, "Angels Round the Throne Are Praising" the most conspicuous for praise, and, "What Shall We Render? the most joyous.

The daughter of the Rev. W. Rooker, fifty years a minister at Tavistock, Elizabeth was born there in 1812. She was married to Mr. Parson in 1844 and died at Plymouth in 1873.

Mrs. M. E. Shelly

Another sweet hymn, set in a very tender key, which the majority of us will never forget, is that of Mary Evans Jackson, to give her her maiden name:

> Lord, a little band and lowly,
> We are come to sing to Thee;
> Thou art great and high and holy:
> O how solemn we should be!

The daughter of John Jackson of Manchester, Miss M. E. Jackson was born at Stockport, Cheshire, and married in 1846 Mr. J. W. Shelly, of Great Yarmouth.

Strange to say, this most effective hymn was not a labored composition, but was composed in a moment of inspiration. Here is Mrs. Shelly's account of her hymn: "At a Sunday school meeting in Manchester, the Rev. John Curven, one evening, gave a lecture on singing. He sang a very pretty and simple tune, to which he said he had no suitable words, and wished that someone would write a hymn to it. I wrote these verses and gave them to him after the close of the meeting."

Among other hymns for children composed by Mrs. Shelly, mention can be made of "Father, Let Thy Benediction," and "Lord, Help Us, As We Sing." The Rev. John Curven wrote only two hymns, one of which is very popular, namely, "I'm a Little Pilgrim." This gifted singer for whom "Lord, a Little Band and Lowly" was written did much to stimulate children's hymnody by the publication of "The Child's Own Hymn Book," which was the first collection deserving of such a title.

Mrs. C. F. Alexander

In 1848 Mrs. C. F. Alexander published her "Hymns for Children," which at once created a new school, and became its model. She saw that hymns for children should be not only in plain language, but that they should be picturesque, moving, and not confined to the severe meters which had long been the case. W. Garrett-Horder figures that before her there is no writer, save Thomas Rawson Taylor, who fully realized this.

It is by Mrs. Alexander's hymns for children that she will always be best remembered and loved. She wrote many of them for her own children – she had four – two sons and two daughters. They were her critics and she wrote what they liked best. What hymns could be more suitable or lovely for children, than her Christmas one: "Once in Royal David's City"; or the one that speaks so touchingly of the Holy Innocents: "We Are But Little Children Weak"; or that joyous and happy one: "All Things Bright and Beautiful"; or that sweet picture hymn: "Every Morning the Red Sun Rises Warm and Bright"; or the moving Good Friday one, as we may call it: "There Is a Green Hill Far Away," which is considered to be the choicest and best of her hymns? There is a beautiful hymn, not generally known as it is not included in her published works. It was written for a Liverpool clergyman, and is especially picturesque. Here is its first verse:

> Once in the town of Bethlehem,
> Far away across the sea,
> There was laid a little Baby,
> On a Virgin Mother's knee.

Mrs. Alexander had every right to be considered the children's hymnist par excellence. Her hymns, some four hundred in number, are known wherever the Gospel is preached. And they have found their way into innumerable translations. A missionary in Central Africa tells how he heard Mrs. Alexander's hymns sung by half-clad Africans in a language she had never known.

Briefly stated, the outstanding facts of her life are as follows: she was born in Ireland in 1823, her father being Major Humphreys of the Royal Marines, who fought at the battle of Copenhagen. At nine, she began to write verses, but belonging to a household where the children were not allowed to assert themselves, Cecil Frances used to hide her poems under a carpet. One day news of them reached her father's ears. He was pleased with her efforts, and instituted a box for their reception, the contents of which he read aloud on Saturday evenings. Her mother and her friends, amongst whom she counted Dean Hook, the famous Vicar of Leeds, and Mr. Keble author of *The Christian Year*, all encouraged her to write.

In 1850 she married the Rev. William Alexander, afterward Bishop of Derry, and later Archbishop of Armagh. After many years of earnest work she went to her rest in 1895, at the age of 72. She was buried in the city cemetery of Londonderry.

It was Mrs. Alexander who wrote that fine poem *The Burial of Moses*, of which Tennyson said that it was one of the poems of which he would have been proud to be the author.

Mary L. Duncan

Another woman hymnist who has the reputation of being the authoress of one of the best known of children's hymns is Mary Duncan.

She wrote a hymn which in points

of simplicity and beauty has never been surpassed. Its opening verse reads thus:

Jesus, tender Shepherd, hear me;
Bless Thy little lamb tonight;
Through the darkness be Thou near me;
Watch my sleep till morning light.

This tender prayer-hymn was included in her tiny book, *Rhymes for My Children,* being composed, it is generally believed, three years after her marriage in 1839, when she was barely twenty-five years of age. Two or three months after writing the above hymn Mrs. Duncan caught a severe cold which developed into pneumonia, and a few days later her young life was closed.

She was the daughter of Rev. Robert Lundie, Parish Minister of Kelso, being born there in April, 1814. In 1836 she was married to the Rev. W. W. Duncan, of Cleish, Kinrosshire, where at the end of December, 1839, she took a chill resulting in her death on 5 January 1840.

Says Dr. Julian, "her gifts and graces were early consecrated to her Master's service. She was a devoted wife and mother, and a true helpmeet to her husband in his parochial work. Her hymns, most written for her children between July and December, 1839, appeared, in 1841 in her *Memoir,* by her mother, and were issued separately in 1842, as *Rhymes for My Children,* to the number of twenty-three."

Anne H. Shepherd

One of the greatest hymns about heaven which all children love to sing is the most effective lyric written by Mrs. Shepherd:

Around the throne of God, in heaven,
Thousands of children stand;
Children whose sins are all forgiven,
A holy, happy band.
Singing, glory, glory, glory.

It was first of all included in her little book, *Hymns Adapted for the Comprehension of Infant Minds,* in which were sixty-four of her hymns. Of these hymns, "Around the Throne" has by far the widest acceptance, and is to be found in almost every hymnbook for children. It enjoys an extensive use in this and other countries. Dr. Moffat translated it into the Bechuana language for his Kuruman College in 1838.

Anne H. Shepherd was the daughter of the Rev. E. H. Houlditch, Rector of Speen, Berkshire, being born at Cowes, Isle of Wight, 11 September 1809. In 1843 she married Mr. S. Saville Shepherd. She died at Blackheath, Kent, 7 January 1857.

Frances R. Havergal

This most gifted hymnist is well-known for her addition of a few precious gems to the growing collection of children's hymns. Her version of the Lord's Prayer is both tender and concise. It begins thus:

God in heaven, hear our singing.
Only little ones are we,
Yet, a great petition bringing,
Father, now we come to Thee.

Another beautiful song which, although more like an address to a child than a hymn, is of great merit. Its opening verse is:

God will take care of you, All through the day
Jesus is near you, to keep you from ill;
Walking or resting, at work or at play,
Jesus is with you, and watching you still.

There is another hymn from the pen of Miss Havergal which is most popular in the English-speaking world. It is —

Golden harps are sounding,
Angel voices ring,
Pearly gates are opened,
Opened for the King.

Her sister gives the following account of the writing of this hymn: "When visiting at Perry Barr, Frances walked to the boy's schoolroom, and, being very tired, she leaned against the playground wall while Mr. Snepp, a gentleman who was with her, went in. Returning in ten minutes he found her scribbling on an old envelope. At his request she handed him the hymn just pencilled, *Golden harps are sounding.*"

A few days later Miss Havergal composed a special tune for this hymn, and it was this same tune, *Hermas,* that the gifted poetess sang a few moments before she died. Frances Ridley Havergal was the daughter of the Rev. W.H. Havergal, being born at Astley, Worcestershire in December, 1836. She died at Caswall Bay, Swansea, 3 June 1879.

Jane E. Leeson

Little is known of this gifted hymnist except that she was born in 1807, and died in 1882. Miss Leeson however wrote many verses for children many of which were included in her *Infant Hymnings.* Dr. Julian reckons that "Loving Shepherd of Thy Sheep" is her most popular hymn. All of her hymns are remarkable for the suitability of their ideas. For example here is the first verse of her hymn on Christ blessing little children:

Sweet the lessons Jesus taught,
When to Him fond parents brought
Babes for whom they blessing sought —
Little ones, like me.

Other of her verses for children include, "A Little Child May Know"; "Dear Saviour, to Thy Little Lambs"; "Saviour, Teach Me Day by Day."

Andrew Young

We have now lighted upon the author of that bright hymn on heaven, loved by all Sunday school scholars, namely,

There is a happy land
Far, far away.

Instead of the first "far" we should sing "not" for the happy land is not far away. There is only a veil between heaven and ourselves. J.S. Curwen in his *Biographical Notes* accounts for the origin of this famous children's hymn thus — "The story of the origin of this hymn, kindly supplied by Mr. Colin Brown, of Glasgow, is interesting. One of the songs which the Indian palanquin bearers sing as they go, was set to English words about thirty years ago.

"It became very popular, its burden being 'There is a happy land, where care's unknown.' This song was sung one evening by a lady in Edinburgh, and heard by Mr. Young, then teacher of Niddry School. Being much touched by the beauty of the music, and of the opening idea of the words, Mr. Young was led to write the exquisite hymn 'There Is a Happy Land, Far, Far, Away,' to suit the music."

Mr. Young wrote several sweet hymns but none has gained so much popularity as the one above which has been translated into many languages and dialects.

Andrew Young was born in Edinburgh in 1807. At the early age of twenty-three he was appointed Head Master of Niddry St. School, Edinburgh, where, in less than ten years he increased the number of pupils from eighty to six hundred. In 1840 he became Principal English Master at Madras College, St. Andrew's where his success as a teacher was no less remarkable. He retired in 1853, and being a great lover of children devoted the rest of his life to Sunday school work in connection with the Greenside Parish Sabbath Schools. He died on 30 November 1889.

John Burton, Sr.

This author is known as John Burton, Sr., to distinguish him from another of the same name, who is known as John Burton Jr. There was no connection between the two. The latter was born in 1803, at Stoutford, in Essex, where he carried on business as a cooper for about fifty years. He was a most gifted hymn-writer for children, and several pieces have attained a measure of fame such as "O Thou That Hearest Prayer"; "Come Let Us Sing Our Maker's Praise"; "Pilgrims We Are and Strangers."

John Burton, Sr., was born in 1773 at Nottingham. He was a Baptist, and closely identified with Sunday school work. In 1802 he published *Hymns for Sunday Schools,* a hymnal containing ninety-six hymns of his own composition. In 1805 Mr. Burton married, and moved, in 1813, to Leicester, where he died in 1822. He was a friend of the famous Robert Hall, of Cambridge.

Emily E. S. Elliot

Two hymns, poetical and original in form, and having a most extensive use among children, and which both deal with the birth of Christ, have come from the pen of this gifted authoress. The first begins:

There came a little Child to earth
  Long ago!
And the angels proclaimed His birth,
  High and low.

The second is more suitable for those of older age:

Thou didst leave Thy throne
  and Thy kingly crown
When Thou camest to earth
  for me.

Their mutual theme has made these two hymns deservedly popular.

Miss Elliot was the third daughter of the Rev. E. B. Elliot of Brighton, where she was born 22 July 1836. She died at Mildmay, London, 3 August 1897. Many of her hymns have gained a wide acceptance.

Jennette Threlfall

It is to this sweet singer of hymns and other sacred poems we owe one of the finest hymns for children, having every characteristic needful for such a composition:

Hosanna! loud Hosanna!
  The little children sang:
Through pillared court and temple
  The lovely anthem rang.

Jennette Threlfall was born in Blackburn, Lancashire, on 24 March 1821. Orphaned at an early age, she became the beloved friend of several relatives. A sad accident lamed and mutilated her for life, and a second rendered her a helpless invalid. She bore her long, slow sufferings brightly, and to the end retained a gentle, loving, sympathetic heart and always a pleasant smile and word, forgetful of herself. Throughout she was a great reader, and at "idle moments" threw off with ease her sacred poems and hymns. These were sent anonymously to various periodicals.

She died on 30 November 1880, and was interred at Highgate Cemetery 4 December 1880. Both Dean Stanley and Canon Farrar preached memoriam sermons in her honor. In praising her poems Bishop Wordsworth observed: "It is an occasion for great thankfulness to be able to point to poems, such as many of those in the present volume, in which considerable mental powers and graces of composition are blended with pure religious feeling, and hallowed by sound doctrine and fervent devotion."

John Ellerton

John Ellerton is most widely known as a hymnologist, hymn writer and translator. His original hymns number about fifty and his translations from the Latin about ten. The following children's hymn is remarkable for its lyric and its practical tone:

> Day by day we magnify Thee —
> When our hymns in school we raise.
> Daily work begun and ended
> With the daily voice of praise.

This hymn was written to be sung daily at the opening of a National School in Brighton, and is now used in almost every hymn book. A companion hymn begins, "The hours of school are over."

John Ellerton was born in London 16 December 1886, and after being educated at Cambridge, held successive curacies, terminating as Rector of White Roding, 1886. Perhaps the grandest of his own compositions are: "The Day Thou Gavest Lord, Is Ended"; "Saviour Again To Thy Dear Name We Raise"; "Throned Upon the Awful Tree."

In his eulogy of Ellerton's works, Dr. Julian says — "His sympathy with nature, especially in her sadder moods, is great; he loves the facing light and the peace of eve, and lingers in the shadows."

William Walsham How

Who is there who would not like to know something of the man who wrote hymns like "O Jesus, Thou Art Standing"; "For All the Saints Who From Their Labors Rest"; "We Give Thee But Thine Own"? Well, these attaining to a foremost rank, and nearly 60 others, were written by Dr. W. W. How, or Bishop How, the celebrated author of several theological works. And "without any claims to rank as a poet, in the sense in which Cowper and Montgomery were poets, he has sung us songs which will probably outline all his other literary works." He wrote some admirable hymns for children, one of which is most appealing —

> It is a thing most wonderful,
> Almost too wonderful to be,
> That God's own Son should come from heaven,
> And die to save a child like me.

Another of a bolder and more jubilant strain with separate verses for boys and girls is, "Come, Praise Your Lord and Saviour."

Bishop How was born 13 December 1823 at Shrewbury. After taking Holy Orders in 1846 he occupied several important positions, finally becoming Bishop of Wakefield in 1888. He died 10 August 1897.

Anna Warner

Perhaps the first song infant lips are taught to sing is "Jesus Loves Me This I Know." Deep emotion fills a mother's heart as she hears her child lisping the sacred name in this beautiful way. This favorite lyric of the young was written by Miss Anna Warner about 1858. Originally written for the tiny members of her class, it speedily became famous throughout America, and in a short time was taken up by English editors. Miss Warner was especially successful in writing hymns for the young. The following, known as "A Mother's Evening Hymn" is both beautiful and tender.

O little child! lie still and sleep;
Jesus is near, thou need'st not fear
No one need fear whom God doth keep,
By day and night:
Then lay thee down in slumber deep
Till morning light.

Another well-known and much loved hymn among children from her pen is "The World Looks Very Beautiful." The authoress was the daughter of Henry W. Warner, and was born in New York in 1821. She wrote several volumes of poems and hymns, beside numerous novels which have had a large circulation in America.

Benjamin Waugh

The untiring efforts of Benjamin Waugh on behalf of a London Society for the protection of children led him to produce one or two gems in children's hymns. The following, as one can see by reading the entire production, enforces with great tenderness a much-needed idea:

Where is Jesus, little children,
Is He up in Heaven?
Has God taken back the present
Which of old was given?

Another one embodying a tender appeal from the child to the teacher is —

O, who will show me Jesus Christ?
O, who will take my hand?
And lead to Him whose words they say
A child can understand!

This, too, is equally good: "I'll Come to Thee, O Jesus Christ."

Benjamin Waugh was born at Settle, in Yorkshire, 20 February 1839. After his education for the Congregational ministry at Airedale College, Bradford, he held pastorates at Newbury, Berkshire, Greenwich and New Southgate. Of his hymns Dr. Julian says they are exceedingly fresh and unconventional. He was the author of "Sunday Evenings With My Children."

Newman C. Hall

Although, as one writer affirms, there is nothing very distinctive or original about Newman Hall's adult hymns, he has struck a really beautiful note in his "Day Again Is Dawning," which came into his mind while walking down Hampstead Hill. We quote the second verse:

Help me, Lord, to praise Thee,
For my cosy bed;
For my clothes and playthings,
For my daily bread;
For my darling mother,
For my father dear;
For the friends who love me,
Far away and near.

The Rev. N. C. Hall was born at Maidstone 22 May 1816. From 1842 to 1854 he ministered at Hull, and from 1854 he was in charge of the work of Surrey Chapel. In 1876 he became chairman of the Congregational Union of England and Wales. He died 18 February 1902. All of his eighty hymns bear the initials N.H. The most popular are "Friend of Sinners, Lord of Glory"; "Accepting Lord, Thy Gracious Call"; "Hallelujah, Joyful Praise."

Sabine Baring-Gould

This author of "Onward Christian Soldiers" wrote an evening hymn for children remarkable for its simplicity and picturesqueness. It is one of the finest evening hymns for children in our language.

Now the day is over,
Night is drawing nigh,
Shadows of the evening
Steal across the sky.

It was written in 1865 and has increased in its popularity until it has become known in all English-speaking countries. Mr. Baring-Gould wrote the hymn especially for the children in his Sunday school at Horbury Bridge. It was intended for evening singing and was founded on the text taken from Proverbs 3:24, "When thou liest down, thou shalt not be afraid: yea, thou shalt lie down, and thy sleep shall be sweet."

Albert Midlane

Another famous masterpiece and one so easily learned in childhood days and which, as one grows older awakens hallowed memories is — "There's a Friend for Little Children." It was first scribbled in the notebook of Mr. Albert Midlane on 27 February 1859. Coming straight from his heart the verses of this sweet hymn have sung themselves around the world in less than a decade. In the original MS the opening verse began "There's a rest for little children," "friend" being subsequently substituted for "rest." The story of its composition is interesting. During the day Mr. Midlane's mind had been musing on its outline, and in the evening, his family having retired, he set himself to arrange and complete the idea. But time stole on and morning came, and the hymn-writer was still busy. At last the verses were completed, but at serious cost to their composer. The strain of writing "There's a Friend for Little Children" had proven too much for its author, and he fell forward unconscious, his head resting upon the finished hymn. His wife, alarmed at his long absence, came down and found him in a state of collapse. He regained consciousness, but all night work was forbidden for the future. Mr. Midlane was greatly cheered as people wrote to him regarding the helpfulness of his hymn. " 'Thanks,' said a father to me in the public streets, with tears falling from his eyes, as he grasped my hand — 'Thanks for the joy my dear child experienced, as your little hymn cheered her in her last moments.' "

Cathedrals, meeting houses, schools, and cottages have echoed its burden, and have called up the affections to the Father's house of many abodes on high. The hymn appears in collections in nearly every known language, in Chinese characters as well as in dialects of the South Seas. A missionary in Africa sent a book, with a flyleaf paragraph: "Mr. Albert Midlane, from the translator into the Sechwana language of his beautiful hymn 'There's a Friend for Little Children,' with every good wish for light at eventide."

Albert Midlane was born at Newport, Isle of Wight, 23 January 1825 within a short distance of the house in which Thomas Binney penned those beautiful and well-known lines beginning, "Eternal Light, Eternal Light." He was a business man in Newport for over fifty years. It was his Sunday school which did much to shape his early life and which prompted him to poetic efforts. Over 300 pieces came from his inspired pen and as "a whole they are full of spiritual thought, careful in their wording, and often pleasing without reaching the highest form of poetic excellence. A marked feature of these hymns is the constant and happy use of Scripture phraseology."

Samuel T. Coleridge

Perhaps the only hymn for children by one of the great English poets, is the following, so simple and exquisite, by Samuel Taylor Coleridge which he wrote in 1808. The first verse reads —

> Ere on my bed my limbs I lay,
> God grant me grace my prayers to say;

O, God preserve my mother dear
In strength and health for many a year.

S. T. Coleridge was born at St. Mary Ottery, Devonshire, 1772, and died in 1834. Says Mr. Garrett Horder, "It is to be regretted that the greater poets did not consecrate their powers to such a work." What noble verses we might have had, if a man like Charles Kingsley had written verses for children, suffused with the spirit of his lovely poem addressed to a child, which I cannot forbear quoting:

My fairest child, I have no song to give you:
No lark could pipe to skies so dull and grey;
Yet, ere we part, one lesson I can leave you
For every day.

Be good, sweet maid, and let who will be clever:
Do noble things, not dream them all day long;
And so make life, death, and that vast forever
One grand, sweet song.

M. B. Betham-Edwards

No greater success has been reached in hymn writing for children than by Matilda Barbara Betham-Edwards, widely known for her works of fiction. It was she who wrote –

God make my life a little light
Within the world to glow;
A little flame that burneth bright,
Wherever I may go.

Less known, but equally delightful is this evening hymn from her pen –

The little birds now seek their nest;
The baby sleeps on mother's breast.
Thou givest all Thy children rest.
God of the weary.

The authoress was the daughter of Edward Edwards and cousin of Amelia B. Edwards, the Egyptologist. She was born at Westerfield, near Ipswich 4 March 1836.

Catherine Hankey

A children's hymn which never loses its charm even after we grow up is –

Tell me the old, old story,
Of unseen things above.

Probably there is no other hymn for the young that has found its way into languages and dialects the world over like this one written by Miss Catherine Hankey over sixty years ago. "The history of the origin of 'Tell Me the Old, Old Story' I heard from the lips of the writer herself some months ago as she sat and wrote an autograph of the simple and beautiful hymn for reproduction here," says F. A. Jones in his *Famous Hymns*. "The hymn as I first wrote it," said Miss Hankey, "consisted of fifty verses of four lines each. It was divided into two parts – "The Story Wanted" and "The Story Told." I wrote Part 1 toward the end of January, 1866. I was unwell at the time – just recovering from a serious illness – and the second verse really indicates my state of health, for I was literally 'weak and weary.' When I had written the first part, which consisted of eight verses, I laid it aside; and it was not until the following November that I completed the whole hymn. It is, perhaps, strange that the plea for the story, and not the story itself, should become the favorite hymn; but of course the second part is far too long for congregational singing."

Its close association with *Sankey's Songs and Solos* can be traced to the fact that Mr. Sankey saw a reprint of the hymn in an American paper and thinking it would make an attractive addition to his hymnal, sent it to his friend, Mr. William H. Doane, with a request to set it to music. This Mr. Doane did, but instead of conforming to the original he turned the four-lined verses into eight-lined stanzas and added the now well-known refrain. This setting, however, Miss Hankey greatly deprecated as each verse was complete in itself, there being no connecting links between any two of the verses. Still, Mr. Doane's setting immediately "caught on" and has greatly helped in making the hymn known in all parts of the world.

Miss Hankey published several hymns of great beauty and simplicity suitable alike for mission services and Sunday schools, but like many another hymnist, she will be remembered by a single composition. For a striking illustration of the influence "Tell Me the Old, Old Story" has exerted, one is referred to Sankey's volume in which he tells of a young stockbroker utterly broken in life through gambling and drunken dissipation, who was brought to Christ through hearing a vast audience singing – "Remember, I'm the sinner whom Jesus came to save."

Children's Prayers

As soon as children are old enough to understand, they should be taught the meaning and reality of prayer. The simplest explanation is that as the child asks his father for something, the father, because of his superior wisdom will know if the request is good and possible for his boy. If it is what is asked for will be given. So the child is taught to think of God as his heavenly Father to whom he can go with all that concerns him. Then what a sacred sight it is to see a little child at prayer. And how simple, natural, direct and earnest are the prayers of children which, no matter how imperfect they may be, are yet heard and answered by God. As we get older too often we are not as direct and confident in our prayers as we were in childhood days.

D. B. Knox in *The Marvels of Radium,* tells of a nice little girl he knew who lived in County Monaghan, Ireland. She was warmhearted and generous, as one of her prayers proved –

> Oh, Lord, bless the big beggars and help them to take care of the little beggars, and give them all bread and jam and cake for tea.

Then she tried to answer her own prayers by doing without sugar in her tea and without cake, so that she might save pennies to give to the poor and to missions. How her thoughtful care of others must have pleased the heart of Jesus. Then there is another story of a little girl who was so excited about going on holiday, and who, as the family were about to leave home, knelt down and prayed –

> "Good-by, God!
> We're going away.
> Take care of Yourself
> until we come back."

Do you not think God understood such an expression?

Among the many prayers in the Bible (See the author's volume, *All the Prayers of the Bible)* we are only indirectly given the prayers of children and young people.

When Hagar and her son Ishmael were sent away by Abraham into the wilderness and their food and water were exhausted, we read – "God heard the voice of the lad" (Gen. 21:17).

When Ishmael was about fourteen years of age, again it was the lad's voice and his prayers which were heard in heaven and answered.

The little Israelitish slave girl in the house of Naaman the Syrian, though she had been carried away from her own land, yet, doubtless prayed for her master who was a leper. Her words to her mistress were shaped in the form of a prayer — "Would God my lord were with the prophet that is in Samaria!" (II Kings 5:3). How wonderfully her prayer was answered!

The child Samuel prayed, "Speak; for thy servant heareth" (I Sam. 3:10). The intensity of his words must have been pleasing to God. The prayers of children are usually intense and uttered with their perfect trust, for children are trustful.

William Canton in his *Child's Book of Saints,* tells of a poor little orphan girl who lived in a tiny cottage on the edge of the moors. Her mother died when she was four, and her father was lost in the snow one night as he staggered home from the village tavern. Destitute of any training from loving parents, or education of any kind, at night she would repeat a simple prayer she learned when a small child. Although we would not deem it to be a fitting prayer, it was real to her. This was the prayer —

> God bless this house from thatch to floor,
> The Twelve Apostles guard the door,
> The four good Angels watch my bed,
> Two at the foot and two at the head.
> Amen

Such a simple and imperfect prayer was answered by God, for His angels did guard the girl's bed, and the Lord of the apostles Himself guarded her door.

It is necessary to teach children not to be selfish in their prayers, as the little boy was when he used to pray at his bed at night —

> "God bless Father and Mother,
> me and Uncle Tom.
> Us four — no more — Amen."

A godly minister looking back over his own life, and thinking of his childhood days and the simple prayers he used to pray, said of those infant years — "Days of illimitable faith! How glad I am to have known them. Very pleasing to me is the remembrance of that simple piety of childhood, of that prayer which was said so punctually night and morning kneeling by the bedside . . . This, I know, that the bedside where I knelt at this morning and evening devotion became sacred to me as an altar. To this day I never see the little clean bed in which a child is to sleep, but I see also the figure of a child kneeling in prayer at its side; and I for the moment am that child."

Among the many examples of a child's simplicity and directness in prayer, there is the one about a missionary lady who had a little Hindu orphan named Shadi living with her. Daily she taught the little fellow about Jesus, and one night when he was six years old, she told him that he could now try to pray a prayer of his own. What kind of a prayer do you think he framed? Here it is: "Dear Jesus, make me like what you were when you were six years old." Is this not the true essence of prayer, just to ask God to help us to be the best it is possible to be now, and not to forget that He can make us like Himself.

Further, the lesson of the Bible, and of all praying lives is that God hears and answers prayer, even the prayers of the little ones who are precious in His sight. This fact is emphasized in the story of a man who, as he bought a paper from a newsboy said to him —

"Well, my boy, do you ever find it hard work to be good?"

"Yes, sir," said the little fellow.

"Well, so do I. But I have found out how to get help."

"How, sir?" asked the boy.

"I just send a telegram," replied the man. The boy looked surprised. Then the man touched the boy's forehead and said: "What do you do in there?"

"Think," said the boy.

"Can God see what you think?" asked the man.

"Yes," answered the boy.

"Well," said the kind gentleman, "when you want help to sell your papers or to be a good boy, just send a sky-telegram – *Jesus, help me,* and God will see and hear." Some time later the man met the boy again, and immediately the boy said, "I've been trying the sky-telegram during the past few weeks, and I've sold more papers than I ever did before." Children should be taught to take everything to God in prayer.

That –

Prayer is the simplest form of
speech that infant lips can try –

is illustrated by this "Schoolboy's Morning Prayer," which S. P. Bevan, in *Silver Pennies* suggests for boys to use:

> Lord Jesus Christ,
>
> I thank Thee for awakening me to this day and to the beautiful sunlight; for this quiet room and this "comfy" bed, too, I thank Thee. To-day's text is, "Lo, I am with you alway." May this inspire me to be a true boy! Canst Thou and wilt Thou really be with *me?*
>
> When, in a few minutes, I go down to breakfast, may I be quite awake and do my best to keep the talk at table happy. May I find no fault with the food; but so behave as to give dear mother a good start for the day.
>
> At school I long to be stronger in doing right. If I am beaten at sport in recreation-time, may I not sulk, but congratulate him who beats me. May I finish the squabble with Nicholson about that Chinese stamp, and may I, in class, give my whole attention and make more careful notes. I feel that Thou wilt help me; for these are Thy words, "Lo, I am with you alway."
>
> Above all, may I grow in self-control and in the habit of thinking more of others and less of myself. This I ask because I wish to please father, mother, the master, and, most of all, to please Thee, my Saviour.
>
> Amen.

For the guidance of parents who have a desire to teach their little ones to pray, there is a surfeit of beautifully produced small books at their disposal. For instance, the inexpensive series known as *The Ladybird Titles* published in Loughborough, Leicestershire, England, are unique and we cannot speak too highly of them. Already there are over 150 titles all designed for parents to read to their children, or to read themselves. In "Book of Prayers Through the Year" the boys and girls in our homes are taught to increase an awareness of lovely things and worthwhile experiences, and to thank God for them. For instance, under "Rainy Days," children are taught to pray –

> Thank you, God, for rain, and cool, clear water, which we need each day for drinking, for washing and for bathing. Help us not to grumble when a rainy day stops us from going out to play.

Under "Foggy Days," we have the prayer –

> Thank you, God, for mothers and fathers who take extra care of us now that the foggy days have come. Thank you for toys and books which keep us happy when we cannot play outside.

Another set of most interesting, well-illustrated booklets are those published by Collins Clear-Type Press,

London. Titles like *First Prayers – First Hymns – First Graces* are all designed to foster the innocence and wonder of childhood, and are to be warmly recommended for use by parents. There are also two small volumes under the titles *Children's Letters to God* and *More Letters to God,* which are most delightful to read, as well as enlightening as an insight into the child-mind. Actually, the "letters" are "prayers" which selected children were asked to present to God. We cannot but smile over some of the specimens given in their own handwriting –

> Dear God,
>
> I read your book and I like it. Did you write any others? I would like to write a book someday with the same kind of stories. Where do you get your ideas?
>
> Best wishes,
> Sarah

What do you think of this brief request? –

> Dear God,
>
> If you made the rule for kids to take out the garbage – please change it.
>
> Very truly,
> Maurice

Then this letter proves that its very young writer paid attention to what she heard in church –

> Dear God,
>
> Our minister says God is love and when we think good things you are always listening.
>
> Good-by,
> Linda

While so many of these simple requests make one chuckle – as you will if you buy these unique children's books – the one that takes the prize for me, reads –

> Dear God,
>
> I am sorry I was late for Sunday school but I couldn't find my underwear.
>
> Norman

Among the many books containing prayers for children – prayers which parents and teachers can offer on behalf of young ones, or teach them to use for themselves, mention can be made of the section found in *A Chain of Prayer Across the Ages,* published by John Murray, Albemarle Street, London. This compilation by Dr. Selina Fox is a most remarkable coverage of "Forty Centuries of Prayer." Under "Children's Prayers," we are given those the young can be taught to offer under varying circumstances. Here are two examples:

For "Help at Lessons," we have the suggested request –

> O Saviour of the world, help us not to be lazy today. Help us to follow Thy example and work with all our might at anything we do. Let us look on our lessons as work of Thee, which we must do well, to fit us for our afterlife. And if we have any other tasks, let us do them as Thou didst do Thy work, cheerfully, willingly and earnestly. And so bless all we do, dear Lord, that our work may please Thee and those who give it us to do, for Thy sake. Amen.

Under "For Kindness to Animals," we find the prayer –

> O Lord Jesus Christ, who has taught us that without our Father in heaven no sparrow falls to the ground, help us to be very kind to all animals, and our pets. May we remember that Thou wilt one day ask us if we have been good to them. Bless us as we take care of them; for Thy sake. Amen.

Closely allied to prayers is what we call "Saying Grace," or "Blessing at Meals," which is a brief prayer before we partake of food, in which God's blessing is sought and gratitude expressed for the supply of our bodily wants. Ancient Jews, we are informed, began their meals with the benediction of the cup –

> "Blessed be the Lord our God,
> King of the World, who has
> created the fruit of the vine" –

Then the cup was passed to the guests. Next followed the blessing of the bread which the master held in his hand saying –

> "Blessed be the Lord our God,
> King of the World, who has
> produced bread out of the earth."

Evidently, it was an established rule that none of the company should touch anything until he, who broke the bread, first tasted it – a custom observed by Christ, and His apostles, as the miracle of feeding the 5,000 proves (Matt. 14:19; Mark 8:6; Acts 20:11).

In Christian homes, as soon as infants are able to sit in a high chair at the table, they are taught to close their eyes, and clasp their hands, and repeat words of thanks to God. Although not all religious people follow the practice of grace before meals, whether eaten at home or in a restaurant, surely there ought to be no embarrassment about offering thanks before partaking of a meal. Food is a bounty of God, and thanksgiving is proof of a sincere faith, as children should be taught to believe.

Several years ago in America an effort was made to encourage people to say grace before meals when dining in public. Such a commendable practice was started by a minister who, while dining with his wife and two children in a New York State restaurant, overheard people at the next table mention they would like to give the Blessing if they only knew how. This gave the minister the idea of distributing cards containing short prayers that could be used by Protestant, Catholics and Jews in local eating places. The idea spread through several states and the following prayers printed on a card were to be found on restaurant tables.

For those who want to pray a Table Grace.

The prayers are:

> Roman Catholic – "Bless us, O Lord, and these thy gifts, which we are about to receive from thy bounty. Through Christ our Lord. Amen."
>
> Jewish – "Lift up your hands toward the sanctuary and bless the Lord. Blessed art Thou, O Lord our God, King of the universe, who bringest forth bread from the earth."
>
> Protestant – "Bless, O Lord, this food to our use, and us to thy service, and make us ever mindly of the needs of others, in Jesus' name. Amen."

A local printer in Los Angeles, California, believed he had solved the problem of parents who cannot think of suitable words when asked by their children to say grace, by setting in type several old-time prayers before meals and printing them on paper napkins. If a guest is honored by being asked to say the grace, if he knows none, one that is appropriate to all religions is Ophelia's blessing from *Hamlet* –

> "God be at your table."

A poetic grace said to have been uttered spontaneously by a man in 1850, on seeing a schoolroom supper provided for him and his sister by a somewhat frugal aunt, reads –

> O Lord, who made the loaves and fishes,
> Look down upon these two poor dishes,

And though they be exceeding small,
Make them, O Lord, enough for all:
For if they should our tummies fill
I'm sure t'would be a miracle.

The story is told of a grace that caused a good deal of mirth. A previous Duke of Devonshire once caused a gurgle of laughter at a luncheon when he rose to open the proceedings. Looking around and seeing no sign of the Rector of the parish, the Duke said:

"Ladies and Gentlemen, as there appears to be no clergyman present, may the Lord make us truly thankful."

"The Selkirk Grace" appeared in 1650 and reads –

Some have meat and cannot eat;
Some could eat but have no meat;
We have meat and can all eat;
Blest, therefore, be God for our meat.

Robert Burns, the Scottish poet used it this way –

Some hae meat, and canna eat,
And some wad eat that want it;
But we hae meat, and we can eat
And sae the Lord be thankit.

An old Latin form of grace before a meal – *Benedictus benedicat!* means, "May the Blessed One bless!"

What is known as "Hodge's Grace" has a humorous turn –

Heavenly Father, bless us,
And keep us all alive,
Here's ten of us to dinner,
And not enough for five.

Our great Example in "saying grace" is Jesus of whom we read, "When he had given thanks," and children should be taught to give thanks because –

It is very nice to think
The world is full of meat and drink,
With little children saying grace
In every Christian kind of place.

Among many simple forms of giving thanks for our daily food and for all other good things, we have the following different ones –

God bless this food
And make us good
For Jesus' sake. Amen.

Pray we to God, the Almighty Lord,
That sendeth food to beasts and men,
To send His blessing on this board,
To feed us now and ever. Amen.

That there is more than meat and drink in the world to be grateful for is implied in this grace –

Thank you God for the world so sweet,
Thank you for the food we eat,
Thank you for the birds that sing,
Thank you, God, for everything.

Jesus was grateful for everything because He saw God in everything. With this thought in mind we can offer thanks in the verse –

Bless these Thy gifts, most gracious God,
From whom all goodness springs;
Make clean our hearts and feed our souls
With good and joyful things.

If it be true that "every father is a looking glass for his children to dress themselves by," then, if he is a praying father ever grateful to God for His mercies, his children will not find it hard to follow him in giving thanks. The voice of the infant heart whom loving parents must listen for, and respond to, seems to say –

A needy little child am I,
Whose thoughts are never very high;
The gifts for which I pray,
I need them day by day.
The God to whom I say my grace
Has got a very human face.

For human hands I grope,
For human love I hope;
How can I know the love of God is true
Without a little love from such as you.

Children's Literature

The plethora of books today dealing with every phase of child life is a striking evidence of the importance we have come to attach to the spiritual, moral, mental and physical well-being of children. In fact, when one comes to classify such material he hardly knows where to begin. Depending upon the particular phase of child life we want to study, so our choice of reliable guide books, of which there seems to be no end. The two general sections to be observed are Books *for* Children and Books *about* Children. As this volume of ours on childhood has been written from the Biblical standpoint, emphasis will be given to modern literature designed for the spiritual development of children. Mention can be made, however, to standard works available to all on almost every phase of child life.

Childbirth

The over-stressed emphasis on sex education of our times means that children, early in their mental expansion, know all about the facts of their creation. Simplified literature relating to this subject abounds. For the newly married setting up home and contemplating a family, information dealing with embryology, maternal health, obstetrics and birth can be found in any worthwhile medical encyclopedia accessible at any local library. Such gathered information will convince prospective parents that their unborn babe is "curiously wrought," and "fearfully and wonderfully made" (Ps. 139: 13-16). Further, the principles of child care and health from birth until the walking stage are set out for the guidance of parents in any reliable medical manual.

Child Psychology

This feature of child study is concerned with efforts to give a systematic account of how the psycho-physiological processes of children differ from those of adults, of the manner in which they develop from birth to the end of adolescence, and of differences in such functions as observed between one child and another. Almost a hundred years ago Charles Darwin, the English naturalist, began to keep a day-to-day record of the progress of one of his own children, collecting the data as a naturalist studying some strange animal, and then published his findings on child behavior. In 1881 the German psycho-physiologist, Preyer, followed with *The Mind of the Child:* and thereafter, a spate of similar works followed. In course of time, formal training in child psychology was added to the curriculum of universities, colleges and schools. There is now a considerable library of worthwhile volumes on the growth of logical thinking and intelligence of a child, notably, *The Intellectual Growth in Young Children,* by S. Isaacs, published in 1966.

Child Amusement

Before they learn to read and write, children learn and love to play. While outdoors is the natural playground of the child, as the Bible indicates when it speaks about boys and girls, "playing in the streets," there are numerous games and amusements for them indoors as well. Jesus used the illustration of children delighting in playing at marriages and funerals. The study of the origins of children's games is a most fascinating branch both of folklore and ethnology. (See article on this in *Encyclopaedia Britannica,* 1968 Edition.) "Directed play broadens a child's interests, both by teaching him new games and by teaching him how to play, and because it aims at involving all those present, it is particularly valuable in building group feeling." Books in this area are most abundant. In any general bookstore you can find resource books under such titles as —

The Games of Children — Origin and History
Children's Games Throughout the Year
Collections of Games for Children
Complete Book of Games
Games Around the World
Ways to Amuse a Child
Complete Family Fun Book

Child Reading

Books written especially for children are as varied as vast in number. With the development of modern art printing, the production of literature designed for young readers has reached great proportions. You have only to scan the shelves in a large book store under the section allotted to children to believe this. What a marvelous library is now at their disposal! We cannot condemn too strongly those writers with warped minds responsible for the furnishing of the suggestive, smutty books exercising such a pernicious influence over the formative minds of the young. To purposely poison a spring is a most diabolical act. Accessible reading for children should always have a high moral tone — conspicuous by its absence in many horror books of today.

As to the enormous range of wholesome, exciting and beneficial books for children, there are those on a hundred and one themes — history, myths and legends, biography, nature, science, general knowledge, quiz books.

The best series in this category that we know of are those under the title, *Tell Me Why,* containing hundreds of answers to questions boys and girls ask. The author of this series, Arkady Leokum, designed these profitable books under the conviction that knowledge should be the heritage of all, and that their purpose should be not only to impart knowledge, but also to stimulate young, inquiring minds to undertake further search of knowledge. Books of this informative nature should be high on the list of general reading for children.

One of the most fascinating books for a child to have is *The Illustrated Treasury of Children's Literature,* published by Collins, London. Its art work — so appealing to children — is superb. Childhood favorites from hundreds of the world's most popular children's books have been crammed into this one-volume library. Stories, legends, fairy tales, rhymes and poems, plus the 550 colorful pictures, make this remarkable production a book to last a lifetime. As the jacket says, "Parents will renew the sweet friendships of childhood and today's children will treasure this volume to read a generation to their children."

Reference can also be made to the scores of children's magazines of a general and particular nature, which are read with great enthusiasm by both boys and girls. With their school stories, romance, adventure, biography, scientific and biological material many of these weekly or monthly magazines make excellent and profitable material for the young.

Parents and teachers who are concerned about the religious education of children under their care, cannot be too particular about the selection of Christian literature which the young read. John Bunyan, who deplored his youthful reading of "vain" literature, came to write one of the most stirring Christian adventure stories which is next to the Bible in its circulation. Full of pious hope, and of excitement and suspense, this stirring classic has been loved by child and parent alike. For bedtime reading to children *Pilgrim's Progress* is incomparable. Bunyan's work, *Book for Boys and Girls,* written in 1686, was less successful. Many of the juvenile books of a century or so ago, like those of James Janeway's, *Holy and Exemplary Lives,* and *Joyful Deaths of Several Young Children,* were oppressively narrow in their attitude.

Today, Christian parents and Sunday school teachers have a tremendous range of well-written books and magazines to choose from when it comes to the religious instruction of children under their care. From the list of *Helps for Sunday School Teachers,* published by Pickering and Inglis, London, we can heartily commend titles like these at low cost —

Seventy Best Bible Stories
Seventy Familiar Bible Stories
Seventy Less-Known Bible Stories
What to Teach and How to Reach the Young
Through Eye to Heart
Bringing the Child to Christ
Bible Object Lessons

Another series one can most warmly recommend is that published by Arnold and Son, Ltd., Leeds, England, under the general title of *Religious Education.* Ably written by E. W. Crabb, Schoolmaster at Harrow, the purpose of these volumes is to assist day school teachers to expound the Scriptures in the period assigned for the religious training of children.

One of the most unique and fascinating volumes on a library of books suitable for family is that by Gladys Hunt, under the suggestive title, *Honey for a Child's Heart.* We can imagine how many parents like bees will gather around this literary honey-pot. In a remarkable way the authoress deals with those readable books that become the treasures of children. A broad field of fact and fiction, prose and poetry, spiritual and secular, is covered, and in an appealing way she shows how honey for the palate of the young can be gathered from many hives. Whether for the little children, or teen-agers, parents who desire to enrich the minds and lives of their children must secure this instructive yet entertaining book. Gladys Hunt in her coverage of books agrees with the sentiment expressed by Emilie Poulsson that —

> Books are keys to wisdom's treasure;
> Books are gates to the land of pleasure;
> Books are paths that upward lead;
> Books are friends. Come, let us read!

One of the best Bible story books we know of is *Richards Bible Story Book* by Jean Hosking Richards. It is a sensitive retelling of the Bible story geared to children aged 4 through 9 and contains more than 100 *new* illustrations, seventy in full color.

For pastors seeking profitable material for a Sunday morning brief message for children, or unusual themes for a children's service, there is a vast collection of books by various authors designed for such a purpose. In my own library I have over 100 of these most valuable aids, the majority of which are no longer in print. Several years ago, my esteemed publisher, P. J. Zondervan, kindly bought up this collection for me. What a boon many of these children's books have been to me in the preparation of this book now in your hands! One could only wish that many of these most helpful volumes could be reprinted for pulpit and school use today.

Various religious publishing houses carry a most recommendable selection of children's books, not only on Bible stories, but also on the lives of saints, heroes, and missionaries. They are well illustrated and calculated to influence the young for the service of Christ. In fact, there never was a time when so much attractive and profitable material was available for children. Although designed for boys and girls, books and booklets uninterestingly written, poorly produced and lacking picture appeal, are useless in these days when papers, magazines, and books are so pictorial and eye-catching, and written in an appealing style.

Apart from denominational Sunday school magazines, a few of which are liberal in outlook and tend to instill doubt in the minds of the youth rather than faith in the foundational truths of Holy Writ, tribute is due to independent organizations for the most up-to-date conservative Sunday school material they produce. Such material, growing in popularity, although not welcomed denominationally, has had a marked effect upon the spiritual training of children. We have in mind *The Scripture Press; The Union Gospel Press; Gospel Light; Scripture Union; Peloubet's Notes;* and *Rozell's Sunday School Commentary,* the material of which is not only well-written but also true to the unfeigned faith young Timothy embraced and came to preach and defend. Because of the importance of Bible teaching in the religious training of the young, it is essential to have the most helpful aids possible.

We end on the thought expressed in various ways throughout our study, namely, that parents, pastors and teachers are here in Christ's stead to point the children around them to the heavenly Father. They are the lambs who must be taught to follow the Good Shepherd by His undershepherds. "The Father of our Lord Jesus Christ, of whom the whole family in heaven and earth is named," is not here in person to care for the boys and girls forming a family. Earthly parents are the representatives of the heavenly Parent in the care and culture of children, and if they fail in their sacred task and trust, He has no other plan. In a very real sense, God is saying to the heart of every father, mother, teacher, pastor – "Take this child away, and nurse it for me, and I will give thee thy wages" (Exod 2:9). The greatest reward we can have for such loving, patient "nursing," is to see the children we are responsible for, embracing the Saviour and growing up into His stature. And He alone is sufficient for these things.